THE BRITISH LIBRARY STUDIES IN MEDIEVAL CULTURE

Views of Transition

VIEWS OF TRANSITION

Liturgy and Illumination in Medieval Spain

Rose Walker

THE BRITISH LIBRARY

AND

UNIVERSITY OF TORONTO PRESS

1998

To my mother and father

FRONT OF JACKET: Silos Beatus, London,
British Library, Add. MS 11695, fol. 21.
Christ's appearance in the clouds (detail).

BACK OF JACKET: London, British Library,
Add. MS 30845, fol. 127V (detail).

FIRST PUBLISHED 1998 BY
THE BRITISH LIBRARY
GREAT RUSSELL STREET
LONDON WC1B 3DG

British Library Cataloguing in Publication Data
A catalogue record for this title is available from the British Library

ISBN 0 7123 4523 X

PUBLISHED IN NORTH AMERICA IN 1998 BY
UNIVERSITY OF TORONTO PRESS INCORPORATED
TORONTO AND BUFFALO

Canadian Cataloguing in Publication Data
is available from University of Toronto Press

ISBN 0 8020 4368 2

DESIGNED AND TYPESET BY
A.H. JOLLY (EDITORIAL) LTD.
YELVERTOFT. NORTHANTS NN6 7LF

PRINTED IN GREAT BRITAIN

CONTENTS

LIST OF ILLUSTRATIONS

Colour Plates

Figures

Tables

ACKNOWLEDGEMENTS

I am exceedingly grateful to the staff of the Students' Room in the Manuscript Department of the British Library for their reliable efficiency, and above all to Michelle Brown and Scot McKendrick, the editors of this series; also to the Biblioteca Nacional and the Real Academia de la Historia in Madrid, and the Biblioteca at the Universidad de Salamanca for providing microfilms and microfiche; to the Central Research Fund of the University of London for enabling me to undertake research in Spain; to John Lowden, who supervised the thesis which forms the basis of this book, especially for his patience and precision; to all the other staff at the Courtauld Institute of Art who have offered me support and encouragement; and to my husband, Lawrence Leonard, for keeping the rest of my life intact.

The author and publisher would like to express their thanks to the following libraries who have kindly provided photographs and granted permission to reproduce them in this book.

Florence, Biblioteca Medicea Laurenziana (FIG. no. 24)

London, British Library (FIG. nos 1–23; 25–50; 64; PL. nos 1–6, 10)

London, Courtauld Institute of Art (FIG. no. 60; photograph by George Zarnecki)

Madrid, Biblioteca Nacional (PL. no. 7, FIG. nos 51, 52, 55–7)

Madrid, Real Academia de la Historia (PL. no. 8; FIG. nos 53, 54)

Paris, Bibliothèque Nationale (FIG. no. 58)

Salamanca, Biblioteca de la Universidad (PL. no. 9; FIG. nos 59, 61–65)

VIEWS OF TRANSITION

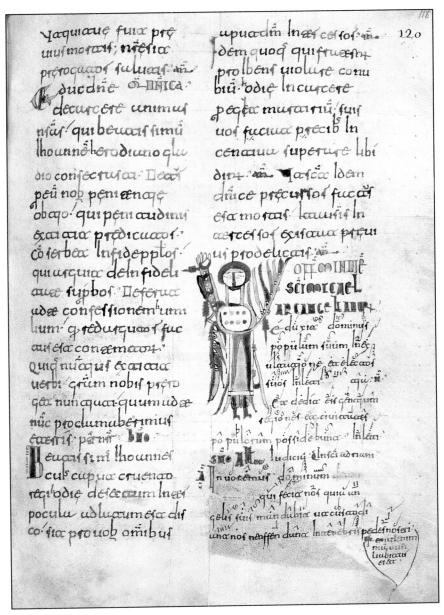

PLATE I London, British Library, Add. MS 30845, fol. 118

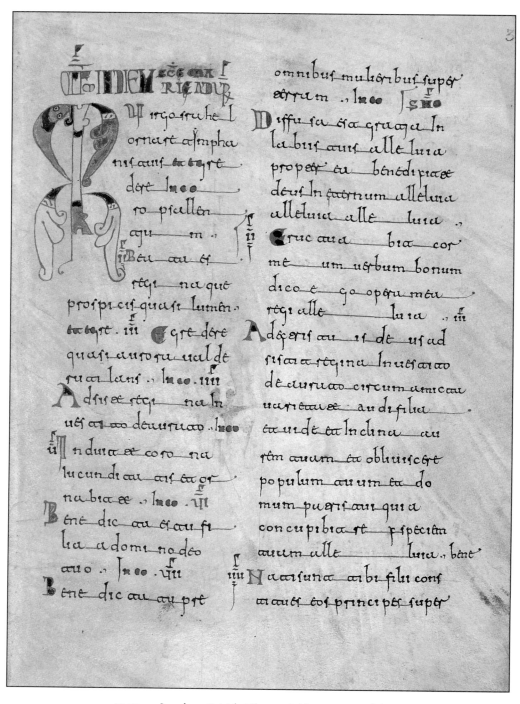

PLATE 2 London, British Library, Add. MS 30844, fol. 33

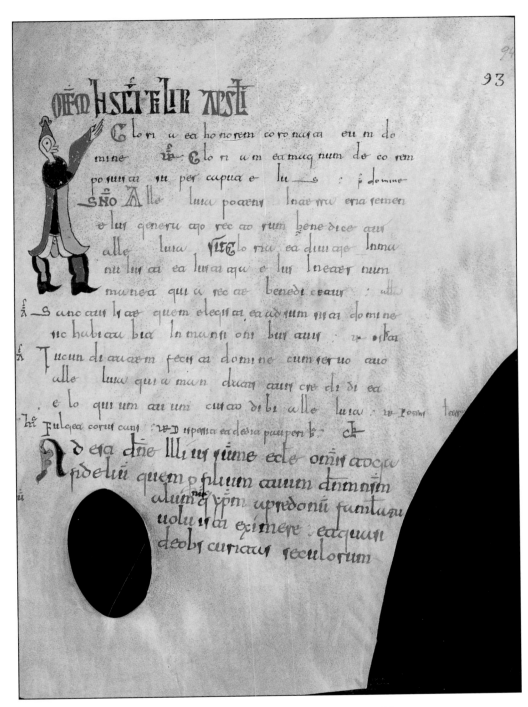

PLATE 3 London, British Library, Add. MS 30846, fol. 94

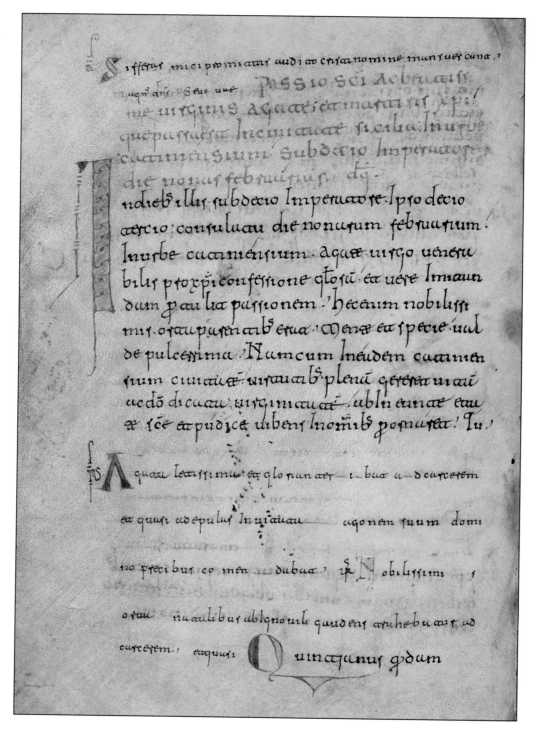

PLATE 4 London, British Library, Add. MS 30847, fol. 113v

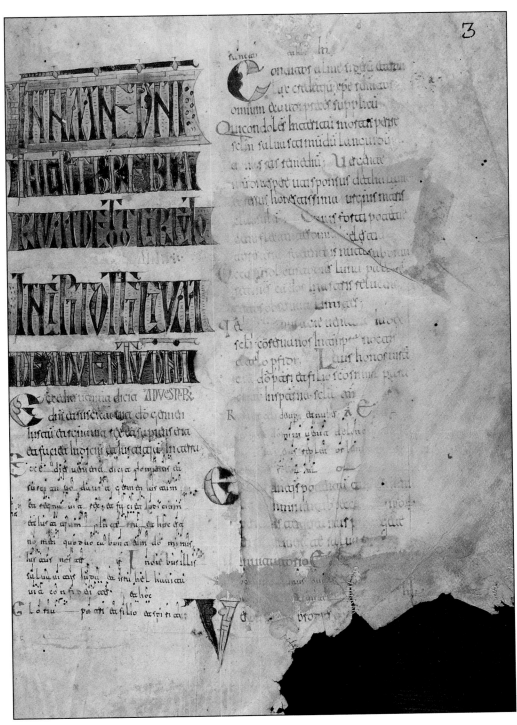

PLATE 5 London, British Library, Add. MS 30848, fol. 3

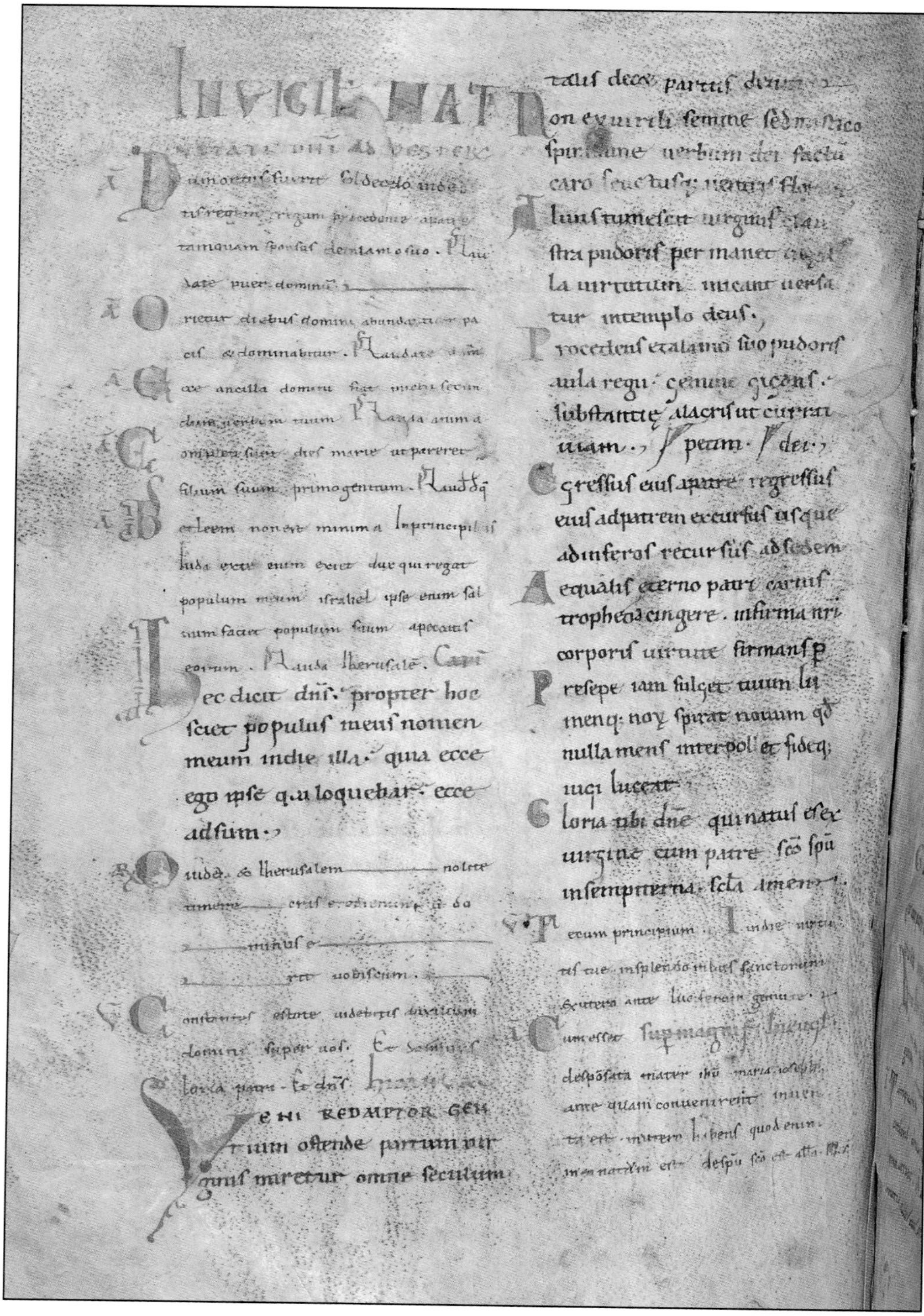

PLATE 6 London, British Library, Add. MS 30849, fol. 27v

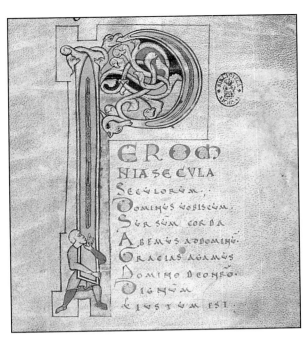

PLATE 7 Madrid, Biblioteca Nacional, MS Vitr. 20–8, fol. 1

PLATE 8 Madrid, Real Academia de la Historia, Aemilianensis. 18, fol. 13

PLATE 9 Salamanca, Biblioteca de la Universidad, MS 2637, fol. 2

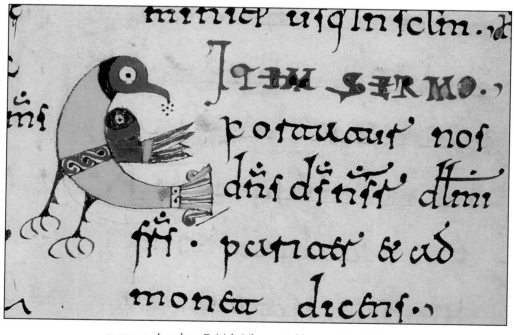

PLATE 10 London, British Library, Add. MS 30844, fol. 41v

INTRODUCTION

————◄○►————

Discourses of Change and Stasis

C HANGE WAS a difficult concept in medieval society. The introduction of anything different was open to the immediate charge of innovation (*novitas*), which could be used as a ready reproach against an opponent. As with accusations of 'racism' or 'sexism' today, there was no defence except denial; it was unacceptable to take the stance that 'new' was 'good'.[1] The modern appetite for 'the new', embedded in discourses of biological evolution and technological progress, was entirely lacking.

This condemnatory category was, moreover, well established, and examples can be found as early as the fourth century in the writings of Eusebius, who speaks of 'those … driven by the desire of innovation to an extremity of error'.[2] It is not surprising, therefore, that innovation was a standard accusation against heretics.[3] It was also used in argument by theologians like Bernard of Clairvaux, who decried *'novitas'* as *'mater temeritatis, soror superstitionis, filia levitatis'* in a letter to the Canons of Lyon, criticising them for introducing the feast of the Conception of the Virgin.[4] Peter Abelard threw the same charge at St Bernard and the Cistercians:

> *Vos quippe quasi noviter exorti, ac de novitate plurimum gaudentes, praeter consuetudinem omnem tam clericorum quam monachorum longe ante habitum, et nunc quoque permanentem, novis quibusdam decretis aliter apud vos divinum officium instituistis agi … haec vestra novitas aut singularitas ab antiquitate recedat aliorum*[5]

If change was not permissible in the Middle Ages, but did perforce occur, how was it made acceptable? I hope through this study of one particular innovation to make some contribution to the understanding of that broad question and the conflicts within it. For this purpose the innovation in question had to have processes which could be examined and also needed to be of clear importance to those who were affected by it. The tensions between presentation and practice had to be evident. The major liturgical change in Spain from the Mozarabic[6] to the Roman liturgy, which was formally initiated at the Council of Burgos in 1080, seemed to provide a suitable subject from the practical and the theoretical angles. Indeed *novitas* was especially controversial in a liturgical context, as the quotations from St Bernard and Peter Abelard show.[7]

The liturgy was an important, indeed pivotal, medieval institution. As the authorised means of mediation between the human and divine spheres, it was invested with the ability to accomplish absolution and thereby salvation on behalf of its participants, specified individuals and the Church as a whole. Monks entrusted with the performance of the liturgy were regarded as occupying a liminal position; with privileged access to 'the sacred' they made reparation on behalf of the living and the dead. By this same means saints could also be prevailed upon to intercede with God to lessen the suffering of the souls of the dead.

The gifts of land and goods to monasteries made in exchange ostensibly only for the liturgical intercession of the monks, whether through the Mozarabic or Roman liturgy, are a crude measure of the value placed on the intercessory power of the liturgy and the status earned by those who could obtain direct access to it.[8] A document of Alfonso VI, dated 1073, encapsulates the exchange:

> *parva pro magnis, terrena pro celestibus, cupientes expiari flagicia nostra per eorum suffragia credo salvari ab* *extuanti ardore, quia, quamvis parum dedi, magnum in retribucione iustorum a Domino reddetur*[9]

These donations brought wealth and reputation to the abbeys concerned, which in turn vied with one another to attract wealthy and influential patrons through the promotion or acquisition of relics and the miracles which they appeared to work. It was, therefore, essential for a monastery to be seen to employ an effective and authorised liturgy.

To those who performed it, the liturgy, was, moreover, their duty towards God, their *Opus Dei*, and the distillation and sanctioned exposition of doctrine. It was also the repository and condensed formulation of moral standards expressed through scriptural and hagiographical models, while on a practical level it gave structure to the day and the year.[10] Any change to the liturgy therefore had the potential to be seen as a threat to a monastery's very identity and essential values.

The liturgical change will be studied through close analysis of text and image in manuscripts of the Mozarabic and Roman liturgies produced in Spain before, during and after the change in the liturgy. The first part of this book (Chapters 1–3) will deal with manuscripts containing texts for the offices in which all monks could participate, while the second part (Chapters 4–6) will examine manuscripts containing texts for the mass, where the role of the celebrant was paramount. The texts will be interrogated for detailed information on the form and structure of the change, its extent and its application. In particular, manuscripts will be compared in search of an impression of the pace of the change and some indication of the processes used to advance it. The codices will themselves be considered as exemplifications of the liturgies which they contain, rather than being compared with some theoretical 'ideal' text, for *a priori* assumptions about 'the Mozarabic' or 'the Roman' liturgy are – as we shall see – problematic.

The presentation and decoration of the liturgical text will then be examined to determine the ways in which the change was expressed and made visible. These manuscripts are not richly illuminated and contain almost no narrative element. In every case the artistic contribution is tied explicitly to the text as an elaboration of it, usually in the form of an illuminated initial or heading; there are no free-standing miniatures. Thus the analysis will concentrate on the totality of the decorated text as image.

The liturgical change has frequently received mention in studies of eleventh- and twelfth-century Spanish art as one of the contributory factors in the development of Romanesque art in Spain.[11] This association was made most forcefully by Meyer Schapiro in his seminal article of 1939.[12] In that article he examined the interaction of the Mozarabic and Romanesque styles within two major works of art produced at the abbey of Silos at the end of the eleventh or beginning of the twelfth century: the Commentary of Beatus on the Apocalypse (British Library, Add. MS 11695)[13], and the sculpture of the cloisters at Silos, including the capitals and reliefs. Schapiro first identified and defined certain stylistic qualities of Mozarabic and Romanesque art, and then pointed out Romanesque elements in the predominantly Mozarabic manuscript as well as Mozarabic elements in the Romanesque sculpture. On a semiological level he recognised that the new artistic forms could have emerged as a negation rather than a development of the older art, and that the continuance of the old beside the new could be an affirmation of an opposed or declining culture. He did not treat this as an absolute opposition, but spoke of the abbey as 'responsive and self-adjusting'. Nevertheless Schapiro attributed the production of the Silos Beatus, not completed until 1109 in the old Mozarabic style, to the affirmation of 'an independent, though weakened, monastic tradition … subjected to a new liturgy and rule, imposed from above'. He also equated the 'luxurious, aristocratic appearance' of the abbey not only with its royal patronage and wealth, but also with the elaborateness of the new liturgy. This function of style has since been questioned,[14] and the present study will be circumspect in its assumptions about the legitimacy of linking style and ideology.

Schapiro acknowledged that he had compared two works of art which were different in genre as well as in style, but offered this difference in a positive light as a metaphor of the qualities of the Mozarabic style – intimate, traditional, native, Apocalyptic, fantastic, exegetical – as opposed to the Romanesque – monumental, expansive, public, international. He did not, however, study the liturgical change in detail, and made only passing reference to the liturgical manuscripts in the Silos corpus. Indeed Werckmeister has maintained that, despite the scholarly historical context which he provided, Schapiro took an anti-religious stance derived from Marxism and dominated by consideration of the secular world.[15]

The present study, by staying very close to the central liturgical texts, focuses specifically on the liturgical change, and places the debate firmly in its liturgical and sacred context. It is, in my view, these liturgical manuscripts – rather than the more spectacular Beatus manuscript – that can give us a view of the liturgical change from the perspective of those who had to put it into practice. They also offer a view of the Romanesque style employed in a more intimate context than the Silos cloister, and hence a more appropriate point of comparison. Finally, this approach offers a different perspective from the more usual viewpoint of historians of medieval Spain, who have primarily studied the elite who imposed the change.

This book will focus on the northern Spanish kingdoms of León and Castile, as it was through their ruler, Alfonso VI, that the decision to change the rite was made. The two kingdoms had been joined since 1037 under Fernando I, by inheritance King of Castile and by conquest King of León. Alfonso VI also ruled Galicia from 1073, but that area will not be considered here, due both to the lack of suitable manuscript material and to the religious domination of that region by the secular cathedral of Santiago de Compostela, which makes it a special case.

The intention to introduce the Roman liturgy into Spain emanated from the papacy, and it was pursued by Pope Gregory VII with tenacity. His arguments are laid out in the letters which he wrote concerning affairs in Spain between 1074 and 1081, spanning the time from the early approaches to Alfonso VI until after the official acceptance of the Roman liturgy at the Council of Burgos in 1080. The most useful of these letters for our purpose is that which Gregory VII addressed jointly, in 1074, to Sancho IV of Navarre, Alfonso VI of Castile, and the bishops of both kingdoms.[16] It is initially surprising that the Pope should have linked the kings in this way, as Sancho and Alfonso both ruled in their own right and did not share territory. Between them, however they ruled the northern kingdoms of Spain (León, Castile, Navarre), which had once been united, together with Aragón, under the rule of their mutual grandfather, Sancho the Great (1000–1035). Sancho the Great had been in regular contact with Abbot Odilo of Cluny in the early eleventh century, and he had even sent a group of Spanish monks, including one called Paternus, to study at Cluny.[17] When Paternus returned in c.1021, Sancho had made him abbot of San Juan de la Peña in Aragón, where he probably introduced Cluniac customs. These reforms seem to have been limited: in broad geographical terms to Aragón and Navarre, and in scope since they did not extend to introducing the Roman liturgy. We can deduce this from a separate letter which Gregory VII sent to Sancho Ramírez V of Aragón, another grandson of Sancho the Great, again in 1074. In this letter Gregory acknowledged Sancho Ramírez's *fidelitas* towards the apostles Peter and Paul and the *Romanam Ecclesiam*, and accepted the king's declaration that by encouragement and direction he would bring about the introduction of the Roman liturgy in Aragón. That is to say, it was still not accomplished by 1074.[18]

Alfonso VI's father, Fernando I, had initiated an annual *census* to Cluny from the kingdom of Castile,[19] drawn from the immense wealth which he had exacted from the Arab *taifas*. In return Fernando had received major liturgical commemorations from the abbey on a level with those given to the German emperors. By this one action Fernando placed himself and his family within the ambit of the aristocracy of Europe and – although he may not have seen it in those terms – legitimised the use of the Roman liturgy to achieve his family's salvation. For his own use, however, the King retained the Mozarabic liturgy, as can be seen from his Prayer Book, which contained not only Mozarabic prayers, but also the Mozarabic arrangement of the psalms.[20]

Gregory VII may have addressed Sancho IV and Alfonso VI jointly in 1074 because of their familial link with Sancho Ramírez, who had already demonstrated his support of the papacy and of the Roman liturgy. In 1068 Sancho Ramírez had visited Rome and acknowledged the claims of Pope Alexander II; he had made his kingdom a papal fief and by 1071 the Roman liturgy had been introduced at the abbey of San Juan de la Peña.[21] Gregory might, therefore, have hoped that the other two grandsons might follow suit.

Another reason for the joint letter to Sancho IV and Alfonso may have been that it was intended as a statement to a wide public of the arguments for the change in the liturgy. Its message was just as applicable in Navarre as in Castile. Moreover, by writing to the bishops, as well as the kings, Gregory seems to have been addressing all influential parties, intending that no-one should be ignorant of his wishes.

The letter is not only a clear exposition of the reasons why the Roman liturgy should be 're-introduced' into Spain. It also includes most of the themes of Gregory's comprehensive programme of reform, although not referring to its essence, the freedom of the Church from temporal control in the form of *libertas romana*.[22] The objectives of Gregorian Reform are freely invoked: the desire for *renovatio*, a return to the ways of the early Church,[23] the ideal of uniformity within the Church, and abhorrence of ecclesiastical corruption, especially simony. Nevertheless it is a welcoming letter in its tone, with no threat of punishment against those who have used the Mozarabic liturgy in the past. Provided that the Spanish are willing now to return to 'Mother Church', they will be received like long-lost children.[24]

At the beginning of the letter of 1074, Gregory refers to St Paul's declared intention to visit Spain (Rom.15:24) and to the tradition that St Peter and St Paul had sent seven bishops from Rome to instruct the Spanish people. He asserts that they had shown how *ordinem et officium in divinis cultis* were to be conducted, and that Spain had *concordiam cum Romana urbe ... in religione et ordine divinii officii*.[25] He thus places Spain firmly in the world of the apostolic Church: it had originally been in accord with the very founders of the Church in its worship and its liturgy, and it truly belonged in concord with Rome. It was essential for Gregory's line of reasoning that he establish – even if only by assertion – that the Spanish had indeed used the Roman liturgy at the time of their conversion, and that any change now would be a return to earlier practice. There would then be no possibility of regarding the change as innovation; it would be merely a return to an earlier state. On a philosophical level he was advancing the doctrine of dissimilarity, whereby the divide between the nature of something at its creation and its present state could be bridged so that it resumed its original image.[26]

In his letter Gregory then compressed and dismissed nearly seven hundred years of Spanish history in thirty-six words.[27] For him this was the period of separation from the church of Rome, when Spain was successively assaulted by the madness of the Priscillianists and the treachery of the Arians, overrun by Goths and invaded by Saracens. To understand his attitude it has to be assumed that Gregory was accepting as a premise the idea that the Mozarabic liturgy in current use was tainted with heresy. This view probably originated with the Adoptionist controversy in Spain in the eighth century.[28] Adoptionism had been condemned at several of Charlemagne's church councils, including that at Frankfurt (794), where it had been implied that the Spanish had been punished for the heresy by the infidels' conquest of Spain.[29] Interest in the heresy was perpetuated among the Frankish clergy by Charlemagne's *Epistola ad Elipandum*, and by other tracts such as Paulinus of Aquileia's *Libellus Sacro syllabus contra Elipandum et ceteros episcopos*.[30]

Gregory was also undoubtedly influenced by the actions of his predecessor, Pope Alexander II, who had expressed his concern, in a letter of 18 October 1071 to the abbot of San Juan de la Peña, that parts of Spain had deviated from Catholic unity and, in particular, had strayed in matters of ecclesiastical discipline and liturgy.[31] Alexander II had sent the legate, Hugh Candidus, to the kingdom of Aragón in 1065, and again in 1071, with the mission to put an end to simony and to reform the 'confused' liturgy.[32] As soon as Gregory assumed the papacy in 1073, he appointed Hugh Candidus as his principal legate in Spain, so he was likely to have been well acquainted with the background to 'the Spanish problem' and primed to view the Mozarabic liturgy as irregular.[33] Although Gregory's letter does not actually accuse the Spanish church of heresy, it is clear from later correspondence that he believed them guilty of more than mere confusion, when he speaks of *'tantum periculum'*, and *'in tali errore'*.[34] In his pursuit of the issue he was thus continuing and expanding the policy of Alexander II, and glossing it with his own reforming ambitions.

Gregory's letter of 1074 continues by urging the Spanish, like good children cut off from their mother, to return to the security of *'matrem ... vestram Romanam Ecclesiam'*. They are to use not the divine service of Toledo, but that of the Roman Church, 'founded by Peter and Paul through Christ on the firm rock, against which the gates of hell, that is the tongues of heretics can never prevail'.[35] Membership of the Church of Rome provided the only authentic, secure community, outside which there were only spiritual and social outcasts. Gregory supported this argument with references to four recognised authorities. The first was Pope Innocent I, who had said in a letter to bishop Decentius of Gubbio:[36]

> If the priests of the Lord really wished to preserve ecclesiastical uses intact, as received from the Holy Apostles, no diversity and no variation would be found in the [eucharistic] rite and [other] ceremonial ... it is incumbent on [all western Churches] to follow what the Roman Church observes, from which they doubtless took their own beginning, lest by favouring adventitious opinions, they overlook the real source of their own institutions.

As a standard entry in collections of canon-law, this letter was a well-tried argument for uniformity based on Roman usage.

The second authority cited is Pope Hormisdas (514–23) who had written on three occasions to Spanish bishops: the reference seems to be specifically to the letter addressed to Sallustius, bishop of Baetica – that is Seville – described in Gregory VII's letter as *'Hispalensem'*.[37] This letter appealed to Sallustius to be vigilant in ensuring that the rules and decrees formulated at councils in the past were obeyed, and included an emphatic condemnation of all heretics. The other two letters to all the bishops of Spain also contained useful material for Gregory VII's case, and their arguments may also have been implied. One made three main points: that priests must be ordained according to *statuta canonum*; that simony must not be allowed; and that annual councils must be held.[38] The other contained a strong statement against the creed of some Greek clerics, followers of the heretic Acacius, who, Hormisdas expected, would try to be accepted in Spain. His endorsement of the Roman Church and the papacy as established by Christ (Matt. XVI), *quia in sede apostolica extra maculam semper est catholica servata religio*, foreshadowed Gregory VII's stance.[39]

The other two sources used by Gregory were Spanish church councils of Toledo and Braga.[40] This was presumably in reference to the canons of the IV Council of Toledo (633), which had legislated for uniformity in usage and in liturgical formulas for masses and sacraments, and for the offices of vespers and matins.[41] Before this similar requirements had already been formulated at the second Council of Braga in 563 concerning chant in the offices, and the *ordo* of the mass including specifically the *lectiones*.[42]

By using these various authorities Gregory was appealing to the recurring ideal of unity in religious practices and usage, which had been sought (but not achieved) throughout the history of reform in the Church. For example Charlemagne, according to the Monk of St Gall,[43] was disturbed to find 'that all his provinces, and indeed his cities and even the smaller localities, continued to differ in the way they worshipped God, and particularly in the rhythm of their chanting'. According to the biography he attempted to correct this by asking the Pope to send him some monks to teach in his cathedrals, but it transpired that these monks all taught different systems, and the only way in which he managed to bring any conformity to the use of the chant was to send two Frankish monks to Rome and then employ them to teach at different cathedrals by means of standard antiphonaries. In spite of, and partly because of, such attempts the Roman liturgy became hybridised and a Romano-Frankish liturgy came to exist in various versions, even in Rome.[44] Nonetheless this did not prevent the persistence of the ideal of uniformity.

The Mozarabic liturgy, it should be noted, was still not itself uniform five hundred years after the canons of the Council of Toledo, which had declared the intention of making it so. Although scholars have reconstructed the liturgy from the various texts which survive, the editions are eclectic,[45] and two disparate traditions have been identified, known as 'A' and 'B', in the system of pericopes.[46] Yet even within these, variations exist between texts from different areas and different dates.

There is, however, no hint in Gregory's letter of 1074 that the Roman liturgy is other than uniform; it seems to require no further definition. The Mozarabic liturgy is not itself mentioned, either as *gothica* or *more Toletano*; it is merely made clear that any liturgy which is not 'Roman' is heretical. The appeal ends by reminding the readers that Spanish bishops had already promised to introduce the Roman liturgy. Gregory then concluded on a practical note relating to his reforming interests, by confirming a decision regarding a bishop who had been found guilty of simony.[47]

The whole communication is confidently directive; it does not attempt to deal with the Mozarabic liturgy or to suggest that a revised version might be acceptable. Only a complete change to the Roman liturgy will do. It is a thinly-veiled ordinance delivered from a distance, and there is no attempt to understand the position of the Church in Spain. Its tone may be welcoming, but its implications are uncompromising, showing little regard for the sensitivies of the rulers, bishops, priests and monks of Spain, let alone the practicalities of replacing one liturgy with another.

In particular, Gregory does not seem to have realised that the Spanish kings – probably from the time of Alfonso II – claimed continuity with the Visigoths (whom Gregory regarded as among the villains) as their legitimate heirs. Although they may have admitted the Arian failings of the first Visigothic rulers, the Spanish chronicles proclaimed the steadfast maintenance of orthodoxy after the conversion of Reccared in 587. By the ninth century the Visigothic kingdom had become the subject of a Neo-Gothic myth,[48] as a time to which the later kings of Asturias, León and Castile could look back with nostalgia and recall when they had ruled all of the old Roman *Hispania*. The *crónica albedense* says that Alfonso II (791–842), king of Asturias and León, re-established in Oviedo the ceremonies of the Visigoths in the church and the palace.[49] It has been generally accepted that this 'myth' was expressed visually by Alfonso II, especially in his church of Santullano.[50] John Williams has argued that this 'myth' was still potent in the eleventh century and that Fernando I, Alfonso VI's father, employed this same tradition in establishing himself as King of León.[51] Since Fernando had acquired León, to add to his kingdom of Castile, only through his marriage to Sancha, and had, therefore, no claim to the lineage by birth, he needed to establish his Leonese identity and to link himself clearly with the associated 'Neo-Gothic' imperial aspirations. Williams argued that he did this through a policy of revivalism, using Sancha's position as the last surviving descendent of Alfonso III, and expressing the policy through, among other possibilities, his choice of design for the church of San Isidoro at León. The supporting evidence for such a policy includes a passage from the *Historia Silense*, which says that Sancha had urged Fernando to use the church of St John the Baptist in León, where her father and brother were buried,[52] as his dynastic burial place, rather than his family mausolea in San Salvator at Oña, in Navarre, or in San Pedro de Arlanza, in Castile, as he had previously planned. Maybe the very choice of Alfonso as the name of Fernando and Sancha's son was another instance of this desire to associate with the Gothic past, recalling as it does the two most successful of the Asturian and Leonese monarchs as well as three other kings in the line.[53] The *Historia Silense* goes as far as to describe Alfonso VI as *ex illustri Gotorum prosapia ortus*,[54] and proceeds to catalogue this ancestry in considerable detail. We have no way of knowing to what extent Alfonso believed Gregory's version of Spanish history in the letter of 1074, or how he reconciled his Gothic inheritance with the papal arguments. Nevertheless Alfonso acted and the change began.

In 1078 the Chronicle of Burgos records *Intravit romana lex in Hispania*.[55] In November 1079, Gregory wrote a congratulatory letter to Alfonso: 'my most dear son in Christ … glorious king of the Spanish'.[56] He then to some extent mitigated the compliment by referring immediately to 'blessed Peter, leader of the apostles, … to whom [God] subjecting all principates and powers of the world, gave the right of binding and loosing in heaven and on earth', promoting his own position with somewhat megalomaniac rhetoric.[57] He praised Alfonso for rescuing his people from so many years of blindness and ignorance, but also stated explicitly the penalties for any back-sliding:

> just as there is certain hope of salvation for those who remain strong in their observance of the faith and doctrine of this holy apostolic see, so for those who turn from the track of its harmony and unity, there threatens certain damnation.[58]

The letter says that it is accompanied by a gift, a small gold key *ex more sanctorum*, with the blessing of St Peter.[59] When speaking of the gift, Gregory recalls how God freed St Peter from prison. He may have intended thereby to refer specifically to Alfonso's rescue from prison. After being defeated in battle by his brother, King Sancho II of Castile, Alfonso had been deposed and imprisoned in Burgos. When he was finally restored to his throne in 1072, after exile in Toledo, Alfonso attributed his release to St Peter and the intercession of the monks at Cluny – perhaps a figurative means of indicating that the abbot of Cluny had helped to negotiate his freedom.[60] Gratitude or fulfilment of a vow may, therefore, have been among the motives which led Alfonso to give the abbey of San Isidoro de las Dueñas to Cluny in 1073, and Gregory's gift in 1079 may thus have been as much a reminder of Alfonso's obligation, as a recognition of his achievement.

Gregory employed the image of curing blindness in a letter to Alfonso VI in 1080, and likened him to the sun emitting heavenly rays: *velut sol quidam in occiduis natus, orientem versus coelestis luminis radios emittebat.*[61] Here Gregory is employing the imagery of light in darkness, one of the topoi characteristic of the rhetoric of Gregorian Reform, which was keen to plunder such long-established symbols of revelation. Similar imagery was used, for example, by Cardinal Matthew of Albano in a letter to the abbots at Reims, whom he described as being 'like bright lights and shining stars' banishing the darkness which obscured the monastic order. Other similes rooted in the natural order were used to promote reform and renewal at the end of the eleventh century to make it seem familiar and part of God's creation; these included fire, reflowering, the weather and the seasons, as well as the opposition of night and day.[62]

The last recorded papal letter concerning the introduction of the Roman liturgy was written in 1081, when the introduction seemed securely under way. Gregory praised Alfonso and then reverted to the maternal imagery of his first letter: 'you have brought about the reception of the liturgy of the holy Roman Church, the mother of all, into the churches of your kingdom and ensured that it is celebrated according to the ancient custom'.[63] The letter is a clear statement of the consummation of Gregory's plan. In the coda Gregory encapsulates his view of the satisfactorily resolved situation, everything now in its appropriate place:

> May Almighty God, … who gives salvation to kings, through the merits of the most high lady Mary, mother of God, and of all the saints, by the authority of the blessed apostles Peter and Paul – although we are unworthy because of whatever offences – absolve you and your faithful in Christ from all sins, and may He give you victory over your enemies visible and invisible. May He always illumine your mind, so that, by careful study of His goodness and human weakness, you may despise worldly glory and come to eternal glory through our guide, blessed Peter.[64]

This examination of the arguments for the change in the liturgy, as expressed by their proposer, has shown them to be contained within the general assumptions of the Gregorian Reform programme, the desire to return to the ways of the *ecclesia primitiva*, to Mother Church in the person of the Virgin Mary, to the church of the Apostles. There is also evidence of Gregory's belief that St Peter, in the person of the Pope, was over all earthly kings, but there is no mention in these letters specifically of *libertas ecclesiae*. Indeed the specifics of the Reform, such as the removal of simony and the promotion of celibacy, are not argued in these letters; it was presumably left to the papal legates to disseminate these.

This is a suitable point to consider briefly some iconographic expressions of Gregorian Reform. Gregorian iconography has been explored by several scholars, including Hélène Toubert and Ernst Kitzinger.[65] Many of Toubert's studies have concentrated on Rome, where, she argues, the Gregorian movement involved a revival of interest in the decorative motifs of the early Church, which were elaborated upon and fused with more contemporary preoccupations to celebrate *Ecclesia* and ideas of *renovatio*.[66] In France on the other hand, particularly in churches associated with Cluny, she has found images of papal authority expressed through events in the life of St Peter, especially in representations of the *traditio legis*.[67] She has also studied the importance of the Gregorian Reform movement in the development of images, especially those of *Ecclesia*. These include *Ecclesia* personified with *Synagoga* or alone as *Mater Ecclesia* – sometimes conflated with Marian imagery, or more allegorical images such as the Vine springing from the Cross/Tree of Life.[68]

Kitzinger suggested that there was a significant difference between 'the Gregorian phase proper of the Reform movement and the subsequent phase of consolidation and triumph'. This could be seen, according to him, in the lack of direct 'visual manifestos', that is actual depictions of papal authority, in Gregory's own time. He pointed to the use instead of oblique visual expressions, such as the revival of devices and themes of early Christian art.[69] Both Toubert and Kitzinger offer examples of such revivalism, but not all examples of the use of antique themes in Romanesque art can be attributed to political or ideological motives, and we must be especially circumspect in attributing any semiological significance to such examples.

Most of Toubert's examples come from large-scale works, such as wall-paintings or sculptural programmes, rather than from manuscripts, so it may be inappropriate to expect direct, prominent Gregorian imagery in more intimate liturgical manuscripts of the period. Small-scale subtle indicators are more likely to be found in the objects of this study. It should also be noted that Spain did not share in the development of very large richly-illustrated bibles with historiated initials, which took place from the end of the eleventh century in France, Italy, Germany and England. Brieger has linked this development to the Gregorian reform movement in general, and has suggested that it may even have been initiated by Gregory VII.[70] The bibles which survive from medieval Spain (outside Catalonia) cannot be connected with the liturgical change, however, since they were produced before the eleventh century or after 1150, that is, well outside the period when the change was being implemented.

No one figure expresses for us the views of those who may have opposed the liturgical change in the way that Gregory sums up the reasons for it. Considering that any who resisted the change were on the losing side and are unlikely to have been encouraged to express their views, it is surprising that any contrary arguments survive. But there is evidence of resistance: in comments made in a letter by Alfonso VI, in some Spanish chronicles, and again in the correspondence of Gregory VII. In 1077 Alfonso wrote to Abbot Hugh of Cluny 'concerning the Roman liturgy, which we have accepted on your instructions' (note that he does not say 'on Gregory VII's instructions'). The letter asks for Hugh's patronage (*paternitas*) in persuading the Pope to send once more his legate, Gerald, 'so that he may amend what needs amending and correct what needs correcting', because 'our land is utterly bereft'.[71]

The *Chronicon Burgense, Annales Compostellani* and the twelfth-century *Chronicon Nájera* all confirm this impression of resistance to change by recording a trial by duel between a Toledan knight and a Castilian knight to decide between the two rites on 9 April 1077, Palm Sunday.[72] The *Chronicon Burgense* and the *Chronicon Nájera* say the Castilian won, but the result is not clear in the *Annales Compostellani*. The *Chronicon Nájera* adds the more colourful story of a trial by fire, where the Mozarabic book is said to have leapt from the flames. At this point the king intervened, kicking it back into the fire and uttering the verse: *Ad libitum regum flectuntur cornua legum*. This unsympathetic description of Alfonso's behaviour seems at variance with his concern expressed in the letter to Hugh, unless the letter merely reflects guilt at the aggressive way in which he had attempted to implement the change, which may have stimulated equally vehement resistance.

When Gregory described opposition to the change in a letter of 1080, it was in terms of a major crisis. The whole enterprise was at risk, 'a hundred thousand men, who through our diligent efforts had began to return to the way of truth, have fallen back into their former error'.[73] This refers to events in that year, when the King's adviser, a Cluniac monk named Robert, was managing the introduction of the Roman liturgy at the royal monastery of Sahagún. According to a charter, also of 1080, Alfonso had chosen this abbey as the centre of the reform programme.[74] The charter laid down that the customs of Cluny were to be used there, that Robert, Alfonso's adviser, was to be abbot, and that he was to supervise the change to Cluniac ways.[75] Robert, however, seems to have given in to the resistance of the monks at Sahagún, who themselves subsequently left the monastery.[76]

These are, however, events described by those who were mainly in favour of the change. For arguments against the abandonment of the Mozarabic liturgy we have only two texts, which originated in one place, the abbey of San Millán de la Cogolla. This abbey had been in the kingdom of Navarre until 1076, so it could have observed Cluniac customs – excluding the liturgical requirements – since their possible introduction by Sancho the Great in c.1022. It had not used the Roman liturgy, as is testified by the surviving manuscripts from its scriptorium. In 1077 the Riojan area including San Millán passed to Alfonso, and the abbey seems then to have come under the same pressure to introduce the Roman liturgy as the other abbeys in his kingdom.

One of the texts concerning the liturgy is inserted in the *Codex Aemilianensis*, now in the library of the Escorial.[77] It is presented not as a defence of the liturgy, but rather as a description of historical events. Historians, however, have doubted its veracity and have viewed it as a deliberate attempt to construct a more convenient past.[78] The narrative operates largely on the premise that papal approbation is sufficient for validation of the liturgy. The first part, headed *De missa apostolica in Spania ducta*, refers to the same mission described by Gregory, the introduction of the apostolic liturgy to Spain by the first seven apostles. In this version, however, the apostolic liturgy is identified with the Mozarabic liturgy, although it is allowed that it was 'enriched' by the great Spanish doctors. Thus this document employs the same appeal as that used by Gregory: authorisation through association with the first apostles. The second and third sections, *De officio ispane ecclesie in Roma laudato et confirmato*, purport to describe two papal approvals of the Mozarabic liturgy: the first is the supposed commission of a priest from Santiago de Compostela, called Zanello, to report to Pope John X (914–28) on ecclesiastical discipline in Spain and on the orthodoxy of the liturgy. He is said to have declared that everything was in accord with Roman usage, but to have recommended that the *secreta misse* should conform to that in the Apostolic Church. David has argued that even this refers not to Rome, but to the usage of Santiago de Compostela.[79]

The third section concerns a more recent event, the supposed approbation of the Mozarabic rite by Pope Alexander II (1061–73). It tells how the papal legate Hugh Candidus had attempted to destroy the liturgy, but, in common with others who tried, had had to abandon the attempt. The Spanish Church had then sent three bishops, Munio of Calahorra, Simeon of Oca, and Fortunio of Alvara, to Rome with a *Liber Ordinum* from Albelda, a *Liber Orationum* and *Antiphonium* from Hirache and a *Sacramentarium* from Santa Gema. The Pope and the abbot of St Benedict are said to have examined the books and declared them Catholic and free of heresy. The Pope and the Council had then forbidden any disturbance or change to the Spanish liturgy.[80]

In view of Alexander II's comments on the Mozarabic liturgy in his letter to the abbot of San Juan de la Peña, as David and others have maintained, it seems very unlikely that any such approbation could have been given.[81] This view is strengthened by Gregory's complaint to Simeon of Oca that there had even been claims to *his* approval.[82] The text was composed unquestionably in direct opposition to the introduction of the Roman liturgy in the 1070s or 1080s.

The second text was written at the back of a copy of a Spanish lectionary, a *Liber Comicus*. It eschewed any attempt at altering past events, but concentrated on the arguments for retaining the traditional liturgy (*see* Appendix I).[83] In so doing it adopted the philosophical position which was opposed to change in general and especially to liturgical change. This text is a statement against all change, novelty, and abandonment of tradition. Gregory may have represented his policy as a return to the ways of the early Church, not as an improvement, or innovation, but the San Millán text clearly treats the proposal as 'new' and calls it an apostasy. As Beryl Smalley recognized, Gregory's reforming ideas were constantly open to this accusation, and he took great care to protect himself from it.[84]

At the beginning of the San Millán text the writer quotes St Isidore, in turn quoting the apostle Paul, 'put all things to the test, hold on to what is good'. On an individual level this passage from St Paul urges renewal and offers scriptural authority for those promoting it.[85]

It even uses the word *'novitate'*, albeit in association with *reformamini*. It is, therefore, very likely that the San Millán writer is well aware that this passage from St Paul is used as an argument for change, and he is rebutting that point by showing that it is rather an argument for what is good. He then turns to the Lord's Prayer, pointing out that in it there are seven prayers of sacrifice laid down by evangelical and apostolic doctrine, and that the original reason for this number seems to be either the 'seven-fold universal nature of the Holy Church' or the 'seven-fold gifts of the Spirit, by whose gift the offerings are sanctified'. This passage also has its origins in the writings of St Isidore and refers to the seven prayers of sacrifice of the Mozarabic liturgy.[86]

Having supported the pedigree of the Mozarabic liturgy, the writer turns to attack innovation. Arguing within the confines of typological thought, he appeals to past authorities with the same disregard for anachronism, and suspension of the critical faculty, that Gregory had exhibited. He uses the Council of Gangra: 'We condemn those who raise themselves up against the scriptures and the church canons and introduce new precepts',[87] and Pope Hormisdas's letter to the bishops of Baetica. This allusion was to one of the same letters which Gregory VII mentioned in his letter, and may refer to the phrase:

Prima salus est rectae fidei regulam custodire et a constitutis Patrum nullatenus deviare.[88]

The writer's choice of a Council and of Pope Hormisdas look like a direct answer to Gregory's authorities, which included the same Pope and two Spanish councils, but this is so only in a schematic, rhetorical sense, and there is no direct rebuttal of Gregory's arguments. The writer is more concerned to make his own point, that those who are trying to change the liturgy are guilty of abandoning tradition and of seeking innovation. It suggests, moreover, that the contents of Gregory's letter of 1074 may have had a wide circulation.

The writer then speaks of the burning of missal books, a reference which is not explained or corroborated by any other documentary evidence – except the story of the trial by fire in the *Chronicon Nájera*. He asserts that these books had been praised by the fathers and by St Peter; this is presumably an allusion to the papal approval claimed in the other document from San Millán. He accuses those who had burnt the books of being the true apostates, thereby implying that the churchmen who introduced the Roman liturgy had made similar serious accusations against those who adhered to the Mozarabic liturgy, charging them with the desertion of their faith and rebellion against 'the Church'. The writer continues with excerpts from the missal books, quoting the words which begin some of the Mozarabic *illationes*.[89] *Dignum et iustum est nos tibi semper gratias agere, omnipotens Deus, per Ihesum Christum Filium tuum Dominum nostrum.* The *illatio* is the formula which is equivalent to the Roman preface and these words are similar to those which begin that preface. The passage continues by referring to Christ as the 'only true pontiff and priest without sin'.[90] By this he may have intended to criticize Gregory for his ambitions in the papacy, but the passages also demonstrate theological correctness in their phraseology concerning God the Father and God the Son.

The next section appeals to the Scriptures and speaks of God's revenge on those who fall into apostasy, for which he punished the fallen angels. The author ends with an exhortation to stand firm: 'Let there not be in us, as in some people, the wicked deviousness of infidelity, nor false treachery of mind, nor the sin of perjury, nor heinous attempts at oaths; the souls of the church agree that without resistance those things of ours which have been laid down will be desecrated by deviation, but all can be kept safe by firm resolve.'

This text implies that severe measures were employed to enforce the change to the Roman liturgy and that the opponents of the Mozarabic liturgy may even have resorted to the burning of liturgical books. The last sentence also suggests that the monks may have been required to swear adherence to the new Roman liturgy. No certain conclusions can be drawn, however, because of the heavily rhetorical conception of the piece. Nonetheless this text is a much more thoughtful and impressive response to liturgical reform than the re-invention of history offered in the *Codex Aemilianensis*.

The obvious iconographic expression of these arguments against change would be the continuance of whatever iconography was currently in use; or, as Schapiro proposed, the persistence of the current style. It is, however, difficult for a modern viewer to distinguish when continuity is the result of mere habit and when it is a positive statement in favour of *stasis*. We might expect those who wished to preserve the Mozarabic liturgy to return to iconography or styles which had flourished in the revivalist times of Alfonso II or Alfonso III, but the overall tendency of Mozarabic art to recycle its traditions makes specific cases difficult to pin down. Any assertion that the use of a style in itself communicated a specific meaning for those who employed it, or those who viewed it, would require considerable contextual evidence.

This study will concentrate in detail on a small number of manuscripts in the hope that arguments based on nebulous suppositions can be avoided. It is possible, as we shall see, to deal with the Mozarabic liturgy *as it was practised* in a specified area, and with the Roman liturgy *in the form in which it was introduced* into Spain. A picture will be built up from comparisons between manuscripts, especially from the information which they may give us about the methods used to implement the liturgical change. Comparison between text and image, or, more generally, text and its means of presentation, will be investigated for indications of the significance of new practices and new approaches. There is little documentary evidence to help us understand the processes used to introduce the Roman liturgy, but a few passages may help to form the background.

In 1075 it seems that both liturgies may have been in use, at least on official occasions, for when Alfonso VI attended the opening of the *Arca Santa* in Oviedo, the priests who lived there used the Toledan rite, while the others used the Roman.[91] This may show that there was initial tolerance of both liturgies, or that at this early stage only the royal party used the Roman liturgy. It also fits with the statement of the Anónimo of Sahagún that Alfonso made a definite decision to change the liturgy only as late as 1076.[92] Most of the progress in the introduction of the Roman liturgy seems to have been made through the papal legates, Hugh Candidus, Gerald of Ostia and above all Richard of Marseilles, who seems to have been the one with the determination to see the decision finally enacted. Gregory's initial hopes of achieving the change through Spanish bishops, such as Jimeno of Burgos, seem to have secured only pockets of support, not the wholesale change of heart which was required.[93] Jimeno, however, may well have been closely involved in the implementation process, since the final decision to change the liturgy was made at Burgos in 1080. Moreover the choice of this city is somewhat surprising, as it was not at that time an obvious location for a Spanish Church council.[94] The likelihood of Jimeno's involvement is strengthened by his probable royal support, at least from the time of his claim to the see of Oca-Burgos in 1074 until his death in 1082. It may also be significant that Gregory VII had urged him to implement the new liturgy when he had confirmed his claim to the bishopric in 1076, and Jimeno was also chosen to work with the papal legate during the Sahagún crisis, at the end of which he reported the successful resolution to Gregory.[95]

Cluny seems to have played the sympathetic, supportive role for which it was suited. When Paternus had lived at Cluny, according to Ralph Glaber, the Spanish monks were allowed to celebrate the beginning of Advent with the feast of St Acisclus according to their own rite,[96] so it seems that Cluny was prepared to tolerate local variations at least at the beginning of the eleventh century. Although we have the *Consuetudines* produced by Ulrich and Bernard setting out the details of Cluniac liturgical practice,[97] they may themselves represent attempts at standardization in a climate of diversity and hence ought not to be taken at face value. Even Abbot Hugh is known to have been prepared to bend the rules and to alter liturgical practices in a minor way.[98] Thus Cluny may have been too tolerant of different practices to play a firm role in the liturgical change.[99]

Cluny did provide Alfonso VI with a close adviser, Robert, of whom he spoke very warmly and on whom he seems to have depended greatly.[100] During the introduction of the Roman liturgy at the royal monastery of Sahagún, possibly the first abbey to have been chosen for the changeover, Robert seems, however, to have been too weak or too sympathetic to persuade the monks to make the transition. Gregory certainly blamed Robert for the failure, in association with an 'abandoned woman' whose identity has been much disputed, but Gregory's outburst at the mis-management of the affair was also directed at Abbot Hugh of Cluny, to whom he sent a long accusatory letter and another to be forwarded to Alfonso.[101] On this occasion Gregory was not grateful for the arbitration tactics of Cluny, and immediately sent his papal legate, Richard, to take charge. To judge from Gregory's letters to Richard, this legate seems to have been much less flexible and the matter was settled quickly.[102] A monk from one of Cluny's daughter houses, Bernard de la Sauvetat, previously at Cluny and recently prior of St Orens at Auch in Gascony, was appointed abbot, and no more dissension is recorded.[103] Bernard seems to have been an ideal appointment, partly because as a young man he had worked with abbot Hugh at Cluny, and especially because St Orens had also gone through a period of change after becoming subject to Cluny in 1068.[104]

At some stage Cluny seems to have become a model for the liturgical change in general and for the abbey of Sahagún in particular.[105] In the first charter of 1080 from Alfonso to the abbey of Sahagún, the one which precipitated the troubles, Alfonso appointed Robert as abbot and did not give the abbey the freedom from his control which Cluny enjoyed from temporal rulers. There followed, however, a second charter in May 1080, after the Council of Burgos, where the adoption of the Roman liturgy was confirmed. This charter stated that the monastic life of Sahagún had been regulated *per quosdam religiosos viros ad instar Cluniacensis normae monasticae ordinis sancti Benedicti docte eruditos.*[106] The new abbot, Bernard, was described as elected by the monks, and only afterwards appointed by the King in the presence of the papal legate. Alfonso also omitted the customary royal prerogative *ad regendum et defendendum.* By December 1080 Alfonso had advanced even further towards the Cluniac model in accordance with Gregory's highest aim, the freedom of the Church. In this charter Alfonso admitted his desire to promote Sahagún, but also claimed to have freed it 'from the power of men' and 'devoted [it] to the liberty that is proper for the Church'.[107] In 1083 Bernard travelled to Rome, was consecrated abbot, and received a privilege 'which was designed fully, finally, and expressly to make Sahagún the Cluny of Spain', endowing it with the *libertas Romana*, and giving it papal protection in return for a nominal annual *census* of two shillings.[108] The abbey was confirmed in its right freely to elect its own abbot; any Catholic bishop might consecrate the abbot or ordain monks; no bishop could administer sacraments within its walls without the abbot's permission. It was Gregory with his talent for epitomising the culmination of his plans who best described the significance of this event:

> we take this monastery into the safekeeping of our perpetual defence and of Roman liberty, and we lay down that it is to be free from the yoke of every ecclesiastical or secular power. ... It is especially to cleave to the Apostolic See after the pattern and form of Cluny which, in God's providence and under Roman liberty, shines more clearly than daylight through almost all parts of the world, because of the fame of its religion, reputation, and dignity. It is likewise to enjoy a perpetual and an inviolable security. *Thus like Cluny in France,* Sahagún may be illustrious in Spain for its prerogative of liberty. As by the grace of God it will be its peer in religion, so let it be its equal in the confirmation of its rights by the Apostolic See.[109]

Alfonso's support is confirmed by the text of the *fuero*, when in 1085 he founded a town at Sahagún for the benefit of the monastery. He stated that he had 'made it free from every burden to the royal fisc and from every ecclesiastical obligation; for I have given it to the Roman Church and to St Peter in Roman liberty'.[110]

Bernard's continued career is well documented, for in 1086 he became the first archbishop of Toledo after its reconquest, and papal legate to Pope Urban II; in 1088 he was one of those who confirmed the charter which made San Servando at Toledo subject to Saint Victor of Marseilles with '*libertas Romana*'.[111] Was the introduction of the Roman liturgy therefore accomplished by the appointment of French abbots and bishops, or was Bernard an isolated example? The evidence concerning this question is complex and has to be gathered mainly from the confirmation of charters; it has been studied at length by Fletcher, who has shown that there was a significant number of French clergy in important posts in Spain from roughly the time of the liturgical change until the middle of the twelfth century. In particular Bernard seems to have recruited at least six promising French monks, including some through his connection with Gascony, but this is not documented until after his promotion to the archbishopric.[112] They include Jerôme from Périgord who was bishop first at Valencia and then at Salamanca, Bernard who became bishop of Zamora, and Bernard from Agen, bishop of Sigüenza, whose uncle was bishop of Segovia and whose brother was bishop of Palencia. Nevertheless not all bishoprics were held by French clergy or monks, as, for example, Diego Gelmirez retained Santiago, and another Diego held León. Many abbacies, for example at Silos, were held likewise by Spanish monks. Although this gives us some idea of the importance of French clergy a generation after the decision to change the liturgy, we still know very little about those who might have been brought in to facilitate the change itself, to teach the new chant and to supervise the copying of missals, breviaries and other liturgical books. The documentary evidence gives us scant indication of the methods used to implement the change.

It is, therefore, above all in this area of the implementation of the Roman liturgy that study of contemporary manuscripts may help us. By examining the objects which embody the change, we shall attempt to understand its nature. We may be able to learn something of the pace at which the change took place and whether it progressed smoothly or was subject to back-sliding. We shall examine its extent, what forms it took, and whether it affected all aspects of the liturgy. We shall attempt to discover whether the manuscripts conform to certain guidelines or models, or compromise on various fronts. In particular the presentation and decoration of the liturgical texts will give some indication of how the new liturgy was approached.

There is a wide choice of surviving manuscripts of the Mozarabic liturgy, most of them in the Cathedral libraries of Toledo and León, the Biblioteca Nacional and the Real Academia de la Historia at Madrid, the Bibliothèque Nationale in Paris, the British Library in London, and the library of the abbey at Silos.[113] Most art-historical work on Spanish manuscripts has been, and still is, concentrated on the rich and abundant Beatus codices, but they will not be considered here, as they are believed to have been reserved for personal study rather than for liturgical purposes.[114] The books of the Mozarabic liturgy have been studied mainly as part of the attempt to reconstruct that liturgy, rather than for themselves, since their illumination is notably inferior in quantity and quality to that in most of the Beatus manuscripts. They have also been consulted by musicologists for information on their abstruse system of neumes.[115] They have received little previous attention for their layout and decoration.

When we look for manuscripts of the Roman liturgy produced in Spain before the end of the twelfth century the choice is much less wide. This may be because the large numbers of books required would have received heavy use both as exemplars in the scriptorium and in the church. Examples are preserved in the Biblioteca Nacional and the Real Academia de la Historia in Madrid, and in the British Library; there is an isolated book in the University library at Salamanca, and a lectionary at the Ruskin Museum in Sheffield.[116]

The two parts of this book will examine the liturgical manuscripts in two categories:

first, books containing texts for the offices, and second, books containing texts for the mass. The attendant antiphoners, lectionaries, books of prayers, books of hours, and psalters will not be discussed here except in so far as they can illumine an aspect of one of the chosen manuscripts. The decision to exclude them has been made largely because of the material available, as there is an insufficient number of Mozarabic and Roman manuscripts to permit a fruitful comparison. This should not, I feel, invalidate the argument, since the manuscripts for the office and mass are the crucial books which give the core texts of the liturgy.

Notes to Introduction

1   Smalley, B., 'Ecclesiastical Attitudes to Novelty *c.*1100–*c.*1250', in *Church, Society and Politics,* Studies in Church History, vol. 12, Oxford, 1975, pp.113–31. *See also* Kemp, A., *The Estrangement of the Past: a Study in the Origins of Modern Historical Consciousness,* Oxford, 1991.

2   Eusebius of Caesarea, *The Ecclesiastical History,* I.I.1–2, pp.6–7, (Lake, K., trans.), London and New York, 1926, 'the names, the number and the age of those who, driven by the desire of innovation (νεωτεροποιια) to an extremity of error, have heralded themselves as the introducers of Knowledge, falsely so-called, ravaging the flock of Christ unsparingly, like grim wolves'.

3   Constable, G., 'Renewal and Reform in Religious Life – Concepts and Realities', in Benson, R.L. and Constable, G. (eds.), *Renaissance and Renewal in the Twelfth Century,* Oxford, 1982, p.65 and n.146, and Moore, R.I., *The Formation of a Persecuting Society: Power and Deviance in Western Europe, 950–1250,* Oxford, 1987, p.71, 'the heretic was always accused of innovation'.

4   Migne, J.P., *Patrologia Latina,* Paris, 1844–64 (hereafter *PL*) 182, col. 336 (1140).

5   *PL* 178, col. 339, 'You who seem to have only sprung up recently, delighting greatly in your novelty, outside the long-established custom of both clerics and monks, have now also set up among yourselves, by some new decrees, a divine office. ... this innovation or individuality of yours retreats from the tradition of others'.

6   The word 'Mozarabic' derives from the arabic *musta'rib,* 'would-be-Arab'. In the liturgical context, however there is no implication that the rite is any way Islamic. In this context the term merely denotes the Old Spanish liturgy. The word has also acquired a broader meaning designating the culture of Christian early medieval Spain. *See* Werckmeister, O.K., 'Art of the Frontier: Mozarabic Monasticism', in *The Art of Medieval Spain* AD *500–1200,* The Metropolitan Museum of Art, New York, 1993, p.121.

7   St. Bernard specifically raises this point in the same letter, although he is referring to the introduction of only one feast: *PL* 182, col. 333, *Praesertim in officiis ecclesiasticis haud facile unquam repentinis visa est novitatibus acquiescere ... Nunquid Patribus doctiores, aut devotiores sumus?*

8   The instances are numerous. For examples involving the Mozarabic liturgy *see* Vivancos Gómez, M.C., *Documentación del Monasterio de Santo Domingo de Silos (954–1254),* Burgos, 1988, p.3 ff. Cluny was the major beneficiary employing the Roman liturgy; *see* Bishko, C.J., 'Liturgical Intercession at Cluny for the King-Emperors of León', in *Studia Monastica,* 3, 1961, p.54 ff., and Cowdrey, H.E.J., 'Unions and Confraternity with Cluny', *Journal of Ecclesiastical History,* 16, 1965, pp.152–62.

9   Vivancos Gómez, M.C., *as above* note 8, p.20.

10   Díaz y Díaz, M.C., 'Literary Aspects of the Visigothic Liturgy', in James, E. (ed.), *Visigothic Spain: New Approaches,* Oxford, 1980, p.72.

11   Recently for example: Dodds, J.D., 'Islam, Christianity, and the problem of religious art', in *The Art of Medieval Spain A.D.500–1200,* The Metropolitan Museum of Art, New York, 1993, p.33.

12   Schapiro, M., 'From Mozarabic to Silos', in *Romanesque Art,* London, 1977, pp. 28–101.

13   Subsequently referred to in this study as 'the Silos Beatus'.

14   Recently in this context by Williams, J.W., catalogue entry on the Silos Beatus, in *The Art of Medieval Spain A.D.500–1200,* The Metropolitan Museum of Art, New York, 1993, p.292.

15   Werckmeister, O.K., review of Schapiro, M., *Romanesque Art,* in *Art Quarterly,* n.s. 2, 2, 1979, p.214.

16   Reg. i, ep. LXIV, in *PL* 148, col. 340, *Unde enim non dubitatis vos suscepisse religionis exordium, restat etiam ut inde recipiatis in ecclesiastico ordine divinum officium.*

17   Cowdrey, H.E.J., *The Cluniacs and the Gregorian Reform,* Oxford, 1970, p.215–16, Jotsald, *Vita Odilonis,* i. 7, in *PL* 142, col 902, and Bishko, C.J., 'Fernando I and the Origins of the Leonese-Castilian Alliance with Cluny', in Bishko, C.J., *Studies in Medieval Spanish Frontier History,* London, 1980, pp.3–6.

18   Reg. i, ep. LXIII, in *PL* 148, col. 339, *in quibus quanta fidelitate erga principes apostolorum Petrum et Paulum ac*

Romanam Ecclesiam ferveas satis perspeximus, and *sub ditione tua Romani ordinis officium fieri studio et jussionibus tuis asseris, Romanae Ecclesiae te filium, ac eam concordiam et eamdem amicitiam te nobiscum habere, quam olim reges Hispaniae cum Romanis pontificibus habebant.*

19 Pérez de Urbel, J. and Ruiz-Zorrilla, A.G., *Historia Silense*, Madrid, 1959, p.206.

20 Biblioteca Universitaria de Santiago de Compostela (Rs.1). *See* Férotin, M., *Le Liber Mozarabicus Sacramentorum et les manuscrits mozarabes*, Paris, 1912, vol. VI of Monumenta Ecclesiae Liturgica, Cabrol, Leclercq and Férotin (eds.) , col. 932; this manuscript also includes several 'Mozarabic saints'.

21 Cowdrey, *as above* note 17, p.220, and Bishko, *as above* note 17, p.52.

22 Cowdrey, *as above* note 17, pp.135–41.

23 Kitzinger, E., The Gregorian Reform and the Visual Arts: a Problem of Method, in the *Transactions of the Royal Historical Society*, 5th series, vol. 22, 1972, pp.87–102. Kitzinger raised the question of whether the *renovatio* looked back to the Church of the Apostles or to the Church of Constantine, and for his purposes opted for the latter. In our case, however, the matter is less clear, as Gregory clearly refers to the time of the original conversion in Spain, although the *terminus ante quem* which he uses for his ideal period, the advent of the Priscillianist heresy, did not occur until the end of the third century. Gregory did not himself make the distinction.

24 Reg.i, ep.LXIV, *PL*, col. 340, *sicut bonae soboles, etsi post diuturnas scissuras, demum tamen ut matrem revera vestram Romanam Ecclesiam recognoscatis.*

25 Reg.i, ep.LXIV, *PL* 148, col. 340, *Hispaniam se adiisse significet, ac postea septem episcopos ab urbe Roma ad instruendos Hispaniae populos a Petro et Paulo apostolis directos fuisse, qui destructa idolatria Christianitatem fundaverunt, religionem plantaverunt, ordinem et officium in divinis cultibus agendis ostenderunt, et sanguine suo Ecclesias dedicavere, ... quantam concordiam cum Romana urbe Hispania in religione et ordine divini officii habuisse satis patet.*

26 Constable, *as above* note 3, p.45. *See also* Katzenellenbogen, A., *The Sculptural Programs of Chartres Cathedral*, Baltimore, 1959, p.17, 'divine wisdom can bestow on the seeker of wisdom its own likeness and bring him back to the purity of its own nature.'

27 Reg.i, ep.LXIV, *PL* 148, col. 340, *sed postquam vesania Priscillianistarum diu pollutum, et perfidia Arianorum depravatum, et a Romano ritu separatum, irruentibus prius Gothis, ac demum invadentibus Saracenis, regnum Hispaniae fuit.*

28 The Adoptionist heresy argued that Christ was the adoptive not the natural son of God. One of its principal proponents was Elipandus, bishop of Toledo. Beatus of Liébana, the author of *Commentarius in Apocalypsin*, also wrote several letters to Elipandus arguing against the heresy. *See* Löfstedt, B. (ed.), *Beatus Liebanensis et Eterii Oxomensis, Adversus Elipandum libri duo*, Turnholt, 1984.

29 *PL* 101, col. 1344, *certissime vos illorum sanctissima scripta haereticae pravitatis veneno infecisse, et interseruisse verba, quae nusquam in eorum legimus libris.*

30 McKitterick, R., *The Frankish Church and the Carolingian Reforms, 789–895*, London, 1977, p.37.

31 *PL* 146, 1362, *in partibus Hispaniae, catholicae fidei unitatem a sua plenitudine declinasse, et pene omnes ab ecclesiastica disciplina et divinorum cultu interiorum aberasse.*

32 *PL* 146, col. 1362, *ad correctionem Ecclesiarum Dei ... et integritatem ibi restauravit, Simoniacae haeresis inquinamenta mundavit et confusos ritus divinorum obsequiorum ad regulam canonicam et ordinem reformavit;* and Cowdrey, *as above* note 17, p.220.

33 Bishko, *as above* note 17, p.77.

34 Reg. i, ep.II, *PL* 148, col. 576, *tantum periculum* and *pristinum errorem* in a letter to Abbot Hugh of Cluny. Gregory's language had increased in severity in this later letter. By this time he had met the 'obstinate' opposition which was considered one of the hallmarks of the heretic. *See* Moore, *as above* note 3, p.68.

35 Reg.i, ep.LXIV, *PL* 148, col. 340, *sicut bonae soboles, etsi post diuturnas scissuras, demum tamen ut matrem revera vestram Romanam Ecclesiam recognoscatis, in qua et nos fratres reperiatis, Romanae Eccelsiae ordinem et officium recipiatis, non Toletanae, vel cujuslibet aliae, sed istius quae a Petro et Paulo supra firmam petram per Christum fundata est, et sanguine consecrata, cui portae inferni, id est linguae haereticorum, nunquam praevalere potuerunt, sicut caetera regna Occidentis et Septentrionis, teneatis.*

36 Reg.i, ep.LXIV, *PL* 148, col. 340, *quod Innocentii papae ad Eugubinum directa episcopum vos docet epistola*. For Innocent I's full letter *see PL* 20, col. 551–61, ep.XXV. This translation is taken from Bullough, D.A., 'Roman Books and Carolingian *Renovatio*', in Baker, D. (ed.), *Renaissance and Renewal in Christian History*, Studies in Church History, vol.14, Oxford, 1977, p.24.

37 Reg.i, ep.LXIV, *PL* 148, col. 340, *quod Hormisdae ad Hispalensem missa decreta insinuant*. For Hormisdas's letter *see PL* 63, ep. XXVI, col. 425–6: *paternas igitur regulas et decreta a sanctis definita conciliis omnibus servanda mandamus*.

38 *PL* 63, ep.XXV, col. 423–5.

39 *PL* 63, ep.VI, col. 459–60.

40 Reg.i, ep.LXIV, *PL* 148, col. 340, *quod Toletanum et Bracarense demonstrant concilia*.

41 Mansi, J.D., *Sacrorum Conciliorum Nova et Amplissima Collectio*, vol.10, Graz, 1960, col. 616, can.2, *unus igitur ordo orandi atque psallendi nobis per omnem Hispaniam atque Galliam conservetur, unus modus in missarum solennitatibus, unus in vespertinis matutinisque officiis nec diversa sit ultra in nobis ecclesiastica consuetudo; qui in una fide continemur et regno: hoc enim et antiqui canones decreverunt ut unaquaeque provincia et psallendi et ministrandi parem consuetudinem continent*.

42 Mansi, *as above* note 41, vol 9, col. 777, *capitula*:

   1. *Placuit omnibus communi consensu, ut unus atque idem psallendi ordo in matutinis vel vespertinis officiis teneatur; et non diversae, neque ac privitae, monasteriorum consuetudines cum ecclesiastica regula sint permixtae*.

   2. *Item placuit, ut per solennium dierum vigilias vel missas, omnes easdem et non diversas lectiones in ecclesia legant*.

   4. *Item placuit, ut eodem ordine missae celebrentur ab omnibus*.

43 Jaffé, P., *Monachus Sangallensis de Carolo Magno*, in Bibliotheca Rerum Germanicarum, vol. 4, Monumenta Carolina, Berlin, 1867, chapter 10, pp.639–641. Trans. Thorpe, L., *Two Lives of Charlemagne*, Harmondsworth, Middx., 1969, p.102. *See also* McKitterick, R., 'Unity and Diversity in the Carolingian Church', in Swanson, R.N. (ed.), *Unity and Diversity in the Church*, Studies in Church History, vol.32, Oxford, 1996, pp.59–82.

44 Vogel, C, *Medieval Liturgy: An Introduction to the Sources*, Washington, 1986, p.61, and Waddell, C., 'The Reform of the Liturgy from a Renaissance Perspective', in Benson and Constable *(eds.)*, *as above* note 3, Oxford, 1982, p.88, p.92–4.

45 Especially Férotin, *as above* note 20; *see* col. 3–4 for the manuscripts used, and Férotin, M., *Le Liber ordinum en usage dans l'église wisigothique et mozarabe d'Espagne du cinquième au onzième siècle*, Paris, 1904.

46 Pinell, J., 'Liturgia Hispanica', in *Diccionario de Historia Eclesiastica*, Aldea Vaquero, Q., Marin Martinez, T. and Vives Gatell, J. (ed.), vol. 2, Madrid, 1970, pp.1304–5.

47 Reg. i, ep.LXIV, col. 340, *quod etiam episcopi vestri ad nos nuper venientes juxta constitutionem concilii per scripta sua facere promiserunt, et in manu nostra firmaverunt. ... depositionem et excommunicationem quam Geraldus Ostiensis episcopus cum Rembaldo in Munionem simoniacum ... ratum esse decrevimus, atque firmavimus*.

48 Linehan, P.A., 'Religion, Nationalism and National Identity in Medieval Spain and Portugal', in Mews, S. (ed.), Religion and National Identity, *Studies in Church History*, vol.18, Oxford, 1982, p.171.

49 Gil Fernández, J., Moralejo, J. L., and Ruiz de la Peña, J. L., *Crónicas asturianas: Crónica Albeldense*, Universidad de Oviedo, Publicaciones del Departamento de Historia Medieval, 2, Oviedo, 1985, p.174: *'omnemque Gotorum ordinem sicuti Toleto fuerat, tam in eclesia, quam palatio in Quetao cuncta statuit'*. Williams, J.W., 'Orientations: Christian Spain and the art of its neighbours', in *The Art of Medieval Spain A.D.500–1200*, The Metropolitan Museum of Art, New York, 1993. Williams points out that the chronicle was written in the reign of Alfonso III and may therefore itself constitute a fabricated past.

50 Schlunck, H., 'La Iglesia de San Julián de los Prados (Oviedo) y la arquitectura de Alfonso el Casto', in *Estudios sobre la monarquia asturiana. Colección de trabajos realizada con motivo del XI centenario de Alfonso II el Casto, celebrado en 1942*, (2 ed. Oviedo 1971) pp.405–65. *See* Williams, *as above* note 49, pp.13–25.

51 Williams, J.W., 'San Isidoro in León: Evidence for a New History', in *Art Bulletin*, vol. 55, no.2, 1973, p.178

52 Pérez de Urbel, J. and Ruiz-Zorrilla, A.G., *as above* note 19, pp.197–8, *'sepulturam regum ecclesiam fieri Legione persuadet, uby et eorundem corpora iuste magnificeque humari debeant. Decreuerat Fernandus rex, vel Omnie, quem locum carum semper habebat, siue in ecclesia beati Petri de Aslanza (Arlanza), corpus suum sepulture tradere;*

porro Sancia regina, quonium in Legionenssy regum ciminterio pater suus digne memorie Adefonsus princeps et eius frater Veremudus serenissimus rex in Christo quiescebant, ut quoque et ipsa et eiusdem vir cum eis post mortem quiescerent, pro viribus laborabat. Rex igitur peticioni fidissime coniugis annuens, deputantur cementarii, qui assidue operam dent tam dignissimo labori.'

53 Geary, P.J., *Living with the Dead in the Middle Ages*, Ithaca and London, 1994, p.88.

54 *Historia Silense, as above* note 19, p.119.

55 For the *Chronicon Burgense* , *see* Flórez, H. (ed.) *España Sagrada*, Madrid, 1749–1879, t.23, p.310. The Chronicon de Cardeña gives 'entró la ley Romana en España' for the same year, *see* Flórez, H., (ed.) *España Sagrada*, Madrid, 1749–1879, t.23, p.372.

56 Reg.vii, ep. VI, *PL* 148, col. 549, *charissimo in Christo filio … glorioso regi Hispaniarum.*

57 Reg.vii, ep. VI, *PL* 148, col. 549, *B. Petro apostolorum principi … cui omnes principatus et potestates orbis terrarum subjiciens, jus ligandi atque solvendi in coelo et in terra contradidit.*

58 Reg.vii, ep. VI, *PL* 148, col. 550, *quia sicut certa spes salutis est his qui in observatione fidei et doctrinae hujus sanctae apostolicae sedis permanent, ita illis qui ab ejus concordia et unitate exorbitaverint, haud dubiae damnationis terror imminet.*

59 Reg.vii, ep. VI, *PL* 148, col. 550, *ex more sanctorum misimus vobis claviculam auream in qua de catenis beati Petri benedictio continetur.*

60 Reg.vii, ep. VI, *PL* 148, col. 550, *omnipotens Deus qui illum admirabili potentia a nexibus ferreis liberavit. See also* Cowdrey, *as above* note 17, pp.226–7, Bishko, *as above* note 17, p.77, and *Chronica de Nájera*, 10, Cirot, J. (ed.), *Bulletin hispanique*, xi, 1909, 273.

61 Reg. viii, ep. III, *PL* 148, col. 577; the biblical reference is Mt.13:43 *tunc iusti fulgebunt sicut sol in regno Patris eorum.*

62 Constable, *as above* note 3, p.42.

63 Reg. ix, ep.II, PL 148, col. 605, *in ecclesiis regni tui matris omnium sanctae Romanae Ecclesiae ordinem recipi, et ex antiquo more celebrari effeceris. See also*: col. 606 *multisque gentibus e cunctis mundi partibus ad gremium matris sanctae Romanae Ecclesiae venientibus ad honorem tuum clare manifestat.*

64 Reg. ix, ep.II, PL 148, col. 606, *Omnipotens Deus … qui dat salutem regibus, meritis altissimae dominae genitricis Dei Mariae, omniumque sanctorum, auctoritate beatorum apostolorum Petri et Pauli nobis licet indignis per eos qualicunque commissa, te tuosque fideles in Christo ab omnibus peccatis absolvat, detque tibi victoriam de inimicis visibilibus et invisibilibus. Mentem tuam semper illuminet, ut, ejus bonitatem et humanam fragilitatem diligenter perspiciendo, mundi gloriam despicias, et ad aeternam beato Petro duce pervenias.*

65 Toubert, H., *Un Art Dirigé*, Paris, 1990, and Kitzinger, E., *as above* note 23.

66 Toubert, 'Le renouveau paléochretien à Rome au début du XIIe siècle', in Toubert, *as above* note 65, pp.239–310.

67 Toubert,H., 'Dogme et pouvoir dans l'iconographie grégorienne. Les peintures de la Trinité de Vendôme', in Toubert, *as above* note 65, pp.365–402; *see also* Palazzo, E., 'L'iconographie des fresques de Berzé-la-Ville dans le contexte de la Reforme Grégorienne et de la liturgie Clunisienne', in *Les Cahiers de Saint-Michel de Cuxa*,no.19, 1988, pp.169–86.

68 Toubert, H., 'Les representations de L'Ecclesia dans l'art des Xe–XIIe siècles', in Toubert, *as above* note 65, pp.37–63.

69 Kitzinger, *as above* note 23.

70 Brieger, P.H., 'Bible Illustration and Gregorian Reform', in Cuming, G.J. (ed.), *Studies in Church History*, vol. 2, Oxford, 1963, pp.154–64.

71 *PL* 159, col. 939, *de Romano autem officio, quod tua jussione accepimus, sciatis nostram terram admodum desolatam esse: unde.vestram deprecor paternitatem, quatenus faciatis ut domnus papa nobis suum mittat cardinalem, videlicet domnum Giraldum, ut ea quae sunt, emendanda emendet, et ea quae sunt corrigenda corrigat.*

72 For the *Chronicon Burgense, see* Flórez, *as above*, note 55, p.309, for *Annales Compostellani, see* Flórez, p.320, for *Chronica de Nájera*, 10, Cirot, J. (ed.), *Bulletin hispanique*, 11, 1909, p.277.

73 Reg.viii, ep.II, *PL* 148, col. 576, *centum millia hominum, qui laboris nostri diligentia ad viam veritatis redire coeperant … in pristinum errorem redacere.*

74 Cowdrey, *as above* note 17, pp.230–44.

75 Fita, F., 'El concilio nacional de Burgos en 1080', in *Boletín de la real academia de la historia*, 49, 1906, pp.341–6.

76 Reg. viii, ep.II, *PL* 148, col. 576, *Quanta impietas a monasterio vestro per Roberti monachi vestri praesumptionem exierit … monachi in eisdem partibus injuste dispersi ad proprium redeant monasterium et nulla ibidem ordinatio vires obtineat nisi quae legati nostri fuerit auctoritate probata.*

77 Biblioteca de la Escorial, MS d.I, fol. 395v.

78 David, P., *Études historiques sur la Galice et le Portugal du VIe au XIIe siècle*, Lisbon, 1947, pp.393–4, and King, A., *Liturgies of the Primatial Sees*, London, 1957, p.499–502.

79 David, *as above* note 78, pp.112–14.

80 Biblioteca de la Escorial, MS d.I, fol. 395v, *officium Hispaniae ecclesiae inquietaret vel mutare presumeret.*

81 David, P., *as above* note 78, pp.394–5. Reilly has maintained that the event was unlikely to have been fabricated; *see* Reilly, B.F., *The Kingdom of León-Castilla under King Alfonso VI, 1065–1109*, Princeton, 1988, p.96 n.12. The medieval propensity for forgery, however, renders this argument less convincing than David's.

82 Reg. iii, ep. XVIII, *PL* 148, col. 449, *Quod autem filii mortis dicunt se a nobis litteras accepisse, sciatis per omnia falsum esse. Procura ergo ut Romanus ordo per totam Hispaniam et Galiciam, et ubicunque poteris, in omnibus rectius teneatur.*

83 Madrid, Real Academia de la Historia, Aem. 22, fol. 195. *See* Pérez de Urbel, J., 'El último defensor de la liturgia mozárabe', in *Miscellanea Liturgica in honorem L. Cuniberti Mohlberg*, vol. 2, Rome, 1949, pp.189–97.

84 Smalley, B., *as above* note 1.

85 Rom.12:2, *et nolite conformari huic saeculo sed reformamini in novitate sensus vestri ut probetis quae sit voluntas Dei bona et placens et perfecta.* See also Constable, *as above* note 3, p.37.

86 St. Isidore, *De Ecclesiasticiis*, Lib. I, ch. XV, *PL* 83, col. 752–3.

87 Hefele, C.J., *Histoire des Conciles*, t.1, partie.2, Paris, 1907, pp.1042–3, epilogue.

88 *PL* 63, ep.LI, col. 459–60. Pope Hormisdas also spoke pejoratively of novelty in a letter describing the Scythians as 'despisers of ancient authorities; seekers after novelty', and this nuance may also be implied in our text.

89 Férotin, *as above* note 20, col. 981.

90 Férotin, *as above* note 20, col. 419, *pontificum Pontifex et sacerdotum Sacerdos, Christe Ihesu.* This is the closest form of words which I can find in Férotin's edition.

91 García Larragueta, S., *Colección de documentos de la catedral de Oviedo*, Oviedo, 1962, p.214: *Clericis toletanis illic habitantibus et reliquis ritum romanum tenentibus.* The date and status of this document (no.72) is now in doubt, *see* Reilly, B.F.,'The Chancery of Alfonso VI of León and Castile (1065–1109)', in Reilly, B.F., (ed.), *Santiago, Saint-Denis and Saint Peter: The Reception of the Roman Liturgy in León-Castille in 1080*, New York, 1985, pp.7 and 25 n.43.

92 Anon Sahagún in Escalona, R., *Historia del Real Monasterio de Sahagún* (facsimile edition), León, 1982, Appendix I, p.299.

93 Reg.iii, ep.XVIII, May 1076, *PL* 148, col. 448–9. *See also* Cowdrey, *as above* note 17, p.226, note 1.

94 Ruiz, T.F., 'Burgos and the Council of 1080', in Reilly, B.F.(ed.), *as above* note 91, pp.121–30. Burgos was not yet one of the most flourishing centres, but it did have strategic importance.

95 Reilly, B.F., *as above* note 81, pp.82, 99–100, 103, 112 and 143.

96 France, J. (ed.), *Radulfi Glabri, Historiarum Libri Quinque, Ralph Glaber, Historiarum*, Oxford, 1989, pp.114–15. Glaber added, however, that this irregular practice gave the Cluniac monks bad dreams.

97 Ulrich of Cluny, *Antiquiores consuetudines monasterii Cluniacensis*, *PL* 149, col. 635–778 and Bernard of

Cluny, 'Ordo Cluniacensis per Bernardum saeculi XI scriptorium', in Herrgott, M., (ed.), Vetus disciplina monastica, Paris, 1726, pp.134–364.

98 Hunt, N., Cluny under Saint Hugh 1049–1109, London, 1967, p.95 and p.113 'He introduced the Veni Creator into the Pentecostal liturgy, a directive to sing the Mass of Our Lady on Saturdays if no other feast occurred, and extra antiphons on the feast of SS. Peter and Paul.'

99 Hunt, as above note 98, p.114.

100 PL 159, col. 938, 'Robertum quem super omnes monachos teneo excellentiorem et chariorem' and col. 939, 'vellem … domnum Robertum omnino in nostris partibus adesse vellem eum mecum in vita et in morte'.

101 Reg. viii, ep. II, PL 148, col. 576, to Hugh of Cluny: 'qui diabolica suggestione Hispaniensi Ecclesiae tantum periculum invexit, ab introitu ecclesiae, et ab omni ministerio rerum vestrarum, separetis, donec ad vos redeat, et temeritatis suae dignam ultionem suscipiat. Regem quoque illius fraude deceptum diligenter litteris tuis intelligere facias beati Petri iram et indignationem, atque, si non resipuerit, gravissimam adversum se et regnum suum ultionem provocasse, quod legatum Romanae Ecclesiae indecenter tractavit, et falsitati potius quam veritati credidit. … si culpam suam non correxerit, esse excommunicaturos, et quotquot sunt in partibus Hispaniae fideles sancti Petri ad confusionem suam sollicitaturos'.

Reg. viii, ep.III, PL 148, col. 577, to Alfonso: 'diabolus tuae saluti et omnium qui per te salvandi erant, more suo invidens, per membrum suum, quemdam Robertum pseudomonachum, et per antiquam adjutricem suam, perditam feminam, viriles animos tuos a recto itinere deturbavit … nefandissimum Robertum monachum seductorem tui et perturbatorem regni, ab introitu ecclesiae separatum, intra claustra monasterii Cluniacensis in poenitentiam retrudi decernimus'.

102 Reg. viii, ep.IV, PL 148, col. 578.

103 Williams, J.W., 'Cluny and Spain', Gesta, vol. 27, 1988, p.60, and Garand, M-C., 'Le Scriptorium de Cluny, carrefour d'influences au XIe siècle: Le manuscrit Paris, B.N. Nouv. Acq. Lat. 1548', in Journal des Savants, 1977, p.264–7. Garand's evidence suggests that the same Bernard acted as scribe for a donation to Cluny in 1066, signing as Bernardus monachus Auxiensis. In 1078 he was sent to St. Orens as prior. There is an unpublished thesis on Bernard: Robin, M., Bernard de La Sauvetat, abbé de Sahagún, archevêque de Tolède (v.1040–1124) et la réforme clunisienne en Espagne au XIe et XIIe siècle, École nationale des chartes, Positions des thèses … de … 1907. See also Rivera Recio, J.F, La Iglesia de Toledo en el siglo XII (1086–1208), vol. 1, Rome, 1966, pp.127–33.

104 Cowdrey, as above note 17, pp.97–101. St. Orens was given to Cluny by Count Aimeric of Auch and his brother. The abbey was favoured by Hugh Candidus, the papal legate, who exempted it from certain tithes and, unusually, gave the prior an archdeacon's rights over the abbey's churches.

105 For the general history of Sahagún see Escalona, R., Historia del real monasterio de Sahagún, Madrid, 1782, (facsimile edition), León, 1982.

106 Fita, F., 'El concilio nacional de Burgos en 1080', in Boletín de la real academia de la historia, 49, 1906, pp.349–51, 'per electionem fratrum ibidem commorantium Bernardum in eodem praefato monasterio abbatem constitui in praesentia Ricardi Romanae ecclesiae cardinalis'.

107 Fita, as above note 106, pp.356–9, 'quatinus qui humana erat sub potestate sepultus per me quasi a morte resuscitaretur, ecclesiasticae libertati donandus'.

108 Cowdrey, as above note 17, p.241.

109 Cowdrey, as above note 17, pp.241–2. Reilly, B.F., 'The Chancery of Alfonso VI', in Reilly, B.F., as above note 91, pp.111–12, has doubts about the authenticity of this charter, but still places it at Sahagún by 1110–1120.

110 Cowdrey, as above note 17, p.242, 'dedi enim eam Romanae ecclesiae et beato Petro in libertate Romana'. See also Muñoz y Romero, T., Colección de fueros municipales y cartas pueblas i, Madrid, 1847, pp.302–3.

111 Cowdrey, as above note 17, p.244. See also Rivera Recio, as above note 103, pp.133–96.

112 Fletcher, R.A., The Episcopate in the Kingdom of León in the Twelfth Century, Oxford, 1978, pp.37–8, and pp.77–9.

113 Férotin, as above note 20.

114 Werckmeister, O., 'The First Romanesque Beatus Manuscripts and the Liturgy of Death', in Actas del simposio para el estudio de los códices del 'Comentario al Apocalypsis' de Beato de Liébana, vol.2, Madrid, 1980, pp.167–200.

115   For example, Suñol, G., *Introduction à la paléographie Grégorienne*, Tournai, 1935, pp.317–52, and Fernández de la Cuesta, I., 'Notas paleográficas al antifonario silense del Museo Britanico, MS Add. 30850', in *Homenaje a Fray J. Pérez de Urbel*, OSB, Studia Silense 3, vol. 1, Silos, 1976, pp.233–56.

116   Whitehill, W.M., 'The Manuscripts of Santo Domingo de Silos (à la recherche du temps perdu)', in *Homenaje a Fray Justo Pérez de Urbel*, OSB, Studia Silense 3, vol. 1, Silos, 1976, pp.271–303, and Janini, J, *Manuscritos litúrgicos de las bibliotecas de España*, t.1 Castilla y Navarra, Burgos, 1977.

PART ONE

THE MONASTIC OFFICE
Adjustment on the Margins?

CHAPTER ONE

—◄◦►—

A Question of Choice
Selected Officia *Manuscripts from Castile*

The Choice of Manuscripts

THE PRESENT STUDY requires that we proceed at all times from at least one 'Mozarabic' manuscript and one 'Roman' manuscript if the liturgy before the change is to be compared with that after the change. They must cover the same period of the liturgical year, be intended for broadly similar liturgical purposes, and have a well-documented origin and provenance. This will enable us to put the change 'under the microscope' in the most precise way possible. Obviously it is more satisfactory if we have more than one manuscript from the two liturgies, conforming to the criteria above. It is therefore very fortunate that a readily accessible group of manuscripts from the Silos corpus between them fulfil all our requirements.[1] They are now in the British Library as Add. MS 30844, Add. MS 30845, Add. MS 30846, Add. MS 30847, Add. MS 30848 and Add. MS 30849.

The provenance of these manuscripts is unusually well-documented. On 1 June 1878 there was a major sale of fifty-five manuscripts from the abbey of Silos at the auction house of Bachelin-Deflorenne in Paris. Some of the manuscripts were not sold on that day and were disposed of subsequently. Twenty-two of the manuscripts were purchased by the Bibliothèque Nationale, but none of these are collections of *officia* texts. The British Library (or British Museum as it was then) purchased thirteen books. Of these one is an *Antiphonarium* (Add. 30850), one a *Homilarium* and Penitential (Add. 30853), and another a *Psalterium* (Add. 30851); of the remaining six, three are described in the Catalogue as Offices and Masses (Add. 30844, Add. 30845, and Add. 30846) and three as Breviaries (Add. 30847, Add. 30848 and Add. 30849).[2] The contents are given in Table 1.

The manuscripts reached the auction rooms after several intermediate resting places. The nineteenth century was a time of great political turmoil in Spain resulting in the Carlist Wars, and the then abbot of Silos, Echevarria, had taken steps to protect the library of the abbey by hiding the books in the village of Silos.[6] Abbot Blanco, who succeeded Echevarria in 1857, was not so careful, however, and handed over all the manuscripts to San Martín de Madrid, a dependency of Silos. That abbey itself required considerable work, and thus expense, to make it habitable, and a decision was made to sell the manuscripts.

TABLE I
A Summary of the Contents of the *Officia* Manuscripts

Manuscripts Containing the Mozarabic Liturgy[3]

MANUSCRIPT	TITLE ON SPINE	CONTENTS[4]
Add. 30844	*Officia Toletana* Codice 1	fols 1–32v: *lectiones* from St Ildefonsus's *De Virginitate perpetua sancte Marie* (beginning now at *Quare non credis*) fols 33–172v: *officia et missae* for the feast of *S. Maria* to that of *missae* for the feast of *Catedra S. Petri* and from Ascension to the preparation for Pentecost fols 173–177: part of a *Liber Canticorum* (*Letanias Canonicas*)
Add. 30845	*Officia Toletana* Codex 2	fols 1–161v: *officia et missae* for *S. Quiricus* to *S. Milanus; Translatio S. Saturnini, de Letanias Canonicas, S. Cristina* and *S. Bartolomeus* added at the end; *f*ols 86*bis* is a fragment; fols 89–92v *missa* for *S. Maria* interpolated
Add. 30846	*Breviarium Toletanum*	fols 1–172 *officia et missae* for Easter to Pentecost made up from two interleaved sections (hereafter section A & B); fol. 173 fragment of a *Passionarium* (*S. Iuliana*)

Manuscripts Containing the Roman Liturgy[5]

MANUSCRIPT	TITLE ON SPINE	CONTENTS
Add. 30847	*Breviarium*	fols. 1–186v *officia* from *Dominica II in Adventum* to *Dominica IV in Quadragesima* including the feasts (and several *passiones*) of saints falling in this period
Add. 30848	*Breviarium*	fols 1–2v calendar; fols 3–279 *officia* from *Dominica II in Adventum Domini* to *Dominica XXIV post S. Trinitatem*, Temporal and Sanctoral; then offices for *SS Apostoli* and *Plurimi Martyres*
Add. 30849	*Breviarium*	fol. 1 fragment containing mass texts; fols 2–4v calendar; fols 5–308 *officia*: Temporal from *Dominica I de Adventu Domini* to *Dominica XIX post Pentecosten*; Sanctoral from *S. Silvestri* to *S. Thome*, and occasional *officia* ending with an office for *SS Virgines*

There are six surviving catalogues of manuscripts held by the abbey of Silos, dating from the eleventh to the eighteenth century.[7] The most complete catalogue is that written in 1772 by Hernández;[8] it includes sufficiently detailed information on the contents of each manuscript to afford the first opportunity for confident identification of the manuscripts in this study. This gives us the following concordance:

offitia Toletano Tomo 10 *Quare non credis eidem* ... 1b *Et Pastores erant in regione.* 15 *... letanias Canonicas* ... 170b	Add. 30844
offitia Toletano Tomo 20 *Officium S. Quirici* ... 1b *Missa eiusdem* ... 2 *... Missa S. Bartholomei* ... 160v	Add. 30845
Breviario toledano *de eodem die* ... 1b *Missa* ... 3b *... de Pentecostes..* 161b	Add. 30846
Breviarium *de Adventu* ... 1 *S. Luciae* ... 1b *... Dominica 4a* ... 180	Add. 30847
Breviarium *Calendario* ... 1 *de adventu domini* ... 3 *... officium Plurimi* ... 277b	Add. 30848
Breviarium et Matinuale *Dominica 1a Adventus* ... 1 *Dominica 2a Adventus* ... 3 *... Virginum* ... 300	Add. 30849

When these descriptions are compared with those in Table 1 it can be seen that the manuscripts concerned are the same: so we can be sure that all the manuscripts under consideration in this study were at Silos by the eighteenth century. Before this date identification poses more problems.

In her Ph.D. dissertation, Ann Boylan has surveyed the whole Silos corpus and cast doubts on the attribution to the Silos scriptorium of Add. 30844, Add. 30845 and Add. 30846.[9] Boylan argues against the existence of an active scriptorium at Silos before the liturgical change in 1080. She is, therefore, forced to find other possible centres of production for all the pre-1080 manuscripts in the Silos corpus previously thought to have been produced at that abbey. Her suggestions include Valeránica and San Pedro de Cardeña (both very close to Silos) and San Millán de la Cogolla. As will be seen, I do not agree with this position, and, indeed, incline towards the opposite point of view: namely that the Silos scriptorium was active in the eleventh century, but in decline by the early twelfth century. The point is not crucial for the present study, however, for the precise place of origin of the various manuscripts can be left open. Boylan's suggestions are all comfortably within a 50km radius of Silos, which is sufficient for the present purpose. A more exact location would nevertheless be even better, and I will now examine the evidence offered by the medieval catalogues of the Silos scriptorium.

The catalogue from the eleventh century is a list of liturgical books comprising one particular donation. It gives no idea of the other manuscripts which Silos may have owned,[10] but a catalogue from the thirteenth century lists one hundred and four manuscripts owned by the abbey at Silos at that time.[11] The description of the list is *'estos son los libros de la capiscolia'*, that is literally those belonging to the head of the school (*scola*). It may not, therefore, be a list of all the manuscripts owned by the abbey, but rather only those in the chantry. In some abbeys, the *cantor* (choir master) also served as the librarian of the abbey, since service books and bibles were usually the nucleus of the collection. The collections were often broken into three groups: the main collection, service books and the school (scriptorium) library, and very large and very small codices were sometimes catalogued separately.[12] It seems improbable that the thirteenth-century catalogue could, therefore, have been a complete inventory of the books owned by Silos, particularly as it includes only one bible and very few missals. The large number of codices designated as or by implication '*toletano*' moreover gives the impression of an archival rather than a working library.

Boylan has attempted to identify the entries in the earlier catalogues with the surviving manuscripts.[13] It is a difficult task as the descriptions are very vague. Boylan states that [no. 38], described only as *Bebriario*, may be either Add. 30847 or Add. 30848; she says that [no. 29] *Liber de assumptione beate Marie* may likewise be part of Add. 30845 or Silos MS 3; she does not find any likely candidates for Add. 30844, Add. 30846 or Add. 30849. There are, however, other possibilities. Add. 30844 could be identified with [no. 17], one of the *tres libros de Virginitatis beate Marie*, as that is the text which begins the volume; it is certainly at least as convincing as the suggestion for Add. 30845. At least three other breviaries are mentioned in the catalogue: [89] *el officerio viejo*, [90] *el officierio gordiello*, and [91] *el del cuero negro*. The *gordiello* (thick) volume seems an accurate, though brief description of Add.30849; the old breviary could be Add. 30847 or Add. 30848, or even an inaccurate title for Add. 30844, Add. 30845 or Add. 30846. Boylan points to a possible additional 'breviary' in [no. 26] *Liber premiorum*, which she says may be a confused transcription. In view of the brevity and equivocal nature of the descriptions, we can say no more than that there is room in this list for all the manuscripts under consideration here to have been at Silos in the thirteenth century but no possibility of certainty. Before this date we must rely on internal evidence to place these manuscripts at Silos or even within that part of Castile. It will, however, be sufficient for our purposes if they can be localised to that extent, and this is here accepted as an initial working hypothesis.

This chapter will, therefore, examine six manuscripts, all produced in or within the region of the abbey of Silos, all now held in the British Library, and all containing texts which serve the same liturgical purpose in so far as they all contain the offices for at least part of the liturgical year. The contents of all the manuscripts will be looked at in detail in chapter two, but it is immediately clear that there is sufficient overlap in the periods of the liturgical year concerned for detailed comparisons to be made between these manuscripts. Clearly they make a good subject for this comparative study. They will enable us to establish in what areas of the liturgy most adjustment took place and the precise details of those changes. Through their structure and illumination they will also show how the change was expressed.

A Codicological Analysis

A codicological analysis may help to confirm whether or not the manuscripts are products of the same scriptorium. It will not be possible to establish a very precise date for them by palaeographical means, due to the difficulty of dating Visigothic script accurately. Nevertheless, palaeographic details may draw attention to some innovatory practices, and may suggest a tentative chronological sequence for the manuscripts, which can then be tested against other evidence. It has not been my intention, however, to attempt a comprehensive palaeographic study of these six manuscripts. Rather I have concentrated on those features which may suggest that one manuscript is earlier than another, and on any other aspect which may relate to the change in the liturgy. There will be, for example, no attempt to identify systematically how many scribes worked on each book, although it will be essential to establish to what extent these manuscripts are coherent volumes. Particular attention will, however, be paid to any signs of innovation in letter-forms, abbreviations and punctuation.

There is a strict limit to the information which can be gained from a study of the bindings of these manuscripts, as in most instances they were probably rebound when the contents were catalogued in the eighteenth century; Add. 30847 was re-bound by the British Museum in 1965. The size of the manuscripts may be more pertinent. The dimensions and number of folios per manuscript (in their present state) are given in Table 2.

A general tendency for the manuscripts to require more folios if they contain the Roman liturgy is apparent. There is no such correlation in dimension: both the Mozarabic and Roman liturgy appear on the one hand in large books whose size seems to fit them for conspicuous ceremonial use, and on the other in quite small books which seem more suited for personal or private use. This will be taken into account when the possible function of the manuscripts is considered later.

Not one of the manuscripts is now complete. It seems that they were in this state for some time prior to their arrival at the British Museum as the folios which now face the bindings show heavy wear and water stains, as if exposed without the protection of a binding for a

TABLE 2[14]

The Dimensions of the *Officia* Manuscripts

MS	FOLIO SIZE	APPROX. WRITTEN SPACE	NO. OF FOLIOS	NO. OF LINES	NO. OF COLUMNS
Manuscripts containing the Mozarabic Liturgy					
Add.30844	400 x 320mm	280 x 190mm	177	22–24[15]	2
Add.30845	363 x 254mm	295 x 190mm	161	27, but last quire 30	2
Add.30846[16]	285 x 221mm	220 x 160mm	175	section A: 21–22	section A:2
				section B: 21–24	section B:1
Manuscripts containing the Roman Liturgy					
Add.30847	315 x 210mm	240 x 135mm	186	25	1
Add.30848	308 x 270mm	280 x 180mm	279	32–33	2
Add.30849	275 x 200mm	235 x 135mm	308	29–33	2

considerable period. Add. 30844 is the most depleted: it is lacking three whole quires in addition to several folios.[17] The likely contents of some of the lacunae can, however, be deduced from the surrounding text. Fols 173–177 of Add. 30844 have been identified as part of an older manuscript of the *Liber Canticorum* and will not concern us here.[18]

The first thirty-two folios of Add. 30844 contain part of the text of the *De Virginitate perpetua Sancte Marie* of St Ildephonsus arranged as *lectiones*. Codicological evidence confirms that they belong with fols 33–172v and do not come originally from a different manuscript, showing that Add. 30844 is a coherent volume. The ruling and pricking of the folios is the same, the arrangement of the text in two columns is identical and, although the number of lines to a column varies within the manuscript, the variations do not coincide with the textual change from Ildephonsus to *officia*. Moreover the same scribe appears to have worked on the first section and on some of the liturgical passages: the same well-formed script is used again especially for *lectiones*. There is similar use of punctuation, and even the one initial on fol. 32 is similar in style to those in the liturgical part of the manuscript. Thus there is no evidence to show that these folios did not belong to the original manuscript, although it could be significant that even today the manuscript falls open most naturally at fol. 33.

Add. 30845 has not been damaged to the same extent. The recto of the first folio is, however, very worn and contains an isolated antiphon, *Splenduit lucerna tua, Domine*. The manuscript is also incomplete after fol. 7 and after fol. 159. Fols 89–92v are clearly later additions and fol. 86*bis* is a fragment which has been bound in. In addition Díaz y Díaz has argued that the first seven folios came originally from a different manuscript, and this possibility will be discussed in the next two chapters when we look at the text and the illumination. It is true that these first folios have thirty-one ruled lines whereas fols 8–147 have twenty-seven and fols 148–161 have thirty.[19]

Add. 30846 is a more complex case: both fol. 86 and fol. 175 are added fragments, but, more importantly, it has been proposed that the rest of the manuscript was put together from two separate codices, which we will call Section A and Section B.[20] Díaz y Díaz has

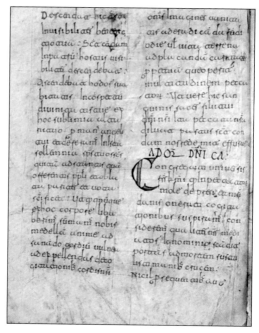

FIG. 1 London, British Library,
Add. MS 30846, fol. 7v

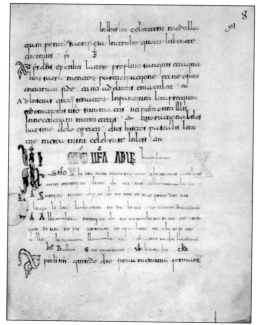

FIG. 2 London, British Library,
Add. MS 30846, fol. 8

identified the constituents, using as the criterion the long-line as opposed to the two-column format and the corresponding ruling pattern. The proposed sections are as follows:

Section A   fols 1–7, 13, 25–56, 74–87
             2 columns, 21/22 ruled lines

Section B   fols 8–12, 14–24, 57–73 and 88–172
             long line, 21–24 ruled lines

As this suggestion has important consequences for our use of this manuscript, I think it is best to confront the questions raised now: was this manuscript originally two separate books? We can first ask whether one section needed to be cut down to fit the other. This was not the case, and since there is no compelling evidence that folio sizes for books, or the sizes of written space, were standardized even within one scriptorium at this date, it seems unlikely from the start that the book is an assembly of two manuscripts – both damaged or otherwise incomplete. I think that this codex is not such an arbitrary amalgamation, and a close examination of the links between the two parts is required.

The first junction suggested by Díaz y Díaz is between fol. 7v and fol. 8 (FIG. 1 and FIG. 2). But before this there is a folio missing between fols 6 and 7, as is shown by an omitted section of text between the *ad Pacem* (*per sanguinem …*) at the end of fol. 6v and the end of the *inlatio* (*… Serafin imnum debite*) at the top of fol. 7. The omission is highlighted by the juxtaposition of flesh (fol. 6v) and hair (fol. 7) sides of the vellum which does not occur elsewhere in the manuscript. It is still possible to see on fol. 6v the transfer of pigment from a red initial, probably an uncial 'd' in the form of a knot, made by a letter on the missing folio. The transition from fol. 7v to fol. 8 is attended by some confusion. The text at the end of fol. 7v is the *ad orationem dominicam* prayer of Easter Monday (feria II), and ends incomplete (*nicil per sequentibus aut ...*), but the text which begins fol. 8 (*In Iherusalem celestem medullata portantes*) is that usually employed for the *ad orationem dominicam* of Easter Tuesday (feria III) and therefore seems to appear here by mistake, for the folio then continues correctly (on line 13) with the *officium* for feria II. There is a marked change of script and decoration between the two pages (from that designated A to that designated B) and an odd blank half line at the top of fol. 8 before the text begins. The manuscript then continues in the B (long-line) format until folio 13.

Four folios are missing after fol. 12 (the stubs remain) and most of the first column of fol. 13 has been scratched out. The text now begins with the rubric at the end of the *missa in die III feria* (*pasche quando baptizatis infantibus albe tolluntur*). While the recto of fol. 13 is written in the script and decorative style of section A, fol. 13v presents a more complex appearance. It is written in the two-column format, but the decoration is closer to that of section B (*see* chapter 3), and the text continues from fol. 13v to fol. 14 without a break. Thus fol. 13/13v seem to incorporate elements from both patterns within one folio. The long-line pattern then reasserts itself until fol. 25.

There are again some difficulties before the next proposed joining point between fol. 24 and fol. 25. Fol. 23v ends abruptly with the first line of the *ad orationem dominicam* prayer (*Respice tuorum fidelium multitudinem*) of the mass for feria IIII. It is not continued on fol. 24 which begins instead with the *officium III Feria*. This text continues on the reverse for four lines (fol. 24v), but the folio is then blank after '*exemplum amen*' until the last line, which gives *IIII feria ad matutinum: Ego dormivi*, the correct introduction to the text on fol. 25. Fol. 25 begins, however, in the two-column format with the antiphon *Quis est iste*, the next expected text entry.

The next change in format is between fol. 56 and fol. 57. The text on fol. 56 ends with *Laudes: Laudate te dominum*, after which there are nine blank lines. No *ad vesperum* is given for the Saturday after the Easter Octave. Fol. 57 begins, clearly in the B format, with a collection of canticles and benedictions *De Resurrectione Domini*, and then hymns for feasts which appear in section A (e.g. *S. Engratia, SS. Torquatus et socii*), and for those in section B (e.g. *S. Filipus, S. Crux*). This section does much to bring together the parts of this manuscript. It does not prove that they were originally one, however, as it could be argued that the missing parts of each book would have contained similar feasts.

The next juxtaposition is between fol. 74 (B) and fol. 75 (A), where there is also a missing folio. Fol. 74v ends with the heading *officium in primo dominico*, and fol. 75 begins in the middle of the gospel reading for that Sunday (*... surrexit a mortuis*). There is also a folio missing at the next changeover, between fol. 87 and fol. 88, but after that, although more than one hand produced the text, the two-column format prevails and there are no more missing folios.

From this examination we can see that the relationship between sections A and B is closer than would be expected from the binding up of folios which originally formed part of two independent, and possibly complete, codices. It is, however, clear that if these two parts were intended from the start to form one manuscript, something went badly wrong in the planning and execution. I would suggest that the examination of the decorative scheme(s) of this manuscript considered in chapter three shows that the two parts were worked on by the same artist at certain points. If this is so, there are consequences for the nature and purpose of this codex. Several of the folios used in its production have holes or other defects, so economy was exercised in its production. At this stage I would like to propose tentatively that this manuscript, with its mangled Latin, may have been the product of the scriptorium school, as this explanation would go some way to explaining its hotch-potch nature and its various flaws. The reason for its preservation remains puzzling.

The three manuscripts containing the Roman liturgy do not pose similar problems. Add. 30847 and Add. 30848 are both clearly coherent volumes, although some folios have been cut from Add. 30847.[21] Add. 30849 has had some extra folios added. Fol. 1 is obviously not an original part of this volume, as it is not of the same size as the other folios in the manuscript and has been folded to fit within the binding. It contains texts for the mass and will thus be considered in part II of this study. The calendar, three folios in the body of the volume, and several at the end (including offices for St Vincent, the Evangelists, and the Virgins) were also interpolated at a later date.

In what follows I will, therefore, be proceeding on the basis that all six manuscripts may be coherent volumes – except for the certainly identified interpolations. An examination of the text and illumination in the next chapters will help to confirm whether or not they were so conceived.

When we examine the techniques employed in the production of the codices, we find few practices consistently in use. All parts of all the manuscripts arrange the vellum in the usual way: HHFF, and the ruling is mostly by hard-point. The only exception is provided by Add. 30849, the calendar of which is ruled in very pale ink. There is considerable variation in ruling patterns. Only Add. 30847 and section B of Add. 30846 are written in long-line format; in both cases one vertical guideline is ruled on each side to contain the single column. The rest of the manuscripts are written in two columns. Add. 30844, Add. 30845 (fols 8–106), Add. 30848 and Add. 30849 all have double guidelines on both sides of the columns. Add. 30845 (fols 1–7 and fols 107–161) has only single vertical guidelines, and in section A of Add. 30846 the side guidelines are double, but those in the centre are single.

Pricking is also carried out in different ways: some of the manuscripts retain pricking only in the outside margins, for example Add. 30846 and Add. 30847, while Add. 30844 has it in the inner margins as well (perhaps because it is the largest manuscript). Add. 30845 also has pricking at the top and bottom of the folios for the vertical guidelines. Some folios in Add. 30846 (section B) and all those in Add. 30848 are pricked, as if by the point of a knife, with vertical slits, whereas Add. 30844 and Add. 30847 and section A of Add. 30846 have round holes as if made by an awl, while both types are found in Add. 30845 and Add. 30849.[22]

The use of catchwords is found in only one of the codices containing the Mozarabic liturgy, Add. 30844 (for example fol. 42v/fol. 43), and one of those containing the Roman liturgy, Add. 30847 (for example fols 86v/87). Guide letters are used in Add. 30847, but only between fol. 66v and fol. 76, and intermittently in Add. 30849, for example on fol. 41, for rubrics. Add. 30848 has numbered quires, as does Add. 30845, at the foot of the recto of the first folio,[23] but this is not the case with any of the other manuscripts.

This analysis shows great diversity of practice and it is certainly not possible to identify a 'house style'. This could be explained if all the manuscripts came in fact from different scriptoria. But it seems more likely that different practices sometimes existed side by side, and that they certainly changed over time. There is, for example, considerable divergence in the practices employed in Add. 30847 and Add. 30848, both of which are certainly products of the Silos scriptorium. Different working practices might be expected in a scriptorium which had drawn its personnel from diverse sources, and Silos could fit this picture. If Santo Domingo revived the abbey in the mid-eleventh century, he may well have welcomed monks skilled as scribes and artists from a variety of neighbouring – or even more distant – abbeys.

As some of these manuscripts may have been have been produced as much as fifty or seventy-five years apart, total uniformity in techniques of book production need not be expected even if they were produced within the same scriptorium. In any case we definitely cannot say that the arrival of the Roman liturgy resulted either in the introduction of specific new techniques or in the standardization of codicological practices. A consideration of the scripts may tell us more.

All the Mozarabic manuscripts and two of the Roman manuscripts are written in Visigothic script and exhibit its typical features: an open letter 'a' formed from two almost identical horns, a closed letter 't' with a bow drawn down to the line which connects with the upper end of the shaft, a short and a long form of the letter 'i' with specific usages, a letter 'r' which has an upturned shoulder-stroke at the end of words, a straight letter 'd' and an uncial 'd' side by side, a narrow uncial 'g' with a long descender, and an uncial 'v', together with the distinctive forms of 'x' and 'z'.[24]

The abbreviations usually associated with the Visigothic script are the bar with a dot above, tagged 'e' for 'æ', a high-set 's' for '–bus' and '–que'. The abbreviation for *per* is the one more familiar in other western scripts as the abbreviation for *pro*, and there is a preference for groups of consonants in the formation of *nomina sacra*.[25]

This script is notoriously difficult to date with any precision, and it is perhaps not surprising (although not helpful) that scholars have sometimes resorted to dating a manuscript to pre- or post-the liturgical change on the basis of its textual contents rather than on the nuances of the script. Even Lowe's attempt to assign manuscripts to the first or second half of the tenth century by the distinction made between the strong and silent 'it' sound has proved unreliable. In very broad terms manuscripts before the tenth century have letters 'h', 'm' and 'n' which turn in their final stroke; the abbreviation for '–us' and '–ue' is formed by '–;' and wedged ascenders occur on the letters 'b', 'd', 'h', 'I' and 'l'. The tenth century provided some of the finest examples of Visigothic script. Scribes like Florentius of

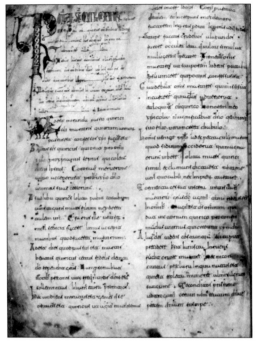

FIG. 3 London, British Library,
Add. MS 30845, fol. IV

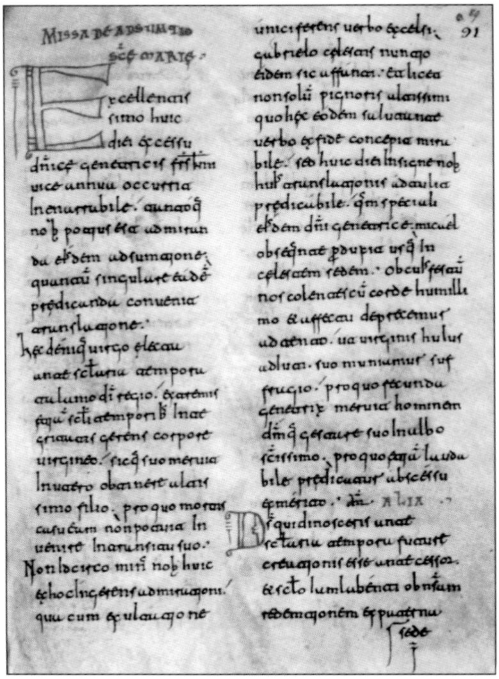

FIG. 4 London, British Library,
Add. MS 30845, fol. 89

Valeránica wrote it with an elegant, graceful *ductus* and with thin, un-wedged ascenders. Millares Carlo describes the eleventh century on the other hand as 'una época en la que se inicia la decadencia'.[26] During this century foreign influences can be detected in many codices above all in the form of abbreviations used. Superscript letters increase: 'u' and 'i' in particular, but also 'o'. The '–us' abbreviation can still be '–;', but also –ꝯ or ─ and '–que' can be '–q;' or –ꝯ.

The scripts of the manuscripts under consideration here vary considerably. Add. 30844 has a clear well-formed script, although not of the highest grade (FIG. 12). It has been dated by Díaz y Díaz to the end of the tenth or beginning of the eleventh century.[27] It has the occasional superscript 'u' (FIG. 26), and it uses more than one abbreviation for '–us' or 'is' including superscript 's' and ─ꞇ (FIG. 26), both of which are also used in the late-eleventh-century manuscript, Add. 30847. So an eleventh century date seems quite plausible for Add. 30844, possibly one even later in the century than Díaz y Díaz proposed.

Díaz y Díaz has dated Add. 30845 to the end of the tenth century (FIG. 3),[28] but at least one of the scribes of this manuscript regularly uses superscript 'u' to abbreviate '–etur', '–amur';[29] and '*quo*' is also abbreviated with a superscript 'o'. The '–*us*' or '–*is*' abbreviation is often ⱬ, rather than the superscript 's' or the curved form used in Add. 30844. As both the superscript 's' and the angular form ⱬ are found in Add. 30848, definitely a late-eleventh-century manuscript, these features suggest that Add. 30845 may also be placed more appro-

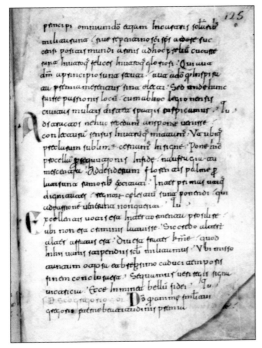

FIG. 5 London, British Library,
Add. MS 30847, fol. 127

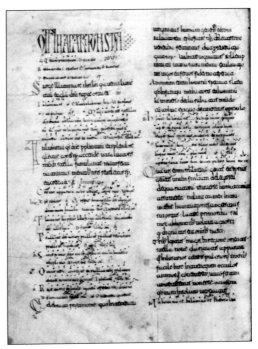

FIG. 6 London, British Library,
Add. MS 30848, fol. 38v

priately in the eleventh century. The first folios are written in well-formed script in a black-brown ink, which changes on fol. 8 to a more informal script in a light brown ink, but the ascenders are picked out in a blacker ink. On fol. 42/fol. 43 there is a reversion to the blacker ink, and a more open script. Fols 89–92v contain the interpolated mass for the Assumption of the Virgin and they are written in a script of a later date (FIG. 4). Several of the corrections in the manuscript are executed in black ink, and it is possible that this is the hand of the master correcting the pupils (FIG. 12).

Both the scripts used in Add. 30846 are ill-formed, almost cursive (FIG. 1 and FIG. 2). The abbreviations in section A include the use of superscript 'u' for '–etur' and superscript 's' and 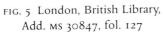 for '–us'. The same features are also found in section B in the hand of more than one scribe. Díaz y Díaz has dated Add. 30846 to the beginning of the eleventh century, but these characteristics suggest that this manuscript could equally well be placed later in that century. Moreover Add. 30845, Add. 30846, Add. 30847 and Add. 30849 – and Add. 11695, the Silos Beatus – all use in headings a capital letter 'D' divided by a cross-bar as an abbreviation for 'De', possibly another indication that there may not have been so many years separating these manuscripts.

There is little to distinguish the Visigothic script used in Add. 30847 (FIG. 5) from that of the Mozarabic manuscripts. The 'decadent' features identified by Millares Carlo are no more in evidence here than in Add. 30845 and Add. 30846; indeed superscript 'u' is less common in this manuscript. Other aspects of this manuscript mark it as a product of the late elev-

FIG. 7 London, British Library,
Add. MS 30849, fol. 42v

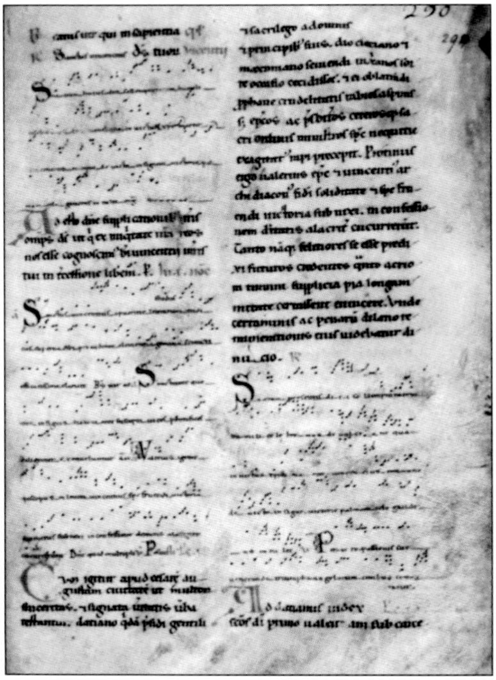

FIG. 8 London, British Library,
Add. MS 30849, fol. 294

enth century: primarily its text but also the introduction of new forms of initial which we will examine in chapter 3. The Visigothic script of Add. 30848 is more distinctive in its general aspect (FIG. 6) being of a higher grade than the script of Add. 30847 and considerably more laterally compressed. In this it has much in common with the more elegant script of the Silos Beatus (FIG. 38, completed 1091) and was probably executed around the same time. The characteristic Visigothic abbreviations are still used in Add. 30847 and Add. 30848, although the line and bar has become very light and fluid in Add. 30848.

Most of Add. 30849 is written by more than one hand in an undeveloped Protogothic script (FIG. 7). The serifs are very weak and the script retains some of the simplicity of Caroline minuscule. The calendar at the beginning of the manuscript, two folios bound into the middle, and several folios at the end are written in a much more developed Protogothic script (FIG. 8).[30] The first script uses the expected Caroline abbreviation forms, but the second script employs a wide range of superscript abbreviations and tironian *'et'*.

The Mozarabic manuscripts punctuate with the *punctus* and the *punctus elevatus* and make particular use of paragraph marks in passages which are to be read aloud. Add. 30844 also uses a distinctive zigzag with an upward stroke, like a neume. There is occasional use of the paragraph mark in Add. 30847 (for example fol. 57v), but such marks no longer appear in Add. 30848 or Add. 30849. The Roman manuscripts, Add. 30848 and Add. 30849, introduce the *punctus versus*, a Caroline feature.[31]

There is considerable variation in the quality of the script, both between manuscripts and within them: some of the finest work is to be found in Add. 30848, which has a very fine, high grade script, often written very small, and somewhat reminiscent of that in Add. 11695. Parts of Add. 30845 and much of Add. 30846, are on the other hand, so roughly written that the script is almost cursive. The other manuscripts are written in functional, clear scripts with no pretentions to high grade status. It is difficult to conclude a great deal from this information, but the low grade of the scripts in Add. 30846 and in parts of Add. 30845 support the notion that these manuscripts could have been produced in the scriptorium school and may not have been intended for liturgical use. Indeed it is a remarkable fact that there are few signs of use on any of these manuscripts: drops of candle wax are largely absent and wear is restricted.

Of particular importance for this study is the use made of liturgical abbreviations in the various manuscripts. This may sound like an arcane subject for enquiry, but I believe it to be of notable help as the different forms used in the manuscripts are measures of consistency and transition. Moreover the subject is one that has not previously been looked at in this way and hence merits a more detailed treatment. Examples of these abbreviations have been taken therefore from all the manuscripts and can be seen in Table 3.

TABLE 3
Liturgical Abbreviations Used in the Office Texts

BL ADD. MS	30844	30845	30846	30847	30848	30849
Ad matutinis	A𝔉	AD 𝔉	AD/𝔉 ad͞m	ad matutiᵍ ad ɸ	in mt�న͞is	in mat⁻
Ad vesperas/um	AD ᵫ	aD ᵫ	AD ᵫ	ad ᵫ	AD ᵫ	AD VESPER
Antiphona	Ā Á Â	aF	Λ ^F	á ã	Á π̃	Á ã
Capitulum				c̃p	c̃p c̄p	captͫ capͤͭ / capͭ CAPI
Collecta				coll		coll
Homelia					hmͭa	
Himnus	ẏm ẏm⁻	ẏs	Iꞣ Iꞣ	Ymnū	hᵫ	h'Ymnum / invͭtatō
Invitatorium				invitatiū	invͭtͤᶜa	ϵLTATOR
Lectio				tc	lc̃o	lc̄oes lco
Nocturno				ïi NETR ïiᴺᶜᵀᵐ ïi NCꝍno / in ll N͞CR	II N͞c	in iii° noct / in ii° noct

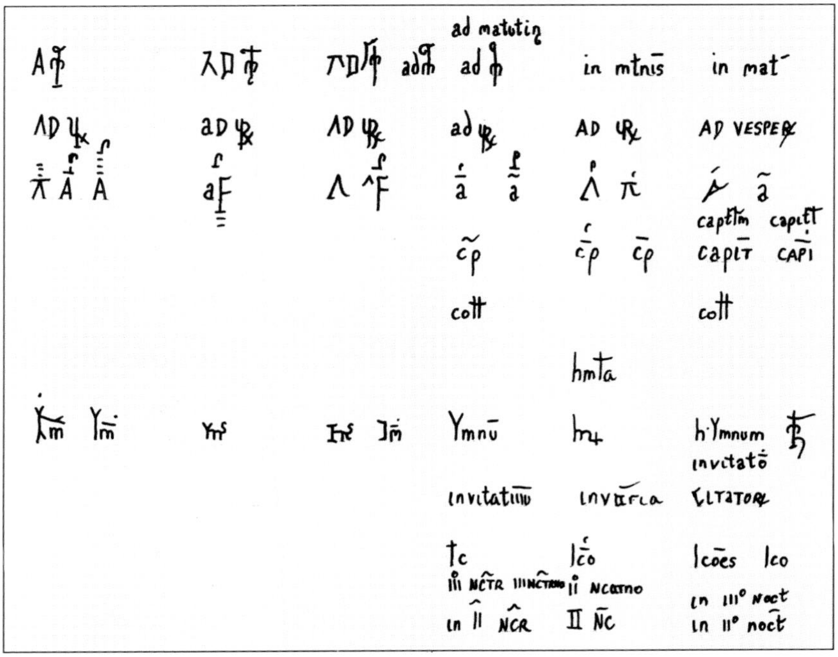

TABLE 3 *(continued)*

BL ADD.	30844	30845	30846	30847	30848	30849
Officium	OFFm	OFFA OFFm OFFm				
Oratio	ozo	ōī	ōī	ōī	ōī	ā
Responsorium	R̄S	R̄S	R̄S	R̄S R̄S Ī	R̄S	R⁄
Sacrificium	SCR	SCF	SCR SCRM			
Sermo						
Sevovae					seuo uae	
Sono	SNO	SNO	SNO SNO			
Versus	R R	R ψ	R VR	ψ	ψ ψ	V̄

The liturgical abbreviations found in Add. 30844, Add. 30845 and Add. 30846 are based on the hook and bar typical of the Visigothic script. In Add. 30844 the bars are frequently multiplied, especially in the abbreviations for *antiphona* and *responsorium*, to give a decorative effect sometimes extending the abbreviation over more than one line. The same feature can be seen in Add. 30845, although more contained versions are also used in this manuscript. Add. 30846 favours the less elaborate forms. The long letters of Visigothic script are also used to form abbreviations, for example the long 'I' in the abbreviation for *himnus*, and an elongated hooked 'T' in that for *matutinis*.

Some of the Visigothic abbreviations do not appear in the Roman breviaries because the words for which they stood are no longer required, for example *sono*. Where a word was used in the Roman text as well as in the Mozarabic, the scribe had to make a decision as to which abbreviation to use. For example Add. 30847 has three abbreviations for *ad matutinis*, one in the Visigothic mould and two in more extended Caroline forms. There are also two versions of the *responsorium* abbreviation in Add. 30847, one Visigothic and one Caroline. The most distinctive Visigothic abbreviations are absent, however, from Add. 30848, and there is only an extended form of *ad matutinis*. Yet the hook and bar persists in this manuscript in a less flamboyant form – for example in the abbreviations for *antiphona*, *responsorium*, and *versus* – and does not give way to the bar and dot more typical of the Caroline script.

The scribes were also faced with the problem of how to handle words which did not feature in the Mozarabic liturgy, for example *nocturno*, *capitulum* and *invitatorium*. Some attempts were made to show these new words in a Visigothic guise, for example the abbreviation for *capitulum* in Add. 30848 has a hook and bar. There was clearly some indecision surrounding this issue: Add. 30847 offers at least three, and Add. 30848 two, different abbreviations for *nocturno*, none of them the same as the Caroline forms found in Add. 30849. The method of abbreviation is, however, closer to that employed in Caroline script than to the Visigothic equivalent.

There also seems to have been some confusion in the minds of the scribes when abbreviating words common to both liturgies. Add. 30847 treats *ad vesperum* in two different ways, either writing it in full or using the Visigothic abbreviation. In the case of *himnum,* however, Add. 30847 opts for a Caroline form, as does Add. 30848 when abbreviating *lectio.* There is a marked change in Add. 30849 which is written in Protogothic script: Caroline abbreviation forms predominate and nearly all Visigothic features have disappeared with the possible exception of a hook and bar used to abbreviate *oratio* and an unusual abbreviation for *himnum.*

In the case of these Roman manuscripts we do not know whether their immediate model(s) would have been in Caroline script, or whether a copy already in Visigothic script was used. Nonetheless we can be certain that at some stage an imported text in Caroline script was transcribed in Visigothic script. This presupposes a scribe who was able to read the Caroline script, including the abbreviations, and to transcribe it into Visigothic script. It seems likely that this scribe would have been from the Spanish tradition, as there would have been little incentive for a foreign scribe to learn to write Visigothic script. Even though no linguistic translation was required, several decisions had to be made consciously or unconsciously during this copying process. One possibility would have been to reproduce the 'imported' manuscript in Caroline script, and then to train those who were to use it to read that script. We know, however, that this option was not chosen, to judge by Add. 30847 and Add. 30848. The decision to transcribe the text into Visigothic script could have been political, and intended to make the manuscript look more familiar and hence more acceptable to those who were to use it. More probably it was pragmatic. Our copyist needed only to be able to read Caroline script, not necessarily to write it, and those who copied him needed neither skill. This would have made the process of producing several codices much easier and quicker, for when he had produced one exemplar of the Roman liturgy in Visigothic script, it could be readily copied by many Spanish scribes. Thus copying the Roman liturgy in Visigothic script may have been a practical necessity in the short term, as there must have been – at least at in the early stages of the change – a severe shortage of Spanish scribes who could write in the 'French' script.[32]

An examination of the orthography of these manuscripts casts further light on the origin of the scribes and their models. The spelling in Add. 30844 and Add. 30845 is remarkably consistent, exhibiting typical Visigothic features such as 'b' for 'v', and 't' for 'd', while that in Add. 30846 can be described as consistently bad. Add. 30847 continues to use Visigothic spelling in many cases, but the hallmark of this manuscript is oscillation: it gives *hoctabas* and *octave* (both on fol. 58), and *octabe* (fol. 66v); *Sebastianus* (fol. 80 and fol. 80v), *Sabastiani* (fol. 80, fol. 80v and fol. 81) and *Savastianus* (fol. 81); *Vincencii* (fol. 89), and *Vincenti* (fol. 90);

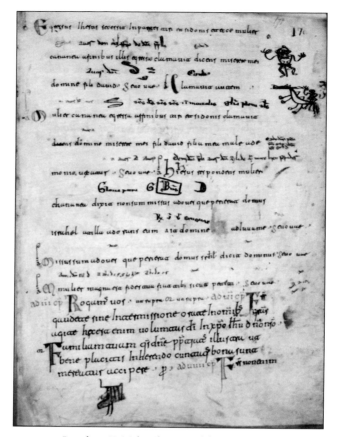

FIG. 9 London, British Library, Add. MS 30847, fol. 171

Stefani and *Stephanus* (fol. 35v), and *horas* (fol. 1) and *oras* (fol. 9). Add. 30848 still has 'b' for 'v', but is not so prone to aberrations, whereas Add. 30849 is generally consistent in suppressing Visigothic elements. It is the scribes of Add. 30847 who again exhibit a state of mind that, either through confusion, the use of more than one model, or a deliberate or subconscious desire to span a divide, results in their using interchangeably not only various letter forms and abbreviations but also spellings. Although totally consistent spelling may not have been prevalent or prized in the eleventh century, it is unusual to find such variability.

We can now begin to assemble a profile of each manuscript. Add. 30844 seems to be a well-produced Mozarabic manuscript, of the kind which could have been kept in a library and possibly used as a model in a scriptorium. There are some problems concerning the nature of Add. 30845, and even more in the case of Add. 30846; we will need other kinds of evidence to help us to understand these manuscripts. They do not appear to have had extensive use, nor are they of a sufficiently high standard to have been ideal models for copying, and their preservation is surprising. At some point they may have become, as they are now, the only volumes at Silos which contained the 'Toledan' offices and masses for these periods of the liturgical year, and they may have been retained for that very reason.

Among the Roman manuscripts Add. 30847 is marked out by its inconsistency in all aspects: its use of abbreviations, script, and orthography is remarkably erratic. None of this is explained by different scribes working on the manuscript, for the variations can occur within the same passage and even in the same line. The overall presentation is far from clean (FIG. 9).[33] Add. 30848 is much more assured in its production and in command of the different forms to be found within it. The innovations (such as the new liturgical abbreviations) seem to have been subsumed into the Visigothic script of this manuscript with considerable sophistication. A dramatic transformation is found in Add. 30849: here the change in script is so complete that all Visigothic elements have disappeared – the link has finally been severed.

So the evidence leads us to a tentative chronological sequence for the Roman manuscripts: beginning with Add. 30847, followed by Add. 30848 and ending with Add. 30849. This must, nevertheless, be surrounded with several caveats. A straightforward linear progression along the scale from Visigothic script to Caroline minuscule may be a distortion as well as a simplification of the historical process. Although originally all the liturgical manuscripts in Spain were written in Visigothic script and eventually they were all written in a Gothic script, it does not follow that the transition was neat, steady and linear.

It seems likely that scribes who were accomplished in the Visigothic script would have continued to use it. One example of this is the Silos Beatus, which was written in a very fine Visigothic script by *Dominico presbiter et ... Munnio presbiter* and finished in 1091 according to its colophon (fol. 265v).[34] In this case we have a dated manuscript demonstrating clearly that Visigothic script was in use a decade after the change to the Roman liturgy and the need for the production of 'Roman' books. We would need to know more about the teaching methods in scriptoria to understand the process of change fully, but presumably scribes from other monasteries who wrote in the 'new' way could have come to teach those in the Spanish monasteries. When the scribes were to learn the new script, instruction would have been required in a different way of forming the letters, and possibly in interpreting some of the abbreviations in the unfamiliar script. It would possibly have been easier to teach the new script to beginners, but at least some of the scribes who had already been trained would have had to learn an additional script. Thus the scribes in the scriptorium would probably not all have been at the same stage in learning the new script, and while some may have found it quite easy to adapt others may have found it almost impossible. Although we do not have any books in this group in which there is Visigothic together with Caroline script,[35] this may be because the scribes selected to co-operate on a manuscript would have been those whose work would look best side by side. We may presume that some general measure of consistency of overall appearance was a usual requirement. Thus there may have been as many different stages along the 'line' from Visigothic to Caroline as there were scribes in the scriptorium. The proposed sequence must, therefore, be regarded with great caution, unless other factors can be found to confirm it.

What else can the codicology of these manuscripts tell us about their nature and purpose? All six manuscripts appear to have been intended to be books for the officiant, in that prominence is given to the read or intoned passages rather than to the sung items. Among the Mozarabic manuscripts Add. 30845 is the only one with neumes. Although the texts of the sung passages in the other Mozarabic manuscripts are written in a smaller script, leaving space for musical notation, no neumes have been written in.[36] Of the Roman manuscripts, Add. 30848 receives musical notation most consistently, and may be called a 'noted breviary' (that is a breviary with musical notation). Add. 30847 and Add. 30849 are also, at least in part, noted breviaries, but here the notation is very sporadic and cannot have been one of the main functions of the manuscripts. In Add. 30848, however, the sung passages are written in such a small script that it is very difficult to believe that they could have been used in a service, especially as the large size of the codex renders it unsuitable for close work. It is even difficult to believe that the sung passages are merely for the officiant to follow the parts of the service in which he did not play the main part. Although the sung passages in the other manuscripts are written in a slightly larger script, they still seem inadequate for performance. It is possible that Andrew Hughes's suggestion concerning noted breviaries in general is relevant here.[37] He argued that although the presence of the text could be explained by the officiant's need to follow, this did not explain why the musical notation was added. He proposed instead that such copies could have been used as reference or master copies. Is this a plausible interpretation in the case of these manuscripts? It would explain why they have survived relatively intact and why there are so few signs of liturgical use. In particular this interpretation fits Add. 30849 very well; it even looks like our modern notion of a reference book with its rather dense layout. Indeed, I believe that this could have been the original status of all three Roman manuscripts, although Add. 30847 and Add. 30848 may have been superseded quite quickly as the liturgical change took hold. This would mean that the differences in size between these three manuscripts are not symptomatic of differences in function, but rather reflect variations in their textual and decorative contents as we shall see in the next two chapters.

Notes to Chapter One

1   Whitehill, *as above* Intro. note 116.

2   Thompson, E.M. *Catalogue of the Additions to the Manuscripts in the British Museum in the Years MDCCCLXXVI–MDCCCLXXXI,* London, 1882 (reprinted 1968), vol.13, pp.119–20.

3   The section of this list which deals with the manuscripts of the Mozarabic liturgy is in broad agreement with Díaz y Díaz, M. C., *Códices Visigóticos en la Monarquía Leonesa,* León, 1983; the description concerning fol. 1–7v of Add. 30845 is however my own.

4   Férotin identified the texts of these codices as the Mozarabic liturgy, *see* Férotin, *as above* Intro. note 20, col. 804–70.

5   Whitehill (*see above* Intro. note 116) identified these texts as belonging to the Roman liturgy, although the original catalogue entry by Thompson (*see above* note 2) assigned them to the Mozarabic liturgy – this has been corrected in the copy kept in the Students' Room of the Department of Manuscripts of the British Library.

6   Besse, J-M, 'Histoire d'un dépôt littéraire, l'abbaye de Silos', in *Revue Bénédictine,* XIV, Abbaye de Maredsous, 1897, pp.210–25 and pp.241–52. *See also* Whitehill, W.M. and Pérez de Urbel, J., 'Los Manuscritos del Real Monasterio de Santo Domingo de Silos', in *Boletín de la Real Academia de la Historia,* t.95, Madrid, 1929, pp.521–601.

7   Boylan, A., *Manuscript Illumination at Santo Domingo de Silos (Xth to XIIth Centuries),* Ph.D. Diss., University of Pittsburgh, 1990, (Ann Arbor, 1992), pp.306–40 gives a helpful summary: a charter of 1067 written into a *Liber Comicus* (Paris, Bibliothèque Nationale, MS N.a.l. 2171, fol. 26); a list, probably compiled in the thirteenth century, written into a manuscript of St Isidore's Etymologies (BN, MS N.a.l. 2169, fol. 16v); a list of manuscripts lent from Silos in the thirteenth century inserted into BN, MS N.a.l. 235, fol. B; an eighteenth-century catalogue (*c.*1770), Silos MS 116a; a list of fifteenth- and sixteenth-century manuscripts and printed books, Silos MS 116b; and a catalogue compiled by Hernández from the indices which he had inserted into all the individual manuscripts.

8   Boylan, *as above* note 7, pp.327–40. Hernández's catalogue is a compilation of the tables of contents which he wrote into the back of each manuscript. These can still be seen in the six manuscripts under consideration here.

9   Boylan, *as above* note 7.

10   Vivancos Gómez, M.C., *as above* Intro. note 8, pp.18–19, no. 16. (1067) '*Antifunario, et Orationum, et Manuale, et Comicum, et Ordinum, et Imnorum, et Oralium, in meos dies ut teneam illos, et postea meo subrino duen Sango; et si postea abuerit duen Sango de sua radice, ut teneas illos; et si tugaberit sua radice, ut veniant ad Sancti Sabastiani*'.

11   This is written on fol. 16v, a blank leaf, in a copy of St. Isidore's *Etymologiae,* now MS N.a.l. 2169 in the Bibliothèque Nationale. The list was first published by Delisle, L., 'Manuscrits de l'abbaye de Silos acquis par la Bibliothèque Nationale', in *Mélanges de paléographie et de bibliographie,* Paris, 1880, pp.53–116. *See also* Férotin, M., *Histoire de l'abbaye de Silos,* Paris, 1897, pp.262–4.

12   Thompson, J, W., *The Medieval Library,* repnt. New York and London, 1965, p.615–16.

13   Boylan, A., *as above* note 7, appendix I, pp.306–40. Her numbers are used here.

14   Most of this information had already been noted by Férotin, *as above* Intro. note 20, col. 804, 820–1, and 842, and Díaz y Díaz, *as above* note 3, pp.402–4.

15   Férotin, *as above* Intro. note 20, col. 804, fol. 1–56: 23/24 lines; fol. 56–94: 23; fol. 95–109: 24, fol. 110–25: 23; fol. 126–37: 22; fol. 138–48: 24; fol. 149–73: 22; and fol. 173–7: 24.

16   The sections of Add.30846 are discussed later in this chapter.

17   Férotin *as above* Intro. note 20, col. 804, two quires missing after fol. 71 and one after fol. 102. The first five folios are missing, and at least twenty others.

18   Férotin, *as above* Intro. note 20, col. 820.

19 Díaz y Díaz, M. C., *as above* note 3, p.404; Díaz y Díaz is incorrect in saying that all the folios after fol. 7 have thirty lines.

20 Díaz y Díaz, *as above* note 3, p.404. Add. 30846: '*Es todavia mas probable que nos encontremos ante un complejo en el que se han mezcalado restos de dos manuscritos, combinados de tal manera que constituyen una aparente unidad.*'

21 For example after fol. 25 and after fol. 84.

22 Jones, L.W., 'Pricking Manuscripts: the Instruments and their Significance', in *Speculum*, 21, 1946, pp.389–403.

23 Férotin, *as above* Intro. note 20, col. 820. They are not found in the first or last quire in Add. 30845.

24 Brown, M.P., *A guide to western historical scripts from antiquity to 1600*, London, 1990, p.46, and Bischoff, B., *Latin Palaeography: Antiquity and the Middle Ages*, Cambridge, 1990, p.97.

25 Bischoff, *as above* note 24, p.97.

26 Millares Carlo, A., *Tratado de Paleografía Española*, vol.I–III, Madrid, 1983, p.139

27 Díaz y Díaz, *as above* note 3, p.402.

28 Díaz y Díaz, *as above* note 3, p.403. Díaz y Díaz assigned fol. 1–7 to the second half of the tenth century, and the rest to the end of that century.

29 *See* Plate 1, for example, column 2 line 9.

30 Fol. 2–4v, fol. 84, fol. 88, fol. 275, fol. 294–308. This script has several features in common with that used in Sal. 2637, a manuscript probably produced at Silos in the mid-twelfth century. (*see* part II).

31 Parkes, M.B., *Pause and Effect. An Introduction to the History of Punctuation in the West*, Scolar Press (Aldershot), 1992, pp.35–40.

32 Schapiro, *as above* Intro. note 12, p.60. According to the thirteenth century catalogue in the library at Silos the new script was thought of as 'French': '*dos reglas de letra fransisca*'.

33 In the thirteenth century several of the blank portions of folios in Add. 30847 were used to record documents. This shows that the book was still in use, even if not liturgical use, at this time. In addition it has suffered from scribbles, which have defaced several of the folios (fol. 69v, fol. 94v, fol. 108v, fol. 170v and fol. 171; *see* FIG. 64). These consist mainly of rough sketches of birds, figures, a lizard and stars, but also include rows of letters, like practice alphabets, not in Visigothic script. The rudimentary and indeed unsophisticated nature of the drawings makes them very difficult to date and they may not even have been executed at the same time as the letters, which are equally difficult to date. It is of interest to note that the subject-matter of the scribbles relates in many cases to elements in the illustration of the Silos Beatus.

34 The Silos Beatus, BL Add. MS 11695, fol. 277v. It is interesting to note that the scribes in this instance were priests and not laymen, and the later illustrator *Petrus prior*. It is surely even more likely that liturgical manuscripts would be written and illuminated by monks or priests.

35 Bischoff, *see above* note 24, refers to a manuscript of Lucan which is written partly in Visigothic and partly in Caroline script, p.126.

36 Suñol, G., *as above* Intro. note 115, p.322; Suñol assigns Add. 30845 to the tenth century and classifies its neumes as: 1st phase Visigothic.

37 Hughes, A., *Medieval Manuscripts for Mass and Office, A Guide to their Organization and Terminology*, Toronto, 1982, p.123.

CHAPTER TWO

———◄◦►———

The Sacred Text

THIS CHAPTER will examine the texts contained in our six manuscripts, beginning with the broad contents and then focusing, in increasing detail, on the texts themselves. [*See* appendix II for a list of the contents of these manuscripts.] This will enable us to see the extent of the change, to analysis its shape and forms, and to isolate the most sensitive issues.

The Manuscripts Defined

Two of the Roman manuscripts (Add. 30848, Add. 30849) are breviaries for the whole liturgical year, but only Add. 30848 has retained its title-page, which clearly describes it as *Brebarium de toto circulo anni*. The text of this manuscript begins on the same page with vespers for the first Sunday in Advent and continues through the liturgical year until the twenty-fourth Sunday after Trinity. The last surviving folios contain two occasional offices and the missing sheets may have contained others. Add. 30849 has lost its title-page and the liturgical text now begins in the middle of the services for the first Sunday of Advent. It ends with eleven occasional *officia*. It is clear then that this manuscript also originally contained services for the whole year beginning at Advent and continuing through to the last Sunday after Pentecost. The custom frequently practised in France at this time – at Cluny and elsewhere – of producing breviaries in two volumes for winter and summer does not seem on this evidence to have been employed in Spain.

The contents of the Mozarabic books were never comprehensive in the same sense. It was usual practice for Mozarabic manuscripts to place offices and masses together under the heading for the feast day in the one volume. So the texts are normally ordered by liturgical day, under which vespers, matins and lauds and then the masses are given. Consequently these manuscripts are usually described as 'mixed books'. The Roman habit, on the other hand, was to have separate books for the mass and the hours: a missal and a breviary. Although we are not going to study the texts for the various masses in part I, their very existence in the Mozarabic codices had an effect on what else could be included. If the masses took up a considerable amount of space, it was obviously not possible to have the whole liturgical year in one volume: it would be impracticably large. Thus the Mozarabic liturgical year could not be presented as a unity, but rather had to appear in a selection of separate volumes.

How was the liturgical year apportioned between these manuscripts? Add. 30844 covers a substantial portion of the liturgical year, stretching from the feast of the Virgin Mary (18 December; *see* appendix III) to Pentecost. It does not, however, cover all parts of that long period with equal thoroughness. The earlier part, from the feast of the Virgin to Epiphany, is given without obvious lacunae, but after that the feasts included seem somewhat random. If one of the main purposes of this manuscript was to cover the first part of the liturgical year, we would expect at least the feast of St Acisclus (17 November), which began the Mozarabic liturgical year, to have been included at the start. It could be argued that the folios containing this feast have been lost, but given the quire structure of the manuscript there do not seem to be sufficient folios missing at the appropriate point for it to have contained even one *officium et missa*.[1] There is, in fact, an important aspect of this manuscript which renders it unlikely that its function was merely to cover the early part of the liturgical year: the inclusion before the liturgical section of the text of St Ildephonsus's *De Virginitate perpetua sancte Marie* arranged in six parts to be read in a liturgical context (fols 1–31v).[2] This is followed by a prayer (*Magnificamus te domine*) addressed to the Virgin (fol. 32 and fol. 32v). The palaeographic evidence, considered in the previous chapter, provides no reason for us to think that the Ildephonsus section originally came from another manuscript, and the liturgical section of the manuscript continues the theme effectively by choosing to begin with the office for the feast of the Virgin. The position of St Ildephonsus's text is also significant. Miscellaneous texts are sometimes added at the end of medieval manuscripts, or on blank pages at the beginning or at the end, but the formal beginning of a manuscript is often its most important section, setting the tone and providing guidance for the rest of the book. So it seems likely from the existence and position of this text that Add. 30844 had some particular connection with the cult of the Virgin.

This supposition can be strengthened by consideration of other manuscripts with parallel collections of liturgical texts. In particular the same prayer was found by Férotin in another manuscript from the Silos corpus (*De Virginitate S. Marie et varia offitia*, Silos MS 5), dated to the eleventh century.[3] This book also begins with the *De Virginitate* divided in the same way into six lessons, and continues with the same *petitio* and the same sermon by St Ildephonsus as that given for the feast day of the Virgin in Add. 30844 (*Exhortatur nos Dominus*).[4] Indeed it is possible that this entire office was composed by Ildephonsus.[5]

There is another Mozarabic manuscript which has similar juxtapositions of St Ildephonsus's tract with offices and masses. It is a Toledan manuscript (Toledo, Cathedral Archive, MS 35.7) entitled *Varia Officia et Missae*.[6] Férotin stated that it originally formed two manuscripts, probably written by the same scribe, '*Sebastianus scriptor*'. The first section contains the *De Virginitate* divided into seven *lectiones* and the mass for the Feast of the Virgin (18 December) and the office for the Assumption of the Virgin.[7]

It appears from these examples that we can reconstruct a Mozarabic tradition of producing books focused on Ildephonsus's text and including other pieces, sometimes *officia et missae*, having a particular connection with the Virgin.[8] Other texts, readings, offices or masses, were added to these books in a variety of ways. We will now examine the other two

Mozarabic manuscripts to see if their conception is similar.

In its present condition Add. 30846 begins with the end of the *Benedictio* for the Easter Mass and continues the temporal cycle until Pentecost. It also contains the texts for the sanctoral feasts which fall within this period: *S. Engratia* (16 April), *S. Torquatus et socii eius* (1 May), St Philip the Apostle (2 May) and that for the Invention of the Holy Cross (3 May). Thus the focus of this manuscript seems to be the fifty days of Eastertide.[9] It did not apparently include Lent, the other fixed period associated with Easter, unless several quires are missing at the beginning for which there is no evidence. The choice of this period may have its roots in canon 43 of the Council of Elvira (314) which stipulated that there should be fifty not forty days after Easter.[10]

Add. 30845 begins now with the office for the feast of *S. Quiricus* (13 June – fols 1–3v) and continues until that of *S. Milanus* on 12 November, that is until just before the beginning of the Mozarabic year. The mass for the Assumption of the Virgin (fols 89–92v) is clearly an addition, probably of the eleventh century, inserted after the original text for the *officium et missa de assumtio sancte marie*. Fol. 86bis is also a fragment which did not originally belong to this codex. It also has texts for the Translation of *S. Saturninus* (1 November), for *S. Cristina* (26 July) and for *S. Bartolomeus* (24 August) added out of order at the end.

Díaz y Díaz has asserted that the first seven folios containing texts for *S. Quiricus* and *S. Hieronimus* are from a different manuscript.[11] However, as the feast of *S. Quiricus* falls naturally in chronological terms before that of *S. Adrianus* and *S. Natalia*, the only textual reason which suggests that these folios are not an integral part of this manuscript is the insertion of the feast of St Jerome – usually celebrated on 7 July – between these two.[12] This reason, however, is not sufficient on its own to secure Díaz y Díaz's position.

In order to define this manuscript, we can say that it deals with the period of the year from the end of Pentecost until just before the first feast of the Mozarabic liturgical year. No major temporal festivals occur in this period and, therefore, Add. 30845 gives only sanctoral feasts. It seems possible that a separate companion volume contained the texts for the twenty Sundays until Advent, as can be seen in a Toledo manuscript (Toledo, Cathedral Archive, MS 35.4) which contains no sanctoral feasts for this period.

We can now see that, even taken together, these three manuscripts leave considerable periods uncovered, including the whole of Lent and all the Sundays after Pentecost. Unfortunately these lacunae are not made good by any other surviving manuscript from the Silos corpus. None of the Mozarabic manuscripts includes the whole liturgical year, nor do they appear to be companion volumes once forming part of a notional set in which the liturgical year was divided chronologically into three or more codices at customary points. If this had been the case we would not expect to find the same feast in more than one volume, as we do for example in Add. 30844 and Add. 30846, which both include the *officium et missa* for the Ascension and for the Sunday after Ascension. It is, of course, possible that such sets did exist, but that our manuscripts, and in particular Add. 30844, were either from different sets or not from sets at all.

There is too much variation among the Mozarabic manuscripts which survive[13] for us to be able to assert confidently that there was even a set pattern which dictated how the liturgical year should be divided. Indeed diversity seems to be the only consistent element; no two of the surviving Mozarabic manuscripts of *officia et missae* cover the same period. The Mozarabic church, in conclusion, seems to have produced non-standardised volumes, each book specifically adapted to particular dedications and usages, and generally idiosyncratic and thematic in conception.

When we look at the Roman manuscripts, the picture is different. Add. 30847 is still not a comprehensive volume. It begins with Advent, but does not continue beyond Quadragesima, and thus covers less then half the liturgical year. Within this period, however, it is thorough, unlike the Mozarabic manuscript, Add. 30844, which covers much of the same period. It may be seen as a transitional stage, for both Add. 30848 and Add. 30849 cover the whole liturgical year. The immediate changeover from multi-volume *officia et missae* to one volume *breviarium* and *missale* does not, therefore, seem to have been a stipulation of the change from Mozarabic to Roman liturgy. Nevertheless the representation of the year in one all-embracing volume was surely a potent symbol when compared to the diverse ways in which texts were presented within the Mozarabic church. The move towards conformity and unity was clearly expressed, consciously or unconsciously, in this codicological alteration.

Another organisational change which can be seen taking place in these six manuscripts concerns the separation of the temporal and sanctoral cycles. There is no clear-cut division between these cycles in most of the manuscripts of the Mozarabic liturgy. Add. 30845, it is true, contains no temporal feasts, but this may be a function of the time of the year which it covers (after Pentecost to before Advent) when there are no major temporal feasts. Both Add. 30844 and Add. 30846, however, mix the temporal and sanctoral cycles. The texts of Add. 30847, on the other hand, fall into blocks, sometimes mixing, but usually grouping, the temporal and sanctoral feasts. The first block proceeds from Advent until Epiphany including the sanctoral feasts of *S. Lucia* and *S. Tome* as well as the saints' days usually included with the temporal cycle. The four Sundays after Epiphany are then given separately and followed by a sanctoral section which begins with St Sebastian, and ends with St Benedict. The Sundays of Septuagesima, Sexagesima and Quinquagesima are together, and followed by the four Sundays of Quadragesima. Again this seems to represent a transitional stage between interleaving the cycles and presenting them as two distinct categories.

In Add. 30848 there is still a tendency to mingle the sanctoral with the temporal. The first block is the same as in Add. 30847 running from Advent to Epiphany, but here the corresponding part of the sanctoral cycle is given separately. The temporal cycle resumes with *dominica post Epiphanie* and continues in this manuscript until Trinity. Major and established saints' feast days again form part of the temporal, including Sts James and Philip, and the Holy Cross. The saints' days for the rest of the year from St John the Baptist (24 June) until St Lucy (12 December) follow in a sanctoral block, and are in turn succeeded by the temporal feasts from *dominica post sanctam trinitatem* until the twenty-fourth Sunday after Trinity.

Finally in Add. 30849 it can be seen that the division is complete: the temporal cycle is

given first, together with the major saints' days: St Stephen, St John, and the Holy Innocents which traditionally form part of it. The sanctoral cycle begins on fol. 232v with the
officium S. Silvestri and ends with the *officium S. Thome*.

This analysis suggests that the split between the temporal and sanctoral cycles may have
evolved quite gradually. In the Mozarabic manuscripts the two cycles are intermixed, although there is sometimes a preponderance of offices from one cycle or the other; in Add.
30847 there is an attempt to separate some of the temporal feasts and to isolate them in
blocks, but some saints' days, like St Lucy's, are still included in the temporal cycle. Whereas
Add. 30848 no longer mixes the two cycles, but divides the liturgical year into substantial
periods, giving the temporal feasts first in each case and following them with a separate
block of sanctoral feasts. Finally Add. 30849 lists the two cycles completely separately. We
seem to have here an example of progressive development, as the two cycles are disentan-
gled partially and unsurely in Add. 30847, clearly but not completely in Add. 30848, and
absolutely in Add. 30849. Again this change does not seem to have been implemented with
any haste.

These manuscripts must also be seen in the context of the general development of the
Roman breviary, which took place during the eleventh and twelfth century. The constituents of the offices had at one time been drawn from a collection of independent codices
including a *collectarium, psalterium, lectionarium, antiphonarium,* and *hymnarium.* This was clearly
cumbersome and, from the ninth century onwards, various attempts were made to combine
some of the elements resulting in, for example, augmented lectionaries. As we have seen,
the practice of the Mozarabic church overcame these difficulties by its use of mixed *officia
et missae* volumes covering only a section of the liturgical year. The breviary as such does not
seem to have been produced until the eleventh century,[14] when it appeared in France, Italy
and Switzerland, as well as in Spain. Salmon, who has traced this development in detail,[15]
suggests two motives, not only the grouping of the different elements, but also the provision of a model for each office. Prior to this it seems that officiants were freer to choose
from the different books.[16] Salmon's examples show that during this period of development
certain items in the offices were written in an abbreviated form so that all the constituents
could be included in one volume. The breviary also seems to have appeared in various
guises during this period sometimes without the full integration of some of the elements.[17]
Compared with many of the examples which Salmon gives from eleventh- and twelfth-
century France and Italy, the Spanish breviaries in this study seem remarkably ordered. The
opportunity which the breviary offered for direction of the offices seems to have been used
gradually but firmly in the implementation of the liturgical change. This may mean in turn
that the demands of the Spanish church played a significant role in the development of the
Roman breviary; it is, however, beyond the scope of this study to establish that.

One implication of the proposed sequence of the three Roman breviaries is that they
could be taken to represent three distinctive stages in the adaptation to the change in the
liturgy: Add. 30847 an initial transitional phase; Add. 30848 an advanced transitional stage;
and Add. 30849 the completion of the change.

The Veneration of Saints

We will now examine another aspect of the texts in these manuscripts, the saints' feasts included in each volume. Before the *officia* themselves are considered, we will look at the calendars. Unfortunately no calendars survive in any of these three Mozarabic manuscripts so it will be necessary to use a composite calendar for the Mozarabic liturgy. One was constructed by Férotin from those Mozarabic manuscripts in which a calendar survives, but this has been superseded by the studies of Vives and Fábrega.[18] Vives and Fábrega do not, however, offer an alternative composite table, but instead give a separate table for each of their nine manuscripts. For our purposes a composite table will be easier to handle, and I have, therefore, constructed one using eight of Vives and Fábrega's manuscripts. In the same way that they decided to omit the famous Córdoba calendar of 961 previously included by Férotin, I have decided to exclude in addition their Catalonian manuscript (Barcelona, MS A.C.A., Ripoll 59), as both were produced outside the geographical area under consideration and are, therefore, unsuitable for this purpose. The new composite table is derived by including every saint's feast which occurs in at least one of the manuscripts assigned by Vives and Fábrega to the tenth century (Biblioteca El Escorial MSS d.I.2 and d.I.1, or Silos MS 4) provided that the feast is also found in at least one of their later manuscripts (Silos MS 3, León Biblioteca Catedral Antiphonarium; or Biblioteca Universitaria de Santiago de Compostela, Rs.1, the Prayer Book of Fernando I and Queen Sancha). I will compare this composite Mozarabic calendar with that of the Roman liturgy as included in Add. 30848 where it is severely damaged, and in Add. 30849, where it is comparatively undamaged [*see* appendix III for a comparative table]. There are some dangers inherent in such a comparison, but so long as they are acknowledged the exercise can still be a valuable one.

I do not wish to prejudge the inquiry by designating too many saints at the beginning as 'Mozarabic', but I do think it is necessary to mention certain key figures who received particular veneration within the Mozarabic liturgy and who are conspicuous in the dedications of important Spanish churches or monasteries.[19] Among such saints should be included *S. Torquatus et socii* (1 May), credited with introducing the Christian faith to Spain, and to whom was dedicated one of the churches at Toledo.[20] We might also include *S. Milanus* (12 November), to whom the great monastery at Cogolla was dedicated, and *S. Acisclus*, whose feast (17 November) coincides with the beginning of Advent in the Mozarabic liturgical year.

In addition there are several Spanish martyrs, who fall into two groups, one of which includes all the early church martyrs who died during the persecutions of Valerian (259) and Diocletian (303) at Tarragona, León, Córdoba, Mérida and at other major towns.[21] Notable among these are *SS. Julianus et Basilissa* (7 January), *S. Babilas* (24 January), *S. Tirsus* (28 January), *S. Eulalia* of Barcelona (12 February), *S. Eulalia* of Mérida (10 December), *SS. Emeterius et Celedon* (3 March), *S. Fructuosus* of Tarragona, *SS. Justa et Rufina* (17 July), *SS. Justus et Pastor* (6 August), *SS. Servandus et Germanus* (23 October), *SS. Vincentus, Sabina et Cristetes* (28 October) and *SS. Facundus et Primitivus* (27 November).

The second group were much more recent (that is mid-ninth century) and the result of a deliberate challenge to the Islamic faith in Córdoba. The foremost in this group was *S. Eulogius* (1 June), and the other celebrated members were: *S. Pelagius* (26 June), *S. Zoilus* (27 June) and *S. Faustus* (13 October).

It is immediately clear from looking at the calendars that these Mozarabic saints were not excluded totally from the Roman manuscripts. St Torquatus and companions still receive mention in the calendar of Add. 30848 on 1st May, although they do not appear in that of Add. 30849. The calendar of Add. 30848 is illegible for the months of September to December, but Add. 30849 includes *S. Emilianus*, and *S. Acisclus*.

Very few of the saints included in the Mozarabic calendar no longer appear in the calendars of our Roman manuscripts. Some of the lacunae, for example St Jerome, are explained by illegible or missing portions of the Roman calendars. This leaves a short list of Mozarabic saints who may have been expressly excluded: *S. Eulogius*, *S. Faustus* (whose feast may also have fallen in the damaged sections of the Roman manuscripts), *S. Fructuosus* of Tarragona, *SS. Facundus et Primitivus*, *SS. Nunilio et Elodia* of Huesca, *S. Pelagius*, *SS. Servandus et Germanus* and *SS. Sabina* and *Cristetes*. These are thus the only Mozarabic saints who do not appear to have been accorded even the meagre recognition of a mention in the calendar of the liturgical year. They are all martyrs and two of them come from the more recent group of Córdoba martyrs, but we cannot say even that this group was intentionally excluded as *S. Zoilus* is included in the calendar of Add. 30849. The most we can say from the evidence of the calendars is that there was a slight but perceptible move away from the commemoration of Spanish martyrs.

It seems on first impression, therefore, that there was no systematic suppression of the most important 'Mozarabic' saints. However, when we put aside the evidence provided by the calendars, and look for texts with which to celebrate the feasts of those saints, a very different picture emerges.

Add. 30844, Add. 30845 and Add. 30846 between them provide texts to celebrate most of the feasts of the Mozarabic saints. Add. 30845 is particularly rich in these texts, containing *officia et missae* for many of the Mozarabic saints, including the ninth-century Córdoban martyrs *S. Zoilus*, *S. Pelagius* and *SS. Faustus, Ianuarius et Martialis*, other Spanish martyrs such as *SS. Servandus et Germanus*, *SS. Iusta et Rufina*, *SS. Iustus et Pastor*, *SS. Vincentus, Sabina et Cristetes* and *S. Eufemia*, as well as *S. Milanus*.

Add. 30846 contains only a few sanctoral feasts, but these include that of *S. Torquatus et socii*. It will be seen from this analysis, however, that some of the noted Mozarabic saints did not receive texts in any of the three manuscripts studied. This may be explained in part by the special nature of Add. 30844 which does not include some of the obvious figures from the earlier part of the liturgical year such as *S. Fructuosus*, *S. Tirsus* and *S. Babilas*.

Add. 30847 seems once again to embody what can be termed an early phase of the transition in that it continues to offer texts for several Mozarabic saints in the form of *passiones*. Only the one *lectio* is offered in each case, however, and we must presume that the common provided the rest of the office. In addition to St Sebastian and St Vincent, who were already venerated by the Roman as well as the Mozarabic church, this manuscript also includes *passiones* for *S. Fructuosus*, *S. Babilas*, *S. Tirsus*, *S. Eulalia* and *SS. Emeterius et Celedon*. When we turn to Add. 30848, a major change can be seen to have occurred, for not a single one of the Mozarabic saints was accorded an *officium*. Add. 30849 is likewise categorical in depriving these saints of proper offices. Again the change in status of the Mozarabic saints does not seem to have been immediate, to judge from Add. 30847. It does not even seem to have been absolute, to the extent that they were still mentioned in calendars. It is even possible that the feasts of these saints may have been celebrated by means of one of the occasional *officia*, such as *in natale unius martyris*, but we have no means of knowing that this was so. The general impression however is clear: although the cults of these saints may not have been totally eradicated, they were certainly not supported and are best thought of as marginalized.

The lack of Mozarabic saints in Add. 30848 and Add. 30849 was more than compensated for by the inclusion of a comprehensive selection of 'Roman' saints. As can be seen from the lists of contents (appendix II), the numbers concerned are very considerable. It is not practical to discuss each of these 'new' saints in turn, and it may even not be helpful, as so many of them are standard in Roman breviaries. I intend instead to approach the possible attitude to saints after the change in the liturgy by a different means: through a consideration of the altar dedications in the new abbey church at Silos in 1088, which occurred only seven years after the official introduction of the Roman liturgy into Spain. This may be an oblique view, but it provides an insight into liturgical practice, and not merely the liturgical theory (if the distinction can be allowed) that is represented in the manuscripts.

The consecration at Silos in 1088 was a major event attended by important ecclesiastical figures from France and Spain, including the Archbishop of Aix-en-Provence from France, the Bishop of Burgos, and the Bishop of Roda from Aragon, all of whom are recorded as consecrating altars in the new church. The text, preserved in a Silos manuscript, is as follows:

> Anno ab Incarnatione Domini millesimo D CCC VIII (*sic*), regnante rege Adefonso in Toleto et in regnis suis, B(ernardo) Tholeti archiepiscopo, dedicata est ecclesia: altari Sancti Sebastiani et Sancti Petri et Sancti Andre a domno Pedro, aquensi [Aix] archiepiscopi; et in dextra techa, Sancte Marie, Sancti Michaelis archangeli et Sancti Iohannis evangeliste, a domno Gomessano, burgensi [Burgos] episcopo; et in sinistra techa, Sancti Martini et Sancti Benedicti et Sancti Nicolai et Sancti Dominici a domno Raimondo, rodense [Roda] episcopo, consecrata sunt, in presentia domni Ricardi, cardinalis romani, regente abba Fortunio, era T C XXVI.[22]

We can take the saints in the order in which they are mentioned in the texts starting with St Sebastian. Although recognised in the Mozarabic calendar and mentioned in various deeds of gift from the tenth century, St Sebastian, patron saint of Silos before Santo Domingo, was not accorded any *officia* or *missa* in the three Mozarabic manuscripts at the centre of this study. This could again be due to the focus of Add. 30844 on the Virgin, as it is this manuscript which might be expected to include the feast day of St Sebastian (20 January) since it covers that period of the year. It could equally be an indication that this manuscript was not in fact produced at Silos, or even that texts concerning the titular saint were written in a separate volume. The only surviving Mozarabic texts for St Sebastian come from the Toledan manuscript (Toledo, Cathedral Archive, MS 35.3), and one of the parish churches in Toledo was dedicated to St Sebastian. None exist from Silos, which may be merely an accident of survival, or it may have been a characteristic of the Mozarabic church to pay less attention to titular saints.

In contrast St Sebastian was honoured on both the day of his *natale* and that of his *passio* in Add. 30847, on the day of his *passio* alone in Add. 30848, and in conjunction with St Fabian in Add. 30849. Because his altar is mentioned first in the text and was consecrated by the senior cleric, emphasis seems to have been given to his continuing – or, we could say, increasing – importance. It was at the very least convenient that Silos had in St Sebastian a patron saint who was also celebrated by the Roman church, and whose cult could be encouraged.

St Sebastian shared his altar at Silos with two other saints, St Peter and St Andrew. Not surprisingly both of the apostles were celebrated in the Mozarabic liturgy. The office and mass for *In Catedra Sancti Petri* is given in Add. 30844, and the feast of St Peter and St Paul is included in Add. 30845. Although none of these Mozarabic manuscripts contain offices for St Andrew, this is likely to be merely because none of these books happens to cover that week of the year. The Roman manuscripts give offices for both saints. Add. 30847 and Add. 30849 include *in Cathedra Sancti Petri*, Add. 30848 and Add. 30849 celebrate his *Natale* and the feast of St Peter *ad Vincula*. Silos held relics of St Peter and St Paul, and they had been mentioned in donations and other official documents of the abbey since the tenth century. The attention paid to St Peter in the manuscripts and at the consecration need not necessarily be seen as an acknowledgement of papal authority – although the papal legate was present – nor as a sign of any Cluniac involvement – although he was that abbey's patron saint. On any level this dedication could not have been safer. As for St Andrew, his feast day falls outside the compass of Add. 30847, but it is included in Add. 30848 and Add. 30849. The list of saints given in Rodrigo Diaz's donation to Silos of 1076 included St Andrew after St Sebastian, St Mary, and St Peter and St Paul.[23] As St Andrew does not appear in earlier donations, one of his relics may well have been acquired by the abbey shortly before that date.

The altar to the right was dedicated to the Virgin Mary, St Michael the Archangel and St John the Evangelist. The Virgin first appears as one of the titular saints of Silos in a donation of 1056, which gives the near-by monastery of St Michael and St Mary to Silos together with '*libros et casulas vel calices*'. It could be that Add. 30844, with its focus on the Virgin, was included among these books, although it is equally plausible that it was produced at Silos with its own dedication in mind. Add. 30845 includes the feast of the Assumption, which does not appear in Add. 30844. This feast received particular attention in Add. 30845 in that an extra mass *de Adsumtio Sancte Marie* was added during the eleventh century (fols 89–92v).[24] A parallel interpolation occurs in another manuscript in the Silos corpus (Silos MS 3, *Ritus et Missae/Liber Ordinum*), where the *officium* and an extended narration of the Assumption of the Virgin was added, probably in the second half of the elev-

enth century (fols 180–201).[25] The treatment of Marian texts in these three Mozarabic manuscripts from the Silos corpus may constitute the beginnings of a case for a developing cult
of the Virgin in the region of Silos in the eleventh century.

The Roman manuscripts discontinued the Mozarabic feast of the Virgin and in Add.
30847 the *officium* is instead *in Purificatione Sancte Marie*. Add. 30848 demonstrates the expansion of the cult by celebrating the *Purificatio, Annunciatio* and *Assumptio*, and Add. 30849
further extended this to include her *Nativitas*. There is additional evidence of an expanded
cult of the Virgin in the number of wooden statues of the Virgin dating from the late
eleventh or twelfth century found in this area of northern Spain.[26] The museum at Silos
includes among its examples the Virgen del Paraíso, which, it is claimed, dates from the
eleventh century. With its hieratic pose this is a clear representation of the Virgin and Child
as *Sedes Sapientiae*. The Virgin is crowned and holds the child-man Christ on her left knee. In
accordance with this iconography he holds a book, but the right arm which we would
expect to see raised in blessing has been lost. In this statue Christ is also crowned. This
extends the imagery to that of Mary as *Theotokos*, as Queen of Heaven, and as *Ecclesia*, a
conflation which fitted well with Gregorian ideals.[27] At Silos itself the Virgin seems to have
featured increasingly in its sculptural programmes, for example she appears in six of the
eight sculptured pier reliefs in the cloisters, the latest two of which focus on her.[28] A surviving tympanum of the church may represent the culmination of this process in the twelfth
century,[29] and it may be significant that the subject of this tympanum is the Presentation in
the Temple,[30] which was celebrated in the Roman liturgy with the Purification of the Virgin. The ceremony centred around the *benedictio candelae* with its associations of light, renewal and rebirth out of the darkness of sin.

So the dedication of this altar at Silos was probably a re-dedication, not an introduction
but an example of continuity. It is also of interest that the altar was shared with St Michael.
The feast of St Michael the Archangel appears in Add. 30845, Add. 30848 and Add. 30849.
His association with the Virgin here may be due to a traditional connection with the near-
by monastery of St Michael and St Mary (given to Silos in 1056), but he also has a narrative
connection with the Virgin. The archangel plays a liminal role in the Virgin's assumption,
conducting her from earth to heaven; this story is told at some length in Silos MS 3.[31] Nor is
the inclusion of St John the Evangelist in this dedication controversial; it may be because of
his scriptural connection with the Virgin. His feast appears in the Mozarabic manuscript
Add. 30844, as well as in Add. 30847. Add. 30848 and Add. 30849.

Thus, as with Sts Peter and Sebastian, the evidence here is of continuity without any
necessary 'pro-Roman' undertone. Thus far the evidence could be interpreted as a policy of
safety through rapprochement, or at least of consolidation, whereby prominence was given
to saints who had received particular veneration within the Mozarabic liturgy provided they
were also due a similar or higher level of cult within the Roman liturgy. It would have made
sense to concentrate on areas where there was already natural accord.

The third altar was dedicated to four apparently unconnected saints, St Martin, St Benedict,
St Nicholas and Santo Domingo. The veneration of St Martin of Tours was well established

in Spain, and this dedication is not necessarily an indication of increased contact with that abbey. He had been mentioned in deeds of gift to Silos since the mid-eleventh century, and was not an importation of the new liturgy. His *sacratio* is celebrated in Add. 30845 together with his feast day, which is also included in Add. 30848 and Add. 30849.

The other three dedications, however, are to 'new' saints. St Benedict has no services in the Mozarabic manuscripts, and appears for the first time in Add. 30847, a status which was confirmed in Add. 30848 and in Add. 30849 where his translation and octave were included. His monastic rule seems to have been introduced into Silos during the tenth century, and Santo Domingo may have used it as the basis of his reform of the abbey. It is, however, not mentioned in Grimaldo's *Vita Dominici Silensis*. So St Benedict's presence among these dedications does appear as the positive statement of a new regime, and one which is mirrored in his appearance in the Roman liturgical manuscripts.

St Nicholas is included only in Add. 30848, and his appearance in the consecration list is particularly surprising in that his name does not appear in any of the surviving donation documents of the time. His feasts are acknowledged in three of the Mozarabic calendars used by Vives and Fábrega, two of them possibly originating in Silos, and an altar was also dedicated to him in the cathedral of Burgos in 1092.[32] His cult increased in popularity throughout Europe during the eleventh century, and it seems that Spain shared in this. St Nicholas was a patron of travellers at sea and prisoners of war; in Spain the former may have been of interest to pilgrims and the latter of significance in the continuing war against the Moors.[33]

None of the manuscripts contains an office for Santo Domingo. He had become abbot of Silos in 1041, and remained there until his death on 20 December 1073. He was canonised in 1076. A service for him does exist in a Roman antiphonal, which is also in the British Library (Add. 30850). He is, however, mentioned in the calendar of Add. 30849 as *Dominici abbatis* and the calendar of Add. 30848 may have included Santo Domingo, but that section is lost. Add. 30847 has no calendar and again does not include any office for Santo Domingo. So it seems that the cult of Santo Domingo grew only slowly; he does not seem to have been named as joint titular saint until as late as 1118, and the abbey of Silos was not exclusively *Sancti Dominici* even towards the end of the twelfth century.[34] Santo Domingo died in 1073 before he could be called upon to take a role in the introduction of the Roman liturgy. Nevertheless he seems to have been given a rejuvenating and reforming brief on his appointment as abbot at Silos by Fernando I,[35] and this more recent experience of change may have made the process easier at Silos than it was apparently at San Millán, where Santo Domingo had been prior before coming to Silos.[36] The amount of building which is attributed to him suggests that Silos was a centre of development under his abbacy.[37] He may, however, have died before the liturgical problem became acute. His inclusion in this dedication is not only prime evidence of his growing cult, but it may also imply that giving prominence to a new cult was intended to distract the attention of the monks from their old liturgical habits. Santo Domingo was ideal for this role, as he had brought considerable success to the monastery and made several changes.

Santo Domingo's inclusion can also be contrasted with St Emilian's omission from these dedications. The notable Spanish abbot, patron saint of the great Mozarabic abbey at Cogolla, had also been associated with Silos since the tenth century, and had been mentioned as recently as 1076 in Rodrigo Diaz's donation to Silos. It is striking, therefore, that St Emilian received no mention in the dedications of 1088. There is also no office for his feast day in any of the Roman manuscripts, although he is included in the calendar of Add. 30849.

The role of the cults of saints in the liturgical change was thus one of subtle shifts alongside a solid base of continuity. The end result was, nevertheless, a dramatic change in cult activity. The moves are again well illustrated by our selection of manuscripts, which show an underlying progression.

The Structure and Text of the Office

We will now examine the contents of the manuscripts more closely by comparing the constituents of a typical *officium* in the Mozarabic and Roman liturgies. [*See* Table 4]

TABLE 4

A Comparison of the Constituents of the Mozarabic and Roman Offices

MOZARABIC	ROMAN
Vesperum Commune[38]	*Vesperum*
Vespertinum	*Capitulum*
Sono	*Versus*
Antiphona I	*Hymnus*
Antiphona II (*Alleluiaticum*)	*Antiphona*
Antiphona III (*Laudes*)[not always given]	*Oratio*
Hymnus	
Completoria	
Benedictio	
Psallendum	
Oratio [rarely given]	
	[*In matutinis*]
	Nocturno I:
	Invitatorium
	Antiphona I
	[Up to 6 antiphons]
	Versus
	Lectio [OT]
	Responsorium
	Versus
	Lectio [OT]
	Responsorium

MOZARABIC	ROMAN
	versus
	Lectio [OT]
	Responsorium
	Versus
	Lectio [OT]
	Responsorium
	Versus
	Nocturno II:
	Antiphonae
	[from 1–6]
	Versus
	Lectio
	Responsorium
	Versus
	Lectio
	Responsorium
	Versus
	Lectio
	Responsorium
	Lectio
	Responsorium
	Versus
	Nocturno III:
	(*ad cantica*)
	Antiphona
	Lectio
	Responsorium
	Versus
	Lectio
	Homilia
	Responsorium
	Versus
	Lectio
	Responsorium
	Versus
	Lectio
	Responsorium
	Versus
	Lectio
	Responsorium
	Versus
Matutinum	*In Matutinis et*
Festivale	*laudibus*[39]

MOZARABIC	ROMAN
Antiphona et oratio	*Antiphona (x5)*
Antiphona et oratio	*Capitulum*
Antiphona et oratio	*Responsorium*
Responsoria et oratio	*Versus*
(this pattern may be repeated	
up to seven times depending on	
the importance of the festival)	
Antiphona (Psalm 50)	*Hymnus*
Antiphona et Canticum	*Versus*
Benedictiones	*In evangelio*
Laudes	*Responsorium*
Sono	*Benedictus*
Hymnus	*Oratio*
Completoria	
Benedictio	
Psallendum	

It is at this point that we will come closest to being able to assess the degree of liturgical change. What we want to know is whether the liturgy really changed or was change limited to the way in which it was presented and packaged?

The order in which the offices are given in the Mozarabic manuscripts is generally: *Ad Vesperum, Ad Matutinum, [Ad Missa]*, although Add. 30846 gives matins in advance of vespers for all the *feriae* and *sabbato* entries.[40] *Letanias Canonicas* in Add. 30845, and *Letanias Apostolicas* in Add. 30846, are the only feasts to have texts for *ad III, ad VI, ad VIIII* in the Mozarabic books. The three Roman breviaries also begin with vespers followed by matins and lauds, and then *per omnes oras diei* sometimes listed separately as *ad III, ad VI*, and *ad VIIII*, and on occasion a second office for vespers. There is one oddity which is shared by both Add. 30847 and Add. 30848 which also appears to some extent in Add. 30849. Although the headings are very clear, especially in Add. 30847 and Add. 30848, the only heading which divides the end of vespers from the beginning of matins is *nocturno I*, and there is no mention of matins as such until the beginning of what should be more accurately described as *laudes* when the heading *in matutinis et laudibus* is used. At first glance it appears, therefore, that vespers includes the three nocturns (which should instead be headed matins), and that matins and lauds form one short office.

It is difficult to explain this apparent misunderstanding in the early Roman breviaries. Such an arrangement is not found for example in breviaries from Moissac or Ripoll which were produced in areas which might have provided models for the new liturgical books.[41] If on the other hand we look back to the headings in the Mozarabic manuscripts, they do not include lauds, but give only *ad matutinum*. This, however, introduces an office which is close to the Roman lauds. It may be, therefore, that the scribes who copied the early Spanish breviaries could recognise vespers as similar to the Mozarabic office of the same name, but applied the heading *in matutinis et laudibus* to the office of lauds because it resembled the office of matins with which they were familiar. The nocturns, which were presumably new to them, were left without an overall heading as they did not correspond to any office in the Mozarabic liturgy.[42] This contention – that the scribes were working with the Mozarabic framework still in their minds – would also explain why *ad vesperum* is the dominant heading in the Roman breviaries: it is included in the overall introductory heading in 'Mozarabic' fashion.

It is also interesting to note that this possible misinterpretation is found also towards the beginning of Add. 30849, although it is not found later in the manuscript. Thus this idiosyncrasy is one of the common factors among the three Roman breviaries in this study, and suggests a link between them unless it can be proved to be a common phenomenon.[43] It seems that in these three books the Roman liturgy was presented within a framework which was in part Mozarabic. There is, however, no indication that this was deliberate. It is more likely that it was an error made by scribes who were still thinking of liturgical elements from a Mozarabic point of view and who had not as yet mastered the Roman structure.

If we look beyond the heading level and examine the constituents of the offices, we can see where the differences between the Mozarabic and Roman offices were concentrated. Férotin used Add. 30844, Add. 30845 and Add. 30846 among other manuscripts to construct standard formats for matins and vespers in the Mozarabic liturgy.[44] It is important to note, however, that the manuscripts themselves do not conform to these patterns in all respects or on all occasions. For example, none of the *officia* in these manuscripts contain a *lectio*, not even Add. 30846 which is the only Mozarabic manuscript among these three to include *officia* for Sundays and therefore the only one which would be expected to offer a reading during matins. Férotin's *communale* model is given in Table 4 (the *dominicale* version contains a reading).

The most obvious difference between the two liturgies is the growth of the night office of matins, mainly through the inclusion of readings.[45] Within the Mozarabic liturgy matins consisted mainly of sung items set around the psalms which formed the original *raison d'être* of the office. The Roman matins on the other hand are constructed around their readings as much as around the psalms – each nocturn containing a reading, scriptural and often homiletic, split into sections and divided by responses. Monastic observance usually employed four sections and secular custom three. Thus it appears no exaggeration to conclude that the fundamental structure and nature of matins changed as part of the move from the Mozarabic to the Roman liturgy.

Other changes in vespers and matins appear to be less significant and more a matter of terminology. The *vespertinum, sono, psallendum* and *completorium* no longer appear under those names in the Roman manuscripts, although the first three are all response anthems, not fundamentally different in function from the *responsoria* which are found in the Roman manuscripts. I do not propose to go into any further detail concerning any changes in the sung elements of the office, since the musicological aspects of the change are outside the scope of this study.[46] For our purposes it is sufficient to note that there is no evidence of any evolution in these structural changes; one system seems to have been substituted for the other in its entirety. But what of the actual texts? Under the guise of altered terminologies and changed structures, are the texts fundamentally the same?

Before we compare the Mozarabic texts with the Roman, it is necessary to establish first whether there is conformity within the liturgies as they are recorded in these manuscripts. There is only a small degree of overlap in the contents of the Mozarabic manuscripts, but both Add. 30844 and Add. 30846 contain *officia* for *in Ascensione Domini*, and this can give us some indication of the degree of uniformity within this liturgy as practised in this part of northern Spain. In this case the same texts are given for most of the items with only minor variants appearing in the sung items towards the end of the office. For example Add. 30846 includes a hymn which is missing in Add. 30844, and different texts are given for the concluding *Psallendum* anthem. If we go on to compare the mass texts given in each case, we see that they are also close, although Add. 30846 excludes several items, especially when the texts for the second mass are compared. If these manuscripts are in turn compared to the Toledo manuscripts (Toledo, Cathedral Archive, MS 35.4 and MS 35.6), the textual agreement continues, showing that with minor variants the Mozarabic liturgy was remarkably consistent. These do not seem to have been isolated instances, as Férotin's edition of the *Liber Sacramentorum* shows by its relative lack of textual variants.

Are the Roman texts in agreement with one another, or do they diverge to such an extent that the very notion of a 'Roman' text is misleading? There is a great deal of overlap among these manuscripts, so it has been necessary to select certain feasts for comparison. It would have been convenient if one of these could have been the Ascension, but this choice was not suitable since the feast of Ascension is not included in Add. 30847. I have instead chosen three feasts to test for uniformity: the Fourth Sunday in Advent, as it is not a major feast but nevertheless a more important part of the temporal cycle than a typical *feria*; the *Vigilia Natalis Domini* which, as a major feast, would be more likely to be an object of convergence; and a sanctoral feast, the *passio* of St Thomas. For reasons which will become apparent I will consider Add. 30847 and Add. 30848 initially and Add. 30849 afterwards.

A comparison of the constituent elements of the offices for *dominica IIII de Adventu Domini* reveals the following: the *capitulum* is the same, *Ecce dominus in fortitudine*, in both Add. 30847 and Add. 30848, although the *responsorium* and *versus* which follow differ in each case. The hymn, *Conditor alme*, is again common to both manuscripts, but the *versus* varies. The antiphon, *Ave Maria gratia plena*, appears in both, followed by the *Magnificat* and the prayer, *Excita Domine qui potentiam tuam*. The *invitatorium* of the first nocturn begins at this point in both manuscripts, although with different texts and different antiphons. The Old Testament reading which follows in four sections is common to both, but the responses and verses which surround it are placed differently. The case is the same in the second and third nocturns: the *lectiones* are standard, but the sung elements vary. It is not until the five antiphons at the beginning of *in matutinis et laudibus* that the two manuscripts again concur. Add. 30848 also gives the services for the *feriae* in full rather than abbreviating them to *per omnes oras diei*.

If we consider the sample sanctoral feast, that of St Thomas, we find that there is total agreement between the two manuscripts for the first section of vespers, but not thereafter. The major feast *in Vigilia Natalis Domini* has very similar texts up to the third nocturn of vespers, when they diverge greatly. If these two manuscripts are then compared with, for example, the Breviary of Ripoll (Paris, BN, MS lat.742),[47] or the Breviary of Cluny (Paris, BN, MS lat.12601 Summer),[48] it is clear that they are much closer to each other than to either of these manuscripts.

Add. 30849 divides its readings into three sections rather than four, which may suggest that this manuscript contains secular rather than monastic offices.[49] This obviously raises questions about the provenance of the manuscript. It does not, however, rule out the possibility that it was executed at Silos. It is even quite probable that the monastic scriptorium would have produced liturgical books for secular use, perhaps for churches in its locality. The mention of Santo Domingo in the calendar – and the lack of any other saint with such a distinctive localising implication – certainly places this manuscript in the region of Silos. Moreover the character of this manuscript, as noted in the previous chapter, suggested a reference use, which would accord with a manuscript held in a monastic scriptorium but used to produce other manuscripts for churches in its area.

There are extremely few instances where the contents of all three breviaries agree, and Add. 30847 and Add. 30849 have almost no items in common. There is, however, more in common between Add. 30848 and Add. 30849, although this is largely because they both draw from the same collection of homilies, as we shall see below. In addition they share the occasional antiphon, response, versus, and hymn. Sometimes the similarities are more substantial: for example, they both give the same five antiphons for *in matutinis et laudibus* on the third Sunday of Advent, but on the whole it is the differences which are most evident. This may show that Add. 30849 emanated from a different scriptorium, or it may be because this manuscript is for secular use and therefore had a different model, or it may be because it was produced at a later date. It certainly demonstrates that the Roman offices were not absolutely uniform at this time, and that several variations were allowed, especially of the sung elements. We cannot, therefore, speak of a 'Roman' breviary text. There was instead a range of approved texts during this developmental phase, from which scribes drew to produce individual breviaries.

A comparison of the Mozarabic and Roman manuscripts, however, shows a much more striking contrast. It is possible to find occasional sung elements which are shared by the Mozarabic and Roman liturgies, but these parallels seem to attest to the distant common roots of the two liturgies rather than to indicate any progressive introduction of the new liturgy or retention of elements of the old. The Roman books are all clearly in a different category from the Mozarabic books. It appears, therefore, that one set of books was set aside and another set, radically different in structure and content, was introduced.

Readings and Sermons

The most striking change of all in terms of content in these liturgical manuscripts was the introduction of readings in the Roman books. As there are no readings in the Mozarabic manuscripts for any of the offices, the contrast is an absolute one between their presence in the Roman manuscripts as opposed to their absence from the Mozarabic manuscripts. It may indeed be that the *lectio*, as a new element in matins, was the distinguishing feature *par excellence* of the new liturgy. *Lectiones* are given in four of the manuscripts used by Férotin in his analysis of the Mozarabic office, but none of these manuscripts are traditional *officia et missae*. All are dated to the eleventh century, and two of them are manuscripts with royal connections, whereas the other two, a psalter and a *Liber Ordinum*, come from Silos.[50]

From the small section of the liturgical year which we have just considered, it appears that the readings are also the most consistent aspect of the Roman liturgy as it was introduced into Spain in these manuscripts. It may be useful to examine them further. The *lectiones* and *homeliae* from Advent until Epiphany in Add. 30847, Add. 30848 and Add. 30849, and those from Easter until Pentecost from Add. 30848 and Add. 30849 are listed in appendix IV. Although there are discrepancies in the choice of readings, the overall impression is of a common structure, above all in the selection of gospel readings.

The readings certainly offered the greatest opportunity for exposition through the homilies which would have accompanied the New Testament, and some of the Old Testament, pericopes. Homilies had played an important part in the Carolingian ecclesiastical reforms, and, as we shall see, some of the same homilies were used in the Spanish manuscripts.[51]

Comparison among the three manuscripts of the Roman liturgy reveals a possible development. Add. 30847 draws most of its homilies from the collection of Smaragdus, supplemented by some from that of Paul the Deacon and others which do not figure in either collection. Add. 30848 is clearly related to Add. 30847 in the choice of texts for *lectiones* and *homeliae* for many feasts, since it also includes several identical homilies from the collection of Smaragdus; but it also seems to be related to Add. 30849 in that on several occasions it agrees with this manuscript rather than with Add. 30847. The points at which it agrees with Add. 30849 are usually where both have a homily from the collection of Paul the Deacon. Add. 30849 has no homilies from Smaragdus; nearly all the homilies in this manuscript come from Paul the Deacon. We have, therefore, an apparent evolution from almost complete reliance on Smaragdus to almost complete use of Paul the Deacon. We cannot assume, however, that this is necessarily a linear sequence, as we would have expected the extremely popular collection of Paul the Deacon to be the favoured choice from the beginning.

The collection of Paul the Deacon formed the basis of most collections of homilies in French manuscripts at this time. He had been a central figure in Charlemagne's reform of the Gallic liturgy, and had been commissioned to compose the collection, in two volumes, to be the 'authorized version' in the genre.[52] His collection continued to be used either alone, or in combination with other collections, throughout France certainly until the twelfth century. We can be sure that it was also known in its entirety in Spain, for – aside from the selection available in Add. 30849 – almost the whole collection (with only minor variants) appears in an eleventh-century Spanish *Homeliarum* (Sheffield, Ruskin Museum, codex 7), published by Louis Brou.[53] Unfortunately this manuscript has not been localised.

The system employed at Cluny, in so far as the meagre surviving evidence can tell us, seems to have been based heavily on the collection of Paul the Deacon.[54] The Cluniac manuscripts studied by Étaix contain no homilies of Smaragdus, and the similarities between these manuscripts and Add. 30847 and Add. 30848 are limited in the main to the routine use of readings from Isaiah in Advent and Epiphany, except where Add. 30848 uses Paul the Deacon.[55] There is, on the other hand, considerable agreement between the Cluniac manuscripts and Add. 30849, because of the increased number of occasions when that manuscript uses Paul the Deacon. This suggests that a decision may have been made not to impose the use of Paul the Deacon's collection immediately, but for some reason to opt for the selection of Smaragdus initially and then to introduce Paul the Deacon's collection gradually.

Add. 30847 is probably the earliest exemplar of the Roman liturgy in our group of manuscripts, and it exhibits a marked preference for homilies from the collection of Smaragdus. Like Paul the Deacon, Smaragdus was a typical Carolingian collector, gathering an anthology of patristic texts for his *Collectiones in epistolas et evangelia* (from which the homilies are drawn),[56] and for his *Diadema monachorum*, a 'reader' for monks.[57] His homilies had been very popular in the ninth century and had contributed to the homiletic collections of the school of Auxerre,[58] and been used again by Aelfric in the reform of the church in England at the end of the tenth century.

Add. 30847 and Add. 30848 are not, however, the only Spanish manuscripts of this time to use homilies from Smaragdus. A considerable selection can also be seen in two *homilaria* also attributed to the abbey of Silos (Paris, BN, MS N.a.l. 2176 and its copy, Paris, BN, MS N.a.l. 2177).[59] Most of the homilies contained in Add. 30848 and Add. 30849 are also to be found in N.a.l. 2176 and N.a.l. 2177, but not all. Nevertheless the connection is very close.[60] In addition there are two fragmentary manuscripts now in the library of Burgos Cathedral (cod. 1 and cod. 2), which contain a similar but not identical group of Smaragdus homilies.[61] The use of this collection does seem to have been characteristic of a stage in the liturgical change in Castile. What was its likely origin?

Several manuscripts of Smaragdus's *Collectiones* survive, but none of them comes from the areas which are known to have supplied personnel for the liturgical change, namely Gascony and Burgundy.[62] Some come from Normandy, St Bertin and St Omer, and two from near Orléans. Another is the famous Smaragdus manuscript illuminated by Florentius of Valeránica in the tenth century, now at Córdoba (Córdoba Cathedral, Cod.1.).[63] The prior existence of this text in Spain, especially in such a luxurious manuscript, might help to explain why these homilies were chosen for the early Roman manuscripts in this area rather than those of Paul the Deacon.[64] The homilies are, however, standard excerpts from the *Collectiones*, and were presumably copied into our manuscripts already in that form rather than from a complete text of Smaragdus. The collection of homilies by Hrabanus Maurus for the Emperor Lothair (847–855) might have been a model, as it also draws frequently from the collection of Smaragdus, but in general there is very little similarity between the collection of Hrabanus Maurus and the 'Spanish' choice of Smaragdus.[65] We should perhaps look instead for a Spanish origin for this selection, as the Spanish examples form the bulk of the surviving manuscripts which have Smaragdus's text already divided into homilies. Moreover Smaragdus's writings – albeit not to our knowledge the *Collectiones* – had played a significant role in tenth-century reform efforts in Castile and Navarre.[66]

In the earlier period, Smaragdus's commentary on the Rule of St Benedict had been drawn on heavily to formulate at least one Spanish monastic rule,[67] and there are also manuscripts of Smaragdus's commentary among the manuscripts from Silos.[68] In this text Smaragdus celebrated the *vita apostolica* and described the apostles as monks and the true authors of the cenobitic life.[69] This statement fitted well with the idea of reform as a return to the primitive church and to monasticism as its truest expression. Moreover some of the contents of Smaragdus's homilies accorded particularly well with the literary ideas of Gregorian Reform. In particular he selected some passages which used light symbolism, including the passage from Isaiah:

> *Populus gentium qui ambulabat in tenebris vidit lucem magnam habitantibus in regione umbrae mortis lux orta est* [70]

and his commentary on a passage for Epiphany:

> *nos omnes ambulamus in apostolorum luce, quae lucet in mundo, et tenebrae eam non comprehenderunt reges ... ambulent in splendore nascentis Ecclesiae.* [71]

Provided that they were drawn from patristic writings, there seems to have been no restriction set on the choice of homilies in the Roman liturgy. Even the *Ordines Romani* agreed in authorising a free choice in this area, and those implementing the liturgical change seem to have exercised their freedom.[72] Our manuscripts include only one homily which was also found in the Mozarabic homiliary,[73] but Paris, BN, MS N.a.l. 2176 and BN, MS N.a.l. 2177 include more and thus suggest that there was a period of transition; these manuscripts include twelve homilies which can also be found in the eleventh-century Mozarabic *homiliarium*, BL., MS Add. 30853,[74] and even one which appears in Add. 30844, the homily for *in festo circumcisionis Domini: huius solemnitatis expositionem vestris auditibus insinuare.* This tolerance did not last, however, and no later manuscripts retain Mozarabic homilies.[75]

Add. 30848 also includes excerpts from Beatus's Commentary on the Apocalypse used as *lectiones* for the four Sundays after the Easter octave. Together these passages form a considerable part of the *Interpretatio* section of the Commentary, where Beatus summarizes the more detailed exegesis of the later chapters. As far as I know, the Mozarabic liturgy did not employ Beatus's text in this way even as mass readings, although – as we shall see in part II – the reading of the Book of the Apocalypse itself during Easter Week and up to the Sunday after Ascension was an important feature of that liturgy. Beatus's text was clearly not part of the Roman liturgy in any recognisable guise, and its use in this context may be unique. What was its significance?

Beatus's text had become a major force in northern Spanish monastic life soon after it was written at the end of the eighth century, and the numerous richly illuminated copies which have survived attest to its continued importance. The text was drawn from various patristic writings, Jerome, Augustine, Gregory and Isidore as well as from the Commentary by Tyconius.[76] It may, therefore, have been considered acceptable material for office readings, which seem to have been defined broadly as scriptural or 'patristic'. During a time of transition the use of such a familiar work would surely have been very helpful, a way of incorporating an established spiritual text into the new liturgy. Even if it was an attempt to infiltrate a Mozarabic text into the Roman liturgy, it may not have been recognised as such, precisely because Beatus's text was *not* used in the Mozarabic liturgy.

The choice of this text may have had additional resonances. Beatus was otherwise known as the opponent of Elipandus, who had supported the Adoptionist heresy, and thus as a champion of orthodoxy.[77] The debate had ended with the excommunication of Elipandus and a break with the current spiritual hegemony of Toledo in favour of the more nebulous tradition of the Visigothic church. Both these aspects may have made Beatus seem a good choice at a time when orthodoxy had to be re-established and the *mos toletanus* repudiated.

If we examine the passages chosen for the readings in Add. 30848, it seems even more likely that Beatus's text had relevant associations beyond its familiarity. The selection starts at the beginning of the *interpretatio*, with the vision of God enthroned in heaven worshipped by the twenty-four elders and the four animal forms of the evangelists; it continues with the four horses of the Apocalypse, the opening of the seven seals, and the sounding of four of the seven trumpets. The reading for the second Sunday follows on from the previous Sunday without a break and tells of the next two trumpets and the mighty angel with a book. It then jumps briefly to the introduction of the seven plagues, the *indignatio Dei*, and then back a little to the 'woman clothed with the sun' and the 'great red dragon', that is Satan cast out. The reading for the third Sunday is even more of a patchwork, beginning with an earlier description of the sounding of the seventh trumpet and the celestial liturgy, and the opening of the temple of God. It then skips forward briefly to tell of Elias and the fall of Babylon, returning to a longer passage on the prophecy and assumption of the two witnesses Elias and Moses. One more section completes the selection for this Sunday: the seven phials of God's anger, that is the seven spiritual plagues. The readings for the fourth Sunday run to the end of the *interpretatio*, again including only certain passages, but this time in the correct order: the pouring of six of the phials and the 'unclean spirits like frogs'; the seventh phial and the division of Babylon; the whore of Babylon; the fall of Babylon; 'The Word of God' on the white horse; the binding of Satan; the reign of the martyrs; and finally the new Jerusalem.[78]

If these are compared with the selection of pericopes from the Book of the Apocalypse used in the Mozarabic masses (*see* appendix VI), there are very few passages in common. It is, therefore, unlikely that the function of the readings was the same in both cases. The selection of readings used in the Mozarabic masses is clearly typologically related to the Resurrection and concentrate on images such as the victory of the Lamb. The passages in Add. 30848 have a very different focus, above all because of the addition of Beatus's exegesis which is ecclesiological and Christological.[79] In the first reading Beatus gives allegorical meanings to the four horses of the Apocalypse: the first is *ecclesia*, the second horse represents 'people against the Church' and its rider is the Devil; the third is 'spiritual famine in the Church', and the rider is the false prophet; whereas the fourth is death. The sun is also said to represent 'the Church' and the smoke which obscures it 'the words of evil men who bring about blindness'. Beatus presents the Church as under attack from the *bestiae* of heresy. The second reading offers signs of hope through penitence, but also introduces the figure of the *draco*, that is the Devil, who attacks the Church through various means including '*malos Christianos*' and '*sacerdotes iniqui*'. The third section deals again with penitence and with the salvation offered to those who hear the two witnesses, that is the *lex et evangelium*, and by the fourth reading it is clear that those who repent will not be sent to hell, but will enter the New Jerusalem, that is the multitude of saints, and that there will be no more tears, death or sadness. The potential significance of such symbols in the context of the liturgical change can hardly have escaped individuals whose mental framework encompassed often much more obscure and convoluted connections. What we do not know is how the labels were attached. The location of the text in a Roman liturgical manuscript suggests that the 'wicked priests' were not those promoting the new liturgy, but the very ambiguity of the text may explain why the use of Beatus in this context did not become a common practice.

The choice of homilies during the period of liturgical change in this area of Castile suggests clear guidance rather than haphazard selection. The use of Beatus in Add. 30848, when linked with the production of the Silos Beatus, suggests choice at the level of the individual abbey. On the other hand the distribution of the 'Smaragdus' manuscripts implies regional direction,[80] for which an obvious candidate is Bishop Jimeno of Burgos.[81] Another possibility is Bernard of Palencia, a city which was at that time a great centre of education; he is thought to be the subject of an undated letter (probably 1081) from Gregory VII to Alfonso VI concerning a proposed candidate for an archbishopric. Gregory objected to the candidate on the grounds that he lacked the essential learning (*litteralis scientie peritia indiget*) which bishops and priests must have to enable them to teach.[82]

Moreover we cannot rule out central direction from Sahagún or even, through there, from Cluny. In any event this strategy for implementing the change seems to have used continuity as far as possible. The use of Smaradgus, an authority whose writings had already been successful in introducing monastic reform in Spain more than a century earlier, suggests an attempt to make the liturgical change appear merely a continuation of the move to the Benedictine rule.

The Use of Rubrication

Before we look at the illumination of these manuscripts, I should like to give some consideration to one of the areas where the dividing line between decoration and text is most indistinct, that of rubrication. Rubrics, in the sense of direction signs used in the text to divide or highlight particular sections, appear in all these manuscripts, but they are used in different ways. The rubrics in the Mozarabic manuscripts are brief and to the point; the longest introduce the *lectiones,* usually giving the book of the Bible from which they come.

Only Add. 30846 has an extended rubric (fol. 13), which describes some of the actions in the ceremony of baptism.[83]

If we turn to Add. 30847, there is a marked difference. Apart from the standard use of rubrication to highlight the beginnings of liturgical formulae and readings, there are especially long headings to introduce the feast days of martyrs, giving the place and date of their martyrdom:

passio sancti/e … (virginis) et martiris christi que passus/a est in civitate … sub … die …

In addition Add. 30847 makes extensive use of rubrics to highlight passages within the pericopes and accompanying homilies. In particular this manuscript gives in full an example of the type of description which Paul the Deacon used before the homilies in his collection (fol. 13v):[84]

homelia lectionis eiusdem habita ad populum in baselica sancti petri apostoli.

This form of words was an integral part of the collection of Paul the Deacon and its use survived in the editions produced at Cluny, where similar phrases introduce many of the homilies.[85] It had presumably been used by Paul the Deacon to give authority to his choice of homily by emphasising that the very same text was used in Rome. It is a clear case of the notion of Rome as model, which was the mainstay of the Carolingian liturgical reform. It may have been used in Add. 30847 for the same reason, and may indicate that those who introduced the Roman liturgy into Spain made free use of earlier models of reform and renewal, including the association with Rome itself as a touchstone of authenticity. It is also possible that the isolated use here is attributable merely to the copying process. There are very few homilies from this collection in Add. 30847, but two other such introductory descriptions are used, one standard: *homelia lectionis eiusdem bede presbytri* (fol. 19), the other very specific: *lectio ecclesiastica de mirabilibus sancti stefani martyris christi ex libris de civitate beati agustini episcopi.*[86] The Smaragdus homilies were not originally written with this type of introduction and receive none in Add. 30847. Add. 30848 assumes more knowledge on the part of its readers and introduces the homilies simply with *homelia eiusdem lectionis.*

Most of the other extended rubrications in Add. 30847 highlight scriptural passages which – with one exception – form part of the homilies of Smaragdus. The rubrication may have been used here merely to help the reader find the biblical words among the exegesis, but, if this is so, it is not clear why this practice is not applied to all the biblical phrases and not continued throughout the manuscript; the examples are all within just over forty folios, less than a quarter of the whole. Thus, this kind of rubrication is found in the readings for only five feasts: the Saturday before Christmas, *Vigilia Natalis Domini* and the feast itself, *Adsumtio Ioannis Apostoli, Natalis SS. Innocentium Parvorum,* and *Apparicio Domini.* This use of rubrication appears to be a feature of this section of the manuscript rather than a deliberate attempt to highlight these feasts in particular, as if at this point the scribe was copying from a manuscript which had the same characteristic.[87] Despite the practical reason for this rubrication, it may nevertheless be worthwhile considering which passages were highlighted, since there are other biblical phrases in the homilies which were not picked out in this way (for a list of the *lectiones* and homilies concerned *see* appendix IV).

The first passage to receive this treatment (Luke 3:3) occurs in the homily of Paul the Deacon for the Saturday before Christmas:

Et venit in omnem regionem Iordanis predicans babtismum
penitentie in remissionem peccatorum (fol. 20v).

The immediate importance of this passage is its encapsulation of the doctrine of redemption through baptism, the washing away of original sin through membership of the church made possible by Christ's incarnation and death.

All three of the homilies given for *Natalis Domini* also have highlighted sections of text:

Nocturno I
fol. 27v   *Populus gentium qui ambulabat in tenebris vidit lucem magnam (Is.9:2)*
fol. 28   *habitantibus in regione (Is.9:2)*
fol. 28v   *multiplicavitur eius Imperium et pacis non erit finis (Is.9:7)*

Nocturno II
fol. 30v   *per quem fecit inquit et saecula (Heb.1:2)*

Nocturno III
fol. 32v   *et verbum erat aput deum et deum erat verbum (Jo.1:1)*
fol. 32v   *hoc erat in principio apud deum omnia per ipsum facta sunt et sine ipso*
               factum est nicil (Jo.1:2–3)

The passage from Isaiah foretells the coming of the Messiah and the joy that will attend it. The excerpt from St Paul's letter to the Hebrews, as is shown in the homily, testifies to Christ's co-substance with God and his role in creation. This is further emphasised by the passages from the gospel of St John which deal more explicitly with the doctrine of the *logos*.

The highlighted excerpts from the homilies for the feast of St John's assumption come from the passage in St John's gospel in which Christ foretells that event, and the homily refers to the divine wisdom which John derived from reclining against Christ.

Nocturno III
fol. 48   *conversus Petrus vidit illum discipulum quem diligebat Ihesus sequentem*
               [hinc] (Io.21.20)
fol. 48v   *+ Qui recubuit in cena super pectus eius (Io.21:20)*
fol. 49   *hunc ergo quum vidisset petrus dicit ad Ihesum Domine: hic autem quid*
               (Io.21:21)

Both the phrases which receive rubrication in the homily for the feast of the Holy Innocents are from the Apocalypse:

Nocturno I
fol. 53v   *Tumquam vocem aquarum: et tamquam vocem tonitus*
               magnus (Apc.14:2)
fol. 54v   *et ante quattuor animalia (Apc.14:3)*

They both come from the passage which describes the Lamb standing on Mount Sion with the hundred and forty-four thousand redeemed – who, like the monks, had been chaste – singing 'a new song' before the four evangelists.

The last feast where the homilies have this kind of rubrication is Epiphany. The first passage comes from Isaiah prophesying the coming of the Messiah as light dispelling darkness; while the other opens Matthew's account of the visit of the magi:

Nocturno I
fol. 60v   *Et gloria domini super te orta est* (*Is. 60.1*)

Nocturno III
fol. 63v   *In diebus herodis regis* (*Mt.2:1*)

As all these rubricated phrases are scripture but not all the scriptural phrases receive rubrication, is it possible to identify any other common factor? Most of the passages seem to have some doctrinal significance, but not in any way which immediately unites them. We have already noted the light symbolism used in the passage from Isaiah selected by Smaragdus, and its relevance to the literary ideas of Gregorian reform. The way in which the reader's special attention is drawn to the same passage in this manuscript reinforces the potential importance of this imagery as a mainstay of the reform process. The passage from St Luke regarding baptism and the remission of sins draws attention to another type of renewal, while most of the other passages deal with the incarnation and divine wisdom. It may be helpful to note that in the Mozarabic liturgy John the Baptist was viewed as a bringer of '*universis lumen baptismatis*' and as '*speculum luminis, initium baptismatis*'.[88] It could be argued, therefore, that these passages relate not only to reform in general, but more specifically to the liturgical change represented as the coming of light into darkness. These rubricated phrases are, however, not sufficient on their own to justify this interpretation, but they do suggest a possible didactic, almost propagandist aspect to Add. 30847, which is not found in any of the other manuscripts.

Add. 30848 is generally much more restrained in its use of rubrication. There is only one vestige of the Add. 30847 phenomenon, this time in the Smaragdus homily for the Nativity where now only the word *gentium* received rubrication. The decision to highlight this passage above all the others may indicate its special importance. Otherwise a great deal more knowledge and understanding is taken for granted by the scribes of this manuscript. The main exception to this is in the texts for the period around Easter, where great attention is paid to the correct performance of the offices. Most of these instructions concern what is, or is not, to be sung at this time, whether antiphons, *capitula*, hymns, glorias or psalms, and all are of a practical rather than ideological nature.[89]

Apart from this Add. 30848 highlights one other passage with several alternating lines of red and blue ink: this describes the *passio* of *S. Dionisius* and his connection with the Pope, St Clement (fols 203v–204). The reason for drawing attention to this particular passage is not clear. *S. Dionisius* – or more familiarly St Denis – was quintessentially a French saint, martyred in Paris with Rusticus and Eleutherius in the sixth century, and the titular saint of the French kings' dynastic mausoleum. This may give us a clue to the origin of one of the models for Add. 30848, which is otherwise lacking in Gallic saints beyond the more usual St Martin. If this was mere adherence to a model, we might expect other Gallic saints to be included (as we shall see is the case in the missals – appendix V). Perhaps the exceptional attention paid to St Denis instead reflects one of the other identities which were conflated to form the personality of this saint. The original martyr was confounded with Dionysius the Areopagite (Acts 17:34), who is described as being converted by St Paul and thus carried the authority of the early church. This figure was in turn believed to be the author of a body of anonymous mystical works from the third century, now known as Pseudo-Dionysius. These include three major treatises: 'The Celestial Hierarchy', 'The Ecclesiastical Hierarchy' and 'The Divine Names'.

These works were known at Cluny from the tenth century through the translations of Eriugena and were still popular in the eleventh and twelfth centuries.[90] They seem to have been written originally for a monastic community and much of the contents relates to the liturgy.[91] They might, therefore, have been considered relevant to the problem of the liturgical change. Moreover the texts combined elements of Platonic and Neo-Platonic as well as Christian thought, several of which have resonances with ideas of Gregorian reform in general and with the arguments which had been put forward for the liturgical change in Spain.

We have seen the use of light symbolism in the letters of Gregory VII and in the homilies of Smaragdus. This symbolism is much more explicit in the works of Pseudo-Dionysius where Light is one of the divine names of God:

> Of course God himself is really the source of illumination for those who are illuminated, for he is truly and really Light itself.[92]

Furthermore in 'The Ecclesiatical Hierarchy', the sacrament of baptism, described in great detail, is called the 'rite of illumination'.

Another theological conception which fits the framework of ideas used to promote the liturgical change can be found in 'The Celestial Hierarchy'. The concept of procession and return was at the centre of Pseudo-Dionysian doctrine, and it was given an important historical dimension by Eriugena who related it to Creation and the Second Coming.[93] Gregory employed this idea in a concrete yet mythical way, suggesting that the use of the Roman liturgy would be a 'return' rather than an innovation or change. It should be noted, however, that Gregory chose the maternal symbol of 'Mother Church' rather than the paternal model used by Pseudo-Dionysus:

> Inspired by the Father, each procession of the Light spreads itself generously toward us, and, in its power to unify, it stirs us by lifting us up. It returns us back to the oneness and deifying simplicity of the Father who gathers us in.[94]

There is also a passage in 'The Celestial Hierarchy' which could be taken to refer typologically to the idea that the occupation of Spain by the Saracens was a punishment for heresy:

Now God, out of his Fatherly love for humanity, chastised Israel so as to return it to the road of salvation. In order to cause a change of heart he handed Israel over to the vengeance of the barbarian nations. This was to ensure that the men who were under his special providence would be transformed for the better. Later in his kindness, he released Israel from captivity and restored it to its former state of contentment.[95]

Thus it is possible to see how this text might have seemed significant and helpful to those faced with the problem of implementing the liturgical change. Moreover Pseudo-Dionysius proposed detailed hierarchies on earth and in heaven which could be seen as bestowing spiritual authority on the upper echelons of the church. Knowles described this as 'a vast hierarchy of laymen, monks, priests and bishops on earth, and in heaven of the orders of angelic beings, each order in heaven and on earth having its function, and each receiving from above the illumination, sacramental or intellectual as the case may be, that it passes on to those in the degree beneath itself.'[96] This may have seemed an ideal model for those who were to pass on the illumination of the Roman church to those in the darkness of ignorance. It also seems likely that this conceptual framework emanated from Cluny, as there is no evidence for a copy of Eriugena's text in Spain at that time. The ideas drawn from it seem to have operated as a broad intellectual back-drop to the implementation of the new liturgy, rather than as a text for the consumption of those undergoing the change. This may have been partly because some of the concepts of Pseudo-Dionysius would have been unsuitable, possibly even confusing. For example, although 'darkness' is used in the biblical sense as a metaphor for ignorance, sin and evil, in Pseudo-Dionysius there is also a mystical darkness which transcends light and is an object of aspiration.[97]

In contrast to both the other breviaries, Add. 30849 is routine in its use of rubrication and no lines or passages are picked out in any particular way.

Thus we seem to have another possible developmental sequence in the use of rubrication. The Mozarabic manuscripts use very little, as would be expected in such a well-established liturgy. Instructions for liturgical performance were reserved for specific volumes such as the *Liber Ordinum*; they were not necessary in every manuscript. Add. 30847 employs a considerable amount of rubrication and deploys it in a very particular way. Its emphasis appears to be doctrinal. Add. 30848 has passed beyond this stage, and is more concerned with the minutiae of liturgical performance. Add. 30849 has returned to the position of the Mozarabic books, and the Roman liturgy is now familiar and entrenched.

Notes to Chapter Two

1   Férotin, *see above* Intro. note 20, col. 804, says that there is only one folio missing between fol. 32v and fol. 33. That is likely to have completed the text of the *petitio* which is incomplete on 32v, and to have included an introductory page for the liturgical section of the manuscript.

2   The surviving folios give the following readings: IIII *Quare non credis*, V *Et pastores erat in regione*, VI *Si de nativitate*. Férotin, *see above* Intro. note 20, col. 755, says that the lessons were read at matins and at mass before the epistle.

3   It has proved difficult to agree on an interpretation for the written date of this manuscript. Férotin, *see above* Intro. note 20, col. 803, believed that the date in the colophon should be read as 1059, but Díaz y Díaz, *see above* Ch. 1 note 3, no. 209, pp.473–5 has dated it to 1094 that is after the liturgical change which seems unlikely. Whitehill and Pérez de Urbel, *see above* Ch. 1 note 6, p.530, thought 1009.

4   This manuscript also contains offices for St Martin, St Michael, a life of St Martin by Sulpicius Severus divided into four lessons to be read at the night office, a mass for St Martin and a letter of Sulpicius Severus *Ad Basulam*. Férotin, *see above* Intro. note 20, col. 802–3.

5   Brou, L., 'Les plus anciennes prières liturgiques adressées à la Vierge en occident', *Hispania Sacra*, 3, 1950, pp.371–81. Brou shows that several Marian prayers in the Mozarabic liturgy as well as the office of 18 December were probably composed by Ildephonsus, as they are based on the *De Virginitate* in thought, theological preoccupation and even style. The *De Virginitate* is also the main text in the Parma Ildephonsus (Palatine Library of Parma, MS 1650), a manuscript, which Schapiro argued, was probably produced at Cluny, and may have been given to Alfonso VI by Hugh of Cluny. *See* Schapiro, M., *The Parma Ildephonsus, A Romanesque Illuminated Manuscript from Cluny and Related Works*, New York, 1964. The other text in this manuscript is a eulogy of Ildefonsus by Julian, bishop of Toledo. As Schapiro pointed out, however, Ildefonsus is the focus of this manuscript, not the Virgin Mary.

6   Férotin, *see above* Intro. note 20, col. 754. This manuscript divides Ildephonsus's text into seven lessons resulting in different divisions: IIII *At vero quia ex defensoribus*, V *Ecce impleta est* VI *Ecce ista nativitas* VII *At nunc venio ad te*.

7   Férotin, *see above* Intro. note 20, col. 754, dates this manuscript to the ninth or tenth century, at least one hundred years prior to Add. 30844, whereas Janini (*see* Janini, J. and Gonzálvez, R., *Catálogo de los manuscritos litúrgicos de la Catedral de Toledo*, Toledo, 1977, p.103–4, no. 78) places it in the eleventh or twelfth century. The associated offices and masses are similar to those in Add. 30844: including *missa in die sancte Marie*, *officia*: *in diem Nativitatis Domini*, *in diem sancti Stephani*, *in diem Sancti Iohannis*, *in diem circumcisionis domini*, and *in apparitionis domini*, although the Toledan manuscript also contains [*officium*] *in caput anni*, *ordo ad comendandum corpora defunctorum* and *officium in adsumtio sancte Marie*. Given the homogeneous script, it seems possible that this codex is a also coherent volume and not two manuscripts.

8   Ildephonsus was believed to have experienced a miracle in which the Virgin reached down from heaven and gave him a chasuble as he prayed at her altar. This assured him a place beside St Isidore as one of the saintly members of the Mozarabic church. *See* Hernández, F.J., 'La cathédrale, instrument d'assimilation' in Cardaillac, L., (ed.), *Tolède, XIIᵉ–XIIIᵉ: Musulmans, chrétiens et juifs: Le Savoir et la tolérance*, Paris, 1991, p.77. *See also* Braegelmann, A., *The Life and Writings of Saint Ildefonsus of Toledo*, Washington, 1942.

9   Vogel, *see above* Intro. note 44, p.311.

10 Vogel, *see above* Intro. note 44, p.311 n.105 and n.106.

11 Díaz y Díaz, *see above* Ch. 1 note 3, p.403.

12 Even that may be explicable, as there is a feast of St Jerome on 13 June in the Russian church.

13 Férotin, *as above* Intro. note 20, has a detailed summary of all the surviving manuscripts of the Mozarabic liturgy known to him.

14 Gy, P.-M., 'La mise en page du bréviaire', in Martin, H.-J. and Vezin, J. (eds.), *Mise en page et mise en texte du livre manuscrit*, Paris, 1990, pp.117–20. The breviary was above all a book-form of the thirteenth century, still relatively rare in the eleventh and twelfth centuries.

15   Salmon, P., *L'office divin au moyen age: Histoire de la formation du bréviaire du IXe au XVIe siècle*, Paris, 1967.

16   Salmon, *as above* note 15, p.85.

17   Gy, *as above* note 14, p.117, and Salmon, *as above* note 15, pp.79–80.

18   Férotin, *see above* Intro. note 20, p.XLV–LIII; and Vives, J. and Fábrega, A., Calendarios hispánicos anteriores al siglo XII, in *Hispania Sacra*, vol.2, 1949, pp.119–46, and pp.339–80. These include two manuscripts from the Silos corpus, designated by Férotin as eleventh century: *Ritus et Missae*, Silos MS 3 (pre-1064), and *Liber Ordinum*, Silos MS 4 (1022 or 1052).

19   For a general survey *see* David, *as above* Intro. note 78, pp.185–224.

20   Férotin, *as above* Intro. note 20, p.XXVI, note 1.

21   García Rodríguez, C., *El culto de los santos en la España Romana y Visigoda*, Madrid, 1966, p.242 ff.

22   BN (Paris) MS N.a.l. 2169 fol. 37 bis v. *See* Vivancos Gómez, *as above* Intro. note 8, p.30, no. 25.

23   Vivancos Gómez, *see above* Intro. note 8, pp.21–3, no. 18, '*in domum Sanctorum Sebastiani et comitum eius et Sancte Marie Virginis et Sanctorum apostolorum Petri et Pauli et Sancti Andree apostoli et Sancti Martini episcopi et confessoris Christi necnon Sancti Emiliani presbyteri et Sancti Filippi apostoli*'.

24   Férotin, *see above* Intro. note 20, col. 592, n.1. Férotin says of this mass 'La doctrine catholique sur la Mère de Dieu est admirablement exposée dans cette messe, surtout dans l'*Inlatio*.'

25   Díaz y Díaz, *see above* Ch. 1 note 3, pp.471–3, states that this manuscript was produced at Silos in the eleventh century.

26   For a parallel development in France, *see* Forsyth, I.F., *The Throne of Wisdom: Wood Sculptures of the Madonna in Romanesque France*, Princeton, 1972.

27   For a full explanation of this iconography, *see* Katzenellenbogen, *as above* Intro. note 26, pp.11–17. *See also* Schiller, G., *The Iconography of Christian Art*, vol.I, London, 1971, pp.23–5.

28   That is, all except those on the north-west pier (the Journey to Emmaus and the Doubting of Thomas). The six are the Ascension, Pentecost, the Entombment and Resurrection, the Descent from the Cross, and the two late-twelfth-century panels, the Tree of Jesse and the Coronation of the Virgin.

29   For the tympanum *see* Yarza Luaces, J., 'Nuevos Hallazgos Románicos en el Monasterio de Silos', in *Goya*, no. 46, Madrid, 1970, pp.342–5. This tympanum probably came from the principal portal at the west facade. There was also a major portal on the north side of the church leading from the pilgrims' porch into the lower church. This is believed to have had representations of the Nativity, the Circumcision, the Adoration of the Magi, the Massacre of the Innocents and the Marriage of Cana. *See* Whitehill, W.M., 'The Destroyed Church of Santo Domingo de Silos', in *The Art Bulletin*, 14, 1932, pp.337–8.

30   For a general survey of this iconography and its association with the *Purificatio*, *see* Schiller, *as above* note 27, pp.90–4.

31   The text is given in full in Férotin, *see above* Intro. note 20, col. 786–95.

32   Moralejo, S., 'On the Road, the Camino de Santiago', in *The Art of Medieval Spain A.D.500–1200*, The Metropolitan Museum of Art, New York, 1993, p.179. Vives and Fábrega, *as above*, note 18, pp.146, 361 and 379.

33   Schapiro, *as above* Intro. note 12, p.97, note 209.

34   Vivancos Gómez, *as above* Intro. note 8, p.107, no. 75 *et al.*

35   Schapiro, *as above* Intro. note 12, p.61.

36   Valcárcel, V., La '*Vita Dominici Siliensis*' de Grimaldo, Logroño, 1982. For Santo Domingo's time at San Millán *see* p.193, and p.211. Grimaldo purports to quote Fernando I's instructions to Domingo, describing the situation of Silos as '*monasterii Exiliensis statum quondam fuisse gloriosum; at nunc, exigentibus peccatis ac negligenciis inhabitancium, pene est redactum ad nihilum*'; it was to be '*in Dei servicio restauretur et in facultatibus necessariis corporibus reintegraretur*', p.232. Grimaldo also describes Domingo's reforms in general terms: '*Adeptus ergo vir beatus regimen Exiliensis cenobii, sedulus et pervigil pertractabat anxia sollicitudine animi quomodo domum Dei, sibi creditam, omni divina religione et humana sustentione pene destitutam, priori decori et honestati restitueret et talem concionem fratrum in ea coadunaret, qui Deo debite officium venerationis diurno nocturnoque tempore persolveret et regularia iura sacre religionis adimpleret.*'

37   Valcárcel, *as above* note 36, p.298, *'ecclesiam et omnia monasterii habitacula ... reedificaverit et pristino melioratoque decori restituerit'*.

38   Férotin, *as above* Intro. note 20, pp.LXIX–LXX

39   Hughes, *as above* Ch. 1 note 37, p.xxx, para. 23–25. Hughes states that there is no standard format for Matins in the Roman liturgy, and that before the thirteenth century 'the liturgy is fraught with great variability and uncertainty of order and of precise text'.

40   Comparison with manuscripts from Toledo shows that this is customary. *See* for example Toledo MS 35.4 in Férotin, *as above* Intro. note 20, col. 692–5.

41   For Moissac I consulted British Library, Harley MS 2914, which has very few headings. A model like this could have led to the confusion in the early Spanish breviaries. For Ripoll, *see* Lemairié, J., *Le brévaire de Ripoll*, Abadía de Montserrat, 1965, where the headings are much more clearly *I Vesp., Matut., Laudes, and II Vesp.*

42   Hughes, *as above* note 36, p.15, para. 113. *'Laudes matutinales'* was a standard heading, but there was no *'et'*. Nocturns can be found in some Mozarabic manuscripts, for example a prayer book which belonged to Fernando I and Sancha *(ordo ad celebrandum nocturnos)*, *see* Ch. 6 note 33 below, but they do not appear in any of the manuscripts under consideration in this study.

43   Further study of this issue is beyond the scope of this study, but I would be very interested to learn of any other examples.

44   Férotin, *as above* Intro. note 20, pp.LXI–LXXI.

45   Salmon, *as above* note 15, p.26, note 1: this lack of readings accords with the office as said by the Eastern church.

46   For an examination of the musicological aspects of the liturgical change, *see* Fernández de la Cuesta, I., *as above* Intro. note 115.

47   Lemairié, *as above* note 41.

48   Leroquais, V., *Les breviaires des bibliothèques françaises*, Paris, 1934. This manuscript probably dates from the end of the eleventh century.

49   Hughes, *as above* Ch. 1 note 37, para.300.

50   Férotin, *as above* Intro. note 20, col. 870–80 (Psalter), col. 769–83 *(Ritus et Missae/Liber Ordinum)*, col. 925–30 (1059), col. 931–6 (1055).

51   McKitterick, *as above* Intro. note 30, p.90, [homilies were] 'the distinctive contribution to the didactic material of the church, for they were from the first designed to be of practical assistance in the Carolingian reforms.'

52   Vogel, *as above* Intro. note 44, p.364, *'quia ad nocturnale officium ... in duobus voluminibus per totius anni circulum congruentes cuique festivitati distincte et absque vitiis nobis obtulit lectiones ... auctoritate constabilimus vestraeque religioni in Christi ecclesiis tradimus ad legendum'* and McKitterick, *as above* Intro. note 30, p.93.

53   Brou, L., 'Un nouvel homiliaire en écriture wisigothique – le codex Sheffield 'Ruskin Museum' 7', in *Hispania Sacra*, 2, 1949, pp.147–91 This homilary, with only seven exceptions, follows the system of Paul the Deacon.

54   Étaix, R., Le lectionnaire de l'office à Cluny in *Recherches Augustiniennes*, vol. 11, Paris, 1976, pp.91–159.

55   Is.:I.1 is the first reading in Add. 30848 as at Cluny. The reading from Luke 21:25 *(Erunt signa in sole)* appears with the homily of Paul the Deacon in the manuscripts from Cluny, and in Add. 30848 and Add. 30849.

56   *PL* 102, 13–552, col. 21–2.

57   Lawrence, C.H., *Medieval Monasticism*, London and New York, (2nd edition), 1989, p.82.

58   Barré, H., *Les homéliaires Carolingiens de l'école d'Auxerre*, Vatican, 1962. The reading *'Populus gentium qui ambulabat in tenebris'* also appears in this collection.

59   Étaix, R., 'Homiliaires wisigothiques provenant de Silos à la Bibliothèque Nationale de Paris', in *Hispania Sacra*, 12, 1959, pp.213–20.

60   The Paris manuscripts also contain the homily, *In exordio satis ostendit generationem*, which also appears in Add. 30848. It is part of the collection by Hrabanus Maurus (In Matt. PL 107 col. 731–2), *see* Étaix *as above* note 59, p.214.

61   Mansilla, D., 'Dos Códices visigóticos de la catedral de Burgos', in *Hispania Sacra*, 2, 1949, pp.381–418. *See also* Pinell, J.M., 'Boletín de Liturgia Hispano-Visigótica (1949–1956)' in *Hispania Sacra*, 9, 1956, pp.405–28, for a survey of literature on sermons used in the Mozarabic liturgy and during the early period of liturgical change. He mentioned also three folios from the Colegiata de Santillana del Mar containing part of the collection of Paul the Deacon and a fragment from Valvanera containing part of the collection of Smaradgus. Another example was mentioned by Leclercq, J., 'Les manuscrits des bibliothèques d'Espagne, Notes de Voyages', in *Scriptorium*, 3, 1949, pp.141, a homilary dated to the eleventh century now in the library at Córdoba – provenance not given – consisting of homilies of Smaragdus up to fol. 180, followed by homilies of Paul the Deacon to fol. 454.

62   For a study of Smaragdus and a complete list of his surviving manuscripts *see* Rädle, F., *Studien zu Smaragd von Saint-Mihiel*, Munich, 1974, pp.120 ff.

63   Williams, J.W., 'A Contribution to the History of the Castilian Monastery of Valeránica and the Scribe Florentius', in *Madrider Mitteilungen*, 2, 1970, p.234.

64   There is a connection between this manuscript of Florentius and the abbey of Silos. Whitehill, W.M. and Pérez de Urbel, J., *as above* Ch. 1 note 6, pp.532–3 n.1, noted that there was very similar wording in the colophons of Silos MS 3 (fol. 177), the Silos Beatus (London, British Library, Add. MS 11695, fol. 278), and Florentius's Córdoba Smaragdus.

65   Étaix, R., 'L'homéliaire composé par Raban Maur pour l'empereur Lothaire', in *Recherches Augustiniennes*, vol. 19, Paris, 1984, pp.211–40.

66   Bishko, C.J., 'Salvus of Albelda and Frontier Monasticism in Tenth Century Navarre', in *Speculum*, no. 23, 1948, pp.584–5 (repr. *Studies in Medieval Spanish Frontier History*).

67   Bishko, *as above* note 66, pp.570–3. Bishko has identified a San Millán manuscript, *Libellus a regula sancti Benedicti subtractus* (Madrid, Real Academia de la Historia, Aem.62) as a Spanish monastic rule devised – he suggests by Abbot Salvus of San Martín de Albelda – for a community of women near Nájera. It should be noted that this rule was carefully adapted to the Spanish tradition and omitted the instructions in Smaragdus's text on the performance of the daily office, substituting the Mozarabic canonical hours. It also left out the chapters on discipline in favour of the Spanish penitential, and the sections on reception, guests, and priests.

68   There are two copies in Silos MS 1 *(In Regulam Sancti Benedicti et alia scripta)*, one from the late ninth century (fol. 1–177) and another from the mid-tenth century (fol. 177–271); the manuscript is Castilian but the scriptorium is not known. There are also other fragments in the Silos archive probably from Santa María de Nájera. *See* Bishko, *as above* note 66, p.586. Although none of these manuscripts can be attributed to the Silos scriptorium, the abbey of Silos, in common with the rest of Castile and Navarre, does seem to have been subject to some form of the Benedictine rule at least since the mid-tenth century. *See* Linage Conde, A., *Los origenes del monacato benedictino en la península ibérica*, León, 1973, vol. 2, pp.617–21.

69   Lawrence, *as above* note 57, p.149.

70   *PL* 102, col. 21. This passage continues with a possible antitype for the liturgical change: '*primo terra Zebulon et Nephthalim Scribarum et Pharisaeorum erroribus est liberata, et gravissimum traditionum Judaicarum jugum excussit de cervicibus suis'.*

71   *PL* 102, col. 68–9.

72   Vogel, *as above* Intro. note 44, p.364, '*Tractatus patrum, sermones atque homeliae ad ipsum diem pertinentes ... and sermones vel omeliae catholicorum patrum'.*

73   *Hodie fratres kmi natale illorum infantum* for the feast of the Holy Innocents; this is also found, however, in the collection of Alan of Farfa, and so may not derive from the Toledan selection.

74   Étaix, *as above* note 59, pp.214–17. These are the homilies for the day of circumcision, and the full set for *hilaria pasche*, the third, fourth, fifth, sixth *feriae* and *sabbato*, then *in octavas Pasche, I Dominico post octavas Pasche, II Dominico post octavas Pasche, III Dominico post octavas Pasche.*

75   Brou, *as above* note 53, p.189, '*Disparu sans retour, les nombreux sermons, presque tous anonymes, mais*

dont beaucoup sont de saveur espagnole incontestable, qui figuraient dans l'homiliaire de Tolède, au XIe siècle encore!'

76 Williams, *as above* Intro. note 49, p.17.

77 Williams, J., *The Illustrated Beatus*, vol.I, London, 1994, pp.13–15. Beatus's Commentary on the Apocalypse was, however, written probably ten years before his arguments with Elipandus over the Adoptionist heresy.

78 The last reading ends with a short section which does not come from Beatus: *Gratia vobis et pax a deo qui est et qui erat et qui venturus est, et septem spiritibus qui in conspectu troni eius sunt et ab Ihesu Christo qui est testis fidelis primogenitus mortuorum. Et princeps regum terre; qui dilexit nos et lavit nos a peccatis nostris in sanguine suo et fecit nostrum regnum sacerdotes deo et patri suo; ipsi gloria in saecula saeculorum. amen.*

79 Matter, E.A., 'The Apocalypse in Early Medieval Exegisis', in Emmerson, R.K., and McGinn, B. (eds.), *The Apocalypse in the Middle Ages*, Ithaca and London, 1992, pp.45–6. Beatus's Commentary has received relatively little scholarly attention, Matter considers, possibly because of its 'extremely dense character ... or perhaps because of its equally extreme topicality'.

80 In the tenth century Smaragdus seems to have been used originally in Castile and from there passed into Navarre. There was apparently no tradition of using this author in the kingdoms of Asturias and León. Bishko, *as above* note 66, p.588.

81 Reilly, *as above* Intro. note 81, pp.100–12 and p.143. Jimeno's death in 1082 may rule him out as a candidate. His successor was Gomez, who seems to have continued his approach.

82 Wright, R., *Late Latin and Early Romance in Spain and Carolingian France*, Liverpool, 1982, pp.212–13. Wright maintained that the '*litterae*' to which Gregory referred was knowledge of a pronunciation method, which gave one sound to each written letter *(littera),* and of the script which elucidated it. This had been familiar in France since the Carolingian period, but was new to Spain.

83 '*explicita missa, adplicantur ad cancellos infantes et decantur hec antifona cum suis versiculis. Et lecta eorundem manus impositione, tolluntur eius albe et soluit eos diaconus: et ibunt in pace'.*

84 The homily is from the collection of Paul the Deacon, '*Ex huius nobis lectionis verbis fratres karissimi Iohannes humilitas'.*

85 *See,* for example, Étaix, *as above* note 54, pp.103–5, Cluny lectionaries use *homelia lectionis eiusdem b. Gregorii papae habita ad populum in basilica [Petri apostoli/s. Mariae].*

86 The phrase *lectio ecclesiastica* does not appear in the *Homilarium* published by Brou. The designation here is *sermo.*

87 For example the biblical text of Smaragdus's *Collectiones in epistolas et evangelia* in *PL* 102, is distinguished from the homiletic text by the use of italic print.

88 *See* the mass for John the Baptist in Add. 30845, given in Férotin, *as above* Intro. note 20, col. 352. Also the antiphon in the office is '*Iohannes erat lucerna'.*

89 For example:

fol. 118v

non dicantur te deum laudamus set statim incipiatur antiphona

– non dicatur capitulum neque hymnum nec versi sed statim incipiatur antiphona et extinguatur lumen

– explicita antiphona simul 100 psalmo Inquoat: (kyrie)

– prostrati dicantur preces cum silentio absque dominus vobiscum

fol. 119

Qui statim eleventur a terra et inluminentur ecclesia

– post nonas inquoatur missa et communio dicatur neque dominus vobis cum sed post comunio incipiatur antiphona ex vespera

fol. 125

ad iii sub una gloria

fol. 125v

processio ad fontem hac antiphona de cantando cum suo psalmo

90 Hearn, M.F., *Romanesque Sculpture*, Oxford, 1981, p.187. Raoul Glaber speaks of continuing interest in the work of Eriugena in the early eleventh century. We also know that there was a manuscript of *expositiones Iohannis Scoti super ierarchias sancti Dionisii Ariopagite* in the library at Cluny. It now contains only the text of *'The Celestial Hierarchy'*, together with Eriugena's commentary, but presumably also once included 'The Ecclesiastical Hierarchy'. It has been dated to the tenth century and is now in the Bibliothèque Nationale (Paris) as N.a.l. 1490. *See* Delisle, L., *Inventaire des Manuscrits de la Bibliothèque Nationale - Fonds de Cluni*, Paris, 1884, no. 110, pp.185–6.

91 Louth, A., *Denys the Areopagite*, Wilton CT, 1989, p.18 and p.29.

92 Pseudo-Dionysius, 'The Celestial Hierarchy', in *The Complete Works*, Luibheid, C. (trans.), London, 1987, Ch. 13, 301D, p.178. In 'The Divine Names' Light is also described as dispelling ignorance and error: 'it drives from souls the ignorance and the error squatting there. ... It clears away the fog of ignorance from the eyes of the mind and it stirs and unwraps those covered over by the burden of darkness.'; *see The Complete Works*, as above p.75.

93 Rorem, P., *Pseudo-Dionysius – A Commentary on the Texts and an Introduction to Their Influence*, New York and Oxford, 1993, p.171.

94 Pseudo-Dionysius, *as above* note 92, Ch.1, 120B, p.145.

95 Pseudo-Dionysius, *as above* note 92, ch.8, 241A, p.168.

96 Knowles, D., *The Evolution of Medieval Thought*, London, 1962

97 O'Meara, J.J., *Eriugena*, Oxford, 1988, p.67.

CHAPTER THREE

———◄◦►———

The Sacred Text Made Visual

I N THE TWO previous chapters we have explored the differences in the conceptual structure of the manuscripts in this study, and the differences between the texts of the
Mozarabic and Roman liturgies as they are given in these books. This chapter will
consider the text as image through the interaction of text and illumination.

The decorative element in all these six manuscripts is highly calligraphic in nature, and it is
likely to have been executed by the scribes who wrote the text. Thus the text and decoration
are very closely connected, and the illumination consists mainly of initials and titles integrated into the text. No full-page miniatures have survived, and it is doubtful whether any
were included in the first place. The lacunae in the body of some of the manuscripts are
unlikely to have included miniatures, and were probably occupied by folios with more decorated headings and initials in keeping with the overall design of the manuscripts.

If there were *pages de garde*, they have been lost, and arguments as to their previous
existence must rest entirely on other extant liturgical manuscripts. We have one example of
the 'Mozarabic' practice – with a Silos connection – among the first four folios of a Mozarabic
antiphonarium bound into the Silos Beatus. These folios have been published in detail by
Brou.[1] They are too luxurious to give a fair indication of any introductory folios which our
more modest Mozarabic manuscripts might have had, but their iconography is of interest.
They include two representations of the Cross of Oviedo (fol. 2v and fol. 3v), one of which
probably came from the front of the original manuscript and the other from the end. This
image, with minor variations, formed a central part of the iconography of the beleaguered
Asturian kingdom of northern Spain from its inception. Alfonso II had commissioned the
gold reliquary Cross of Angels possibly to enhance his role as Christian conqueror, and
Alfonso III likewise donated the Cross of Victory to Oviedo Cathedral.[2] The cross in these
guises had thus acquired great political significance, and its use in liturgical manuscripts
demonstrates the extent of the identification of the king with the Church. The close recip-
rocal nature of that relationship is further demonstrated by the *ordo* in the Mozarabic liturgy
for the king going into battle.[3]

After the Cross of Oviedo there is a full-page miniature of a *vespertinum* monogram (fol.
4), that is the abbreviation which introduces the first word of the first antiphon. Several
smaller examples are found in the Mozarabic manuscripts in this study. The final display

folio (fol. 4v) consists of the word LUX arranged as a monogram. This is the first word of the first antiphon for the first office of the Mozarabic liturgical year, the feast of *S. Acisclus*.[4] As most of Brou's parallels for these folios come from other antiphonaries, we do not know if similar *pages de garde* would have begun and ended *officia et missae*. We can say only that it seems quite likely that something similar but less lavish could have been used. The Mozarabic manuscripts may also have had colophons possibly naming the scribes and artists in the Spanish fashion.[5] These are also unfortunately lost.

The Roman breviaries are less likely to have had elaborate *pages de garde*, as their probable models, breviaries produced in France at this time, seem to have lacked full-page miniatures. If we look at the eleventh- or early-twelfth-century examples offered by Leroquais,[6] we see that they are quite plain, fronted only by calendars or other miscellaneous textual material.

We have found that the text of each of our six manuscripts is identifiably that of either the Mozarabic or the Roman liturgy – there is no compromise position. There is, however, evidence of a gradual transition in the structure of the manuscripts and in the feast days included. We will now examine to what extent the nature of the text determines the nature of its presentation.

We have seen already that there is no correlation between script and liturgical text; to our knowledge the Mozarabic liturgy was never written in Caroline minuscule, but the Roman liturgy was written in several instances in Visigothic script. There is thus no clear evidence of any semiological significance in the choice of script. Was the decision on which script to use paralleled by the choice of style: 'Mozarabic' for Visigothic and 'Romanesque' for Protogothic? Or did the texts of the Mozarabic liturgy receive only 'Mozarabic' decoration,[7] while the texts of the Roman liturgy were decorated in a 'Romanesque' manner? Or were the combinations less predictable? The following pages attempt to answer these questions. It should be noted from the start, however, that the emphasis will be on the ways in which the illumination was used, not merely an attempt to designate certain stylistic features as 'Mozarabic' or 'Romanesque'.

Manuscripts of the Mozarabic Liturgy

I will begin with an examination of the manuscripts of the Mozarabic liturgy. At first glance these manuscripts seem to differ considerably from one another partly because of the variation in overall quality. Closer examination, however, reveals important similarities. By studying these similarities I will try to establish whether these manuscripts exemplify a common approach to the illumination of liturgical manuscripts. The issue of the origin of these manuscripts, although not essential to this study, is of broader interest and will also be discussed further in this chapter.

One of the characteristics common to these three Mozarabic manuscripts is their use of colour contrasts. All three of the manuscripts fit John Williams's apt phrase concerning Leonese manuscript illumination, that it was 'clearly established by line but chiefly conceived in terms of colour'.[8] In Add. 30844 a bright red is used for rubrication, headings and

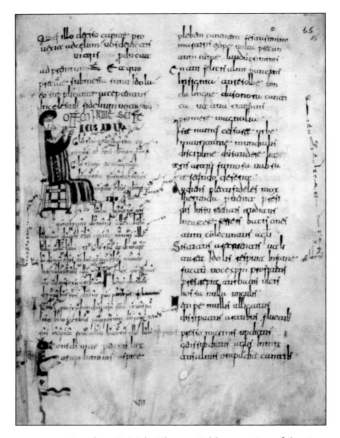

FIG. 10 London, British Library, Add. MS 30845, fol. 56

initials; a light or bright yellow, a bluey-green, and a dark blue are also employed exten-
sively as infill colours (PLATE 2). These colours form the four-colour chord familiar from
tenth-century 'Mozarabic' illumination.[9] In addition there are occasional uses on initials of
a light or dark mauve (e.g. fol. 70v and fol. 71v). These colours are usually used together in
groups, so the folios are enlivened by the constant contrast of red/yellow/green/blue. This
system of infill for the liturgical abbreviations which mark sections, and in the illumination
of headings and initials, forms a continuous theme throughout the manuscript and helps to
make it clear and legible.

Add. 30845 presents a rather different aspect, using predominantly greens, a light brown,
and a dull red (PLATE 1). At some points, red and black are used in close proximity, uncertainly mixed, to result in a patchy purple (fol. 1v and fol. 2, fol. 100 and fol. 158), which
seems to develop into the more confident use of a dark purple by fol. 161v. On fol. 55 a
yellow is introduced which is used with a bright green on fol. 56 (FIG. 10) and occasionally
thereafter. The emphasis in this manuscript is again on tonal contrasts, but these are not so
striking since the pigments used are duller. The interpolated section containing the mass for
the Assumption of the Virgin (fols 89–92v) has only red outline initials (FIG. 4) and looks

FIG. 11 London, British Library, Add. MS 30846, fol. IV

FIG. 12 London, British Library, Add. MS 30844, fol. 57

quite different. The general deployment of the colours, especially through infill is, however, very similar to that of Add. 30844.

The colour contrasts used in Add. 30846 (folios of section A) are similar to those in Add. 30845: a deep red, a very light brown and a mid-green (FIG. 11), while the other folios (section B) have more in common with Add. 30844, using brighter colours – a bright red, green and yellow – as well as, occasionally, black in a decorative context (PLATE 3). On fol. 22v, fol. 23v and fol. 87 there is also an unexpected appearance of a deep blue with a metallic sheen.

The unifying design of each of these Mozarabic manuscripts can thus be viewed as a reflection of the textual synthesis of the office with the mass. Both types of text are unified in the book by the use of a common colour-based theme.

All three Mozarabic manuscripts have prominent headings, often contained in an actual or notional frame, and sometimes using letter patterns to achieve this compressed blocked effect. We can no longer gain a full picture of the impact of the programme of headings in Add. 30844, however, as several of the folios in this manuscript which should have contained headings have been lost: i.e. those of the *officia* for the Nativity, the feast of St Stephen, the Circumcision, and Epiphany. It is indeed very possible that these contained some of the best examples of decoration, and that they may have been torn out for that specific reason by collectors – especially as in most cases the folios in question have been cut from the manuscript. Nevertheless a sufficient number of other headings remain to give a clear indication of the methods employed.

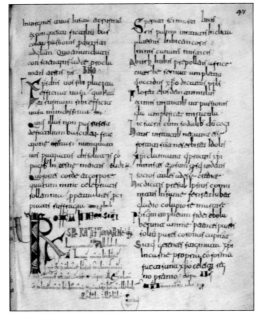

FIG. 13 London, British Library,
Add. MS 30845, fol. 47

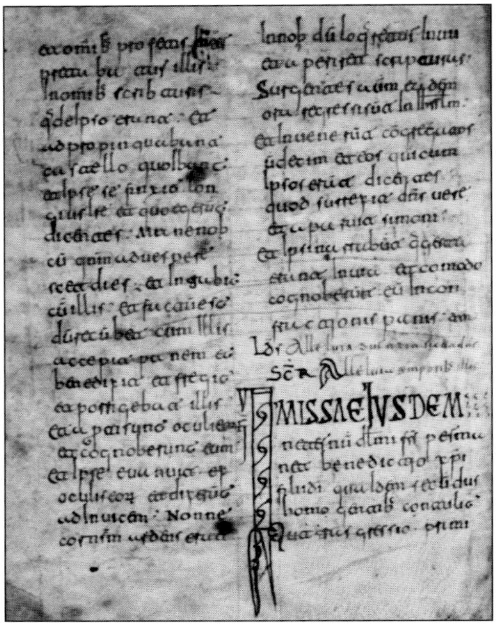

FIG. 14 London, British Library,
Add. MS 30846, fol. 5v

Add. 30844 has headings to introduce the office for each feast day. They are usually placed at the top of folios or at least not encumbered by the surrounding text. A frame consisting of a simple red border, with an outline leaf extending on the right-hand side, may sometimes surround the letters (fol. 57, FIG. 12); in other cases the letters are written only as if surrounded by a frame. The words of the titles, suitably abbreviated, are written in capitals with great attention to the space and patterns created, extending some tall letters and abbreviations above the line and arranging other smaller letters sometimes one above the other. The heading often occupies only one line, but sometimes uses several more. The abbreviation which states that the first office is vespers, *ad vpr*, frequently appears below, but may be included in the frame.

The headings in Add. 30845 are not as bold nor as carefully executed as those in Add. 30844. Only occasionally are they blocked on one line with ascenders and abbreviations extending from a notional frame; there are no frames as such in this manuscript. Generally the headings are well sited at the top or in the centre of folios and stand out clearly from the text. There are a few exceptions, for example on fol. 43v where the heading is placed at the bottom of the page, but here the *vespertinum* monogram is reserved for a commanding position at the top of the following folio. Nearly all the headings are conceived of in the same broad terms, as a line or lines highlighted by the application of colour. Exceptionally, on fol. 64, the heading is integrated into the figurative *vespertinum* monogram and the letters arranged around the figures. There is considerable variation in the execution of the headings in this manuscript and there seems to be a constant desire to experiment and to mix

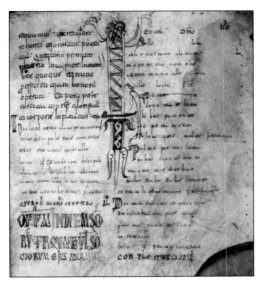

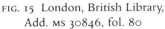

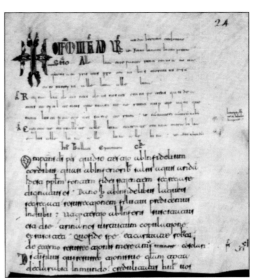

FIG. 15 London, British Library,
Add. MS 30846, fol. 80

FIG. 16 London, British Library,
Add. MS 30846, fol. 24

approaches using various letter forms, abbreviations, colour contrasts, line lengths and forms.
One simple form of two-line heading occurs throughout much of the manuscript, for example on fol. 47, where the first line is in red letters infilled with green and the second line
is in red letters infilled with brown (FIG. 13). Letter or infill colours may also be alternated
within the lines (fol. 96), and the patterns can become quite elaborate. On fol. 118 Add.
30845 has a five-line heading introducing the reading for the mass of St Michael. A different
technique is used here and colour washes are placed behind the red lettering (PLATE 1).[10]
There are several very bold headings over the next few folios using strong contrasts oppos-
ing red, black and yellow ochre. The interpolated folios (fols 89–92v) are not part of this
pattern. Here the heading for *missa de Adsumtio Sancte Marie* is written on two lines in red
capitals (FIG. 4); there is no infill and only the initial 'm' extends above the ruled line,
otherwise the heading is neatly blocked. These folios may show that there was a change in
the approach to illuminating liturgical manuscripts even before the change in the liturgy.
There is no attempt here to make the interpolated pages appear part of the original manuscript, and the style used employs very little decoration. In the rest of the manuscript the
mass texts do not receive separate headings, but are merely marked by the rubric for the first
prayer *ad missam*; this may not even appear on a separate line.

In both sections (A and B)[11] of Add. 30846 the headings are executed using colour in
much the same way as it was used in Add. 30845. Different colours are used for different
sections of the heading, sometimes alternating and sometimes as if moving through a
spectrum. Most of the headings in Add. 30846 involve very little patterning of letters, but
examples can be found on fol. 74v (A) and on fol. 59 (B). The headings in section A usually
use two colours (chosen from red, green and brown), sometimes alternating on the line (fol.

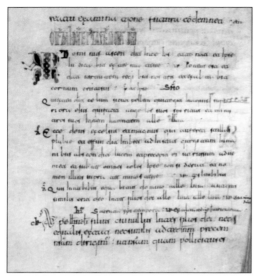

FIG. 17 London, British Library,
Add. MS 30846, fol. 124v

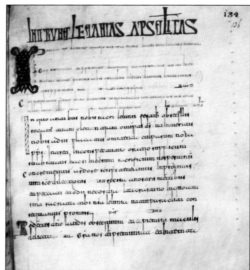

FIG. 18 London, British Library,
Add. MS 30846, fol. 136

5v) (FIG. 14). The headings are used for *officia, missae* and *ad matutinum* without particular prominence being given to one kind of heading, and are sometimes omitted altogether (fol. 54v, fol. 55).

There are two types of heading in section A, one in the earlier folios using mainly red and green thin letters on one to five lines. Occasionally the pattern is varied, as on fol. 39 where the heading is written round the *vespertinum* monogram. Occasionally the heading is finished with a decorative block of commas at the end of the line (fol. 5v, FIG. 14) again in one or two colours. The second type of heading in section A is larger, more sprawling, and usually written in robust outline letters, for example on fol. 80 (FIG. 15) or on fol. 43v; it may also be finished with blocks of decorative commas.

Most of the headings in Section B are written in a much tighter, neater, laterally compressed style. The device of alternating or grading colours continues to a greater effect because of the more dramatic colour contrasts. The examples vary from a simple version on fol. 8 moving from green to red (FIG. 2) – or a three-colour example on fol. 21 where red becomes yellow which gives way to green – to that on fol. 24 which uses more than one colour even in the first word (FIG. 16). There are also occasional delicate precise headings written in brown ink in section B, for example fol. 124v (FIG. 17).

A third kind of heading appears in both A and B sections of the manuscript, linking them at their time of production. The most elaborate example occurs on fol. 136 for *Incipiunt Letanias Apostolicas* (FIG. 18). This heading is written in solid red letters with a thicker pen (or brush) than was used elsewhere. It incorporates a distinctive type of letter 'T' with a vegetal left-hand stroke reaching down to the ruled line, as well as sweeping curves in the letter 'S'. The heading in red for *sabbato ad missa* on fol. 41 (FIG. 19) is clearly by the same hand, as it

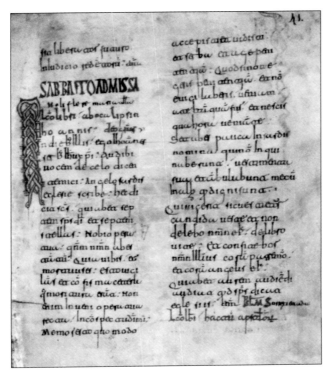

FIG. 19 London, British Library, Add. MS 30846, fol. 41

exhibits the same letter 'T' and letter 'S', as well as the same *ductus*. The initials which accompany these headings on fol. 41 and fol. 136 are also by the same artist; they use the same red ink and have the same 'kufic' border.[12]

From this analysis it seems that headings are used in the Mozarabic manuscripts simply to guide the reader through the text. They are not a visual map of the liturgical year, and do not give obvious prominence to the major feasts of the church year or to particular saints. The emphasis continues to be on the rhythm of the book, and variations seem to be incidental.

If there is a primary distinguishing feature in the decoration of these Mozarabic manuscripts, it is the *vespertinum* monogram. It is the main recipient of decoration in these manuscripts, and serves as a sign to direct the reader to the beginning of each *officium* entry. In many cases it is elaborated to such an extent that the *VPR* abbreviation from which it is formed is indecipherable, becoming instead a highly ornamental abstract feature. This device was presumably so familiar to the users of Mozarabic liturgical manuscripts that it did not need to be legible: its function as a marker for the beginning of the first item of the first office of each day in the manuscript must have been accepted to the extent that the artist could free himself from the restraints of the letters themselves without impairing the effectiveness of the sign.

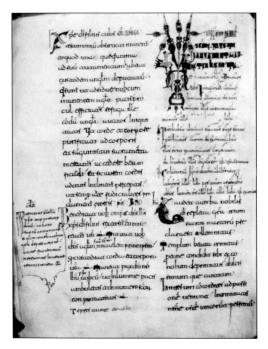

FIG. 20 London, British Library,
Add. MS 30845, fol. 127v

FIG. 21 London, British Library,
Add. MS 30845, fol. 5v

These monograms, and the balance between them and the title headings of each *officium*, are an important part of the decorative scheme of Add. 30844: the monograms occupy from three to eight lines of the written space in length and are roughly half that in width; as an ensemble with the title they are the largest decorative elements in the manuscript. They are usually treated in one of two ways. The example on fol. 33 is typical of one of the styles used (PLATE 2). The central stem is formed as an initial 'I': filled mostly with yellow, it has a blue band near each end, and the lower compartment is filled with green. The potentially harsh outline is broken by two nodules on the right and two indentations, one on the top and one on the base. A simple penwork flourish extends below, and a simple curl comes from the top. The rest of the letter is formed by four curving sections arranged symmetrically around the stem. The upper two touch the stem at the top and in the middle; the lower two curve out gently from the centre. That at the top left has two eyes, transforming it into a representation of a fish. This zoomorphic tendency had been a feature of Mozarabic illumination from the tenth century, when the features were usually drawn by compasses, but here the line is freehand.[13] The other sections, blue and yellow or blue and green, are organic curls. The *vespertinum* monogram on fol. 57 (FIG. 12) is related to that on fol. 33, but the curves on the left are formed respectively by a bird and a snake; palmettes emerge from the downward curve on the right, which has interlace decoration, as does the stem. The monogram is carefully executed, its effect striking and memorable.

The other *vespertinum* monograms in Add. 30844 are purely geometric. These tend to be

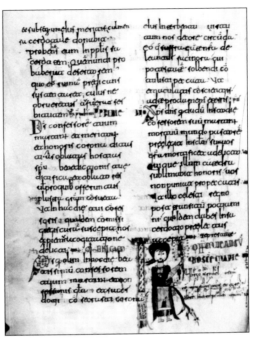

FIG. 22 London, British Library,
Add. MS 30845, fol. 96

FIG. 23 London, British Library,
Add. MS 30845, fol. 83v

less well executed, such as that on fol. 138. The central stem is roughly drawn and the curves have been simplified to form two upward-reaching 'arms' at the top, a cross-bar through the middle and two 'legs' at the base which extend horizontally before turning down. The outline is in red and there is pale yellow and blue infill. The only other decoration is a series of dots which give the monogram a rudimentary sense of body. The monogram for the feast of St James the Less, fol. 93v, is merely in black outline, as is that for *De Letanias ante Pentecosten.*

The *vespertinum* monograms in Add. 30845 are drawn in three main ways: geometric, 'tree-like' and figurative. The geometric variety are usually based on a central shaft like a letter 'I' (fol. IV, FIG. 3; and fol. 47, FIG. 13), which can have a core in the form of a spiral or zig-zag column. The ends of the shaft may be decorated with triangular sections or with a row of stripes. The rest of the sign is formed by strokes or curved sections, which may be embellished with vegetal scrolls or delicate leaf outlines. The 'tree-like' designs are much more exotic (fol. 13, fol. 38, fol. 52v, fol. 71, fol. 107 and fol. 136v). They are like fantastic trophies, with decorative devices hanging from the branches and birds or animals inhabiting them. The monogram for *officium in diem Sanctorum Fausti, Ianuarii et Martialis* (fol. 127v, FIG. 20) is one of the most complex: it springs from a stepped 'platform' from which hang palmettes and another possibly vegetal extension. The central shaft is narrow and soon divides into three upward lines and two downward ones which 'flower' into long thin 'leaves'. A bird perches on each of these and pecks at the foliate shapes which hang from the 'branches' above. These same branches divide yet again into three. Somewhat similar trees can be found in the Conciliar Codex of Albelda (Escorial, Biblioteca del Monasterio, MS d.I.2, fol. 142) where they are labelled '*arbor cum docalibus*' – tree with gifts – and '*vascula in ramiis*' – vessels on branches. This link with the illumination of such an authoritative codex suggests that these trees may have had a particular votive significance.[14]

The figurative *Vespertinum* monograms are the most distinctive feature of Add. 30845. They are in many cases barely recognisable as monograms, but all perform that function to introduce the *vespertinum* antiphon.[15] They are formed of calligraphic and geometric units and are found throughout the manuscript (fol. 5v–fol. 160v) in various forms. The figure, possibly depicting Jerome, on fol. 5v (FIG. 21) can be analysed into its constituent parts: an angular paragraph mark forms a large hood, presumably representing a mitre, his arm is two sides of a square, the lower part of the body is an upside-down triangle and the lower section of the clothing is stripes with curved ends. These stripes have the appearance of feathers, and a similar effect can be found in Leonese manuscript illumination as early as the León Bible of 920 (León Cathedral, cod. 6). The whole figure is highly schematic. The head and face are based on curves rather than straight lines, including a bulging curve for the back of the head. The only recognisable facial features are an eye (a circle with a dot) and, among the three bulbous curves of the profile, a beard. The feet are formed by two small oblong blocks. The fingers are individually but crudely drawn and those of the right hand pass through the crosier which the figure holds. This crosier is formed from a letter 'T' with a left loop, extended down to a pointed end with three pairs of nodules along the shaft. The figure is decorated with a heart motif and with rough zigzag lines. It is possible to see the basic form of the *vespertinum* monogram in this figure which offers the fundamental components: branches reaching up to the left and the right which are formed by the mitre and the raised left arm, and two reaching downwards which are formed by the body and the staff; these four are linked by the right arm reaching across to grasp the staff. Some of the other monograms are very like that on fol. 5v, so similar that it is difficult to believe that they were not all executed by the same artist; these are found on fol. 81 (*officium Sacrationis S. Martini*), fol. 96 (*officium S. Genesi*) (FIG. 22), fol. 144v (*officium S. Milani*) and fol. 160v (*officium S. Bartolomei*). The last two are especially close to that on fol. 5v, which indicates that this codex is an integral volume, and that fols 1–7v are not from another manuscript as Díaz y Díaz proposed.[16]

There are also other figurative monograms which differ from the type exemplified on fol. 5v to varying degrees. Some are seated and hold up processional crosses, such as those on fol. 29v (*officium SS. Petri et Pauli*), fol. 56 (*officium S. Felicis*), fol. 100 (*officium S. Augustini*), others stand as that on fol. 139 (*officium Sacrationis S. Martini*). Others involve two figures, fol. 42 (*SS. Iusti et Rufine*), fol. 64 (*SS. Iusti et Pastoris*) and fol. 130 (*officium SS. Cosme et Damiani*), and some use a different type of figure, usually facing front, with a round face decorated with two bright red dots, for example fol. 83v (*officium S. Marie*) (FIG. 23, here the monogram is easier to decipher). There are, however, motifs shared by some of the figures with both facial types, and it seems to me likely that one artist did execute both types. The face of the

FIG. 24 Florence, Biblioteca Medicea Laurenziana,
MS Ashb. 17, fol. 66

figure of *S. Felix* on fol. 56 (FIG. 10) is depicted full-face as well as in profile. This phenom-
enon can also be seen in another Silos manuscript, MS 5, in a León manuscript now in León
Cathedral, MS 6, fol. 154, and in an eleventh-century Toledan manuscript, Florence, Biblioteca
Laurenziana MS Ashb.17 (FIG. 24).[17]

As soon as it is realised that these figures represent *VPR* monograms, several of the
previously inexplicable aspects of them become clearer. In particular the varied 'attributes'
which they hold are explained, at least to some extent, as forming necessary or helpful
functional parts of the monograms. On the whole these 'attributes' seem general rather than
specific, as each is used for more than one figure. For example the processional crosses,
mentioned above, form the upper right-hand branch of the monogram, and similarly the

flowering stems held by the figures on fol. 83 (*officium S. Marie*) (FIG. 23), fol. 144v (*officium S. Milani*), and fol. 130v (*officium SS. Cosme & Damiani*) complete the upper section of the monogram. St Michael the Archangel (fol. 118) is portrayed with one wing pointing upwards and one downwards, a feature which is found occasionally in other Mozarabic manuscripts; in this case, however, it is not merely a convention, but cleverly enables the wings to form two of the arms of the monogram (PLATE 1).

Several figures hold staffs or crosiers which are variations on that held by the figure on fol. 5v (*S. Martinus* (fol. 81), *S. Genesus* (fol. 96, FIG. 22) and *S. Bartolomeus* (fol. 160v)). Such staffs appear in other Mozarabic manuscripts held by abbots, bishops or kings.[18] Other attributes remain difficult to identify, for example the object held by *S. Martinus* (fol. 139) which has a handle and a horn-shaped base. St Michael holds something similar and two more hang from his wings (PLATE 1). *S. Eufemia*, St John the Baptist and *S. Saturninus* also hold similar unidentified objects.

Unlike Add. 30845, all the *vespertinum* monograms in Add. 30846 are geometric and/or vegetal in conception. Moreover they are nearly all clearly *VPR* monograms with defined central shafts, two vegetal scrolls on the left-hand side, a bow on the top right-hand side and a downward stroke on the lower right-hand side with a cross stroke to complete the abbreviation. The difference between the two main types which appear respectively in section A and section B is a combination of size and colour. Several of those in section A are drawn in outline, usually brown or red, with only occasional infill (fol. 1v, FIG. 11). They occupy, typically, some six or eight ruled lines. Others are much larger and rougher in execution, for example fol. 44 (15-lines), fol. 80 (17-lines, FIG. 15), and fol. 87v (11-lines). Exceptionally, that on fol. 80 also includes a rudimentary drawing of a bird.

Those in section B are mainly much smaller, usually no more than five or six lines, and much more contained and concentrated in their use of pattern and colour. The outline is usually brown, but red, green, yellow and brown are used to define the decoration, and the natural colour of the vellum is also used to effect (fol. 24, FIG. 16). There are also some very small *VPR* monograms towards the end of the manuscript (FIG. 17) – only one–three lines in depth – (fol. 121v, fol. 124v, fol. 144). There are, however, some noticeable exceptions to this restrained impression in Section B. For example, the monogram for Pentecost on fol. 163v uses large crescents of bright green. These are 'framed' by a thin strip of yellow which edges all the blocks and extends into bands of interlace, which are set against a red background. In the central shaft there is a cable motif with square edges in red, green and 'white'. The bands or compartments of interlace derive from Frankish models and were added to the repertoire of 'Mozarabic' motifs in the tenth century.[19]

The *vespertinum* monogram is, therefore, the identifying feature of the Mozarabic liturgical manuscript *par excellence*. Although the decoration applied to them does not generally seem to indicate a hierarchy of feasts, the notable exception to this is the number of finely illuminated monograms used to introduce offices connected with the Virgin in Add. 30844. It is possible, however, that this tells us more about the nature of that particular manuscript, and does not demonstrate a wider tendency to privilege particular texts in this way.

In addition to these distinct Mozarabic decorative features, these three manuscripts are also articulated by initials. Each manuscript establishes a hierarchy, applying initials of different sizes to different passages. Small initials, of one or two lines in height, are used to begin the sung passages and prayers, but certain liturgical items consistently receive large initials. These items are, in the main, mass rather than office texts (the *missa* prayer, each *lectio*, and sermons) and will be studied when we look at the illumination of mass texts in part II. It is appropriate, however, to consider the character of the initials at this point, as it forms part of the overall scheme of illumination in each of these manuscripts. There is, moreover, one element of the office which consistently receives a large decorated initial when it is included: the hymn.

Like the monograms, the initials in Add. 30844 are mostly geometric. They employ a wide range of Mozarabic motifs including multiple scrolls, interlace panels, spirals within columns, penwork, and interlocking blocks arranged like steps; they are also frequently zoomorphic, resolving into fish, birds and snakes. All these decorative devices had appeared in Mozarabic manuscripts by the end of the tenth century, and the zoomorphic tendency even before this. In addition there are some initials which are based on the Valeranican style demonstrated notably by Florentius in the tenth century; some of these have open flowing interlace, while others have a much more delicate tracery of interlace which is drawn in outline only; the shaded areas are given depth by the application of several small circles – the Valeranican stencil motif (fol. 98, fol. 104). The large hymn initials provide examples of most of these motifs. The fluid, organic style of the other *vespertinum* monograms can also be seen in the initials: for example on fol. 33v (FIG. 25) there is a geometrical vegetal initial 'A' introducing the hymn *A solis ortus*, which has its two main bars augmented by several excrescences of a plastic organic kind. These are decorated with infill in green, blue, yellow and red. The Valeranican repertoire may explain the appendages, which could be simplified and abstract forms of the elaborate palmettes and other vegetal scrolls which distinguish some of the initials produced by that scriptorium. Some of the other hymn initials use 'bristles', small black penwork dashes, usually in groups of three, which give an explosive effect (fol. 86v – FIG. 26, fol. 149); these were used a great deal in Leonese manuscript illumination.[20]

The initials of Add. 30845 are different in character, but draw from the same repertoire of compartments, foliate scrolls, penwork, nodules and indentations, and zoomorphic forms. The hymn initials are often in the form of a bird, for example fols 1v and 127v (FIGS 3 and 20). The character of this manuscript is perhaps best exemplified by three distinctive minor initials – not introducing hymns – on fol. 12, fol. 22v, and fol. 28. These are formed by a head with a neck but no body, from which emerges an arm to form the uncial letter 'D'. The heads are full face and use the line-and-dot method of representing hair and red dots on cheeks. The other known examples of this rather bizarre conception are in two Toledan manuscripts, a Mozarabic breviary (Madrid, BN, cod. 10001, fol. 34) and a conciliar manuscript (Madrid, BN, cod. 1872, fol. 144).[21] This feature lends support to the idea that one of the artists who illuminated this manuscript was working within a southern 'Mozarabic'

FIG. 25 London, British Library,
Add. MS 30844, fol. 33v

FIG. 26 London, British Library,
Add. MS 30844, fol. 86v

tradition, and was possibly an immigrant from Toledo or other Islamic territory. Add. 30845 also has a selection of initials formed by four-legged lion-like animals, for example at the base of fol. 56 (FIG. 10) beginning the hymn *Fons dei vitae*.[22] The tops and bases of letter-shafts in this manuscript are treated with fantastic 'Mozarabic' embellishments, feather-like tops, hood-like tops, palmettes and other foliate scrolls, and pendants (FIG. 20).[23] Towards the end of the manuscript there are three initials which stand out as different: they are all letter 'O's, and one of them introduces a hymn (fol. 145). They have bold, bright, well-defined angular designs: on fol. 108v a detailed chequer-board pattern in alternating dark red and light brown, and on fol. 132v a square of red and yellow basket-weave ornamented on the outside with green beads. On fol. 145 the letter is formed by a ring of cable painted in black, deep red and ochre making a dramatic contrast with the vellum which shows through as small white beads; the centre is filled by a cross with triangular arms striped in ochre and red. Similar motifs can be seen in the Silos Beatus: the basket-weave in the bowl of a letter 'D' (fol. 8v) and the chequer-board pattern as the background to the full page miniature *page de garde* (fol. 6 – this may have been intended to form an acrostic page).

Add. 30846 offers further variations of 'Mozarabic' decoration. One of the distinctive aspects of the initials in section A is the use of figures, similar in conception but even less well executed than those which form the monograms in Add. 30845. They are crudely drawn, only in black or red outline, but occupy several lines, for example a 13-line 'I' on fol. 28 (FIG. 27). The decision to use figurative initials, however rough in execution, suggests that they may have had some emblematic significance; found also in Add. 30845, these

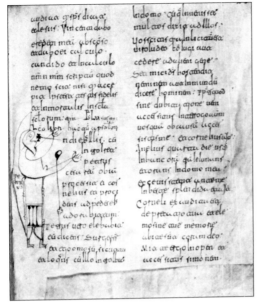
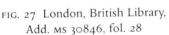

FIG. 27 London, British Library,
Add. MS 30846, fol. 28

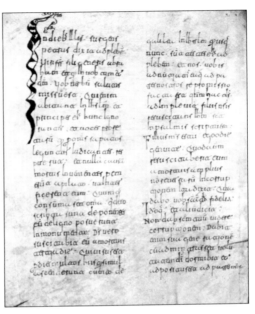

FIG. 28 London, British Library,
Add. MS 30846, fol. 41v

schematic figures might in some way have represented the authority of the Mozarabic church. Long letter 'I's are a standard feature of Mozarabic manuscripts and Add. 30846 offers several other examples, including some in the form of snakes with their heads at the top of the letter and their bodies waving downwards (fol. 35 and fol. 41v, FIG. 28); a similar letter-form can be seen in the San Millán manuscript (Madrid, Real Academia de la Historia, Aem. 22, fol. 123, 1073).[24] There are, however, no hymns in this section.

Add. 30846 (section B) uses some Valeranican features not found in the other two Mozarabic manuscripts, in particular animal-head terminals which appear from fol. 57 onwards; these are neat, quite small and executed in bright colours (fol. 57v).[25] In this same section there are zoomorphic initials of birds and fish, and some of the birds are executed in a fashion very similar to those in the León Bible (AD 920), fol. 211.[26] On fol. 43v and fol. 44v there are two letter 'O's which use the distinctive Valeranican cross-hatching motif.

One figure on fol. 94 (PLATE 3) is totally different from the other initials in section A and B:[27] it is made of clear-cut blocks of colour: green, red, and black. It wears black boots which are decorated with a red and yellow blocks, and a small pointed hat. The lower body is striped vertically like a schematic letter 'A' in red and yellow, the shoulder is almost a circle and one arm reaches upwards. The facial features are, as usual, rudimentary. To the modern eye this looks very like a clown, and this suggestion is supported by another clown-like figure in the *Codex Aemilianensis* (a San Millán manuscript), swinging from a bar – although in this case the figure is half clown/man and half beast.[28]

The hymns in Add. 30846 are concentrated in fol. 63–fol. 74, that is in Section B. The initials are therefore all quite small, and precisely executed. They are mainly geometric and foliate, but that on fol. 67v includes animal-head terminals. Moreover, the 'P' beginning *Pange lingua* on fol. 70 is formed by a small figure which has similarities to the 'clown' on fol. 94.

Despite the different styles used in these three manuscripts and the variable quality, we have seen that they share a similar system of decoration. They have clear layouts, picked out in colour contrasts, prominent headings for each *officium*, and a distinctive sign to direct the reader to the texts for each new feast day. This system was applied regularly throughout the manuscripts, highlighting certain elements of the text, for example the hymns, but often with little regard for the feast in question. A larger initial often seems to have been employed for the sake of the design of the manuscript, or as a result of the decorative repertoire associated with the particular letter. Add. 30844, with its Marian bias, is the only one of these manuscripts to give noticeably richer decoration to particular feasts, in this case those associated with the Virgin.

If we take an overview of the artistic style of these manuscripts, one of the common features is that they all draw on various strands of Mozarabic decorative tradition. The individual styles used may all be termed 'Mozarabic', since they can all be seen – often separately – in manuscripts of tenth-century Spain. Spanish illuminators often retained traditional motifs while mixing them with new ideas, and this habit had developed into a rich eclectic style, especially at San Millán de la Cogolla in the late tenth century. In the eleventh century the practice of drawing on the tenth-century repertoire seems to have continued not only at San Millán but in Castile in general. Different motifs seem to have been used side by side, without a great deal of synthesis, and there is little which is identifiably eleventh-century.[29] This tendency may have been increased at Silos, if monks from a number of different scriptoria came to work there. Introspection and regeneration had long been features of 'Mozarabic' art – even more than is usually associated with an artistic tradition which relies on copying. Evidence of this can be seen in the continuance of its compartmentalised church architecture and the persistence of the decorative form of the Beatus manuscripts. Other manuscripts were also copied almost as facsimiles; for example a copy of St Ildephonsus's *De Virginitate S. Marie* (Florence, Biblioteca Laurenziana, MS Ash. 17) was executed in Toledo in 1067, but it is so close in style to manuscripts of the tenth century that if it were not for the date given in the colophon it would have been placed much earlier (FIG. 24).[30] It follows from this that there is no reason to presume that the Mozarabic manuscripts in this study should be dated to the tenth century merely because they look 'primitive'. I propose, on the basis of their style, and with supporting palaeographic evidence, that all three date from the eleventh century, with Add. 30846 probably significantly later than the others.

None of these manuscripts can be localised precisely by their contents, and none of them has a surviving colophon to place it confidently within a scriptorium. The circumstantial evidence places all three at Silos and no other scriptorium has been confidently proposed for them. Díaz y Díaz has ascribed Add. 30844 to the scriptorium at Silos; he made no attributions for Add. 30845 or Add. 30846, only pointing to 'Riojan' influence in the former and the extreme diversity of the latter.[31] Boylan places none of these manuscripts at Silos, as her thesis doubts the existence of a flourishing scriptorium at Silos before the change in the liturgy. She describes the initials of Add. 30844 as 'too varied to be able to attribute them to a particular scriptorium', Add. 30845 as having 'parallels with the early work of Cardeña only in its anthropomorphic initials, while the rest were derived from Toledan manuscripts' and parts of Add. 30846 as 'may be successfully compared with Silos, MS 7, another liturgical codex, which, like Add. 30846, is unlocalized'.[32] However, Boylan's dismantling of Silos as a centre of production raises more problems than it solves.

The abbacy of Santo Domingo at Silos (1041–1073) was a time of great development, and of powerful political connections. It seems improbable that such a major institution as the reformed abbey would not have had its own scriptorium. Silos was sufficiently important – and sufficiently wealthy – to have Santo Domingo's body translated in the presence of Alfonso VI in 1076. There are two documents which mention books being given to Silos,[33] but this certainly does not imply that there was no scriptorium at the monastery at the time. The first document records the donation of the whole of the neighbouring abbey of St Michael and St Mary to Silos in 1056. Some books, little caskets (possibly for relics) and chalices were included. The second is specifically a gift of liturgical books in 1067 by Don Sanzo de Tabladillo. They are specified as for his personal use in the monastery, and after his death for the personal use of members of his family. This does not suggest that the monastery as a whole was short of liturgical manuscripts, indeed rather the opposite.

Both Add. 30844 and Add. 30845 have features which make it conceivable that they could have been given to the abbey as part of the donation of 1056. Add. 30844 has strong Marian associations, and in Add. 30845 it is the *officium* and *missa* of St Michael which receive the most extravagant decoration. It is, however, equally possible that both manuscripts were produced at Silos, perhaps after the donation of 1056, which may have included relics of the Virgin and St Michael. The joint altar dedication to the Virgin and St Michael in 1088 shows that Silos continued to attach special importance to both these saints. In any event it seems likely that Dominic would have built up a scriptorium at Silos as soon as he had the necessary resources, and that one would have been well in place by the middle of the century. Domingo is likely to have welcomed scribes from other monasteries when setting up the scriptorium, perhaps especially from his previous abbey of San Millán and possibly immigrants from Moorish territory, which could explain the presence of differing workshop practices and artistic styles in these manuscripts.[34] It is thus quite possible that all three of our manuscripts were produced there. In any event there is no reason to suppose they were produced far from Silos.

Add. 30846 is the most inscrutable of the Mozarabic manuscripts. Why is it so difficult to make sense of this manuscript? The text is in places unusable, and generally of a low level. The two parts are in most ways different and yet joined by some common features as well as by physical means; for example one scribe worked on both sections. Its folios are small, limiting the scope for illumination in the Mozarabic tradition, and produced on low-quality vellum. Why would such a manuscript be preserved? It could have been produced as the result of school exercises, but it would have made a poor model for others to follow, which would argue against its preservation. One clue may, I think, be found in the few folios which contain the unusual blue and the dull yellow inks (fols 22–23v), for these same colours are found in Add. 30847, a manuscript of the Roman liturgy. Is it possible that Add. 30846 was preserved for reasons of nostalgia because it was one of the last Mozarabic products of the scriptorium? The possible connection is strengthened by the form of the geometric and vegetal initials which are the subject of these particular coloured inks, as they are similar to some of the initials in Add. 30847 – for example the letter 'D' on fol. 22v of Add. 30846 has some similarities with the letter 'D' on fol. 127 of Add. 30847 (FIG. 5). It is conceivable that this manuscript was being produced at Silos at the very time of the change in the liturgy. We do not know what happened when the edict of 1080 was issued, but it seems likely that production of manuscripts of the Mozarabic liturgy would have been halted more or less immediately. Given the time taken to write and illuminate a manuscript, there must have been some, even many, only partly finished. What happened to these books? It would presumably have taken time to organise the distribution of models of the Roman liturgy, to train the scribes to read them, and to produce working copies for the monastery. This transitional situation seems the most likely one in which an oddity such as Add. 30846 might have been produced and valued sufficiently to ensure its survival.

Manuscripts of the Roman Liturgy

If we turn from the colourful pages of the Mozarabic manuscripts to the first Roman manuscript, Add. 30847, the change in decoration is dramatic even though the script is still Visigothic. Indeed, it is difficult even to speak of a decorative scheme, as there is so little illumination. The most striking feature on reading this manuscript after the Mozarabic ones is the comparative lack of visual structure. The headings are written in plain rustic capitals with occasional letters in lower case. They are in red ink with no infill and are not immediately distinguishable from the rubrics: they almost are rubrics. The headings are also very much part of the text blocks; there is no considered placing: they fall as required, and there is no particular spacing around them. Most significantly, there are no *vespertinum* monograms; only the rubrication serves to draw the reader to the beginning of each office.

Even the colour-scheme is insipid, and the yellows, bluey-greens, orange, greeny-blue and light brown all lack impact. Towards the end of the manuscript the colours dim to a duller yellow and a darker blue. There is very occasional infill in the rubric, for example *SABBATO* (fol. 20), and in two headings *DOMINICA IN LXMA ad vesperum* (fol. 133v, FIG. 29) and *In Purificatione Sancte Marie*. Perhaps these titles needed to be highlighted in this way because they did not even begin a new line.

The initials are drawn mainly in red outline (FIG. 29) – occasionally in black outline (fol. 7v, FIG. 30)– and several of them are filled with one or two colours in the 'Mozarabic' manner. The colours used are yellow, orange and blue, but the juxtapositions are not as

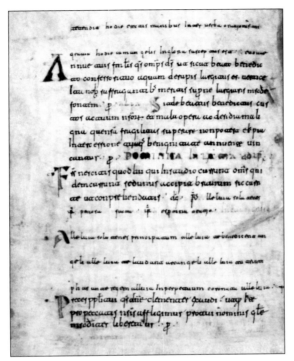

FIG. 29 London, British Library, Add. MS 30847, fol. 133v

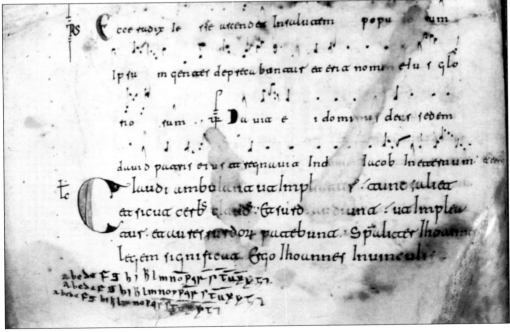

FIG. 30 London, British Library, Add. MS 30847, fol. 7v

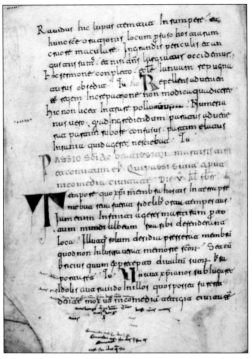

FIG. 31 London, British Library,
Add. MS 30847, fol. 170v

FIG. 32 London, British Library,
Add. MS 30847, fol. 120v

strong as in the Mozarabic manuscripts and so the impact is not so great. Most of the initials which begin the readings, responses, and hymns have two-colour infill, whereas those which introduce the antiphons and verses seem to vary between one-colour infill and no infill at all.

The inconsistent nature of this manuscript, shown in the orthography and the letter-forms of the script, is further demonstrated by its initials. For example there are two forms of the letter 'T': that familiar from the Mozarabic manuscripts, a fluid curving letter where the cross-bar rises and then dips to the left (fol. 170v, FIG. 31), and a new type with severe angles, its top a straight line weighted by a downward pointing triangle at each end (fol. 120v, FIG. 32). There are also two forms of the letter 'A': one fluid uncial type and the other straight, both seen on fol. 133v (FIG. 29); on fol. 5v there is also a lower-case initial 'A' with nodule decoration and a foliate scroll for a bowl. Likewise there are two forms of the letter 'V', uncial on fol. 126v and straight on fol. 10. The letter 'E' appears most often in its uncial form, but there is also a straight version (fol. 109v) in red outline. In other cases only the Visigothic forms are used. These include a small version of the long 'I' with restrained penwork and only occasionally showing faint red lines indicating compartments (fol. 62, fol. 80v); one of the most elaborate is that on fol. 118v which has stepped compartmentalisation. Another on fol. 113v (PLATE 4) has the spiral motif in turquoise, yellow and red. The other Visigothic uncial letter forms are a plain vegetal letter 'h' (fol. 75)

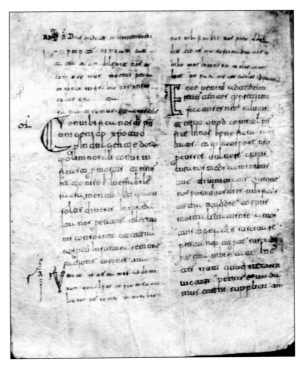

FIG. 33 London, British Library,
Add. MS 30846, fol. 52v

and an 'm' (fol. 154v); there are very few straight forms of these letters in Add. 30847 (fol. 25v and fol. 107v respectively). Taken together, it is possible that the discrepancy in style is due to two scribes working on the initials, one in the 'Mozarabic' tradition and the other using 'new' patterns, possibly a little uncertainly.

In spite of the survival of Visigothic initial forms in this manuscript, there are few matches with our Mozarabic manuscripts. The penwork on several of the initials is like that used in Add. 30844, and similar compartments and nodules are used, but the initials are not identical in form on any occasion. There are also similarities with the initials in Add. 30846; for example the letter 'C' on fol. 52v of Add. 30846 (FIG. 33) has some structural parallels with that on fol. 7v (FIG. 30) in Add. 30847. The terminals of the letters are, however, quite different, which is typical of the kind of variations between these manuscripts. We could say that the theme is the same, but the individual expressions differ. Another parallel is between the straight letter 'E' in Add. 30847 (fol. 109v) and the 'E' initial in the interpolated section of Add. 30845 (fol. 89, FIG. 4).

The lack of decoration in Add. 30847 may be symptomatic of a desire or even of an instruction to suppress or tone down any identifiably 'Mozarabic' ornament. The initials may still be based on Visigothic letters, but, as the manuscript is written in this script, it was presumably permissible to use these. There is, however, no sign of an attempt to incorporate conspicuously 'Romanesque' decoration in Add. 30847. Alternatively the paucity of ornament may be due largely to the speed with which it had to be produced. In any case, there is a striking contrast with the Mozarabic manuscripts – especially Add. 30846 – in which rudimentary decoration, even of a crude type, was preferred to no decoration. The lack of decoration in Add. 30847 may thus indicate a stylistic phase where the 'Mozarabic' was no longer acceptable, but the techniques required to execute the 'Romanesque' had not been mastered.

If Add. 30848 is, in textual and palaeographic terms, the next manuscript in the putative sequence, its scheme of decoration is surprising. The mixing of letter-forms continues to the extent that two forms of the letter 'A' can be seen only lines apart on fol. 6v where one begins *Ad I* and the other *Ad III*. More letters are found in the straight version in this manuscript: there is an 'M' with a flat top and vertical shafts, and a 'G' also formed from straight lines. There are again no monograms. Thus far it follows the pattern of Add. 30847. In contrast, Add. 30848 has a very tight and quite elaborate decorative structure. This is immediately apparent on the title-page and confirmed by headings throughout the text.

The title of the manuscript, *In nomine Domini / incipit brebi / arium de toto circulo / anni / incipit officium / de Adventu Domini*, takes up more than half of one of the columns on fol. 3 (PLATE 5). It is divided into six lines as shown by the obliques above. The first line is abbreviated in the usual way and its abbreviation marks are made into a decorative device such that they form a 'bar' across the top of the title, broken at intervals by irregular blobs from the top of which small 'T' shapes project slightly above the bar. Below this, the lines of text are enclosed in rectangles which curve in at the ends. The total effect is a little like banners suspended from a horizontal pole. This effect is heightened by the alternation of colours: blocks with a ground colour of light brown for the top line, blue for the second, red for the third. The short fourth line is not part of the pattern, which resumes in the fifth line repeating dark blue, and then light brown for the sixth. The letters are reversed out over the ground, dark blue against light brown, light brown against dark blue, and dark blue against red. All the letters were originally drawn in red outline and this is still faintly visible and gives definition to the shapes. Some of the letters extend outside the frame. All the backgrounds are textured with calligraphic decoration: lines and commas, dashes, or step-like patterns. The end of line one is decorated with a series of very small circles.

Aside from the banner design itself, we have met all these principles in the Mozarabic manuscripts, the alternating colours in a multi-line heading, the frame and the detailed calligraphic features. The total effect from the assembling of all these parts is, however, very different from any of the manuscripts we have examined. Guilmain includes some examples of 'banner' headings in his survey. The León Bible (AD 960), for example, has the same shaped blocks and similar disposition of letters, but they are set into a very large initial and do not hang from above.[35] The Beatus manuscript now in the Museo de la Catedral in Gerona (MS 7, fol. 20v) has the same device of a bar across the top linked to the enlarged abbreviation marks, but the title is laid out as if on a whole canvas, not on separate banners, and also attached to a large initial.[36] This manuscript is thought to have been produced in southern León, possibly at Tábara in 975.

Although many of the components of this title-page would be familiar, and even *courant*, to those experiencing the change in the liturgy at the end of the eleventh century, the banner design itself may have looked especially antique. As far as we know, no such headings seem to have been used at Silos in the recent past. Although on one level everyone would have known that this manuscript was not old, the method of decoration may have been intended to give it a sense of the traditional, to endow it with some of the authority which the past had always supplied for the kingdoms of northern Spain. I do not think that the tradition of 'Mozarabic' art as revivalist – or more properly regenerative – undermines this argument. It rather reinforces it, for where manuscripts have customarily been copied in an old-fashioned style reminiscent of their models – and the Silos Beatus is itself an important example – to apply what looks like the same treatment to a new text becomes a major statement. It is a way of creating the impression of a tradition even where one did not exist, a way of altering the past to serve the needs of the present.

Most of the headings in Add. 30848 are plainer than that on the title-page. They are nevertheless all easily distinguishable from the text, well-spaced and written in the same majuscule Visigothic script and usually contained in the banner-like frames. The distribution of headings forms a very distinct hierarchy which emphasises Easter and its associated festivals, and to a lesser extent Christmas. Prominence is also given to the Assumption of the Virgin, and to the first Sunday after Trinity, a feast which did not even appear in the Mozarabic manuscripts. This feature, whereby certain texts are promoted over others, is in marked contrast to the use of headings in the Mozarabic manuscripts.

Some of the headings are only in red ink on one line, as on fol. 13v (*feria iiii in quatuor tempora*), or on two lines (*officium in Apparitionis Domini* – fol. 38v (Fig. 6) and *officium in Ascensionis Domini* – fol. 153v). Some have line-and-circle decoration at the right-hand end of the frame (fol. 38v. Fig. 6). Several alternate red and blue on one line: St Lucy (fol. 224v), St Andrew (fol. 218v), *dominica in Quinquagesima* (fol. 92), and *dominica in Quadragesima* (fol. 95v). Others, apparently a further stage up the hierarchy, alternate colours over two lines (*officium in Sanctorum Apostolorum Filippi et Iacobi et de aliis Sanctis, officium de Sancto Iohanne Baptista* and *officium Sancti Petri*). *Officium de Sancta Trinitate* belongs to this category, but also has the circle-and-line decoration.

The most elaborate banner headings are reserved for major feasts. *Vespera Natalis Domini* (fol. 24, Fig. 34), *officium in Ramis Palmarum* (fol. 112v) and *officium in Assumtione Sancte Marie* (fol. 179v) all fall into the first category of these, as they receive a banner heading and matching initials on one folio. The Palm Sunday heading has yellow letters on a blue background on line one, and blue letters on a yellow ground on the second line. The letters are fairly plain but include a vegetal letter 'O', and a geometrical 'A' with one section marked out towards the bottom of the right-hand shaft with a round nodule at the point where the triangle, which forms the bottom of the left-hand shaft, meets the single line linking it to the other shaft. The *Ad vesperum* title is written out on a separate line underneath and initials in blue and yellow accompany it. A similar heading introduces the *officium in Assumtione*: the first 'banner' occupying two lines with a yellowy-brown background and blue letters, while

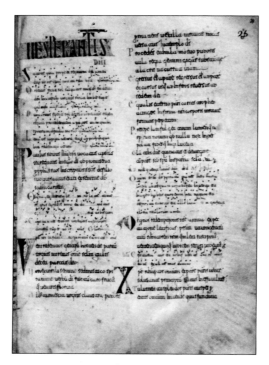

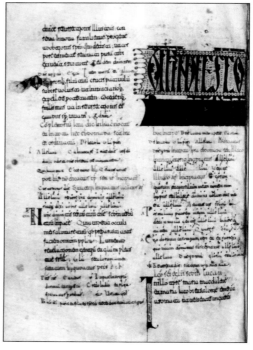

FIG. 34 London, British Library,
Add. MS 30848, fol. 24

FIG. 35 London, British Library,
Add. MS 30848, fol. 123v

the second occupies only one line, but is more dramatic with a blue-green ground and red letters. Here sympathetic initials in blue and yellowy-brown with touches of red are found only on the same folio (fol. 179v). It is of particular interest that a Marian feast should be singled out for this higher level of decoration, as it supports the view that further development of the cult of the Virgin was one of the characteristics of the liturgical change.

The full banner heading and double-page spread, where the initials on the same page as the heading are illuminated in related colours and those on the facing page likewise, is reserved for Easter, Pentecost and for the first Sunday after Trinity. *Officium Pasche* on fol. 123v (FIG. 35) has one large 'banner' (with cords and suspension rings at the left) of five and a half lines in yellow with blue letters followed by a three-line band in blue with brick-red letters. As on fol. 3 the backgrounds are given depth by the use of dashes both horizontal and vertical, waves, and rows of squares with dots in the middle. The letters are vegetal and geometric. The left-hand edge of one of the frames is again decorated with lines finishing in circles, and the end itself is zigzagged. The initials on fol. 123v are in yellow and blue, while on the facing page (fol. 124) there is a pair of initials in yellow and blue and another in red and blue. The feast of Pentecost (fol. 158) receives similar treatment, the first line having a light brown ground and blue letters, the second reversing this. The decorative devices used here are similar to those on fol. 123v. Initials in brown and blue appear on this and the facing page (fol. 157v). Fol. 229v (FIG. 36) has a banner heading for *Dominica prima*

FIG. 36 London, British Library,
Add. MS 30848, fol. 229v

FIG. 37 London, British Library,
Add. MS 30848, fol. 230

post Sancta Trinitate, in yellow letters on a blue ground and initials drawn in red outline and filled with the same yellow and blue on the same folio and on the facing page (FIG. 37). The emphasis given to this feast is somewhat surprising, but may highlight the long section of Sundays after Trinity which did not appear in this form in Mozarabic manuscripts.

The style of this manuscript is not drawn from several 'Mozarabic' traditions, like the Mozarabic manuscripts in this study, but is instead homogeneous. Several stylistic details link the decoration of Add. 30848 to that in the Silos Beatus, not least the use of alternating red and blue in the headings,[37] and the line-and-circle motif which decorates some of them. Small sections of the banner-type blocks – the mainstay of Add. 30848's decorative scheme – are also used for PAX, LUX, LEX, REX in the Cross of Oviedo miniature in the Silos Beatus (fol. 277). Boylan has attributed this miniature to Munnius, a priest at Silos, who according to one of the colophons wrote much of the text of the Silos Beatus (fol. 277v). There are also clear parallels in some of the geometric initials, which include compartments and some small vegetal features.[38] For example both Add. 30848 and the Silos Beatus have ball decoration at narrow points on some geometric letters, a continental ornamentation which does not appear in any of the Mozarabic manuscripts nor in Add. 30847.[39] More specifically there are three initials towards the end of the Silos Beatus (a 'P' on fol. 264v, and an 'I' and a 'Q' on fol. 274v) (FIG. 38) which are very close to examples in Add. 30848 (fol. 24, FIG. 34 and fol. 230, FIG. 37). Apart from the step motif, ball decoration, eyed

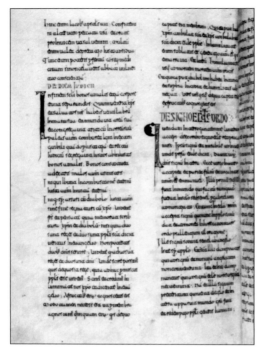

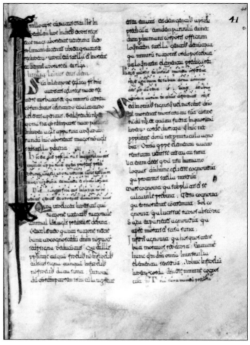

FIG. 38 London, British Library,
Add. MS 11695, fol. 274v

FIG. 39 London, British Library,
Add. MS 30848, fol. 40

panels and vegetal scrolls, the most telling feature is the use of colour. These initials, in both manuscripts, are executed in black outline and filled with dull metallic blue and dull yellow blocks.[40] Boylan also thought that Munnius was probably responsible for some of the initials in Add. 30847, and the close textual relationship between these two manuscripts which we established in chapter 2 helps to confirm this suggestion.

It is likely, therefore, that Munnius worked on Add. 30847, Add. 30848 and the Silos Beatus. His contribution to Add. 30847 seems to have been limited to a few initials. His work on the Silos Beatus, however, was apparently much more substantial, although primarily as a scribe rather than an illuminator. He may have been totally responsible for Add. 30848. The connections between the Silos Beatus and Add. 30848 – shown not only by their illumination but also by the use of part of Beatus's text in Add. 30848 – may tell us something about the Silos Beatus, as well as helping us to localise and date Add. 30848. If some of the ideas and imagery contained in Beatus were harnessed in support of the new liturgy (*see* chapter 2), this may have enabled Spanish scribes and illuminators to justify the production of a lavish manuscript of such a significant Spanish text. If the Silos Beatus is placed within the context of the liturgical change, this might also explain why the Beatus received only non-figurative decoration during its first campaign (completed in 1091), and was left largely without illumination until the second campaign of 1109, when the major full-page miniatures of the Beatus tradition were executed.

Most of the initials in Add. 30848 are plain and similar in conception to those in Add. 30847. They also share some distinctive features such as the use of an 'L' initial drawn on its side (fol. 31 in Add. 30847 and fol. 245v in Add. 30848). There are, however, more examples of full-blown 'Mozarabic' initials in Add. 30848; these are mainly examples of the long 'I', for example a ten-line shaft with three-line penwork on fol. 97, and another letter 'I' on fol. 40 (FIG. 39), which takes up nearly the whole length of the folio beyond the written space. This letter is one of the few to receive interlace decoration; it has simple yellow and black interlace, like a greek-key pattern, along the shaft, and more complex interlace at the top and bottom.

Add. 30848 is a manuscript of great importance for this study. It was decorated in an identifiably 'Mozarabic' style, but not one in recent use. This style was not only 'antique', but it was deployed in ways which were not 'Mozarabic'. All these decorative devices were familiar in manuscripts of the tenth century, but they were always accompanied by zoomorphic or figurative features. In Add. 30848 the figurative and zoomorphic elements were excluded. The Mozarabic manuscripts had received roughly even decoration through-out, but certain texts in Add. 30848 are privileged over others by receiving conspicuously more ornament. This manuscript is a paradox, and the reaction it evoked from its readers is a matter for considerable speculation.

The last manuscript in this proposed sequence, Add. 30849, looks immediately different, as it is written in Caroline/Protogothic script. Beyond this, however, it shares many decorative features with the other two Roman codices. Like Add. 30847 it is restrained in terms of ornament; it is even more dense in layout. There are no monograms, and the headings are restricted in the main to one-line majuscules in red (FIG. 43). The grandest is the two-line heading for *In Vigilia Nativitatis Domini* (fol. 27v, PLATE 6). This uses the same technique as Add. 30848 in presenting a display page where the infill colours of the heading are reflected in the initials on the rest of the folio. Like Add. 30848, part of this manuscript (fols 1–64) employs 'Mozarabic' decorative techniques – although, as in Add. 30848, never the figurative or zoomorphic motifs. The decoration of the headings and initials in this section is mark-edly different from that in the rest of the manuscript, as it is the only part to employ infill technique.[41] The infill technique here, however, is less precisely applied than that used in the Mozarabic manuscripts. The outline is in black or red and two infill colours are usually used, a pinky red, a dark sky blue or a pale yellow, but the colour is not applied to fill the whole space inside the letter and it is as if it has been applied roughly with a brush (FIG. 40). The colours and the contrasts used are nevertheless reminiscent of the washed-out shades in Add. 30847.

Some of the initial forms also recall those of Add. 30847 and Add. 30848. In particular the letter 'T' on fol. 71v has a cross-bar formed from two triangles, as does that on fol. 120v of Add. 30847, and the letter 'P' on fol. 18 of Add. 30849 has step motif in the shaft, as does the letter 'P' which so clearly links Add. 30848 with the Silos Beatus. As with the comparison between Add. 30847 and Add. 30848, it is possible to identify several common components and shapes, penwork, collars, nodules and curved sections, which Add. 30849

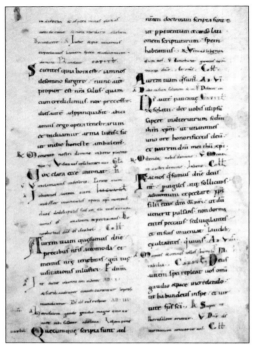

FIG. 40 London, British Library,
Add. MS 30849, fol. 14v

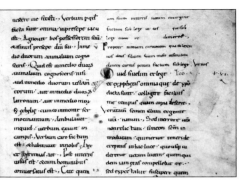

FIG. 41 London, British Library,
Add. MS 30849, fol. 17

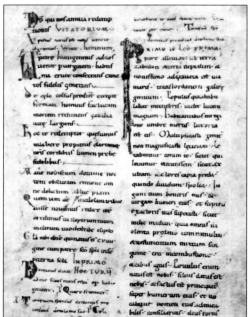

FIG. 42 London, British Library,
Add. MS 30849, fol. 28

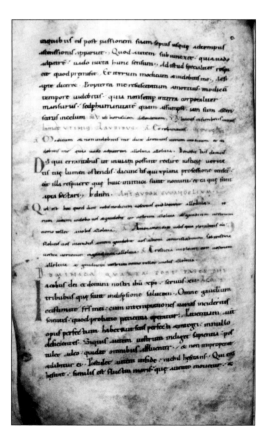

FIG. 43 London, British Library,
Add. MS 30849, fol. 160v

shares with them – there is even a textured trumpet flower (fol. 17, Fig. 41) which is reminiscent of those in the Silos Beatus (fol. 8). As in Add. 30847, most of the initials are small, one-, two- or three-line capital letters, and they are used to introduce the *capitula*, hymns, readings and homilies. In spite of this it is not possible to point to any two *identical* letter forms found in both Add. 30849 and one of the other manuscripts. Nevertheless the similarities make it likely that Add. 30849 is related to the other two Roman manuscripts.

Up to fol. 64, Add. 30849 has some 'Mozarabic' initials, which have more in common with those in some of the Mozarabic manuscripts than with the initials in Add. 30848. This is partly due to the roughness of their execution, as these initials are crudely drawn in outline, often in black ink. On fol. 9 there is a long 'I' – although it is still short in 'Mozarabic' terms – which is decorated with the step motif and penwork technique familiar from the Mozarabic manuscripts. On fol. 28 (Fig. 42) there is a letter 'P' with a long shaft which seems to have been freely drawn with curls at the top and bottom and compartments and pendants in the 'Mozarabic' fashion. The 'Q' on fol. 13v has comma 'hair' around it, as if the artist is familiar with the 'Mozarabic' habit of making such letters into heads. There are several other initials in this section with 'Mozarabic' motifs such as scalloping, zig-zag decoration and foliate pendants. These look very like some of the unidentified attributes associated with the figures in Add. 30845, where they also appear as pendants or cross-bars in initials. It is perhaps these strange pendants which link the decoration of this manuscript most closely with the 'Mozarabic' tradition, as the other elements are not really sufficiently specific.[42]

The other initials in Add. 30849 are mainly solid red letters, sometimes decorated with balls on the stem or with single-line penwork flourishes (fols 160v–161, Fig. 43). Some of these red initials have in addition foliate decoration (for example fol. 74v and fol. 100), varying from the plain to the fantastical, which seem to fuse 'Mozarabic' and continental forms. One of the most elaborate examples is a letter 'H' (fol. 102, Fig. 44). The letter itself is formed of two uprights, the left slightly higher than the right, and a cross-bar, potentially very simple, but ornamented in a quite fanciful way with numerous excrescences: there is penwork on the left, not unlike that often used on a 'Mozarabic' letter 'I', and the cross-bar has an arch in the centre. Foliate or even floral growths extend from the top of the left shaft and the bottom of the right, while a more 'Mozarabic' piece of vegetation hangs from the cross-bar. The letter is drawn in brown/black outline and has red infill. The 'Mozarabic' features have been seen in Add. 30845, but one of the closest parallels for the other aspects comes from the *Codex Calixtinus* (Santiago de Compostela, Archivo de la Catedral, no shelf number, siglum C). The origin of this manuscript, France or Spain, is the subject of scholarly debate, as parallels have been suggested on both side of the Pyrenees, and Add. 30849 may be one more argument on the Spanish side.[43] The parallel letter 'H' in the *Codex Calixtinus* is on fol. 18; although it lacks the 'Mozarabic' elements, having instead more flowing penwork outlines and nothing below the cross-bar, it is in other aspects very similar.

Add. 30849 presents us with a conundrum. On the one hand it is strikingly different from the other manuscripts in its use of Protogothic script and it seems to have more familiarity

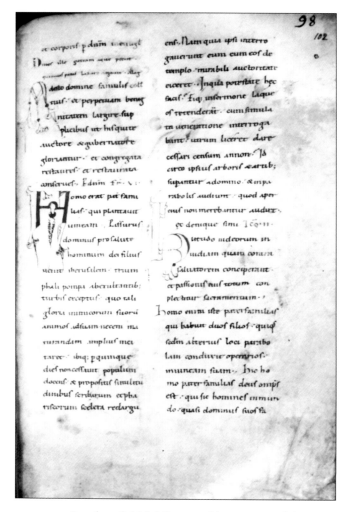

FIG. 44 London, British Library, Add. MS 30849, fol. 102

generally with continental initial styles. On the other hand this manuscript retains many 'Mozarabic' elements, many more than Add. 30847. These 'Mozarabic' features are not the spectacular ones used in the 'banner' titles of Add. 30848, but they contain suggestions of the exotic southern 'Mozarabic' style used in Add. 30845. Again, however, all figurative and zoomorphic elements are missing; only the decorative details remain. It is as if the scribes were instructed to avoid using explicit 'Mozarabic' decoration with the traditional associations of its figurative and zoomorphic styles, but allowed to use the old decorative motifs which were less easily categorized. Given the calligraphic nature of 'Mozarabic' decoration, it seems highly unlikely that the scribes of this manuscript – or indeed those of Add. 30847 and Add. 30848 – would have been unable to produce rudimentary zoomorphic and figurative illumination. We can only speculate as to the reasons for the prevalence of the abstract. The scribes could have made the decision because they felt that the more explicit 'Mozarabic' decorative style was inappropriate for the new liturgy, or because they were directed not to use it. They may, on the other hand, have been trying to come as close as possible to the models they were given, while still re-interpreting them to some extent in their own terms. To the modern viewer these manuscripts do not advertise their Roman nature, and it is interesting to note that they were even mis-catalogued originally in the British Museum as Mozarabic manuscripts. In semiological terms, therefore, they are muted.

As a result of the palaeographical and textual analysis in the first two chapters of this part I have proposed a chronological sequence for these manuscripts. This happens to be in accordance with the numbers assigned to them in the catalogue of the British Library, although there is no indication that such a chronological sequence was proposed by Thompson. There is nothing in the decoration of these manuscripts which directly contradicts this sequence or opens it to further question. Yet the textual and structural development which has been shown to have taken place in the course of these manuscripts is not paralleled in any simple way by the changes in the methods and styles of decoration. There is no linear development from 'Mozarabic' to 'Romanesque' style in these manuscripts. Instead the interaction of the text and its presentation is quite complex.

The various ways in which the Roman texts are illuminated seems to express the different attempts of those who produced liturgical manuscripts to try come to terms with the new liturgy. Add. 30847 represents a fairly early stage in the transition when the reader was led through the text by clear guidelines with the minimum of distraction. 'Mozarabic' decoration is almost entirely absent, whether through choice or compulsion. This phase would accord with Kitzinger's comments on the visual expression of Gregorian Reform,[44] that during the process of change there were unlikely to be direct 'visual manifestos', any iconographic expression would be expected to be oblique. There is very little in the decoration of this manuscript which could be described as 'new'; its hallmark is merely paucity of ornament.

Add. 30848 exhibits another approach to assimilating the liturgical change, probably later, after the first protestations had died away. In its use of 'Mozarabic' designs which had fallen into disuse it is specifically archaising. In a culture which produced forged documents with considerable frequency,[45] it would have been a minor fiction to illuminate a manuscript as if it came of a long 'Mozarabic' lineage. In any event the decorative scheme of Add. 30848 subsumes the Roman liturgy into a Castilian vocabulary and thereby expresses acceptance, whether or not the new liturgy had been fully accepted in practice.

In contrast Add. 30849 is essentially a Roman manuscript in content and style. It does, however, retain a significant number of 'Mozarabic' vestiges. All the initials are geometric or foliate, but some have 'Mozarabic' decorative motifs whereas others use only a continental vocabulary; others add 'Mozarabic' components to the continental letter-forms. The style does not constitute a real synthesis, but may instead show the last efforts to retain some elements of the 'Mozarabic' tradition. Thus Add. 30849 may show a further stage in the

reception of the Roman liturgy, the last phase before the Roman liturgy completely sup-
planted the Mozarabic. This manuscript probably dates from the second quarter of the
twelfth century. By that time any scribe who had been working at the time of the liturgical
change would be very old. This could explain the uncertainty of much of the execution.
This could, however, also be the work of a younger scribe, untrained in these techniques
but exhibiting the traditional regenerative tendencies.

In any event 'Romanesque' styles of illumination were totally dominant in northern
Spain by the middle of the twelfth century. We have no major codices definitely produced
at Silos during the twelfth century, although the missal which will be considered in part II
is one possible example, probably from the middle of the century. The scriptorium at Silos,
built up, I suggest, by Santo Domingo, was certainly still active in the early twelfth century,
when the Silos Beatus was produced, but this spectacular book was still illuminated primarily in the 'Mozarabic' manner – albeit with fine 'Romanesque' elements.[46] It seems likely
that the Silos scriptorium went into relative decline after the change in the liturgy had taken
firm hold and 'Mozarabic' techniques died out. Deprived of this tradition the scriptorium
probably took many years to revitalise, and it never again produced work of the quality of
the Beatus.

Notes to Chapter Three

1   Brou, L., 'Un antiphonaire mozarabe de Silos d'après les fragments du British Museum', in *Hispania Sacra*, vol.5, 1952, pp.341–66.

2   Arbeiter, A., and Noack-Haley, S., 'The Kingdom of Asturias', in *The Art of Medieval Spain A.D.500–1200*, New York, 1993, pp.113–19, and the catalogue entry pp.147–8. The end of the inscription on the back of the cross: HOC SIGNO TUETUR PIUS/HOC SIGNO VINCITUR INIMICUS, alluding to the Vision of Constantine, became the motto of the Asturian kingdom. Whether this association of the cross and victory can be pursued to the extent that this cross can also be called the symbol of the reconquista is still a matter for debate. The case was most strongly put by Menéndez Pidal, R., 'El Lábaro Primitivo de la Reconquista – Cruces Asturianas y Cruces Visigodos', in *Boletín de la Real Academia de la Historia*, 136, pp.275–96.

3   Williams, *as above* Intro. note 49, p.19. For the text, *ordo quando rex cum exercitu ad prelium egreditur, see* Férotin, *as above* note 53, col. 149–53. This is an elaborate ceremony for a warrior king, who is attended by deacons carrying incense and other clergy dressed in white, while the reliquary cross is carried before him. The king prostrates himself in prayer and is embraced by the bishop before departing for battle. Other Visigothic customs – most likely based on Byzantine models – such as the giving of votive crowns, seem to have persisted – or been revived – in the reign of Fernando I. Fernando and Sancha included three votive crowns in their dedication gifts to the church of San Isidoro, as well as two regalia crowns, *see* Williams, J.W., 'León and the Beginnings of the Spanish Romanesque', in *The Art of Medieval Spain* AD *500–1200*, New York, 1993 , p.168. The text (of Carolingian origin) which often accompanies the manuscript miniatures of the Cross of Oviedo consists of the separate words: PAX LUX LEX REX, in itself a juxtaposition of spiritual and royal concepts. *See also* Cid, C., 'Relaciones artisticas entre Santo Domingo de Silos y Oviedo. Las cruces del Beato' in El románico en Silos*: IX centenario de la consagración de la iglesia y claustro, 1088–1988* (Studia Silensia, Series Maior, I) Burgos: Abadía de Silos, 1990, pp.511–25.

4   Brou, *as above* note 1, p.14, n.27.

5   Werckmeister, O.K., *as above* Intro. note 6, p.122–4.

6   Leroquais, *as above* Ch. 2 note 48.

7   In this chapter any reference to the Mozarabic liturgy will appear without quotation marks, but any reference to a putative 'Mozarabic' style of decoration will appear with them.

8   Williams, J.W., *Early Spanish Manuscript Illumination*, New York, 1977, p.15.

9   Werckmeister, *as above* Intro. note 6, pp.127–8.

10 The rubric is '*ex inventione ecclesie sancti Micaelis arcangeli Domini nostri Ihesu Christi in Gargano rupe, in die III kalendas octubres*'. A similar technique can be seen in the Silos Beatus (London, BL Add. MS 11695, fol. 173 and fol. 177).

11 The folio divisions (according to the two- or one-column format) are as follows:
    Section A fol. 1–7, 13, 25–56, 74–87,
    Section B fol. 8–12, 14–24, 57–73 and 88–172.

12 Williams, J.W., 'Tours and Early Medieval Art', in *Florilegium in Honorem Carl Nordenfalk Octogenarium Contextum,* Stockholm, 1987, p.199. Williams suggests that so-called 'kufic' borders may be linked to a Touronian type of border formed by pennons and half discs rather than to Islamic writing, as had previously been thought.

13 Guilmain, J., 'On the chronological development and classification of decorated initials in Latin manuscripts of tenth-century Spain', in *Bulletin of the John Rylands University Library of Manchester*, vol.63, Spring 1981, Pl.I.

14 In this I doubt Reynolds, who translates *docalibus* as halters and believes that they relate to the military tents in the Codex of Albelda. I believe that the more straightforward 't' for 'c' (i.e. *dotalibus*) substitution makes a more plausible explanation. Reynolds, R.E., 'Rites and Signs of Conciliar Decisions in the Early Middle Ages', in *Settimane di Studio del Centro Italiano di Studi sull'alto medioevo* (*Segni e Riti Nella Chiesa*

Altomedievale Occidentale – 1985), Spoleto, 1987, pp.207–44.

15   Férotin does not transcribe these figures as *vespertinum m*onograms. The antiphons which they introduce are however *vespertina* and are marked more clearly as such in other parts of the same manuscript or in other Mozarabic liturgical books given in Férotin, *as above* Intro. note 20.

16   Díaz y Díaz, M. C., *as above* Ch. 1, note 3, p.403.

17   Mentré, M., *La peinture mozarabe*, Paris, 1984, Pl. 21, Fig. e and c.

18   *See* for example illustrations of the *Codex Vigilianus* (fol. 209v – a king, and fol. 331 – a bishop and Antiphonarium of León (fol. 241 – an abbot) in Sánchez Albornoz, C., *Los Estampos de la vida en León durante el siglo X*, Madrid, 1926, p.66, p.75 and p.149 respectively.

19   Williams, *as above* Intro. note 49, p.20.

20   Guilmain, *as above* note 13, Plate I, II and III.

21   These are illustrated in Mentré, *as above* note 17, p.70, and Guilmain, *as above* note 13, Plate I, Fig. 16. An initial from Add. MS 30845 is illustrated in Mentré, M., *El Estilo Mozarabe, La pintura cristiana hispánica entorno al año 1000*, Madrid, 1994, p.66, Fig. 9.

22   *See* part II, p.177.

23   For comparisons *see* Guilmain, *as above* note 13, Plate I, Fig. 21 (Burgos, Archivo Capitular, Expos. Vitr. *Bible*, fol. 33 – from Cardeña, tenth century), Plate I, Fig. 28 (Madrid, Real Academia de la Historia, cod.24, fol. 91v – from San Millán, 917); and Mentré, *as above* note 17, pp.100–2, Plate 4, (Paris, BN, MS N.a.l. 2180, fol. 193, fol. 217v and comparison with León Bible of 920.

24   Boylan, *as above* Ch. 1 note 7, Plate I.

25   Guilmain, *as above* note 13, Plate II, Fig. 6 (Manchester, John Rylands University Library, Lat. MS 89, fol. 397v – Cardeña or Valeránica, *c.*949) and Fig. 7 León Bible (Real Colegiata de San Isidoro, cod. 2, fol. 76v, – Valeránica, 960)

26   Williams, *as above* note 8, Plate 3.

27   It is likely that the same artist did some of the small initials nearby and the small figure on fol. 70.

28   Guilmain, *as above* note 13, Plate IV, Fig. 6 (El Escorial, Real Bibl. del Monasterio, cod. dI.1, fol. 226v, 976–94)

29   Guilmain, *as above* note 13, p.394, p.399, p.400.

30   Williams, *as above* note 8, p.106, Pl.34.

31   Díaz y Díaz, *as above* Ch. 1 note 3, p.404, Add. 30846: 'A juzgar par los oficios conservados, el manuscrito, o su modelo, debio originarse en una zona de notables confluencias, ya que presenta en el contenido influjos leoneses, como el oficio de san Pelayo, junto a otros de innegable origen meridional, o de Valle del Ebro.'

32   Boylan, *as above* Ch. 1 note 7, p.239, p.242, and p.244 respectively.

33   Vivancos Gómez, *as above* Intro. note 8, pp.13–14, no. 11 and pp.18–19, no. 16.

34   It should be noted that Santo Domingo did not found the abbey at Silos, as is suggested by Barbara Drake Boehm, catalogue entry in *The Art of Medieval Spain*, *as above* Intro. note 14, p.277; rather he was invited to restore the abbey. *See above* Ch. 2 note 36.

35   Guilmain, *as above* note 13, Plate II, Fig. 7 (Real Colegiata de San Isidoro cod.2, fol. 76v). A similar arrangement can be found in the Facundus Beatus (Madrid, B.N., MS Vit. 14–2,fol. 30) attached to the first initial of the preface; for an illustration *see* Williams, *as above* Ch. 2 note 77, p.18.

36   Guilmain, *as above* note 13, Plate III, Fig. 1.

37   For example the heading on fol. 131v in Add. 11695.

38   These parallels have also been noted by Boylan, *as above* Ch. 1 note 7, pp.124–6 and p.246; her examples are: Add. 30848, fol. 24 'X' with Add. 11695, fol. 274v 'I'; Add. 30848, fol. 124 'D' with Add. 11695, fol. 274v 'Q'; and Add. 30848, fol. 124 'P' with Add. 11695, fol. 275 'P'. Williams has identified a body of work in the Silos Beatus as that of Munnius: this includes the Cross page, the *de affinitatibus* table, the

Acrostic page (fol. 276, incorporating the text:*Munnius presbiter titulabit hoc)*; and the frames of the colophons. This is quoted by Boylan in advance of the publication of vol.3 of Williams, J., *The Illustrated Beatus: A Corpus of the Illustrations in the Commentary on the Apocalypse*, catalogue entry no. 16.

39   This was common in French manuscripts at this time, and can be seen, for example, in the Moissac lectionary (London, BL, MS Harley 2914).

40   These are the same colours which we found in Add. 30846.

41   Some rubric headings in the earlier part of the manuscript have a line drawn through them, similar to that usually used for an erasure, but these headings seem correct. Moreover the line is in blue or yellow, not red which is the more usual colour for corrections, and is the colour employed for corrections later in the manuscript. This technique is not in the 'Mozarabic' repertoire, nor is it familiar from French manuscripts; the only two parallels of which I am aware are i) a breviary from Vercelli (MS 124), which seems to employ the same technique in highlighting *In illo tempore. See* Suñol, *as above* Intro. note 115, p.192, plate 34; ii) a Commentary of St Augustine on St Paul (Vatican MS lat. 5730, fol. 185v) illustrated in Lemairié, *as above* Ch. 2 note 41, Pl.VII.

42   For example there are freely drawn initials with some decorative similarities in an early twelfth-century breviary and missal from Corbie (Paris, BN., MS lat.11522), illustrated in Gy, *see above* Ch. 2 note 14, Fig. 62 (fol. 2v).

43   Díaz y Díaz, M. C., *El códice Calixtino de la Catedral de Santiago*, Santiago de Compostela, 1988, and Stones, A., 'The Decoration and Illumination of the *Codex Calixtinus* at Santiago de Compostela', in Williams, J. and Stones, A., *The Codex Calixtinus and the Shrine of St. James*, Tübingen, 1992, p.138.

44   *See* Kitzinger, *as above* Intro. note 23.

45   *See Fälschungen im Mittelalter,* teil 1 and 2, Hannover, 1988.

46   The illumination of the Silos Beatus was completed in 1109 by Petrus, who describes himself in his colophon as *domnus Petrus prior*. He does not seem to have begun work on it until the abbacy of Nunnus (*c*.1100–*c*.1106), and he was probably invited to finish the codex by the abbot to whom he was related (*consanguineus*). Thus there was apparently a gap of at least nine years between the completion of the text and some preliminary illumination in 1091 by Munnius and Dominicus, and the beginning of Petrus's large-scale illumination.

PART TWO

THE MASS
The Centre of the Matter

CHAPTER FOUR

Select Survivals
From Mixed Book to Missal

HE EUCHARIST is the focal point of all Christian liturgies, the element prescribed in the gospels by Christ himself. Its position in reform movements has been central. When Charlemagne put together a collection of books necessary for the correct performance of the liturgy, particular effort was expended on the sacramentary, the book which contained the texts for the mass. He sent to Pope Hadrian in Rome requesting a true Roman sacramentary, and received a manuscript from the Pope's personal collection, the *Hadrianum*. Unfortunately this book was intended for the personal use of the Pope and lacked mass texts for ordinary Sundays as well as votive masses.[1] The inadequacies were made good by a supplement to this manuscript, which was probably written by Benedict of Aniane, the great promoter of the Benedictine Rule in the Carolingian empire. Benedict was careful to distinguish his work from the core supplied by the Pope, which was 'obviously the work of the blessed Pope Gregory', and he provided his contribution with a preface giving its purpose and origin.[2] During the tenth century this 'Gregorian' text – which had always existed in more than one form – became mixed again with the Gelasian sacramentary (the sacramentary used by the Franks up to the reign of Charlemagne). It was this combined version which was later taken to Rome and became acknowledged as the authentic *Roman* mass book.[3] The Mozarabic mass texts went through none of these vicissitudes. After the main period of liturgical composition in the sixth and seventh centuries, these texts seem to have remained largely unaltered except for the regional variations which developed.[4]

The Choice of Manuscripts

The purpose of this section is to examine the processes by which the Roman mass texts replaced the Mozarabic. This will be approached through original manuscripts, as in the case of the *officia* texts. Three of the British Library manuscripts already examined will be used again – Add. 30844, Add. 30845, Add. 30846 – as they contain *missae* as well as *officia* in accordance with the usual Mozarabic practice outlined in the previous section. There is no evidence for the existence of a separate book offering texts for the mass in northern Spain before the introduction of the 'Roman' liturgy.[5] These three manuscripts will be used as examples of the presentation of Mozarabic texts for the mass.

It would be ideal for this study if there were also three surviving missals of the Roman liturgy produced at Silos in the late eleventh or early twelfth centuries for purposes of a similar comparison to that undertaken in part I. Unfortunately this is not the case. There is indeed no missal fitting this description in the British Library collection beyond the one folio at the beginning of Add. 30849 which will be considered. The Bibliothèque Nationale in Paris, the Biblioteca Nacional and the library of the Real Academia de la Historia in Madrid and the library at Silos all lack suitable books. One possible example, however, is at present in the library of the University of Salamanca, MS 2637.[6] This manuscript has been connected with Silos by Janini and it is dated by him to the twelfth century.[7] The clearest evidence for the Silos connection is the inclusion of a mass for Santo Domingo, the canonised abbot and titular saint of the abbey at Silos. The codex is not explicitly identified in the eighteenth-century Silos catalogue of Hernández, but there is a possible location for it at no. 79 'dos missales monasticos antiguos'. Yet the identification cannot be made with confidence, as there are no signs of Hernández's work in the manuscript itself. It does not have a list of contents like the other manuscripts from the Silos corpus in the British Library, and the arabic numerals used in the modern foliation do not match those found in the British Library manuscripts. Further evidence for or against the link between this manuscript and Silos will be offered in the course of this study, but, for the moment, the presence of the mass for Santo Domingo is sufficient to place this manuscript at the very least in the region of Silos, and, therefore, to justify its place in this study of manuscripts produced in the kingdom of Alfonso VI.[8] Sal. 2637 has probably always remained in Spain: it was recorded as Cajón 34 at the Colegio de San Bartolome in Salamanca, then as MS 294 at the Biblioteca Palacio Real in Madrid, before coming to the University of Salamanca. Nothing further is known of its provenance.

There are no other surviving missals of an appropriate date with any evidence to connect them to the abbey of Silos. Indeed there are very few surviving missals which originated in northern Spain at the end of the eleventh century or during the twelfth. There appear to be only two further manuscripts which can be dated with some degree of confidence to the relevant period and which also have clear links with a Leonese, Castilian or Riojan monastery.[9] These missals have both been dated to the late eleventh century,[10] and, conveniently for us, both come from monastic centres with significant roles in the introduction of the Roman liturgy. One is the famous Missal of San Facundo, now in the Biblioteca Nacional in Madrid (MS Vitr. 20–8).[11] It is tied by its contents to the royal monastery of Sahagún in that it includes two masses for SS. Facundus and Primitivus, the patron saints of that abbey. The other manuscript has been identified as originating in the monastery of San Millán de Cogolla, and it contains three masses for that titular saint. It is now in the collection of the Real Academia de la Historia in Madrid, Aemilianensis 18.[12] Like the Missal of San Facundo this manuscript has been dated to the end of the eleventh century.[13]

Apart from their appropriate dates and clear origins these manuscripts are also fitted for the present purpose by the political circumstances of the monasteries in which they seem to have been produced. The monastery at Sahagún with its royal connections was, as described in the introduction, at the centre of events at the time of the change in the liturgy. From

1081 it had as its abbot Bernard of Sauvetet, who oversaw the successful implementation of the change at Sahagún and possibly – at least by example – throughout León and Castile. In 1086 Bernard was appointed to the archbishopric of Toledo and on the last folios (fols 134v–135v) of Vitr. 20–8 is written out a copy of a letter to Bernard from Hugh of Cluny, full of advice and guidance on the occasion of his appointment. Although in a different hand from the rest of the manuscript, the script is of a similar date, and the letter provides further evidence for the dating of the manuscript, placing it beyond reasonable doubt in the first years of the liturgical change, specifically to 1081–86. It also suggests a personal link between the missal and Bernard.[14] It seems likely that this manuscript was produced and used initially in 'the Cluny of Spain', where abbot Bernard had successfully introduced the Roman liturgy. As the rest of the manuscript's known history places it in Toledo it seems likely that Bernard took it with him, and it seems to have been kept in the library at the Catedral de Toledo (cod. 35.14) until it passed to the Biblioteca Nacional in Madrid. If we are looking for a possible example of 'good practice', an approved text and method of presentation, we could hardly expect to find a better example than a missal connected with Bernard himself. Such a book would be likely – at least in theory – to have followed any directions which might have been given to him or might have been given by him to others.

The other manuscript, Aem. 18, from the abbey of St Millán de la Cogolla, is described on its cover (dated 12 July 1578) as a possession of that monastery presented to the Bishop of Ciudad Rodrigo, from where it seems to have reached the library of the Real Academia de la Historia. It is the scriptorium of San Millán which is believed to have produced the manuscripts which contain the two texts defending the use of the Mozarabic liturgy described in detail in the introduction. These texts do not enable us to conclude necessarily that San Millán was a stronghold of the Mozarabic liturgy, since they may not be representative and their survival may have been merely a matter of chance, but they are evidence that argued resistance did exist at San Millán. The texts in favour of the Mozarabic liturgy were inserted in a manuscript which contained that liturgy; it is much less likely that signs of resistance will be found in a Roman missal, which is by its very production a sign of capitulation. Nevertheless the text and presentation of this manuscript will be considered, bearing in mind that it was produced in what had been and may still have been an atmosphere of intransigence. In a different way, therefore, Aem. 18 is an intriguing test case for the purposes of this study.

Part II will, therefore, consider in detail six manuscripts, and one isolated folio, all of which contain texts for *missae*. It is likely that four of them originated in or near to the abbey of Silos, while two can be confidently attributed to other known scriptoria. I will again begin with a codicological and palaeographical comparison on the same basis as that conducted in part I.

A Codicological Analysis

The manuscripts of the Mozarabic liturgy under consideration here, it will be recalled, all contain a similar number of folios, but the size of the folios varies greatly (*see* Table 5). The

Roman missals, however, vary greatly in the number of their folios. Vitr. 20–8 is plainly the slimmest volume, Sal. 2637 has over one hundred more folios, and Aem. 18 exceeds Sal. 2637 by almost as many again. This diversity is not counter-balanced by differing folio sizes, as in both Sal. 2637 and Aem. 18 the folios are of a similar size (in height and width), whereas Vitr. 20–8 has the smallest folios as well as the fewest. From its size it is easy to understand how Vitr. 20–8 has been thought to have been a personal missal.[15] The discrepancy between Sal. 2637 and Aem. 18 does not have such a ready explanation, as the function of these two manuscripts is broadly the same. The folio from Add. 30849 is different again in folio size from the other three Roman manuscripts; it is closest to the Mozarabic manuscript Add. 30846.

The table below gives the comparisons:

TABLE 5

The Dimensions of the *Missa* Manuscripts

MS	FOLIO SIZE	APPROX. WRITTEN SPACE	NO. OF FOLIOS	NO. OF LINES	NO. OF COLUMNS
Manuscripts containing the Mozarabic Liturgy					
Add.30844	400 x 320mm	280 x 190mm	177	22–24	2
Add.30845	363 x 254mm	295 x 190mm	161	27, but last quire 30	2
Add.30846	285 x 221mm	220 x 160mm	175	section A: 21–22 section B: 21–24	section A:2 section B:1
Manuscripts containing the Roman Liturgy					
Add.30849	275 x 218mm	210 x 160mm	1	27	2
Vitr.20–8	210 x 110mm	140 x 70mm	136	21	1
Aem.18	375 x 245mm	265 x 170mm	15+350	31	2
Sal.2637	345 x 235mm	265 x 190mm	267	32	2

Aem. 18 has one set of ruled double lines at the sides and three lines in the middle, all reaching to the top of the folio, and pricking is visible in the outer margins. Sal. 2637 is also written in two columns, but there is no visible pricking on the folios, suggesting that it may have been removed by trimming. The ruling is by hard point, with one set of double lines reaching to the top of the folio between the two written columns and another set on the outside of each column. By comparison Vitr. 20–8 is written in one narrow column, with very wide margins. Pricking is visible and ruling is by hard point. The appearance of this manuscript is radically different from Sal. 2637, and indeed from any of the other manuscripts in this study. This is partly due to the treatment of space which is used extravagantly between the lines as well as in the generous margins. The consideration here was not how to fit as much text as possible onto expensive parchment, but rather conspicuous disregard for such parsimony.

The fragment from Add. 30849 (folio 1, FIG. 45) is written in two columns, and retains a

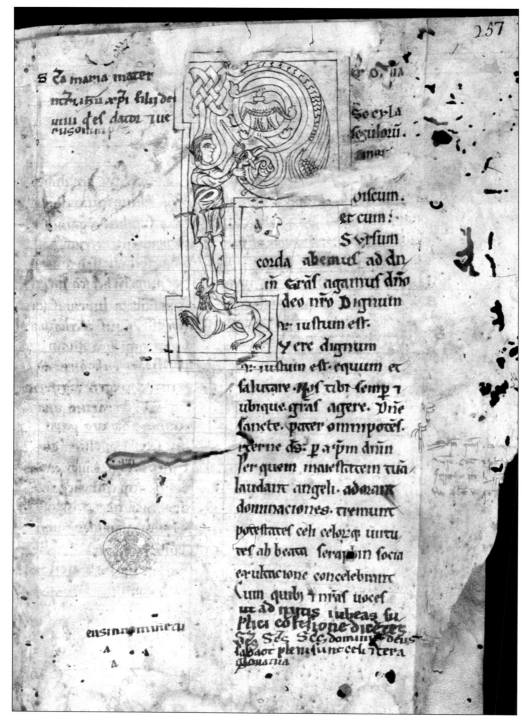

FIG. 45 London, British Library, Add. MS 30849, fol. 1

wide right-hand margin, which renders it 18mm wider than the other folios in the volume. It has been numbered at the top right-hand corner in arabic numerals, at a later date, with the figure 257. The ruling is in very pale ink and is slightly off-centre on the recto, resulting in a narrower column on the right-hand side of the page. The left-hand column is blank, except for some words added by a different scribe in ill-formed script. On the recto there are four vertical rules in the centre of the page, not evenly spaced, as the distance between the two on the right-hand side is smaller, possibly to align with the decorated initial. On the verso there are three vertical rules in the centre of the page. No ruling is visible in the outer margins on the verso or recto, but pricking can be seen in the outer margin, consisting of small slashes which could have been made with the point of a knife rather than the circular points made by an awl.

When this information is put alongside that concerning the manuscripts of the Mozarabic liturgy, Add. 30844, Add. 30845, Add. 30846, no standard practices can be identified. Vitr. 20–8 stands alone, because it is written throughout in one column and so requires simple ruling. The missal from San Millán is also distinguished by the constant use of three central vertical lines, although a similar pattern can be seen on the verso of fol. 1 of Add. 30849. The ruling on the recto of Add. 30849, despite its lack of precision, has, however, more in common with the manuscripts of the Mozarabic liturgy, and the pricking technique used on this folio is the same as that used in section A of Add. 30846 and in the rest of Add. 30849. Sal. 2637 is closer to the Mozarabic manuscripts than to Vitr. 20–8 or Aem. 18, in that it uses two central lines rather than the three used in Aem. 18, but given the general lack of consistency in ruling and pricking practices no reliable conclusions can be drawn.

Aem. 18 is the only one of the Roman manuscripts under consideration here to have been written in Visigothic script, and this is one of the features which have been used to date it to the end of the eleventh century (Fig. 53). Although some Spanish manuscripts were still written in this script in the early twelfth century until *c.* 1125, it gradually gave way to Caroline conventions, and lost its dominant position shortly after 1110.[16] The *terminus post quem* for this manuscript is 1090 when the body of San Felices was moved to the monastery, since the feast of his translation (6 November) is included in the calendar. The usual letter-forms and abbreviations of the Visigothic script are present and there is very little indication of the late date of this manuscript beyond a tendency towards lateral compression and a formal *ductus*, both redolent of Add. 30848. There is, however, a heaviness in the script of Aem. 18 not seen in that manuscript, possibly due to the thickness of the pen-nib used in Aem. 18. In comparison with the Roman breviaries written in Visigothic script (*see* part I), this manuscript is noticeably lacking in the superscript abbreviations which had infiltrated the script during the eleventh century. Although we cannot be sure that the continued use of Visigothic script carried a strong semiotic meaning, because it may have been merely the persistence of a familiar form, it is likely that the introduction of a new script would have had a forceful impact. It is, therefore, of note that Aem.18 is the only missal in this study still written in Visigothic script and that it comes from a monastery with a likely history of conservative attitudes and serious opposition to the change in the rite.

All the other manuscripts of the Roman liturgy are written in a form of Protogothic script. The folio from Add. 30849 has the least accomplished form of this script, being written stiltedly with rather large letter-forms (FIG. 45). In particular it may be useful to note the typically Protogothic flat top of the 't', tall 's', hooked second stroke of the 'h', and pronounced serifs on 'h', 'b'. The letter 'd' appears with and without a serif, and there is a tironian *'et'* as well as a complex knotted ampersand. The more unusual features include several angular forms, the bowls of 'o', 'c', and 'a', the harsh slope of the return stroke of 'g', and the tag at the base of the letter 'v'. There is also a row of letter 'a's written by an even less practised scribe, who also seems to have copied out one section of the text on the recto, which was written by the first scribe on the verso. All these points indicate that this may have been a blank folio subsequently used as a practice sheet.

In contrast the script of Vitr. 20–8 is so accomplished that it has been maintained that it was written by a French, not a Spanish, scribe (FIG. 55).[17] Distinguishing features of the script include the 'st' ligature; the dot placed inside the 'y'; restrained serifs; a knotted ampersand; a backward curve for the tail of the 'g'; and a long left stroke in the 'x'. The abbreviations used are the standard ones associated with this script, the bar, tagged 'e', ˅ for -ur, and, ' for -us. Above all it is a clear, regular, well-formed script with an upright *ductus* consistent with the date of the manuscript, which has comparisons in French manuscripts of the end of the eleventh century. In the light of a study of the Sahagún scriptorium at the end of the eleventh and beginning of the twelfth century it seems indeed unlikely that this script could have been written by a locally-trained scribe. No documents in Caroline script are known from Sahagún before the twelfth century, and the Caroline script does not prevail in documents until as late as 1125.[18]

The script of Sal. 2637 places it, by comparison, in the twelfth century,[19] probably in the second third: the passages which are to be spoken are written in a well-formed Protogothic script with a flowing *ductus*, and the chants in a smaller version of the same. Its distinctive features include the use of tironian *'et'* alongside an unusually tall ampersand, the frequent omission of the dot from lower-case 'i', a 'ii' ending where the second 'i' is taller and the dots are formed by two fine strokes; there is extensive use of superscript abbreviations and the bar abbreviation has become light and flowing. When the script of this manuscript is compared to that used in most of Add. 30849, the twelfth-century breviary described in the previous chapter, it is seen to be a much more developed and confident Protogothic script, employing a much more diverse range of abbreviations. It is closer to the script of the additional folios (except folio 1) in Add. 30849.

When we look at the punctuation used in these manuscripts, it is immediately apparent that many of the differences are linked to the broader distinctions between the Visigothic and Protogothic scripts. All the manuscripts use the *punctus* and *punctus elevatus*, but Aem. 18 is the only one of the manuscripts containing the Roman liturgy to retain the *paragraphus*, found so frequently in the Mozarabic manuscripts.

A comparison between the liturgical abbreviations used in the Mozarabic manuscripts and those in the Roman breviaries offered several helpful insights, and a similar examination of the different usages between the Mozarabic manuscripts and the Roman missals may be equally informative. The results are shown below in Table 6.

TABLE 6
Liturgical Abbreviations Used in the Mass Texts

BL Add.	30844	30845	30846	Vitr. 20–8	Aem. 18	Sal. 2637
Ad missam		ad misse	AD MISSA	Ad millam	AD MISSA	
Ad orationem dominicam	AD ORO DNICA	oī ꝺ̅ꝺ̅nica	AD oī. D̅ꝺ̅ICA			
Ad pacem	Ad Pace	ap Pc̄m	A PACE ad Pc̄m			
Ad prolegendum	AD PP̄L̄m̄					
Benedictio		ꞴN̄O	ꞴN̄O ꞴN̄O Ꞵ Benedict Ꞵ̃		ꞴN̄O	Ꞵ
Clamor	cl̄m		cL̄m̄		c⁺⁺	
Collecta						
In fractione				IN FRacᴛ̃	IN FR̄C	IN FRACTIONE
Inlatio	INLATIO	IꞱᴇ̄ ꞱꞱᴀꞱIꝈ ꞱꞱᴀꞤᴏ ꞱꞱᴀᴛᴏ				
Lectio	Lō Īc̄o	Īc̄o Lecc·ꝺo Īc̄o lec c·ꝺo	ᴌ	Īc Līc	Īc̄o Līc̄o Īc
Missa	c̄m̄	MISSꞱ	MISSA	MISSA	m̄	
Oratio	oī oī	o̊ʀ̊	oī	o̊R	oᴜ	o̊Ro oī
Post communionem				post co̅m̄m	P'c̄m Pc̄o	P'c̄m
Post nomina	Pˢ N̄MN̄a	pˢ n̄m̄a	Pˢᵀ N̄MN̄A			
Post pridie	P PRIDIE	pˢ ppɪꝺ́ɪᴛ	P͛ᴛ Pridie			
Post sanctus	P̄ scs	pˢ.ꞩꞔ̄Ʇ	Pꞥ̊ ꞩꞔꞩ Ꞥ̊ꞩꞔꞩ			
Praefatio				PrᴇFaᴛ̃	PR̄F PꝔꞔ̄ PRꝔCO	p̄facıo
Psallendum	Psᴌ̄m̄	Psᴛ̄m̄	Pꞩ Ꞥ̊̄ PꞩꞱꝰꞺ			
Sacra					scꝚ scꝚA	saꞔ̄ sꞔ̄
Secreta				secꝚ̄		
Sanctus	scs	scs	scs			
Sevovae					Sevovʋe	Sevovae
Super oblata			sup obᴛ			
Super populum			sup popᴛm	SUPER PPᴛM	sup pplm̄	
Vere dignum			⊕	Ꝙ ⊕	⊕	

If this table is compared with Table 3, which showed the liturgical abbreviations used in the office texts, one of the most striking differences is the extent of change in the liturgical vocabulary. The Roman mass texts use very few of the same titles as the Mozarabic texts, and therefore the comparison is often between the Mozarabic examples on the one hand and a complete absence of the terminology in the Roman manuscripts on the other. Similarly there are new titles in the Roman books which did not appear in the Mozarabic texts. In the few cases where the words are shared: *benedictio, lectio,* and *missa,* Aem. 18 – the only one of the Roman missals written in Visigothic script – is usually also the only one of the Roman books to use Visigothic abbreviations. Vitr. 20–8, written in fine Protogothic script, uses only Caroline abbreviations. Sal. 2637 retains one or two abbreviations which might be categorized as Visigothic, in particular the common Mozarabic composite abbreviation *sevovae* (an abstraction from *seculorum Amen,* in which extended form it appears in the Mozarabic manuscripts in this study) which is also found in Aem. 18 but not in Vitr. 20–8.

Where the terminology was not previously in use in the Mozarabic liturgy – for example *prefatio* – Aem. 18 still abbreviates in what might be called a Visigothic manner, or uses a fully extended form. In these cases Sal. 2637, on the other hand, tends to use Caroline forms. There are also differences in vocabulary, and therefore in abbreviations, between the Roman missals. Vitr. 20–8 is alone in avoiding the abbreviation for *officium* as an introduction for the masses, and in using the abbreviation of *secreta* rather than that of *sacra.* In general – but not exclusively – the form of the abbreviations seems to have been determined by the character of the script rather than by the liturgy to which the vocabulary belonged.

The spelling used in the manuscripts of the Mozarabic liturgy was examined in part I and was found to be generally consistent; this was in contrast to the various forms found in the Roman breviaries especially in Add. 30847 and to some extent in Add. 30848. Contrary to this finding, however, the spelling in the missals is, in the main, consistent. The variations which do occur seem to concentrate on the choice of 't' or 'c'. The folio from Add. 30849 exhibits a marked preference for 'c' over 't' as in *exultacione, milicia* and *circumadstancium.* Aem. 18 uses 't' in these words, whereas Vitr. 20–8 has *exultacione,* but *circumadstantium.* Nevertheless, within each manuscript there is a fair degree of consistency, and we do not meet the striking number of variant spellings for proper names which were found, for example, in Add. 30847. The overall impression is one of close copying of the model or adherence to a standard.

As was shown in chapter 2, the 'Mozarabic' books did not contain *officia* for the whole liturgical year; instead the offices for the year were contained in several *sui generis* volumes. What applied to the *officia* necessarily applies equally to the *missae* in these 'mixed books', for the two texts were written one after the other. The mass text for each feast and Sunday included in the manuscript appears after the text for vespers and matins, or any other office given. Thus the *missae* included in the Mozarabic books reflect the overall conception of these books, as outlined in part I.

Of the manuscripts containing the Roman liturgy, the Missal of San Facundo (Vitr. 20–8) is the most complete. It nevertheless lacks any *page de garde* or title-page and begins directly with the preface and canon of the mass, before giving the texts for the temporal and then the sanctoral cycle. These are followed by several common and votive masses. The letter to Bernard ends the volume, and it may have been added to previously blank folios; it now ends in mid-sentence (*confidimus in misericordia dei quoniam*), and there is no colophon.[20]

The single folio bound into the front of Add. 30849 (FIG. 45) also contains the text for the preface and the beginning of the canon of the mass. It clearly does not belong with the rest of Add. 30849, as this folio is of a different size from the other folios and has been folded to enable it to fit within the cover. The isolated folio can give us very few clues as to the full contents of the manuscript to which it once belonged. The page number, 257, clearly does not refer to the folio's present position at the front of the codex, but indicates that it came from the back of another book. It could have once belonged to a missal which contained the preface and canon at the end of the manuscript, as Janini has suggested may have been the case with Sal. 2637.[21] Arguments against this are that the preface and canon did not often come at the end of a missal and, more importantly, that this folio is in a totally unfinished state. It lacks the *Te igitur* to begin the text in the second column on the verso, which now begins with *clementissime pater*, and, more significantly, the text does not continue beyond the end of this prayer, leaving the rest of the column blank.[22]

It may be that this sheet was originally one of the blank folios often left at the end of a codex, which were sometimes subsequently used for scribal notes or even as practice sheets. This folio has certainly received several scribbled additions, including on the recto, top left-hand corner *'sancta maria mater nostra ihesu christi filii dei vivi qui es dator* (*sic*) *et verus omnipotens'*, and at the base of the same column has been written at an angle *'Deus in nomine tu'* with two separate angular letter 'a's. At the base of the right-hand column the text is continued below the original ruled line with an illiterate copy of the formula *'ut admitis* (*sic*).. *et tera* (*sic*) *gloria tua'*, which is also found in the correct form on the verso. It is also possible that the number '257' indicates that it was bound in as a single leaf at the back of a volume before being moved to the front of Add. 30849.

Sal. 2637 retains a title-page stating accurately that *Incipit liber missarum per anni circulum dicendarum*. The mass texts are again separated into those for the temporal followed by the sanctoral, after which the common and votive masses are added. The manuscript ends with a selection of tropes. The sung items in this book receive particular attention throughout, and the addition of the tropes serves to emphasise this. The final folios are missing, and Janini has speculated that the last of them may have contained the canon.[23]

Aem. 18 is a more complex codex. At the beginning some folios (fols 1–5v) from other manuscripts are bound in, including fragments of a Mozarabic calendar and a martyrology. Folios 6–11v contain a full calendar,[24] and the next folio seems originally to have been blank, but was used for later liturgical additions of the mid- to late twelfth century.[25] The missal itself now begins on fol. 13 with vesting prayers; any title-page is unfortunately missing. After these prayers come the preface and canon of the mass, then mass texts for the temporal and sanctoral cycles, a large number of votive masses, and finally more late-twelfth-century additions including a mass for St Thomas of Canterbury. Thus this manuscript is substantially complete in its liturgical contents, but there are no formal closing pages. This manuscript has one unusual textual feature with Mozarabic associations, and the same phenomenon is found to a much lesser degree in Sal. 2637. At the end of the texts for several of the masses it gives a short prayer *ad vesperos*. This could be a limited survival of the Mozarabic *missae et officia* format (*see* part I, p.69), although in no instance is the full office given. However, the surviving ancient sacramentaries also include occasional prayers for the office.[26] It is therefore more likely, in my view, that this feature derived directly from the manuscripts used as models for Aem. 18 and Sal. 2637.

Any discussion of the presentation of the texts for the mass in this period must also take into account the general development from the sacramentary to the plenary missal which was taking place within the Roman church during the eleventh and early twelfth centuries. The sacramentary was defined by its user, for it contained all the texts said by the celebrant for the mass, the sacraments, the liturgical hours, and for the dedication of churches, weddings and other such events. For that reason it did not have readings, chants or detailed directions for the mass ceremony.[27] The plenary missal, however, included all the sung parts of the mass, the readings, and the masses which had previously been included in the pontifical, but not the prayers for the liturgical hours, which were transferred to small separate books such as the *benedictionale* or *collectarium*. It was the conflation of the sacramentary, the lectionary (epistles and gospels) and the antiphonary. Liturgical books ceased to resemble orchestral parts in which each participant had only his contribution, and became instead, like a conductor's score, an over-view of the whole ceremony, and the role of the priest-celebrant became likewise dominant.[28]

The outline of the contents of the manuscripts under examination here shows the nature of each book. The missal of San Facundo is an old-style *sacramentarium*, a book for the celebrant, containing texts for the prayers which he is to read, but no chants or pericopes. The only exception in this manuscript is the inclusion of *lectiones* for Holy Saturday, two of which have musical notation, probably because these would have been read and sung by the celebrant. Sal. 2637 and Aem. 18, on the other hand, are plenary missals including not only the texts to be read by the celebrant, but also the accompanying chants and readings.

Near the beginning of Sal. 2637 there is an antiphon which declares the supposed origin of the book: *Gregorius presul meritis et nomine dignus unde genus ducit summum conscendit honorem renovavit monumenta patrum priorum tunc composuit hunc libellum musice artis scole cantorum.*[29] This sentence was originally part of the prologue of an antiphonary, not a missal, specifically the Roman antiphonary in the form in which it was copied from the time of Charlemagne. The truth of the claim was doubted even in the ninth century, but it continued to be used.[30] It does not act as a strong claim here as it is not even the first antiphon given, but its presence suggests that this manuscript is – or is a copy of – an amalgamation of a Roman antiphonary with other mass texts. The contribution of the antiphonary remains extremely important throughout the book, and may even explain why this book begins directly with Advent.[31] Thus this manuscript shows some of the processes of the fusions which produced the plenary missal.

The differences among the three Roman manuscripts under consideration are, however, dwarfed by the much greater differences to be seen when any of them is compared with any of the Mozarabic manuscripts. The variations among the Roman manuscripts are largely a matter of how much is to be included, depending upon the use for which the book is intended. The profound difference between the Mozarabic and Roman books is more conceptual. It is the result of a move towards a book dedicated to the mass, as opposed to the office, and structured accordingly. As we shall see, this had an immense effect on the presentation of the text.

Notes to Chapter Four

1   McKitterick, *as above* Intro. note 30, pp.130–8.

2   Vogel, *as above* Intro. note 44, p.87, Bernard's preface, *Hucusque.*

3   Vogel, *as above* Intro. note 44, pp.102–4.

4   Férotin, *as above* Intro. note 20, pp.XIV–XVI.

5   Férotin, *as above* Intro. note 20, col. 690–91. The Toledan manuscript which forms the basis of Férotin's edition is a true sacramentary and does not contain *officia*. As Férotin said, it is unique.

6   For the sake of convenience this manuscript will be described as Sal. 2637 during the rest of this study.

7   Janini, *as above* Intro. note 116, pp.236–9, no. 284.

8   By 1073 Alfonso's kingdom covered León, Castile and Galicia, and from 1077 the Rioja area of Navarre.

9   There is a missal from San Isidoro at León, dated by Janini to the last quarter of the twelfth century (*see above* Intro. note 116, p.132, no. 152); this manuscript, however, concentrates on votive masses, which, together with its likely late date, made it unsuitable for this study.

10 For Aem. 18 *see* Janini, *as above* Intro. note 116, pp.150–3, no. 171. For MS Vitr. 20–8 *see* Janini, J. and Serrano, J., *Manuscritos litúrgicos de la Biblioteca Nacional*, Madrid, 1969, pp.248–51, no. 199. For Vitr. 20–8 *see also* John Williams's catalogue entry in *The Art of Medieval Spain*, *as above* Intro. note 14, pp.294–5.

11 The designation of this manuscript during the rest of this study will be Vitr. 20–8.

12 The designation of this manuscript during the rest of this study will be Aem. 18.

13 Janini, *as above* Intro. note 116, p.150.

14 For the full text, as it survives in Vitr.20–8 *see* Férotin. M, 'Une lettre inédite de saint Hugues, abbé de Cluny, à Bernard d'Agen, archevêque de Tolède (1087)', in *Bibliothèque de l'école des chartes*, 61, 1900, pp.339–45; Férotin published later the probable missing end of the letter 'Complément de la lettre de saint Hugues, abbé de Cluny, à Bernard d'Agen, archevêque de Tolède', in *Bibliothèque de l'école des chartes*, lxiii, 1902, pp.682–6.

15 For example, Reynolds, R. E., 'The Ordination Rite in Medieval Spain: Hispanic, Roman, and Hybrid', in Reilly, B.F. (ed.), *Santiago, Saint-Denis and Saint Peter, The Reception of the Roman Liturgy in León-Castile in 1080*, New York, 1985, p.144.

16 Shailor, B.A., 'The Scriptorium of San Sahagún: A Period of Transition', in Reilly, *as above*, note 15, p.44. Shailor found that Visigothic script had died out at Sahagún by *c.*1125, but it should be noted that Shailor's evidence is based on charters not liturgical manuscripts. *See also* Millares Carlo, A., *Tratado de Paleografía Española*, vol. 1 (texto), Madrid, 1983, p.141, and Wright, *as above* Ch. 2 note 82, pp.235–6. Visigothic script survived in Toledo until the second half of the thirteenth century and was used in a charter issued by Doña Sancha, the sister of Alfonso VII in 1158. A private charter of 1155 (León: Archivo de San Isidoro, 298) has been found by Fletcher, *as above* Intro. note 112, p.115, which gives at the foot a kind of conversion table of the two scripts, which may indicate that by this time many found Visigothic script difficult to understand.

17 *See* Janini and Serrano, *as above* note 10, pp.248–9.

18 Shailor, *as above* note 16, p.44.

19 Janini, *as above* Intro. note 116, p.236.

20 For a more detailed summary of contents *see* Janini, *as above* Intro. note 116, pp.249–51.

21 Janini, *as above* Intro. note 116, p.236.

22 *Per omnia secula seculorum ... atque omnium fidelium.*

23 For a more detailed summary of contents *see* Janini, *as above* Intro. note 116, pp.236–9.

24 Janini, J., 'Dos calendarios emilianenses del siglo XI', in *Hispania Sacra* no. 15, 1962, pp.177–95.

25 Janini, *as above* Intro. note 116, p.151.

26 Salmon, *as above* Ch. 2 note 15, p.23.

27 Vogel, *as above* Intro. note 44, p.64.

28 Vogel, *as above* Intro. note 44, pp.105–6.

29 This text originally appeared as the preface to Frankish antiphonaries including the Antiphonary of Compiègne (Paris, BN, Lat. MS 17436), a manuscript connected with Charles the Bald and produced at that abbey in *c.*860/880. *See* Rankin, S., 'Carolingian Music', in McKitterick, R. (ed.), *Carolingian Culture: emulation and innovation*, Cambridge, 1994, pp.277–8.

30 *See* Bullough, D.A., *as above* Intro. note 36, pp.31–2, n.18. Agobard of Lyons said *(PL* 101, col. 1074): 'Seeing that the inscription which serves as the title of the book under discussion [the Antiphonary] proposes the name of one *Gregorius Praesul,* there are not lacking men who therefore feel that the work was composed by blessed Gregory, Pontiff of Rome and most illustrious Doctor'.

31 Vogel, *as above* Intro. note 44, p.358.

CHAPTER FIVE

━━━━━◄◦►━━━━━

The Most Sacred Text

THIS CHAPTER will analyse the contents of the missals in more detail from two angles. First to see the extent of uniformity between the Roman mass texts in view of the different origins of the manuscripts. To assist in the consideration of uniformity we can refer to one of the numerous *ordines* which have been identified in manuscripts to guide the performance of the mass. We will consider a version contemporary with the change in the liturgy, the *Micrologus*. Written by Bernhold of Constance at the end of the eleventh century, the *Micrologus* purports to be a description of correct practice in the execution of the liturgy, as recognised at that time in Germany. Bernhold often refers to *Gregorius papa septimus cum apostolicae sedi praesideret, constituit*, and therefore his treatise may been taken to exemplify one version of Gregorian Reform in action. Reference to this text will enable us to see whether our missals conform to that Gregorian practice. Then we will determine how different the Roman text is from the Mozarabic as seen in these manuscripts. The comparison with the Mozarabic liturgy will examine in particular how the change of rite affected the mass. What forms did the change take, and were the alterations imposed more or less stringently when applied to the mass than to the *officia*?

When we examined the *officia* texts in part I, we found two structural developments between the Mozarabic and Roman books. One was the transition from a volume which contained part of the liturgical year to one which contained the year in its entirety, the other involved a gradual separation of the temporal and sanctoral cycles. The Roman missals in this study show no such signs of transition: in all three of the codices the change is complete. They contain the whole liturgical year and in every case the temporal and sanctoral cycles are completely separate. This may be because these manuscripts are later than the first two Roman breviaries (Add. 30847 and Add. 30848), although this is doubtful in the case of Aem. 18 and highly unlikely for Vitr. 20–8. It is possible, then, that more importance was placed by the reformers on the presentation of mass texts, and that consequently these were given new formats in advance of the less pivotal offices.

It already seems likely that the liturgical change may have affected the mass texts in a different way from that in which it changed the offices. In spite of their likely divergence in function and date the three Roman missals seem to present a united front rather a developmental sequence. We will now examine the contents of each Roman manuscript up to the end of the temporal cycle to see if the consistency extends beyond the outer structure, and to see how the entries differ from those in the Mozarabic manuscripts.

The Temporal Cycle

The most obvious difference among the three Roman missals is in the way in which Vitr. 20–8 begins the temporal cycle. After the preface and the canon of the mass it is the text for the Christmas vigil which opens the temporal cycle in this manuscript. This was also the opening of many Romano-Gallic sacramentaries, and of the *Hadrianum* and the Gelasian sacramentary.[1] After the extraneous folios and the calendar, Aem. 18 – in its now incomplete state – begins the *Missale* in the middle of some vesting prayers. The preface and canon follow, and then the texts for individual feasts, but in this case the first day in the temporal is *Dominica I ante natalem Domini*. Sal. 2637 does not start with the preface and canon, which are missing from it altogether in its present form, but, rather, opens immediately with processional antiphons for Advent and then proceeds with *Dominica Prima in Adventu Domini*. The decision to begin with Advent rather than the Christmas vigil, evident in both these manuscripts, could be seen as a conservative statement in Spanish terms. Although none of the Mozarabic books in this study start at the beginning of the liturgical year, it was a Mozarabic custom to begin with Advent – or more precisely with the feast of *S. Acisclus* just before it – rather than with the Christmas vigil. As we have already noted, however, the Roman antiphonaries began with Advent, and so it is more likely that it was their structure which determined this decision in Aem. 18 and Sal. 2637, rather than Mozarabic retrospection.[2]

There is no precise agreement between the Roman manuscripts as to which masses (and under what titles) should be included for the Christmas period: all the Roman missals offer the V*igilia* (*de Nativitate* in Vitr. 20–8, *Natalis* in Sal. 2637 and Aem.18), but Sal. 2637 also includes the *missa de galli cantu*, and Aem. 18 has *missa de nocte*. In Vitr. 20–8 and Sal. 2637 the mass for Christmas day is straightforwardly *Missa in mane*, whereas Aem. 18 follows its mass of the night with *missa in luce*, and concludes with what became the more usual title by the thirteenth century, *missa maior*. Add. 30844, the only one of our Mozarabic liturgical manuscripts to cover the Christmas period, gives only one mass, which is headed *item ad missam*, a heading which is used for most of the masses in the book. In contrast these Roman missals use a much more symbolic vocabulary, emphasising the coming of the light out of darkness. The imagery of Advent had much in common with that used to promote ideas of religous reform and renewal, and its clear use here, especially in Aem. 18, may be significant in both contexts.

Sal. 2637 also gives a mass for *S. Anastasia* on the same day as Christmas.[3] This addition may be explained by a passage in *Micrologus*:

> *In Nativitate tamen Domini ad missam in mane, Romani orationem de sancta Anastasia adjiciunt, quia stationem in ecclesia eiusdem martyris ad eamdem missam agunt.*[4]

Thus this feature is rooted in ecclesiastical practice specific to the city of Rome: the stational mass which fell on the same day as Christmas was celebrated at the church of *S. Anastasia*. Although this custom could not be re-enacted in other locations, the association had persisted. Apart from this there are several other archaisms in these missals. For example Aem. 18 is the only one of the Roman missals to include *in pascha annotina*, which is mentioned in ch.lvi of the *Micrologus* as the name given by the Romans to the anniversary of Easter:

> *quia antiquitus apud illos, qui in priori Pascha baptizati erant, in sequenti anno eadem die ad ecclesiam convenere, suaeque regenerationis anniversarium diem cum oblationibus solemniter celebraverunt.*[5]

These two examples show Bernhold's attention to the customs of the Roman *ecclesia primitiva*, which accords well with his reformist interests. Their inclusion in our manuscripts could indicate similar concerns among their compilers, but they could equally be accidents of the copying process included without any particular intention. In either case their use shows close adherence to a guide or model. All three missals also use *sabbato in xii lectiones*, the obsolete title for the Ember Saturday of fasting, which does not have twelve readings in any of these manuscripts, and Sal. 2637 continues the use of this terminology by marking the days of fasting, *feria iv* and *feria vi* after Pentecost, as *in quatuor tempora*.[6]

Throughout the liturgical year, there is divergent terminology among the Roman missals as much as between them and the Mozarabic books. For example none of the Roman missals use the word *Apparitio*, used in Add. 30844 and generally in the Mozarabic liturgy. Vitr. 20–8 employs 'theophania' and 'epiphania'; Sal. 2637 uses only 'epiphania' and Aem. 18 uses mainly 'theophania'. The fifth Sunday in Lent is described as *in Passione Domini* in Vitr. 20–8 and in Sal. 2637 (with the variant spelling *pfassione*), but only as *Dominica v* in Aem. 18. Neither term is used in the Mozarabic books. Palm Sunday is called *Dominica in palmis* in Vitr. 20–8, but the term more familiar in Mozarabic liturgical manuscripts, *in ramis* is used in Sal. 2637 and Aem. 18.

The period from the beginning of Lent to the end of Holy Week is set apart in all the Roman missals by the use of rubrication which introduces the ceremonies for three different manifestations of renewal. During this period three separate but parallel rites of passage take place. The most fundamental is Christ's time in the wilderness, his passion and death followed by the ultimate renewal, the Resurrection. Alongside this there are two personal rites of regeneration, baptism at Easter preceded by the preparation of the catechumens during Lent, and the penitential process whereby the penitents were publicly dismissed at the beginning of Lent and welcomed back into the Church on Maundy Thursday.

The main ceremonies of the Passion and Resurrection given in all three Roman missals are the *benedictio palmarum* on Palm Sunday,[7] the *benedictio ignis* on Maundy Thursday, the *ad adorandam crucem* on Good Friday and the *benedictio cerei* on the eve before Easter Sunday. The blessing of the fire and of the paschal candle are both rich in light symbolism,[8] the former including the phrase, 'tu illuminasti omnem mundum', and the later being introduced by the 'Exsultet': '... laetetur et mater ecclesia tanti luminis adornata'. Similar ceremonies existed in the Mozarabic liturgy[9] for they are given in the *Liber Ordinum*,[10] although they do not appear in the Mozarabic manuscripts in this study. There is one exception to this, the rubric in Add. 30846 ending the mass for the catechumens,[11] but none of the Mozarabic manuscripts being examined here includes the preparation or baptism of the catechumens. Vitr. 20–8 and Aem. 18 both give only minimal rubric for these ceremonies. Sal. 2637 is the only one of the Roman missals to give detailed rubric for the Palm Sunday ceremonies (fol. 74v): *ordo in ramis palmarum ad ramos benediciendo sacerdos dicat istos orationes*, continued on fol. 77v with: *usos inter ecclesiam et claudatur ostium ecclesiae.*

Detailed rubrication is found, however, in all three manuscripts for the baptism ceremony, giving the separate prayers over the male and female catechumens, the *benedictio salis*, the major litany, the *benedictio fontis*, the three immersions and anointing with the chrism. Vitr. 20–8 uses more archaic terminology in marking the fourth *feria* after the fourth Sunday in Lent *'in scrutinii'*. This refers to the extensive scrutinies which were at one time applied to the catechumens before they could be baptised.[12] The other rubrics are clearly standard, when compared with those in Roman missals from France of a similar date, and exhibit the importance attached to the correct performance of this ceremony. The Mozarabic rite is in essence the same, but the form of the prayers and instructions differs, most noticeably in the lack of the great Litany.[13] There is also a procedural change implicit in the new ceremony, whereby only a bishop was allowed to perform the laying-on of hands and the first communion.[14] Such a requirement preventing other priests from effecting full baptism would have helped bishops considerably in keeping a firm hold on liturgical practices, necessitating regular visits.

Sal. 2637 is different from the other two earlier missals in the attention which it gives to the rites of the penitents. All the missals include the *benedictio cineris*, but Sal. 2637 gives a context to the basic prayer with the rubric *'hoc expleto prosternentur in terra clerus et populus. Tunc incipiant sacerdos cum clero vii psalmos speciales'* (fol. 30v), that is the seven penitential psalms. The psalms themselves are given in the other missals, but without the rubric which continues in Sal. 2637 after the psalms with *'Finitos psalmos dicetur letania. Post letania Dicat capitulum initium Pater noster.* On fol. 31 the instructions continue in some detail: *'his expletis sacerdos indutur vestimentis albis imponendo cynes capitibus singulorum? inchoeta'* and then *'Clero cantante antiphonas sacerdos dum cineri imposuerit singulis? dicat, clerici cantent antiphonas processionale', 'Finita processione et receptis cyneribus dicat sacerdos hanc orationem',* and *'Quo pacto induat se sacerdos et incipiantur'.* The reconciliation of the penitents on Maundy Thursday is contained in all the missals with the nine intercessory prayers including those for schismatics and heretics and other enemies of the Church.

There are, therefore, more rubrics in what seems to be the latest of the manuscripts under consideration here. It is also clear from this that there are insufficient instructions in the earlier Roman missals to enable a celebrant who was not experienced in the Roman liturgy to conduct it correctly in every detail. For example there are no instructions for the fraction, which is believed to have been very different in the Mozarabic liturgy.[15] It is possible that such instructions were supplied in other books, that is in some form of pontifical, or that they were deliberately not insisted upon at a relatively early stage in the changeover to make the adoption of the new liturgy more acceptable. The instructions which did appear all centre on the penitential and baptismal aspects of Lent and Easter, and may indicate particular emphasis placed on these ceremonies.

There are two feasts added in the temporal cycle which are notable departures from the Mozarabic liturgy. One is a mass *in commemoratione S. Marie*, which Sal. 2637 inserts before Epiphany. This may be another reflection of the growth of the Marian cult over the period of the liturgical change, which we found in part I. The other is the feast *de S. Trinitate*, which makes an appearance in Vitr. 20–8 and again in Sal. 2637, but in Aem. 18 it is found only among the votive masses and the Sunday concerned remains the octave of Pentecost. The introduction of this feast with the change in the liturgy would presumably have had deep resonances for the Mozarabic church. Ever since the disputes over the Adoptionist controversy in the eighth century, great care had been taken to express orthodoxy in statements concerning the nature of the Trinity. The inclusion of this feast would have been a continuance of that tradition.

Since it began with the Nativity, Vitr. 20–8 ends the temporal section with the Sundays of Advent, and with the feast of the Purification of the Virgin. This is marked *IIII Nonas Februari* (2 February), which is its proper place, but its inclusion at this point is exceptional and hence surprising. We would have expected the sanctoral section to abut the temporal, or to find the *dedicatio ecclesiae* here, rather than the *in Purificatione Matris*. It seems, therefore, that this mass may not have been inserted at this point because it had been omitted from the sanctoral, but specifically so as to draw attention to it. We saw in chapter 2 that this feast was also an important introduction into the Roman breviaries. It may be that the *purificatio* was seen as bringing together much of the symbolism of renewal: light in darkness with its dramatic *benedictio candelae*, the Virgin as Mother Church, and purity out of defilement.[16] It is this feast, which was not celebrated in the Mozarabic liturgy, rather than the more obvious one of Easter with its manifold symbolism of renewal, which seems to have been chosen as one of the prime vehicles for the promotion of the liturgical change.

The comparison among the Roman missals shows the extent of agreement between them to be remarkable, with only minor divergences from the common pattern, many of them only a matter of nomenclature. The Roman liturgical year stands as a strong framework to which the texts of the individual masses are grafted. The divergence between the temporal cycle of the Mozarabic and Roman liturgy is more a matter of presentation. Generally the same feasts are celebrated, but the Mozarabic manuscripts do not show the liturgical year as a unity. As we have seen they mingle the temporal with the sanctoral and produce thematic sections which give oblique views of the liturgical year.

The Sanctoral Cycle
[*See* appendix II for the Mozarabic manuscripts and appendix V for the Roman missals.]

All the Roman missals begin the sanctoral cycle with St Silvester and end it with St Thomas. This is a mark of the consistent and comprehensive nature of the Roman missals. The Mozarabic books differ from this and also considerably in the feasts included. We saw in chapter 2 that the Roman breviaries gradually marginalised the Mozarabic cults, and this comparison shows us that the missals were even more rigorous.

Vitr. 20–8 has the smallest number of sanctoral masses, and is also the least adventurous. The only 'Spanish' martyrs – except for those regularly included in the Roman liturgy – who receive a mass in this manuscript are *SS. Facundus* and *Primitivus*, the titular saints of Sahagún. Their inclusion strongly suggests that this book may have been produced for use at Sahagún before Bernard was appointed archbishop of Toledo in 1086. It is thus probably the earliest surviving manuscript connected with the liturgical change. Vitr. 20–8 also includes several masses for the martyr popes, whose feasts Gregory VII had made obligatory.[17] These include St Marcellus, St Urban, St Stephen, St Sixtus, and St Calixtus. All the feasts of St Peter and St Paul are included (*Conversio Sancti Pauli, Cathedra Sancti Petri, Vigilia Apostolorum Petri et Pauli, Natale Apostolorum Petri et Pauli, Commemoratio Sancti Pauli, Octave Apostolorum,* and *ad Sanctum Petrum ad Vinculam*). Their inclusion was presumably acceptable not only to Rome because of the attention given to the papal saint, but also to Cluny as an acknowledgement of its patron saints and thus of Bernard's continuing connection with the abbey. Two feasts are given for St Benedict, whose order had been implemented at Sahagún. The *Nativitas* and *Annunciatio*, together with the *Vigilia* and day of the Assumption, are the fairly extensive range of Marian feasts given in the sanctoral cycle. Otherwise the saints included are mainly apostles, Roman martyrs, and church fathers, with a few established and well-connected Gallic saints such as *S. Saturninus, S. Martinus,* and *S. Dionisius.* The list seems carefully chosen.

Aem. 18 extends the list hardly at all. It includes masses for the martyr popes, Sts Peter and Paul, V*igilia Sancte Marie* and three masses for the Annunciation, as well as one for the Assumption, the Purification, and a mass for St Benedict. Again no Spanish martyrs are included, and *S. Dionisius* and *S. Martinus* are among the few Gallic saints. Another Gallic saint is *S. Albinus*, whose inclusion here is somewhat surprising and may be due to some connection with the abbey at Angers where he was the patron saint. The abbey of San Millán had two patron saints and both are given masses, *S. Emilianus* on his *natale* and on its octave, and San Felices on the day of his *translatio corporis*. In addition this manuscript has a mass for Santo Domingo of Silos, which stands out because of the general absence of 'Spanish' saints. Santo Domingo may be included here because he was once a monk at San Millán, or because he was one of the 'new' saints who had helped to bring about the new order, or for a combination of reasons. The calendar which comes at the beginning of this missal has been published by Janini,[18] and it has similarities with the calendars found in the breviaries. 'Mozarabic' saints are acknowledged here, although they receive no recognition in the body of the missal. This calendar includes the feasts of *SS. Iulianus et Basilissa* (7 January), *S. Torquatus* (1 May), *S. Zoilus* (27 June), *S. Acisclus* (17 November), *SS. Facundus et Primitivus* (27 November), and even the Mozarabic feast of the Virgin on 18 December, but they are all literally on the edge of the manuscript.

Sal. 2637 has a much larger sanctoral cycle. A selection very similar to that given in the other two Roman missals is here augmented to a considerable extent by the feasts of several Gallic saints. These include *S. Richarius* (near Amiens), *S. Arnulfus* (Metz), *S. Audoenus* (Rouen), *S. Leodegarius* (Autun, Burgundy), *S. Sulpicius* (Bourges), *S. Giraldus* (Aurillac, Auvergne), *S. Austremonius* (Clermont, Auvergne), *S. Bricius* (Tours), *S. Fides* (Agen, Aquitaine), and *S. Hilarius* (Poitiers). Even the 'Mozarabic' martyrs *SS. Iulianus* and *Basilissa*, to whom Santullano – the royal church at Oviedo was dedicated – are accorded a proper collect, and therefore presumably a mass. This list has a great deal more in common with the list of offices in Add. 30848 and Add. 30849 than it does with the other missals, although it is not so generous to Spanish martyrs. Sal. 2637 is obviously a much later manuscript than the other two Roman missals and this may explain the divergence between it and them. It could be that there was some back-sliding after the initial efforts to suppress or restrict the Mozarabic cults and that gradually more Gallic saints were venerated to replace the cults of the Mozarabic saints. The Mozarabic church had had a great inclination towards diversity, and the influx of Gallic saints may have gone some way to satisfying the desire generated by this tradition. Moreover the similarity between the saints venerated in Sal. 2637 and in the Roman breviaries strengthens the argument that Sal. 2637 is a product of the Silos scriptorium.

After the sanctoral cycle all three Roman missals give a selection of common and votive masses. In the Mozarabic liturgy these are found in the *Liber Ordinum*, and they do not appear in any of the manuscripts we are examining. The Mozarabic liturgy is noted for the literary quality and number of its votive masses, nearly sixty altogether.[19] Among the Roman votive masses we will be paying particular attention to the commemorative masses, which were used on a regular basis, possibly daily or weekly, and are thus a good indicator of the importance given to their subjects.

Vitr. 20–8 includes five common masses for saints, and then the text for *in dedicatione ecclesiae*. After this there are six commemorative masses: *de Sancta Trinitate, de Sancta Cruce, de Sancta Maria, de Purificatione Matris Dei, de SS. Petro et Pauli, de Sanctis Facundo et Primitivo*, and the catch-all *de Omnis Sanctis*. This reads like a roll-call of orthodoxy, with two Marian masses, one of them another for the Purification; a mass for the Trinity; another mass for the apostles Peter and Paul, and for the titular saints of Sahagún, and a mass for all saints. This selection serves to underline our interpretation of the sanctoral cycle and highlights its most significant aspects. The other nineteen votive masses include the more usual *pro rege, pro infirmis*, and *pro defunctis*. At the end of the manuscript two ordination masses are added, *ad clericum faciendum* and *ad monacum benedicendum*.[20]

Aem. 18 is not party to this restraint. It begins this section with a mass for the anniversary of the dedication of the church and after this it has some thirty common masses, a similar number of commemorative masses and over eighty other votive masses. We will only consider the commemorative masses. They include a daily mass for the patron saint, San Felices, and similarly a long mass for *S. Emilianus* (*Pater Noster*). There are two *de Trinitate* and two for the Virgin, one of which is *in veneratione*; the same prefix is given to the masses for *S. Iohannis Baptista, S. Petrus apostolus, S. Iohannis evangelista; S. Stephanus; S. Laurentius; S. Benedictus, S. Ylarius*; and *S. Martinus*. This varied collection may be explained by the relics held by the abbey, which received two masses of their own. As in Vitr. 20–8 there is also a mass *Sancte Crucis* and for all saints, but there are also several more abstract dedications such as *de Sancta Sapientia, de gratia Spiritus Sancti*, and *de Sancta Caritate*.[21] There is also a group of masses *in memoria Incarnationis, Nativitatis, Aparitionis, Passionis, Resurrectionis, Ascensionis et Adventus Spiritus Sancti*. It is almost as if all the individuality and eccentricity previously found in the Mozarabic church had been concentrated into this massive collection, while the rest of the missal remained much more conformist.

Sal. 2637 has a more modest number of common masses, less than ten, but like Aem. 18 it has an extravagant number of votive masses, as well as several blessings and the text for a nuptial mass. Its selection of commemorative masses is, however, much more limited than Vitr. 20–8 or Aem. 18; it also gives two masses *de Trinitate*, and one each for the Holy Cross, *Sapientia*, *Karitate* and the Holy Spirit, and for the unnamed relics in the church. The only masses in this section for named saints are one for the evangelists and one for St Michael. Further on there are masses for St James, Sts Peter and Paul, *SS. Facundus et Primitivus* and St Stephen hidden among the votive masses. There is nothing for the Virgin, Santo Domingo or St Sebastian, which raises doubts about the manuscript's possible origin at Silos. If we were to follow these clues, we would be looking for a church of St Michael which has links both with Sahagún, as that abbey's patron saints are mentioned, and with Silos, as a mass for Santo Domingo is included in the body of the manuscript. This could be the nunnery of St Michael at Silos attached to the main abbey of St Sebastian and Santo Domingo.[22] Alternatively the lack of commemorative masses in this section of Sal. 2637 could indicate that by this later date all important masses had been transferred to the sanctoral section of the manuscript; only less important masses and those, like so many of the votive masses, verging on superstition, may have remained at the end.

The Structure and Text of the Mass

The formulae of the Mozarabic mass are distinct from those of the Roman liturgy in number and title, and to some extent in function. The Mozarabic mass as laid out in Add. 30844, Add. 30845 and Add. 30846 has nine formulae: *missa, alia, post nomina, ad pacem, inlatio, post sanctus, post pridie, ad orationem Dominicam* and *benedictio*. This is two more than St Isidore speaks of when he describes the seven prayers of sacrifice of the liturgy, omitting the three formulae after the *post sanctus*, but adding the *missa secreta*.[23] It is interesting, therefore, that the defender of the Mozarabic liturgy at the monastery of San Millán (*see* appendix I) also refers to seven prayers of sacrifice rather than nine.

The Mozarabic mass opens with the *missa* prayer,[24] or dismissal of the catechumens, which is followed by another prayer asking for purification and the acceptance of the gifts and prayers of the faithful.[25] These are followed by the reading of the names of the saints, the clergy and the faithful. The third prayer, *post nomina*, often refers to the names just mentioned, and asks for mercy (*veniam*) on behalf of those offering or on behalf of the dead.[26] This is followed by the *ad pacem*, which comes before the kiss of peace, and reconciles all present with the body and blood of Christ in unity.[27] The fifth prayer, *inlatio*, is the preface of the Mozarabic mass. It is preceded by the standard phrases:

> *Aures ad Dominum. RESP. Habemus ad Dominum nostrum. – Sursum corda. RESP. Habemus ad Dominum nostrum. – Deo ac Domino nostro, Patri et Filio et Spiritui Sancto, dignas laudes et gratias referamus. RESP. Equum et iustum, dignum et iustum est*

and is often very long and elaborate. Despite the theological meanderings associated with this formula, which are usually tailored to fit the feast concerned, it is in essence still the celestial panegyric, opening with a version of *'tibi gratias agere'* and concluding with the *sanctus.*[28] The sixth prayer is the *post sanctus*, which is a continuation of the *inlatio*, but is written as a separate piece in the manuscripts which we are examining, and this was found to be a general rule by Férotin.[29]

At this point the *missa secreta* should be given, but it is found in only two surviving manuscripts of the Mozarabic liturgy, as Férotin informs us. One of these is in a manuscript from Silos, the *Liber Ordinum*, and it reads as follows:

> *Dominus noster Ihesus Christus, in qua nocte tradebatur accepit panem at benedixit, et gratias egit ac fregit, deditque discipulis suis dicens: Accipite et manducate: Hoc est corpus meum, quod pro vobis tradetur. Hoc facite in meam commemora+tionem. – Similiter et calicem, postquam cenavit, dicens: Hic calix novum testa-mentum est, quod pro multis effundetur in remissione peccatorum. Et hoc facite quotienscumque biberitis, in meam commemora+tionem. Quotienscumque manducaveritis panem hunc et calicem istum biberitis, mortem Domini annuntiabitis donec veniat in clarita+te de celis. RESP.: Sic credimus, Domine Ihesu.*

It is not found in any of the Mozarabic manuscripts in this study, and its very absence indicates that it was either considered too sacred to be written or that it was the only standard part and, therefore, was so well known that it did not need to be written.[30]

The *Post Pridie* follows invoking the presence of the Holy Spirit at the sacrifice. St Isidore calls this the sixth prayer.[31] Isidore's seventh prayer is the *ad orationem dominicam*, which introduces the Lord's Prayer, and is in turn followed by a usually long embolism, remember-ing the living and the dead.[32] At the end of the mass comes the *Benedictio* – not mentioned by Isidore – which is a three-part blessing of the departing faithful. The foremass is given separately in advance of each mass in the Mozarabic books often under the heading *item ad missam*. This section includes *Ad Prolegendum* and the *lectiones* together with various sung items.

When we look at the equivalent passages in the Roman missals, it is immediately clear that the conception is quite different. Although a similar division between the foremass and the mass itself existed in the Roman liturgy, where the foremass, sometimes known rather confusingly as *officium*, was a separate preparation, the method of presenting the texts is very different in the Roman missals. They separate and highlight the preface and canon, that is to say the beginning of the mass itself, from all the other texts and give them in an isolated section. In view of the clear differentiation in the treatment of these texts by the missals we will examine them separately and first. This will not be possible in the case of Sal. 2637, which, at least in its present state, omits this central standard section.

The Preface is the celestial liturgy, based partly on the vision in the Apocalypse (Apoc. 4:2–11) of God enthroned and surrounded by the *animalia* embodiments of the four evan-gelists who without rest *'in saecula saeculorum'* say *'sanctus sanctus sanctus Dominus Deus omnipotens qui erat et qui est et qui venturus est'*, and the twenty-four elders who similarly say *'dignus es Domine et Deus noster accipere gloriam et honorem et virtutem quia tu creasti omnia et propter voluntatem tuam erant et creata sunt.'* This vision is founded in turn on that in Isaiah (Is.6:1–4) where it is the seraphim who surround the throne and cry *'sanctus sanctus sanctus Dominus exercituum plena est omnis terra gloria eius'*.

In examining the text of the preface I will begin with Vitr. 20–8, as it is probably the most authorised text. Written in capitals on folio 1 of the manuscript it is as follows:

> *Per omnia secula seculorum / Dominus vobiscum / Sursum corda / abemus* (*sic*) *ad Dominum / Gracias agamus* (*sic*) */ Domino Deo nostro / Dignum / et iustum est.*

The *Vere Dignum* continues on the verso:

> *Vere dignum [et iustum est] equum et / salutare. [n]os tibi semper et ubique gracias agere / [Domi]ne sancte pater omnipotens eterne deus [per] Christum dominum nostrum. [per] quem maiestatem tuam laudant angeli. [a]dorant dominationes tremunt potestates. [c]eli celorumque virtutes ac beata seraphin socia exulatacione cum celebrant. [c]um quibus et nostras voces ut admittis iubeas deprecamur; supplici confessione dicentes.*

If this is compared to the preface text on folio 1 of Add. 30849, it can be seen that it is identical except that here the text is completed by the *'sanctus'*:

> *sanctus sanctus sanctus Domine Deus sabaoth. Pleni sunt celi et terra gloria tua. osanna in excelsis. Benedictus qui venit in nomine Domini osanna in excelsis.*

Add. 30849 also continues with an additional section (embolism) for feast days *Et ideo cum angelis et archangelis cum tronis et dominacionibus cumque omni milicia celestis exercitus hymnum gloriae tuae canimus sine fine dicentes: sanctus.* It then offers another embolism *Quam laudant angeli adque archangeli, cherubim quoque et seraphin incenssabili voce proclamant sanctus, sanctus, sanctus [dicentes].* The text of the first part of the preface in Aem. 18 differs from both of the above in that it inserts the response *et cum spiritu tuo* after *Dominus vobiscum.* The writing after *Vere dignum* is badly worn away, but it can be discerned that the text is fundamentally the same as in the previous two manuscripts up to *confessione dicentes.* At this stage the *sanctus* is omitted, but the embolism for feast days, as given in Add. 30849, is added and completed with the full *sanctus.*

The text of the Roman *Prefatio* corresponds to that of the Mozarabic fifth formula, *inlatio,* and shares some standard phrases. In the Mozarabic liturgy, however, this text had as many variants as there were feasts, and it was often extremely long, incorporating passages taken from the Church fathers or from saints' lives. There had been a similar degree of diversity in the Roman liturgy at one time, but the number of prefaces was reduced to ten, including the *prefatio communis,* that is for Christmas, Easter, Epiphany, Ascension, Pentecost, for the feasts of the Apostles, *in natali papae,* Holy Cross, Holy Trinity and Lent. These were the only prefaces allowed in the Decretals, as described by Burchard of Worms at the beginning of the eleventh century.[33] Even Vitr. 20–8, however, extends a little beyond this list, adding the three Marian feasts: Annunciation, Purification and Assumption; and St Stephen and St John the Baptist, in addition to the apostles John the Evangelist and Sts Peter and Paul. Aem. 18 expands this further by including most Sundays, and the feasts of St Matthew, St Michael, St Martin, and one of the patron saints of San Millán de la Cogolla, San Felices, *presbyter.* Sal. 2637 is, however, closer to Vitr. 20–8 and in some cases even more restrained, giving only a short preface for the feast of the Nativity, and the same for Lent, the Ascension and Holy Trinity. In the sanctoral it has a preface for only Sts Peter and Paul and the Assumption of the Virgin. Thus it seems that the accretion of prefaces was one of the ways in which the compilers of missals could escape from the straitjacket of conformity, and it is, therefore, not surprising that Vitr. 20–8 gives fewer variants than Aem. 18. The lack of prefaces in Sal. 2637, the later manuscript, is not so easy to understand.

As Janini has noted there is another variation at this point, in that Aem. 18 inserts after the preface the prayer:

> *Deus qui non mortem sed penitentiam desideras peccatorum … temereamus laudare incul/pabiliter in hoc peregrinatione.*

This does not appear at the corresponding point in Vitr. 20–8 or in Sal. 2637,[34] but more usually among the intercessory prayers which precede the reconciliation of the penitents at Easter, and its presence here could indicate more frequent use of this prayer and therefore of its penitential nuances.[35]

The canon of the mass is the collection of prayers which accompany the act of consecration in the Eucharist. They begin with the *Te igitur*. As given in Vitr. 20.8 it is as follows:

> *Te[igitur] clementissime pater per ihesum Christum filium tuum dominum nostrum supplices rogamus et petimus uti accepta habeas et benedicas haec dona haec munera haec sancta sacrificia illibata [i]n primis quae tibi offerimus pro ecclesia tua sancta catholica quam pacificare custodire adunare et regere digneris toto orbe terrarum una cum famulo tuo papa nostro.illo. et antistite nostro.N. atque rege nostro.N. et omnibus orthodoxis atque catholicae et apostolicae fidei cultoribus*

In Add. 30849 the text seems to be the same, except for the addition of 'sedis apostolicae' after 'papa nostro', although some of the script is worn, especially after 'antistite'. Aem.18 on the other hand omits 'et antistite nostro.N. atque rege nostro.N.', which may be indicative of the attitude of the monks at San Millán to their bishop and their king. On the other hand it may merely show that the model used was older, as both the reference to the bishop and the king were later additions to the text, the king especially not being introduced until the eleventh century.[36] Aem. 18 is the only one of these manuscripts to mark the three *signa crucis* in this passage in accordance with the instructions in the *Micrologus*.[37] The text in the *Micrologus* is identical to that in Vitr. 20–8 up to 'antistite', but it ends at that point. In function the *Te igitur* is closest to the second prayer in the Mozarabic liturgy, usually called only *alia*.

The second prayer of the Roman canon is as follows:

> *Memento domine famulorum.ill. famularumque tuarum ill. et omnium circumadstantium atque omnium fidelium christaniorum quorum tibi fides cognita est et nota devotio pro quibus tibi offerimus. vel qui tibi offerunt hoc sacrificium laudis pro se suisque omnibus pro redemptione animarum suarum. tibi qui reddunt vota sua eterno deo vivo et vero.*

It is in essence a remembrance of the living, for which there is not a named prayer in the Mozarabic liturgy. This text is from Vitr. 20–8, and the folio from Add. 30849 gives the same text up to 'omnium fidelium' where it ends. Aem. 18 also agrees except for the phrase marked in bold below: *Memento domine famulorum ill … famularumque tuarum ill. **et omnium pro quibus decreui orare**, atque omnium fidelium christanorum'*. The text in the *Micrologus* does not feature the phrase marked in bold, but adds after 'suarum', 'pro spe salutis atque incolumitatis suae'.

The next prayer is closely linked to the *memento* and continues its function. The text in Vitr. 20–8 is as follows:

Communicantes et memoriam venerantes ...virginis Mariae Genitricis Dei et Domini nostri ... beatorum apostolorum ac martyrum tuorum, Petri, Pauli, Andreae, Jacobi, Joannis, Thomae, Jacobi, Philippi, Bartholomaei, Mathaei, Simonis et Thaddaei, Lini, Cleti, Clementis, Sixti, Cornelii, Cypriani, Laurentii, Chrysogoni, Joannis et Pauli, Cosmae et Damiani nec non et illorum quorum hodie sollemnitatis in conspectu gloriae tuae celebratur triumphus, et omnium sanctorum tuorum quorum meritis precibusque concedunt ut in omnibus protectionis tuae muniamur auxilio. Per Christum Dominum Nostrum.

Aem. 18 agrees with this word for word, but the *Micrologus* omits '*nec non ... celebratur triumphus*' after '*Damiani*', thus excluding all saints but those actually mentioned.

The *Hanc igitur*, which follows, is another plea for the acceptance of the offerings; there are no variant readings and the texts match that in the *Micrologus*. There are likewise no variations in the *Quam oblationem*, which asks for 'the final hallowing of the earthly gift and ... a plea that it may become the Body and Blood ...'; this has no precise equivalent in the Mozarabic liturgy. Aem. 18 marks this prayer with the *signum crucis* at five points, again as directed in the *Micrologus*.

The *Qui pridie* is the *missa secreta* of the Roman liturgy, the prayer of consecration. The text in Vitr.20–8 is as follows:

Qui pridie quam pateretur accepit panem in sanctas ac venerabiles manus suas et elevatis oculis in coelum ad te deum patrem suum omnipotentem: tibi gratias agens benedixit fregit dedit discipulis suis, dicens: Accipite et manducate ex hoc omnes: hoc est enim corpus meum. Simili modo postea quam coenatum est accipiens et hunc praeclarum calicem in sanctas et venerabiles manus suas item tibi gratias agens benedixit dedit discipulis suis dicens: Accipite et bibite ex hoc omnes: hic est enim calix sanguinis mei novi et eterni testamenti mysterium fidei qui pro vobis pro multis effundetur in remissionem peccatorum. Haec quotiescunque feceritis in mei memoriam facietis

Aem.18 and the *Micrologus* agree with this almost exactly, with only minor variations such as '*postquam*' in the *Micrologus* where Vitr. 20–8 has *postea quam*.

In comparison the text of the Mozarabic liturgy is very different, but even that differs only in turns of phrase, not in essential ideas nor in general vocabulary. The divergence is greatest at the end of the prayer, where the Roman version uses *mysterium fidei*, which is not found anywhere in the Mozarabic prayer. The Mozarabic version on the other hand adds an idea beyond remembrance, that of positive announcement: '*mortem Domini annuntiabitis donec veniat in clarita+te de celis*', and emphasises it with the response: '*Sic credimus, Domine Ihesu*'. This is lost in the Roman prayer.

The next prayer in the Roman mass is the *Unde et memores*, which is an interpretation of the mystery.[38] The texts in the two manuscripts and in the *Micrologus* agree and Aem. 18 again writes in the three crosses as stipulated in the *Micrologus*: '*Hic tres cruces super utrumque simul facit et quartam super oblationem, et quintam super calicem*'. The prayer which follows, the *Super quae propitio*, introduces the antitypes of the sacrifice, Abraham's and Melchizedek's, which are absent from the prayers of the Mozarabic liturgy. Likewise the next prayer of the Roman mass, the *Supplices*, contains another idea not in the Mozarabic liturgy at this point, that of the sacrifice *perferri per manus sancti angeli tui in sublime altare tuum;* that is the transference of the sacrifice to the place of the celestial liturgy. The Mozarabic mass includes a prayer asking for the blessing of the Holy Spirit, but there is no mention of the ascent of the sacrifice. This passage received much theological comment in the medieval period, in particular concerning the likely identity of the angel.[39]

At this point there are two further prayers of remembrance, the *Memento etiam,* for the dead, and the *Nobis quoque,* for 'ourselves'. The *Micrologus* makes provision for names to be inserted here, which may presumably vary in accordance with the wishes of the church or monastery in question. Neither Vitr. 20–8 nor Aem. 18 direct that any particular names should be included here, although Aem. 18 does make provision for their inclusion by the abbreviation *.ill..* In the *Nobis quoque,* however, the standard list of saints and martyrs is supplemented in Vitr. 20–8, as Janini has noted, by *S. Benignus* of Dijon.[40] Neither Aem. 18 nor the *Micrologus* includes *S. Benignus;* both adhere faithfully to the Roman list. Jungmann stated that additions to this list were made during the Middle Ages, although usually at the end of the passage, which is not the case here, and especially in France.[41] The addition of *S. Benignus* is, therefore, a strong indication that the model used, at least for this section, came from Burgundy.

The communion cycle of the Roman mass begins with the *Pater Noster,* introduced by an apology, the *Preceptis.* Vitr. 20–8 differs from the *Micrologus* in ending the prayer at *libera nos a malo. Amen.* It then continues with the *Libera nos, domine,* but in the passage which calls for the intercession of the Virgin Mary, Sts Peter and Paul, and St Andrew, it describes Mary as *genitrice* rather than as *semper virgine;* it also declines to add any other names as the *Micrologus* urges. Aem. 18 continues with *libera nos quaesumus,* which, as we noted, is also used in the Mozarabic liturgy, under the name *ad orationem dominicam,* and also at the same stage in the ceremony, that is during the preparation for communion.

The only other prayer given in Vitr. 20–8 for the mass itself is the *Agnus Dei,* which does not appear in the *Micrologus.* Aem.18, however, continues with prayers for the communion, noted as variants by Janini.[42] They are completely different from those given in the *Micrologus,* but are not throwbacks to the Mozarabic liturgy, which uses different prayers at this point. We know this from fol. 49v of Add. 30844, which gives the full Mozarabic text:

> *Ad commixtionem panis et vini: Sancta sanctis et coniunctio corporis et sanguinis Domini nostri Ihesu Christi edentibus et bibentibus sit in vitam eternam. In civitate Domini ibi sonant iugiter organa sanctorum. Ibi cinnamum et balsamum odor suavissimus in conspectu Dei. Ibi angeli, archangeli hymnum novum decantant ante tronum Dei. Agyos, Agyos, Agyos, cyrie o Theos.*

These florid references to the celestial liturgy are absent from the Roman prayers in Aem. 18 and also from the version in the *Micrologus.*[43]

Aem. 18 also gives, before the preface, texts for the preparation of the clergy in advance of the mass. Fol. 13, the beginning of the missal section of the manuscript, opens with the continuation of some vesting prayers.[44] These do not themselves appear in the *Micrologus,* but there is an instruction which impresses on the reader the importance of the wearing of the correct vestments by the celebrant.[45]

Aem. 18 includes – in accordance with the instruction in the *Micrologus*[46] – a *benedictio agni* in the Easter mass. The text is substantially the same as that found in an eleventh-century Mozarabic *Liber Ordinum* also from San Millán de la Cogolla (Madrid, Real Academia de la Historia, Aem. 56).[47] This is the only prayer from the Mozarabic liturgy which I have been able to identify in any of the Roman books in this study. It does not appear to be a recognised Roman text, as Sal. 2637 also gives a prayer, *benedictio novi agni* (fol. 104v) with a completely different text.[48] In view of the way in which Aem. 18 seems to follow the guidelines set out in the *Micrologus* it is possible that a copy was available at San Millán, and that the scribe, therefore, felt compelled to insert a *benedictio agni* at this point in accordance with the *Micrologus* instructions. As not every Roman missal gives a *benedictio agni* prayer, the version from the Mozarabic *Liber Ordinum* may have been included *faute de mieux*, if the missal which the scribe was copying from did not provide a text for that prayer. Alternatively the Mozarabic version may have been slipped in as a sign of defiance.

From this analysis we can see the considerable uniformity of these essential parts of the Roman mass, and the gulf which separates them in form and content, if not in function, from the Mozarabic formulae. Even allowing for the variants which are given regularly in the Roman missals for the *sacra*, *post communionem*, and occasionally for the preface, this variety does not begin to approach the diversity of the formulae in the Mozarabic liturgy which were individually composed for each mass. Through the comparison with the texts given in the *Micrologus*, we can see that this uniformity was not due to a particular model text introduced into Spain, but was a general hallmark of the Roman liturgy as propagated by the reform movement.

The proper texts given in the temporal and sanctoral cycles include the items of the foremass, which we will consider below, and occasional proper variants for the mass texts. As we have already seen, there are proper prefaces: very few in Vitr. 20–8, more in Aem.18 and in Sal. 2637, but there are also variants most significantly for the *secreta* (labelled *sacra* in Sal. 2637), which is almost always proper, in total opposition to Mozarabic practice. The other variant given regularly in all three missals is the *post communionem*, and occasionally there is a proper *in fractione* or *communio*.

The Foremass and Readings
[*See* appendix VI]

The items of the foremass given in the manuscripts of the Mozarabic liturgy vary to some extent with the importance of the feast, whether *dominica*, *feria*, major church festival or saint's day, but follow a fairly regular pattern. In Add. 30844 each foremass begins with *ad prolegendum*, which is an antiphon; in Add. 30845 this text is sometimes headed *antiphona* or given without a title, and the practice is also variable in Add. 30846. A *versus*, *agios* or *sanctus*, and an *oratio* may follow. Among our manuscripts this occurs only in Add. 30844. The three readings for the *missa* are written out in full, and are usually introduced by '*lectio*' or '*epistola*' together with the relevant book of the Bible. Chants are given, usually before the epistle, and these have the title *clamor* or *psallendum*. Important feasts, for example *de Nativitate Domini* in Add. 30844, may have in addition a benediction, *benedictiones*, again after the first pericope. Add. 30844 is the only one of our manuscripts to give the sermon regularly at this point, but the responses which follow it, *laudes* and *sacrificium*, appear also in the other two manuscripts.

Under the heading for each feast day in the temporal and sanctoral sections Vitr. 20–8 usually gives only the variants for the prayers, as it is a *sacramentarium*. The first prayer is usually introduced by the rubric '*oratio*', and followed by a second, *alia oratio*; these are collects for the day.[49] The next prayer is usually that for the offertory section, '*super oblata*', and the other proper texts for the mass itself are given at this point. Sometimes the *lectiones* are written at the end, although only the *incipit* is given,[50] and occasionally an anthem, entitled *tractus*.[51]

Aem. 18 has a more structured foremass section: within each feast it begins with an antiphon, and then a prayer, both of which are untitled. The first reading follows in full – since this is a plenary missal – introduced by the name of the biblical book but not the word '*lectio*', and then the response which this manuscript calls '*gradual*'. Two more sung items follow, *laudes* and *versus*, before the gospel reading, which is in turn followed by a *versus*. This manuscript also uses the title '*clamor*', in the Mozarabic fashion, for the response between the readings; '*benedictiones*' and '*tractus*' also appear as titles for anthems, the first also having Mozarabic associations while the second is also found in Vitr. 20–8. The offertory prayer ends the foremass items.

The texts in Sal. 2637 also open with an antiphon, and then a prayer with the heading '*oratio*'. The epistle reading follows usually, with only, for example, '*ad Romanos*' as a heading. The response is entitled '*responsorium*', often with a number of *versus*. The gospel reading begins with a similarly brief introduction, and is followed by the offertory anthem. Only *lectiones* are given only for the *feriae*, no proper prayers or chants.

Thus in both the Mozarabic and Roman liturgies the readings are the essence of the foremass, surrounded by prayers and chants. Their importance is diminished only in Vitr. 20–8 because of the sacramentary function of that manuscript: the pericopes were not read by the celebrant and hence would have appeared in a separate lectionary for the use of the deacon who was to deliver them. We now have the opportunity, therefore, to make a detailed comparison between the Roman and Mozarabic *lectiones*, such as was not possible in part I, since there were no readings for the offices in the Mozarabic books.

Appendix VI is a comparison of the readings found in the Roman missals (Sal. 2637 and Aem. 18) with those of the Mozarabic liturgy. I have chosen readings covering the two major festivals of the church, Christmas (including the preceding weeks of Advent) and Easter (including the following period to Pentecost). This provides both a balance of major feast days, for which we might expect the essential texts to have been more stable, and minor days, for which greater variation might be expected. The selected pericopes are from Sal. 2637 although it is noted where Aem. 18 agrees; then the Roman readings are compared with the Mozarabic *lectiones* as given in the *Liber commicus*,[52] with which Add. 30844 agrees (some of the readings in Add. 30846 diverge from this pattern). Add. 30845 is not included here as it does not cover any of the feasts concerned.

This analysis shows us first that there is fundamental agreement between the reading schemes of the Roman missals. There is some variation, it is true, but this occurs mainly in the readings for the less important *feriae*, whereas the readings for the great feasts are much more fixed. When the pericopes of the Mozarabic liturgy are now compared with this Roman scheme there are very few readings that match. Put differently, we can say that there seems to have been no attempt to incorporate any of the readings from that liturgy into the schemes in the Roman missals, and agreement occurs only where the Mozarabic and Roman liturgies already used the same readings. This agreement is primarily in the choice of passages from the gospels, for example during Advent the antitype of the Entry into Jerusalem, the preaching of Christ's precursor John the Baptist, and the descriptions of the events leading to the nativity. There are occasional matches in pericopes from the epistles and in the verse from Isaiah 9:2. Both liturgies follow similar themes of expectancy and preparation, offering various images of renewal, especially in the Old Testament pericopes, but the Mozarabic passages are especially rich in vegetal images of plenty and regeneration as well as the light symbolism found in the Roman pericopes. Only the Roman liturgy includes an eschatological passage during this period, likening Advent to the second coming of Christ 'in a cloud with power and great glory' (Luke 21:25–33). The Mozarabic liturgy concentrates its eschatological references in the period after Easter.

During Easter week the Mozarabic and Roman liturgies have several pericopes in common, telling of the discovery of the Resurrection and of the subsequent appearances of Christ to his disciples. There are, however, marked differences in the overall scheme, as the Mozarabic liturgy uses an integrated selection of readings from the Apocalypse and from Acts throughout Easter Week until the Sunday after Ascension.[53] The apocalyptic theme is continued even in the sanctoral feasts at this time through the feast of *S. Torquatus* and that of the Holy Cross, although it is broken at the feast of Ascension when the Old Testament antitype of Elijah's ascent to heaven is used.[54] This cycle of eighteen readings from the Apocalypse is recognised as one of the distinctive features of the Mozarabic liturgy,[55] together with the pericopes from Acts which are also found in the Gallic liturgy. The selected passages concentrate on the triumphal theme of the Lamb victorious, that is the Resurrection, and on the celebratory images of the New Jerusalem and the Tree of Life.

The Roman missals present a complete theological vision through the selection of readings which they give for the entire liturgical year, a structured exposition of the doctrines of the Roman Church presented in a single volume as a continuous process. The Mozarabic readings on the other hand generally appear together only in the *Liber commicus*. The books under consideration here do not offer a complete series of readings for the year, as they do not contain feasts for the whole liturgical year. Nevertheless the readings given in Add. 30844 are the same as those in the *Liber commicus* from Silos (Paris, BN, MS N.a.l. 2171),[56] and the readings in Add. 30845 are also almost always identical.[57] Add. 30846, the manuscript which contains the apocalyptic cycle of readings over the Easter period, however, diverges from the *Liber commicus* on several occasions while maintaining the same theological emphasis.

The differences between the pericope schemes of the Roman and Mozarabic liturgies, together with the divergent methods of presentation, thus constitute one of the most significant aspects of the liturgical change. It may be that these schemes were reflected in works of art produced at this time in varied media. It is, however, beyond the scope of this study to follow the various avenues of investigation which this offers.

Texts of sermons or homilies exist in the manuscripts of the Mozarabic mass, but not in those of the Roman. This is the reverse of the situation which we found with the *officia* texts in part I, where homilies were not given in the *officia* section of the Mozarabic manuscripts, but did appear in the Roman breviaries.

It is clear from the analyses undertaken in this chapter that the nature of the Roman mass entailed a different kind of liturgical change from that engendered by the Roman offices. We have seen that all Mozarabic features were eventually eradicated uncompromisingly from the Roman breviaries, some apparently immediately and others over a period of transition. In the case of the missals, however, nearly all Mozarabic characteristics and associations seem to disappear right from the beginning. The earliest manuscripts, Vitr. 20–8 and Aem. 18, are no less rigorously Roman than the later codex Sal. 2637. Vitr. 20–8 could be expected to be prescriptive, as it was presumably intended as an exemplar of 'best practice', a personal copy of the kind of sacramentary which had been imposed at the model abbey of Sahagún. Aem. 18 is, however, scarcely less correct, allowing no texts for Mozarabic saints except its patrons, although it does include formulas for vespers. Sal. 2637 shows a relaxation by the mid-twelfth century, the occasional Mozarabic saint reappears, the book begins more familiarly with Advent, and the preface and canon no longer dominate the structure. These apparent Mozarabic elements are, however, probably due to the influence of the structure of the antiphonary on the plenary missal rather than to any significant backsliding; the Roman mass had taken complete hold.

Notes to Chapter Five

1 Vogel, *see above* Intro. note 44, p.76, and p.83.

2 *See* Leroquais, V., *Les Sacramentaires et les missels manuscrits des bibliothèques publiques de France*, Paris, 1924; which shows that not only is there a move from sacramentary to plenary missal during the eleventh and twelfth centuries – as Vogel observed, *see above* Intro. note 44, p.143 n.288 – but there is also a small increase in the number of manuscripts beginning with Advent rather than with the Christmas Vigil.

3 An office for *S. Anastasia* is also found in Add. 30849, the Roman breviary, after the Christmas vigil.

4 Ch.IV in *PL* 151, col. 980.

5 *PL* 151, col. 974–1002.

6 Different patterns of fasting were followed in the Mozarabic liturgy; *see* Férotin, *as above* Intro. note 20, p.LIV.

7 *benedictio ramorum* in Aem. 18.

8 For an overview *see* MacGregor, A.J., *Fire and Light in the Western Triduum, Their use at Tenebrae and at the Paschal Vigil*, Alcuin Club Collection 71, Minnesota, 1992

9 Tyrer, J.W., *Historical Survey of Holy Week its services and ceremonial*, Alcuin Club Collection 29, London, 1932, pp.154–5.

10 Férotin, M., *as above* Intro. note 45. Two benedictions are given for use *in sacrario, benedictio lucernae* (col. 209) and *benedictio cerei* (col. 210) and two more for use at the altar (col. 212, and col. 214).

11 *See* above Ch. 2 note 83.

12 For a full description of the scrutinies and the origins of *Ordo* XI, *see* Andrieu, M., *Les Ordines Romani du haut moyen âge*, vol. 2, Louvain, 1931–1961, pp.380–447.

13 Tyrer, *as above* note 9, p.162.

14 Fisher, J.D.C., *Christian Initiation: Baptism in the Medieval West*, Alcuin Club Collection 47, London, 1965, pp.88–100.

15 There is an elaborate description attributed in the middle ages to Ildephonsus (not the bishop of Toledo) in a piece entitled *Revelatio (PL* 106 col. 881–90). According to this the host was arranged in nine pieces in the shape of a cross, each piece representing one of the stages of the incarnation, life, death and glory of Christ. This is similar to the supposed Mozarabic practice still in use in Toledo. *See* Reynolds, R.E., '*Pseudonymous liturgica* in early medieval canon law collections', in *Fälschungen im Mittelalter,* teil II (Gefälschte Rechtstexte der bestrafte Fälscher), Hannover, 1988, pp.67–77 for the likely origin of this text, which casts doubt on its reliability.

16 Duffy, E., *The Stripping of the Altars*, New Haven CT and London, 1992, p.15, n.11.

17 Davies, J.G. (ed.), *New Dictionary of Liturgy and Worship*, London, 1986, p.143.

18 Janini, J., *as above* Ch. 4 note 24, pp.183–95.

19 Férotin, *as above* Intro. note 45, p.XXIII and col. 277–447.

20 Reynolds, R. E., *as above* Ch. 4 note 15, p.144.

21 Such masses are commonly found in French missals at this time. *See* Leroquais, *as above* note 2.

22 Férotin, D.M., *Recueil des Chartes de l'abbaye de Silos*, Paris, 1897, p.12 n.1.

23 Isidore, 'Etymologies', Lib. VI ch.19, in *PL* 83, col. 252.

24 Férotin, *as above* Intro. note 20, p.XX, '*missa si quis catechumenus remansit exeat fores, et inde missa'.*

25 Férotin, *as above* Intro. note 20, p.XXI, '*Secunda invocationis ad Deum est, ut clementer suscipiat fidelium oblationesque eorum'.*

26 Férotin, *as above* Intro. note 20, p.XXI, ' *Tertia autem effunditur pro offerentibus, sive pro defunctis fidelibus, ut per*

idem sacrificium veniam consequantur'.

27 Férotin, *as above* Intro. note 20, p.XXI, '*Quarta infertur pro osculo pacis, ut caritate reconciliati omnes invicem digne sacramento corporis et sanguinis Christi consocientur, quia non recipit dissensionem cuiusquam Christi indivisibile corpus'.*

28 Férotin, *as above* Intro. note 20, p.XXI–XXII, '*Quinta deinde infertur Inlatio in sanctificatione oblationis:in qua etiam et ad Dei laudem terrestrium creaturarum virtutumque celestium universitas provocatur et Hosanna in excelsis cantatur'.*

29 Férotin, *as above* Intro. note 20, p.XXII.

30 Férotin, *as above* Intro. note 20, pp.XXIV–XXV.

31 Férotin, *as above* Intro. note 20, pp.XXII–XXIII, '*Sexta exhinc succedit conformatio sacramenti: ut oblatio quae Deo offertur sanctificata per Spiritum Sanctum, Christi corpori ac sanguini conformetur'.*

32 Férotin, *as above* Intro. note 20, p.XXIII, '*Ultima est oratio, qua Dominus noster discipulos suos orare instituit, dicens: Pater noster, qui es in celis'.*

33 Jungmann, J.A., *The Mass of the Roman Rite: its Origin and Development*, vol.II, (trans.) New York, 1955, p.119 ff. Pope Urban II added a preface for the Virgin Mary in 1095.

34 Janini, *as above* Intro. note 116, p.151.

35 Hughes, *as above* Ch. 1 note 37, para. 915.

36 Jungmann, *as above* note 33, pp.155–8.

37 Micrologus, *PL* 151, col. 993.

38 Hughes, *as above* Ch. 1 note 37, para. 512, and Jungmann, *as above* note 33, vol.I, p.218.

39 Jungmann, *as above* note 33, vol.I p.232.

40 Janini, *as above* Intro. note 116, p.249, no. 199, '*Nobis quoque peccatoribus … Johanne, Stephano, [M]athia, Barnabas, Ignatio, Alexandro, Marcellino, Petro, Benigno, Felicitate, Perpetua, Agatha, Agnete, Lucia, Cecilia, Anastasia'* (Vitr. 20–8, fol. 5). Dijon was independent of Cluny, but it was strongly influenced by it. *See* Hunt, N., *as above* Intro. note 98, pp.159–60.

41 Jungmann, *as above* note 33, p.256 and note 43.

42 Janini *as above* Intro. note 116, p.151, no. 171 '*Corpus et sanguis domini I.C. non fiant michi ad iudicium, se fiant ad remedium anime mee in vitam eternam. Amen. Fiat nobis commixtio et consecratio corporis et sanguinis d.n.I.C. in vitam eternam. Amen. Domine non sum dignus ut intres sub tectum meum, sed propitius esto michi peccatori, per hanc usurpationem veri corporis et sanguinis tui. Amen. Domine sancte pater, o.e. deus, da michi hoc corpus et sanguinem filii tui d.n. I. C. ita sumere ut merear per hoc remissionem omnium peccatorum accipere, et tuo sancto spiritu repleri. Qui vivis. Domine I.C. filii dei vivi qui ex voluntate patri … et a te numquam separari permittas salvator mundi deus, qui cum eodem … '.*

43 Micrologus, *PL* 151, col. 995, '*Fiat commistio et consecratio corporis et sanguinis Domini nostri Jesu Christi accipientibus nobis in vitam eternam. Amen.'*

44 These are prayers for a succession of vestments: *ad camiciam, ad albam, ad cingulam, ad stolam, ad casulam, ad manipulum.* This is not the vocabulary of the Roman *Ordo* VIII, Andrieu, *as above* note 12, pp.321–2.

45 Micrologus, *PL* 151, col. 982 *in missa sacris vestibus est indutus, sine quibus ad altare juxta Romanum ministrare non debemus.*

46 Micrologus, *PL* 151, col. 1015 '*Juxta Romanam auctoritatem, agnus in Pascha benedicitur, non ad altare, sed ad communem mensam'.*

47 Férotin, *as above* Intro. note 45, col. 224: '*Post celebratam sanctam Pasche sollemnitatem, postquam etiam, transactis sacris ieiuniorum diebus, iam animabus spiritualibus dapibus refectis de mensa tue Maiestatis, offerimus famuli tui, pro huius fragilitate corpusculi aliquantulum reparandi, hance usui nostro concessam creaturam agni: poscentes, ut eum, ore proprio nobis signantibus, benedicas ac dextra tua sanctifices, et universis ex eo ministratis gratiam effici prestes, atque cum gratiarum actione percepta, te Deum, qui es cibus vite et anime nostre, magis magisque et inhianter desideremus et indefesse fruamur.'*

48 '*Deus universe carnis qui noe et filius eius … repleantur omnibus bonis.'*

49   Hughes, *as above* Ch. 1 note 37, para.503–9.

50   For example fol. 40v: *In principio creavit,* and *Factum est in vigilia matutina*, and fol. 41: *Apprehendent vii* and *Haec est hereditas.*

51   For example *Cantemus domino* (fol. 40v); *Vinea facta* and *Attende caelum* (fol. 41).

52   Morin, G., *Liber Comicus* (Anecdota Maredsolana vol.1), Maredsoli, 1893.

53   Gibert Tarruell, J., 'El sistema de lecturas de la cincuenta pascual de la liturgia hispánica, según la tradición B', in *Liturgia y Música Mozárabes*, Instituto de Estudios Visigótico-Mozárabes de San Eugenio – Toledo, Serie D, Núm. 1, (Ponencias y Comunicaciónes presentadas al I Congreso Internacional de Estudios Mozárabes), Toledo, 1975, pp.111–24. This article deals primarily with the Toledan tradition, but it is generally informative about the readings during this period.

54   Morin, *as above* note 53.

55   The reading of the Apocalypse at Easter was prescribed by the Fourth Council of Toledo in 633.

56   Férotin, *as above* Intro. note 20, col. 820.

57   Férotin, *as above* Intro. note 20, col. 842.

CHAPTER SIX

—◄○►—

The Mass Displayed

IN PART I we found that the interaction between the *officia* texts and their presentation was varied and unpredictable. Although identifiable Mozarabic text was absent from the breviaries, there was evidence of gradual transition in the structure of the books and in areas – such as homilies – where the status of a text was less clear-cut. The illumination of the Roman breviaries was characterised by the absence of the vigorous figurative work found in the Mozarabic books; two of the manuscripts had no elaborate decoration. Continental geometric and foliate initial styles, which had already been integrated into the 'Mozarabic' tradition, continued to be used alongside abstract 'Mozarabic' decorative motifs. Only one Roman breviary had an explicitly 'Mozarabic' decorative scheme but even in this case the style was not figurative. Moreover the style did not seem to be the multi-faceted one found in eleventh-century Mozarabic manuscripts, but instead used only a narrow range of the tenth-century abstract 'Mozarabic' visual vocabulary.

Analysis of the Roman mass texts introduced into Spain has shown that this area of the change was more immediate and absolute than that of the offices. Was this different approach reflected in the decoration of the Roman missals? This chapter will address that question, beginning with an examination of the way in which the Mozarabic mass texts were presented.

The Mozarabic Manuscripts

The schemes of illumination of the Mozarabic books encompass both the office and mass texts. Throughout all three manuscripts – although Add. 30844 provides the clearest example – a constant rhythm of rubrication and minor initials with infill colours articulates the texts. Thus the same technique is used for the standard formulae of the *officia* and *missae* integrating the disparate texts into a unified structure. Even if the style of illumination varies – which it does – within each manuscript and sometimes within the texts for one feast, the divide does not come between office and mass, they continue to be treated as an entity. There is also a hierarchy of initials which operates in broadly the same way in each of the manuscripts.

We have seen in chapter 3 that each feast is introduced by a heading together with a *vespertinum* monogram which begins the office text. The items of the office are then introduced by characteristic rubrics and one- or two-line initials with their contrasting infill

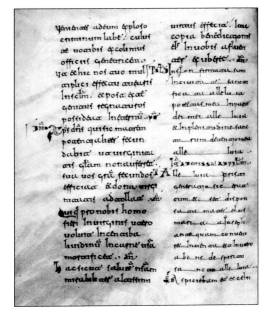

FIG. 46 London, British Library,
Add. MS 30844, fol. 38v

FIG. 47 London, British Library,
Add. MS 30846, fol. 3v

colours, and the occasional larger initial for a hymn. The transition to the foremass is marked in a relatively modest way. The rubric is usually *item ad missa: ad prolegendum*. In Add. 30844 (e.g. fol. 38v, FIG. 46) attention is drawn to the heading by placing it alone on one line and using capital forms for all the letters; in other ways the heading is treated just like the other rubricated labels, being written in red ink and filled with yellow and a greeny-blue. The first letter of the text is given only a one-line initial, in red with yellow infill, similar to those used for the other minor items of the office mass. A slightly larger initial, just over two lines high, is given to the *oratio* text, in red outline blocked with yellow, and light and dark blue ink. Similar schemes can be seen in Add. 30845 (e.g. fol. 19) and Add. 30846 (fol. 3v, FIG. 47), although both these manuscripts favour the briefer heading *Ad missa* or *Missa eiusdem*. Add. 30845 treats the heading in a very routine way, except for using capital letters, and usually follows it with the *antiphona* abbreviation instead of *ad prolegendum*, but it gives more prominence to the *oratio* by using larger initials, for example a three-line 'M' on fol. 2 and a five-line 'A' on fol. 5v. Add. 30846 occasionally elongates the heading to draw attention to it; it achieves this by leaving oddly-placed gaps between the letters (FIG. 47). There is usually no abbreviation after the heading, but occasionally *prolegendum* is used.

It is at this point in all three Mozarabic manuscripts that some of the finest and most elaborate initials appear. They mark the beginning of each *lectio*, Old Testament or Apocalypse, epistle, and gospel. Rubrication is used to give the nature of the reading and the initial is reserved for the first letter of the standard phrase, which is very often the 'I' for '*in illo tempore*' or '*in illis diebus*', or the 'F' for '*fratres*' at the beginning of the epistle. This often

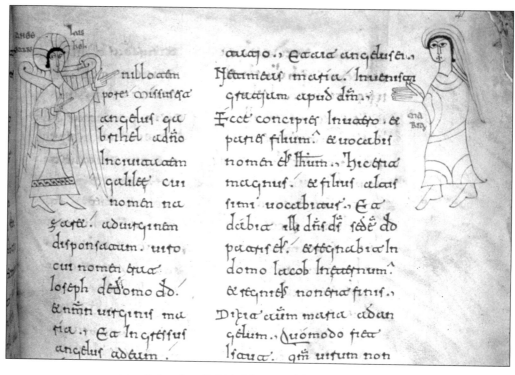

FIG. 48 London, British Library, Add. MS 30844, fol. 41

provides the opportunity for one of the distinctive 'Mozarabic' long 'I's. This Visigothic letter form is both highly functional, being immediately recognisable, and highly decorative. In its most ornate forms, when it is divided into several sections and compartments, it can combine a very large selection of 'Mozarabic' motifs. Moreover the impact of the initials which introduce the readings is all the greater as no other decoration is used throughout these texts. This is well illustrated in Add. 30845 by the ten-line 'I' on fol. 132, the six-line 'I' on fol. 44v (FIG. 50), and by the double-spreads on fols 87v–88 and fols 141v–142. Add. 30844 provides several more good examples.

The ubiquitous 'I' initial can also take other forms. In Add. 30845 (fol. 19) there is one example of a figurative letter 'I' in a style similar to that used in some of the *vespertinum* monograms; Add. 30844 likewise has one example for the gospel reading of the feast of the Virgin which is different in style from all the other initials. This is a figurative initial used to introduce the *lectio* which recounts the story of the Annunciation (fol. 41, FIG. 48). The 'I' of *in illo tempore* is formed by the figure of Gabriel and, even more exceptionally, it is matched by the figure of Mary which does not form a letter. They are located in the top and side margins of the folio. Both figures are drawn only in black outline, except for the hair in each case and the eyes of the Virgin which are filled in. Gabriel has a cross nimbus and striated wings which hang down vertically, a tunic with a rope border and a low belt; two long fingers on each hand point towards Mary. Each figure is labelled: ANGELVS GABRIHEL

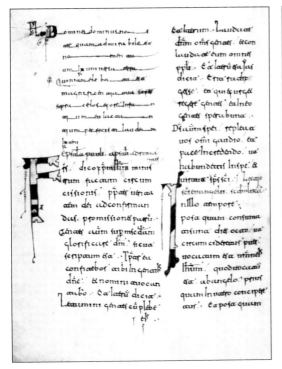

FIG. 49 London, British Library,
Add. MS 30844, fol. 117v

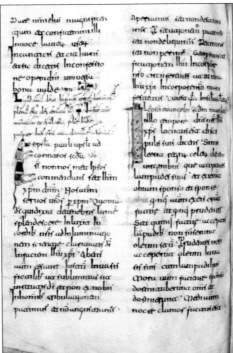

FIG. 50 London, British Library,
Add. MS 30845, fol. 44v

and MARIA respectively. Mary wears a long head-dress and has her hands modestly joined. Her mouth is formed like a small cross. The exceptional use of a figurative initial at this point in the text further emphasises this book's likely connection with the cult of the Virgin. Add. 30846 (section A) has several figurative 'I's closer to the figurative style of Add. 30845 but all large and very crudely drawn. Some are named: for example the figure on fol. 28 (FIG 27), which carries a cross and staff, is labelled '*Petrus*', and indeed the reading concerns St Peter. Similar figures are used for St John (fol. 46v), St Philip (fol. 47v) and *S. Torquatus et socii* (fol. 84v).

The 'F' initials are often geometric, as on fol. 117v (FIG. 49) of Add. 30844, but a zoomorphic form is also used for this letter on several occasions in Add. 30845. On fol. 44v (FIG. 50) a fantastical tiger-like creature with a mane along its back and striped body markings stretches out its four legs to form the central bar of the letter 'F', while the top bar is formed by its head and protruding mouth, and the tail of the letter by its tail. This seems to have been a largely continental letter-form found, for example, in Limoges manuscripts.[1] Four-legged beasts were used in a similar way in Mozarabic manuscripts from the tenth century,[2] but the examples in Add. 30845 seem to relate more closely to the Limoges type: compact, with a mane, the cross-bar of the letter formed by the beast's legs, and a shape probably indicating foliage protruding from the mouth. This association strengthens the argument for an eleventh-century date for Add. 30845.[3]

After the readings, the next item to receive special attention in Add. 30844 is the *sermo*. None of the other Mozarabic manuscripts include homilies, so this manuscript must serve as the only example. The sermon for the feast of the Virgin (fol. 42) is given a heading (*item sermo*) in letters of the same type and size as those of *item ad missa*. It is also given a four-line initial 'E', built ingeniously in the form of two birds (PLATE 10): in red outline with yellow, green and blue infill, the curving body of the letter is formed by a large bird whose head turns towards its tail, and another small bird sits on its back to create the bar of the letter. The other homilies receive headings and initials of a similar size.

The central section of the mass receives a rubricated heading, usually *missa* or *missa eiusdem*, in the standard style. There is no monogram to draw attention to this important point, so the first initial of the *missa* prayer is used to serve the same function. All three of the Mozarabic manuscripts have notable initials serving this purpose. Add. 30844 has a seventeen-line letter 'P' (fol. 83), in yellow interlace of the Valeranican type, to open the mass for St Stephen, and another large letter 'P' on fol. 162v which introduces the mass for Ascension. This is a very elaborate initial and has a blue-black outline with red, blue, green and yellow infill decorated with small bands of interlace, large zoomorphic scrolls ending in birds' heads, and interlocking geometric segments. Add. 30845 does not always use large initials to begin the masses; some are quite compact bird or bird/fish initials and others, for example the 'T' used to begin the mass of *S. Zoilus*, use particularly delicate geometric decoration. Add. 30846 also uses various combinations of geometric, vegetal, and zoomorphic elements in the initials which introduce the *missae*. In section A these are often large, for example the ten-line letter 'H' on fol. 3v (FIG. 47), or the eight-line letter 'P' on fol. 36, which incorporate several of the more exotic geometric motifs. The initials in section B are smaller, but they generally maintain a similar hierarchy, a five-line letter 'D' (fol. 17) being large enough to make the impact required.

The other mass formulae are given the appropriate abbreviated heading in rubric with the usual infill decoration. The initials beginning each prayer vary in size. In Add. 30844 the *missa Sancte Marie* has a four-line initial for the *alia*, a two-line 'E' for the *post nomina*, a five-line 'X' for the *ad pacem,* and two-line letters for the remaining formulae (*inlatio, post sanctus* and *post pridie, ad orationem dominicam, benedictio* and *completuria*). These gradations, however, may not always indicate the relative importance of the formulae, since – within certain limits – the size of the initial seems to be as much a function of the letter concerned as a reflection of the importance of the text. The same phenomenon can be seen in the other two manuscripts.

It is equally difficult in the case of the Mozarabic manuscripts to speak of one feast being given prominence over the others in terms of its illumination. Add. 30845 and Add. 30846 seem to treat each day in a different yet basically equal fashion. Add. 30844 is a more difficult case because of its special association with the Virgin. The texts of the feast of the Virgin, which begin the liturgical section of this manuscript, stand out because they receive some of the largest and most meticulously executed initials. The case is made most strikingly by the individual way in which the Annunciation *lectio* is decorated (Fig. 48). The sudden stark outlines, with no trace of colour, unlike the rest of the manuscript, and the figurative subject matter, also found nowhere else in this manuscript, mark this feast as pre-eminent. The Marian character of Add. 30844 is clearly articulated by its decoration, but the other portions of the manuscript are of a piece and it is hard to discern any further hierarchy of feasts.

From this separate consideration of the decoration of the mass texts from that of the offices in the Mozarabic manuscripts we can reach some conclusions. The mixed structure of the books is mirrored by the integrated decorative schemes. In total the mass texts receive more elaborate illumination than the office texts, largely because of the three major initials used to mark the *lectiones*. Otherwise the heading and *vespertinum* monogram used to begin the office balance the heading and initial used to begin the mass. Although the mass was just as central to the Mozarabic liturgy as to any other Christian liturgy, it is the sacred text, the biblical word delivered in the *lectiones*, which is given prominence in these manu-scripts through the large and elaborate initials which introduce the readings. In contrast the text for the central mystery of the mass itself is not even written.

The Roman Manuscripts
Two of the Roman missals, Vitr. 20–8 and Aem. 18, announce their purpose immediately. The preface and canon of the mass are placed at the front of the codices and receive the kind of illumination which clearly sets them apart. The difference seems so great at this point that it is difficult to believe that we are dealing with the same ritual. There is no trace of the 'Mozarabic' approach to the decoration of these texts.

These manuscripts would presumably have had *pages de garde*, but we cannot usefully speculate on their contents, as no comparable complete manuscripts survive from this period in this part of Spain. Aem. 18 retains its calendar, but any folios before it and the beginning of the liturgical section are missing. In these manuscripts the preface is the quintessential beginning in decorative as well as text terms, and we will deal with it first.

The first folio of Vitr. 20–8 (Plate 7) is dedicated to the common preface. The initial 'P' of *Per omnia secula* starts someway below the top ruled line on the page, but stretches almost to the last ruled line; it does not follow the vertical ruled line to the left but leans slightly to the right. It is set in an irregular stepped frame which is drawn by only a single line and filled – on the right-hand side of the shaft – with a blue wash. The shaft of the letter is formed by a tapering core which is filled with yellow wash, in the centre of which is a narrow strip of interlace. The core is, in turn, encased in a thin outline frame; it is held aloft by a male figure. At the top the frame of the shaft widens into two amorphous entwined bodies, which end in two heads whose mouths grip the shaft. The male figure at the base supports the stem, with legs apart, balancing it, like an acrobat, with his right arm across the front to stop it toppling forward; the left arm also comes across, but the weight of the shaft seems to be steadied by the man's neck while his left hand supports his chin. The figure is drawn in outline in bold sections, and a central block together with the left arm are filled

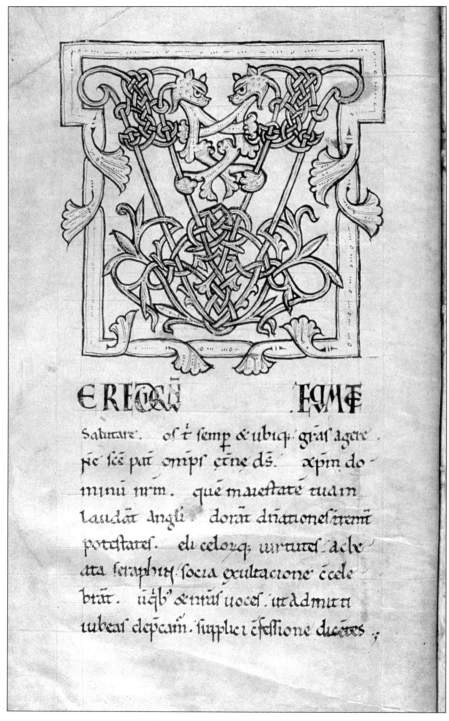

FIG. 51 Madrid, Biblioteca Nacional, MS Vitr. 20–8, fol. 1v

with red. The bowl of the 'P' is filled with thick tendrils drawn in outline, entwining in a free-form manner and ending in leaf profiles and, in three cases, in small beasts' heads. The spaces between the tendrils are filled with blocks of dark green and dark red pigment, or with the yellow and pale blue washes used elsewhere in the initial. The crescent which circumscribes the bowl is, like the shaft, filled with yellow wash in the outer section, but there is a thin core of interlace, and this, in turn, becomes at the base a delicate beast's head. The tendrils which fill the bowl seem to grow from the beast's 'body' as if they are meta-morphosed legs. The tail of this beast is swallowed at the top of the bowl by a more dragon-like head with a hooked beak or mouth. All the beasts' heads have carefully delin-eated eyes and eyebrows.

The text of the preface is written as a display page, in well-spaced letters in red ink filled with yellow wash, filling the space alongside the shaft of the letter 'P'. The letters decrease in size over the first three lines, but then continue as rustic capitals of the size set by the third line (rustic capitals were often used to continue the titles of texts in Protogothic script). The whole forms an elegant though not luxurious display page.

On the verso of the same folio (fol. 1v, FIG. 51) is the *Vere Dignum* text. It is introduced by an initial 'V' set in a thick frame. The whole initial occupies approximately half of the page beginning one line above the top ruled line and continuing for another eleven lines, thus dominating the text. The sides of the frame follow the inner of the two vertical ruled lines at each side of the folio, except for the top portion of the frame, which steps out to align itself with the outer of the ruled lines. The frame is thick and is filled with lines of calligraphic decoration, three short vertical lines alternating with tiny circles or with short wavy hori-zontal lines. The patterns are not regular but merge one into the other. At eight points in the frame foliage sprouts from a mark of two short lines, or one short line and one long trian-gular shape, which resemble the growth points of shrubs just above the leaf scars; this may be a remarkable touch of naturalism. The lengths of foliage are short and end in profile acanthus leaves; they are decorated with dots and thin branching lines. The 'V' of *'Vere'* is drawn in interlace with intricate knots at the top of the shafts and at the base where they meet. The interlace at the base also 'flowers' in that the terminals become foliage with curling leaves and pointed buds. At the top between the shafts there is darker, more robust, knotted foliage which issues from the mouths of two affronted beasts' heads which have a fierce, almost oriental, appearance. The mouths are open very wide, the ears stand proud, the eyes are drawn with a clear eyelid and the faces are decorated with a small arrow motif. The thick stems of foliage, decorated with a three-dot-and-circle motif, divide, cross and terminate in scalloped leaves. Two more wide stems meet these, cross and wrap themselves around the interlace of the letter 'V'. All this is in outline only, drawn in brown/black ink.

The rest of the heading '[V]ere dignum ... [A]equum et' is written in capitals in a pattern where the letter 'U' of *'dignum'* is placed under the preceding letter and the 'I' is set in the bowl of the 'D', while the first 'U' of *'aequum'* is subsumed into the 'Q', and the 'E' of *'et'* intersects the stem of the 'T'. It is possible that the missing words would have been com-pleted in a contrasting colour.

Aem. 18 does not open with such dramatic effect, as the preface is not placed on a display page as in Vitr. 20–8. Instead the folio is cluttered with text, most of which is broken up only by rubricated titles. The left-hand column is occupied by preparatory prayers which continue to the top of the right-hand column, and immediately below these comes the 'P' of *per omnia secula seculorum* (PLATE 8). It is in its size and placing quite a modest initial. Occupying only nine lines of the thirty-one on the page, it is built into the column and is thus rather cramped, although it does extend into the centre margin.

Like the same initial in Vitr. 20–8, the structure of the letter involves a man and a dragon, but it uses those elements in a somewhat different way. Instead of supporting the shaft of the letter, the figure is the shaft. Drawn full-length, the man's hair and forehead extend above the bowl of the letter, while his feet form the base of the shaft. The figure leans slightly to his left, that is towards the bowl, extending his right arm by bending it at the elbow and thus giving balance to the letter. The figure is drawn in a slightly gauche Romanesque style and is depicted with skilful use of colour. He has reddish-brown hair and light-green trousers; his feet are drawn in outline with red ink and filled with yellow, while his bluey-green tunic spreads to his knees like a skirt and has a red border. The bowl of the letter is, as in Vitr. 20–8, formed by a dragon, which here has a blue body with yellow and red wings, the tips of which extend beyond the line of the letter. The lines of text are lengthened or shortened to allow space for the bowl of the letter.[4]

The eight-line *Vere dignum* monogram, which follows, is placed very close to the initial 'P' – indeed they overlap for one line – and it seems that they were executed as a balanced pair. In this instance, however, there is no similarity with the decoration of Vitr. 20–8 with its foliate interlace pouring from beasts' mouths. Instead this monogram is figurative. The main feature is an *agnus dei* set in a slightly oval mandorla, with the lamb facing to the right and holding a cross. The central shaft of the monogram rises from the mandorla and spreads at the top to the left and right in an interlace pattern. The sides of the monogram are formed by two upside-down angels which hold the mandorla, one on each side. The folds of their robes flow out at the top of the monogram and, in defiance of gravity, meet the interlace of the central shaft. Below, their wings spread in opposite directions: the left wing of the angel on the left and the right wing of the one on the right point upwards towards their feet, thus strengthening the sides of the monogram, while the other wing in each case stretches downwards and across until they meet just below the mandorla. The drapery of the angels is green, red and blue with occasional yellow infill.

Not only is the form of this monogram not familiar from Vitr. 20–8, it is also not generally found in missals from France, Italy or elsewhere in medieval Europe, where the most common representation of the monogram is geometric with foliate or interlace decoration.[5] An *agnus dei* is found with two seraphim in association with the *sanctus* text in an Italian twelfth-century missal (Florence, Bibl. Riccard., cod. 299 fol. 100v).[6] However, not only is this manuscript most likely later than Aem. 18 (1113), but here the image is not a monogram, as it falls at the end of the *sanctus* text; it also recalls the vision of Isaiah more accurately than the monogram in Aem. 18, as it represents seraphim not angels. The *agnus dei* in a mandorla is found regularly, however, in the Beatus manuscripts, in the miniatures depicting the adoration of the Lamb (Apoc.5:6–8), but in this representation the Lamb is usually surrounded by the evangelist symbols and by some or all of the twenty-four elders; it is also usually contained within a large circle which is in turn sometimes supported by four angels.[7] In these miniatures, moreover, the mandorla is circular, the Lamb traditionally faces to the left and is depicted, like the angels, in a more schematic way than in Aem. 18. There is another example of this motif surviving from a slightly later period (post–1120) in the sculpture of the tympanum in the south nave door at San Isidoro in León.[8] This image is closer to the depiction in Aem. 18 in that it is supported by two angels, but they are not upside down, the mandorla is circular, and the lamb is facing to the left. Other examples of the *agnus dei* motif have been noted from the ceiling mosaic at San Vitale in Ravenna to Ottonian portable altars,[9] but none is very close to the representation in Aem. 18.

It seems, therefore, that the monogram in Aem. 18 was probably not copied from another missal, but was rather a construction adapted from another context. The Lamb is a clear iconographic expression of the sacrificial aspect of the mass encapsulated in the *agnus dei* text. This aspect rather than the apocalyptic role is paramount here, as it is in the San Isidoro tympanum, which emphasises the point by including the Old Testament antitype of Abraham's sacrifice of Isaac.[10] The angels and the shaft of the monogram were possibly adapted from a situation in which they may have appeared the correct way up, as they seem to have been executed from that angle. It may be of note that this is also the case in one of the eleventh-century miniatures in Romanesque style in the Beatus manuscript from San Millán.[11] Here the angel which is depicted upside down is very similar to the angels represented standing upright, again as if it was executed from the same point of view, that is to say drawn with the page upside down.

The isolated folio 1 from Add. 30849 (FIG. 45) also contains some decoration for the preface, notably again the letter 'P' of the opening *Per omnia saecula saeculorum*. Drawn in outline only, the top of the shaft of the letter is formed by interlace which loops down around the neck of a man; the man's body forms the rest of the shaft. His right foot is swallowed by a lion at the base of the shaft and his left hand emerges at the top to kill a dragon. We have the man-and-dragon theme once more, but in yet another variation. The figure is again Romanesque in his facial features and in the lines and shading which have been used to indicate the folds in his clothing. The dragon again forms the bowl of the letter: its head curling round at the bottom, and its wings curving back so that its tail meets the top of the shaft of the letter. In this version the man pierces the dragon's head from above with a short spear. Another beast's head emerges from the interlace at the top of the shaft and swallows the dragon's tail. The bowl of the letter is filled with tendrils, as is the 'P' on fol. 1 of Vitr. 20–8, but it is dominated by one large foliate structure and there are no more beasts' heads.

This initial also differs in other ways from those in Vitr. 20–8 and Aem. 18. Most significantly, it is drawn only in black ink without any trace of colour and the standard of workmanship is clearly lower than that found in the other manuscripts. In common with the other elements on this folio it looks like a practice attempt with its uncertain lines and ill-formed features. All the elements of a Romanesque initial are there, but it is executed without flow and without feeling for the style. This could of course be mere lack of talent, but there is sufficient achievement, for example in the portrayal of the lion, to indicate promise. Is this an example of a Spanish scribe, inexperienced in the Romanesque style, trying to copy the initial and text from a manuscript of the Roman liturgy which had been supplied as a model?

If a model text or illumination were produced and circulated, we might expect Vitr. 20–8 to have some close relationship to it, as that manuscript belonged to the model abbey of Sahagún and probably to its influential abbot. The presence of the man-and-dragon iconography in both Vitr. 20–8 and Aem. 18 may thus be more than coincidental, especially considering the distance between the two monasteries geographically and, probably, in terms of attitude to the liturgical change. The presence of yet another example – albeit an isolated folio which cannot be confidently localised – bound into a codex which has connections with yet another abbey, Silos, suggests that this iconography may have been particularly significant.

The man-and-dragon iconography, especially in its combative form, has symbolic associations. In the eleventh century the dragon lacked the more charming associations which it later acquired. Then in the words of the Apocalpyse it was '*draconem serpentem antiquum qui est diabolus et Satanas*', an identification familiar in Spain from the Beatus manuscripts.[12] It was also from the mouth of the dragon that the frogs emerged who, according to Beatus, represented those who preached the word of the devil, that is heresy.[13] Could this initial in its earlier forms, as in fol. 1 of Add. 30849, have been taken to represent the defeat of heresy and the victory of orthodoxy? It seems to me possible that there may have been a model text, perhaps containing only the preface and canon, with an initial including this feature circulated to all important abbeys. Yet the other major initials in these two manuscripts are not similar, and it is unsatisfactory to speculate on a putative lost 'original'.

In Vitr. 20–8 (PLATE 7), however, the imagery is definitely not combative. We might almost wonder whether the figure balancing the large letter 'P' with its dragon heads is not meant to be a visual witticism for Bernard's own demanding role in introducing the new liturgy. The figure in Aem. 18 is also not actively fighting the dragon, but almost holding it. These three 'P' initials are thus variations on one theme, but they do not resemble one another visually in any way and could not, in my view, have been copies of a common model. It is unlikely that each of these monasteries would have independently acquired models with this iconography, as it is not a common motif in French missals. Indeed, to my knowledge, no French missals survive from this period with this iconography in the 'P' of the preface,[14] although there are several interlace and foliate examples.[15] The recurrent theme in our Spanish example has an emblematic quality which might have been communicated verbally rather than by means of a visual model. If this is so, this common iconography suggests that there may have been more central control of the liturgical change than has been assumed, at least in the early stages. Even if a model of good practice was not circulated,

clementissime pater per ihm
xpm filium tuum dnm nrm
supplices rogamus ac petimus.
ut accepta habeas & benedicas
hec dona hec munera. hec sca
sacrificia illibata' inprimis

FIG. 52 Madrid, Biblioteca Nacional, MS Vitr. 20–8, fol. 2

it looks at the very least as if some of the iconography may have been prescribed or 'recommended'.

The canon is the central text which contains the act of consecration. It encompasses the essential *missa secreta*, which was not even written down in the Mozarabic books. The first prayer is the '*Te igitur*', which was represented in many French manuscripts since Carolingian times in the form of a calvary, and this is precisely the iconography which we find in Vitr. 20–8. The choice of a crucifixion scene for this position emphasises the function of the mass as an imitation of Christ's sacrifice, a re-enactment *in memoriam*. As we have seen in the previous chapter, the text itself gives antitypes of the sacrifice, Abraham and Isaac and that of the high priest Melchizedek (Heb.5:1–11).[16]

This much-reproduced initial occupies the upper part of fol. 2 in Vitr. 20–8 (FIG. 52). The depiction of Christ on the cross forms the 'T' of *Te igitur*, the first words of the Canon, and occupies the first fourteen ruled lines on the page ending with a horizontal line drawn across the ruled line (the remaining letters [*T*]*e igitur* were not supplied). On the right-hand side of the page the initial aligns with the inner vertical ruled line, while on the left it uses space beyond the ruled lines; thus it is not precisely central on the page, but rather drawn slightly to the left. The execution is highly calligraphic, although the total effect belies the technique. The figure of Christ is constructed from compartments: at the top is the halo and within it a nimbus decorated with tiny circles. The hair below is drawn in eight sections, two frame the face, and the shapes used could almost be leaves in another context; below these, three small crescents on either side show the hair falling across the shoulders. Structure is given to the hair by the use of fine lines, similar to those used on the leaves on fol. 1r. The face is merely the space between the hair sections articulated by delicate features including treatment of the eyes, again similar to that on fol. 1r. The arms and trunk of the body down to the waist form another compartment, and again subtle calligraphic lines, this time curved, and dots are used to indicate the structure of the body. The drapery of the loin-cloth is complex in comparison, as is the knotted girdle which holds it and then falls down the front. All this is accomplished by the careful placing of single lines and variation in their lengths with only one scalloped line to show gathering. Below this section the legs are drawn simply with two outer lines and a single central line; the drapery falls higher over one knee than the other. Two curved faint lines are used to indicate the knees, and two arrow-headed nails secure the feet. The cross is very plainly drawn without decoration and emerges from a hillock decorated with stylised foliage. This is shown by an irregularly scalloped outline broken by a handful of short vertical lines, possibly to indicate grass. Within this are three rows of comma-like curved lines, some of which have fine lines drawn in the curve. The top line faces right, the second left and the third right again, and they link to form a pattern. The stylistic context of this initial is discussed below, but we may note at this point a drawing of Christ crucified on the back cover of a Beatus manuscript from San Millán executed at the end of the eleventh century. Although more fluid, this drawing echoes the initial in Vitr. 20–8 especially in the calligraphic depiction of the hair arranged along the outstretched arms.[17]

Aem. 18, however, does not follow Vitr. 20–8 in using this iconography. Instead the 'TE' of the *Te igitur* is a monogram (fol. 13v, FIG. 53). The letters are set in a 'T'-shaped frame broken by a series of irregular steps which nevertheless resolve into a balanced form. The letters themselves are formed of white interlace set against a plain green ground, which is in turn framed with dark green. This contrast is softened by yellow, red and blue infill. Both ends of the crossbar of the 'T' are decorated with interlace, but the central sections of the shaft and crossbar are divided by stripes, the inner two bands having an irregular step pattern. The letter 'E' of '*Te*' is placed across this portion of the central shaft allowing its interlace and foliate extensions to stand out. This format for the first initial of the canon also has its roots in Carolingian illumination.[18] The folio from Add. 30849 is lacking the 'Te' initial, although space is reserved for it. As only six lines are allowed, it is unlikely that a crucifixion depiction was envisaged. It is more likely that a foliate or interlace initial was planned.

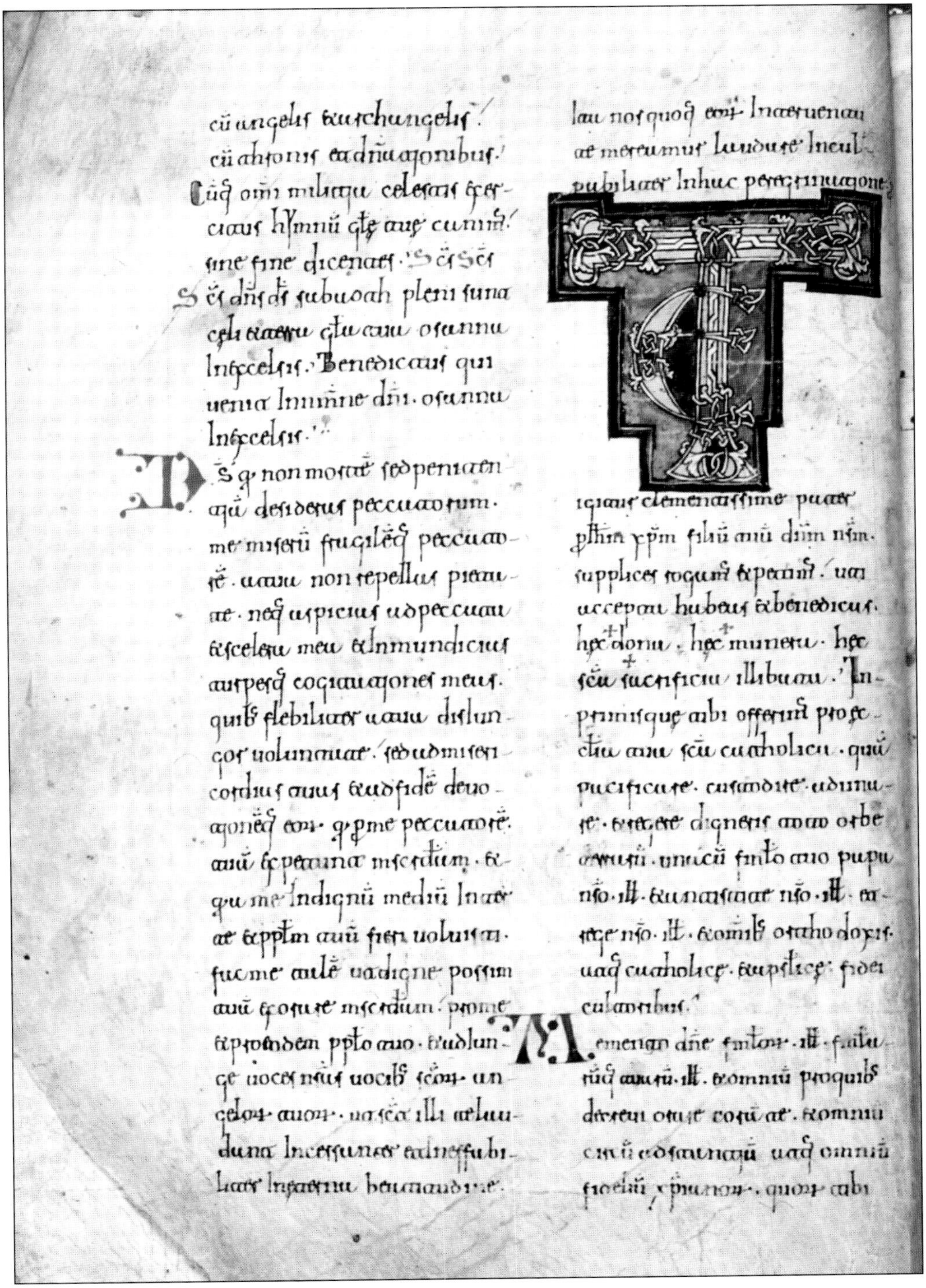

cū angelis & archangelis.
cū thronis & dominationibus.
Cūq omni militia celestis exercitus hymnū gloriæ tuæ canimus.
sine fine dicentes. Scs scs
scs dñs di sabaoth pleni sunt
celi & terra gloria tua. osanna
in excelsis. Benedictus qui
uenit in nomine dñi. osanna
in excelsis.

s q non mortē sed peniten-
tiā desideras peccatorum.
me miserū fragilēq peccato-
rē. tu me non repellas pieta-
te. neq aspicias ad peccata
& scelera mea & inmundicias
aut peruersas cogitationes meas.
quib flebiliter ttantur disiun-
cor uoluntuat. sed ad misera-
cordias tuas & ad fidē devo-
tionēq eor qui pro me peccatore.
tuā septuam misericordiam. &
qui me indignū medium inter-
ce & populum tuū fieri uoluisti.
fac me tale ualdigne possim
tuā exorare misericordiam. pro me
& pro eisdem populo tuo. & ad lun-
ge uoces nras uocib scor an-
gelor tuor. ut inter illos ac lau-
dum incessanter & ineffabi-
liter ingenita benignitate.

lau nos quoq eor interuenien-
& meritum laudare incul-
pabiliter inhuc peregrinatione.

igitur clementissime pater
per ihm xpm filium tuū dñm nrm.
supplices rogamus & petimus. uti
accepta habeas & benedicas.
hec dona. hec munera. hec
scta sacrificia illibata. In
primisque tibi offerimus pro ecclesia tua scta catholica. quā
pacificare. custodire & aduna-
re & regere digneris toto orbe
terrarū. unicū famulo tuo papa
nro. ill. & antistite nro. ill. &
rege nro. ill. & comite ortho doxis.
atq catholice & apostolice fidei
cultoribus.

emento dñe famulor. ill. famu-
larū tuarū. ill. & omnium pro quib
direptu ōrte eor & ad. & omnium
circū adstancium uaq omnium
fidelium xpianor. quor tibi

FIG. 53 Madrid, Real Academia de la Historia, Aemilianensis. 18, fol. 13v

In Vitr. 20–8 rubric headings and initials are the main illumination throughout the remainder of the canon. Each prayer is begun with a majuscule letter set in the left margin, which provides a clear guide to the contents of each page, and otherwise the text is enlivened only by the occasional use of red infill to highlight the first letter of a word, often the name of a saint. Aem. 18 is treated in a similar way; the rest of the section has mainly geometric initials with beads and penwork foliate flourishes, built from standard components. The colours used are red, green and blue with occasional yellow infill. Attention is also drawn to the first words of the prayers by the use of a yellow wash behind the letters. The first letters of the names of apostles, saints and Christ are also highlighted in this way. The prayer *Deus qui non mortem* receives a two-line initial 'D' of the geometric and bead variety found throughout the manuscript.

The illumination of the rest of the mass texts in Vitr. 20–8 and Aem. 18 contains no more major initials of the importance of those used for the preface and canon. Aem. 18 has no further figurative or interlace initials; the remainder of the text, temporal, sanctoral and votive masses, is articulated without differentiation by red geometric initials which are relieved only by ball decoration and occasionally extravagant, foliate flourishes (FIG. 54). The components which make up the letters are often crescent-shaped blocks with inner curves that widen out to a point, or small triangular blocks. These components are familiar to us from some of the geometric initials of the Silos Beatus, and, to a lesser extent, from the Roman breviary, Add. 30848. In this restrained setting the monograms which introduce the proper prefaces, a letter 'V' where the second stroke is made into a cross, are especially noticeable. In the 'Mozarabic' fashion, the most elaborate initials are used to introduce the *lectiones*, for example the 'F' on fol. 15v for '*fratres*' and the 'I' on fol. 16v for '*in illo tempore*'. There are even traces of what could be termed 'Mozarabic' decoration on some of the letter 'I's, for example on fol. VIII(v), i.e. fol. 23v, where a rudimentary spiral fills the shaft of the letter 'I', although similar decoration can also be found in a manuscript from Cluny, Paris, BN, MS N.a.l. 1548, fol. 30. The headings are generally picked out only by rubrication, although some are elongated (fol. VI(v), i.e. fol. 21v, FIG. 54), in the same way as some of the headings in Add. 30846 (FIG. 1). On fol. CXX(v), i.e. fol. 135v, a schematic face is drawn inside one of the letter 'O' initials. The use of heads to form initials was a distinctive feature of the southern tradition of 'Mozarabic' art, as we saw in Add. 30845, but in those cases the heads were usually more elaborate and augmented by one arm. It is possible that this isolated sketch represented a momentary escape from the restrictive non-figurative and bland decorative scheme of the bulk of the manuscript. On the other hand it may merely have been a convenient way of drawing attention to the texts inserted in the margin at this point.

Thus it could be said that the scribes of Aem. 18 occasionally lapsed into 'Mozarabic' habits, or at least that they were not entirely absorbed by the 'Romanesque' approach. A similar propensity can be detected in the initials of the preface and canon. The 'P' initial gives the impression of being carefully copied, rather than freely drawn, and the '*Vere dignum*' initial betrays its artist's training even more by the unconvincing stance of the angels and especially by lapses in the symmetry. The artist of the '*Te igitur*' initial seems

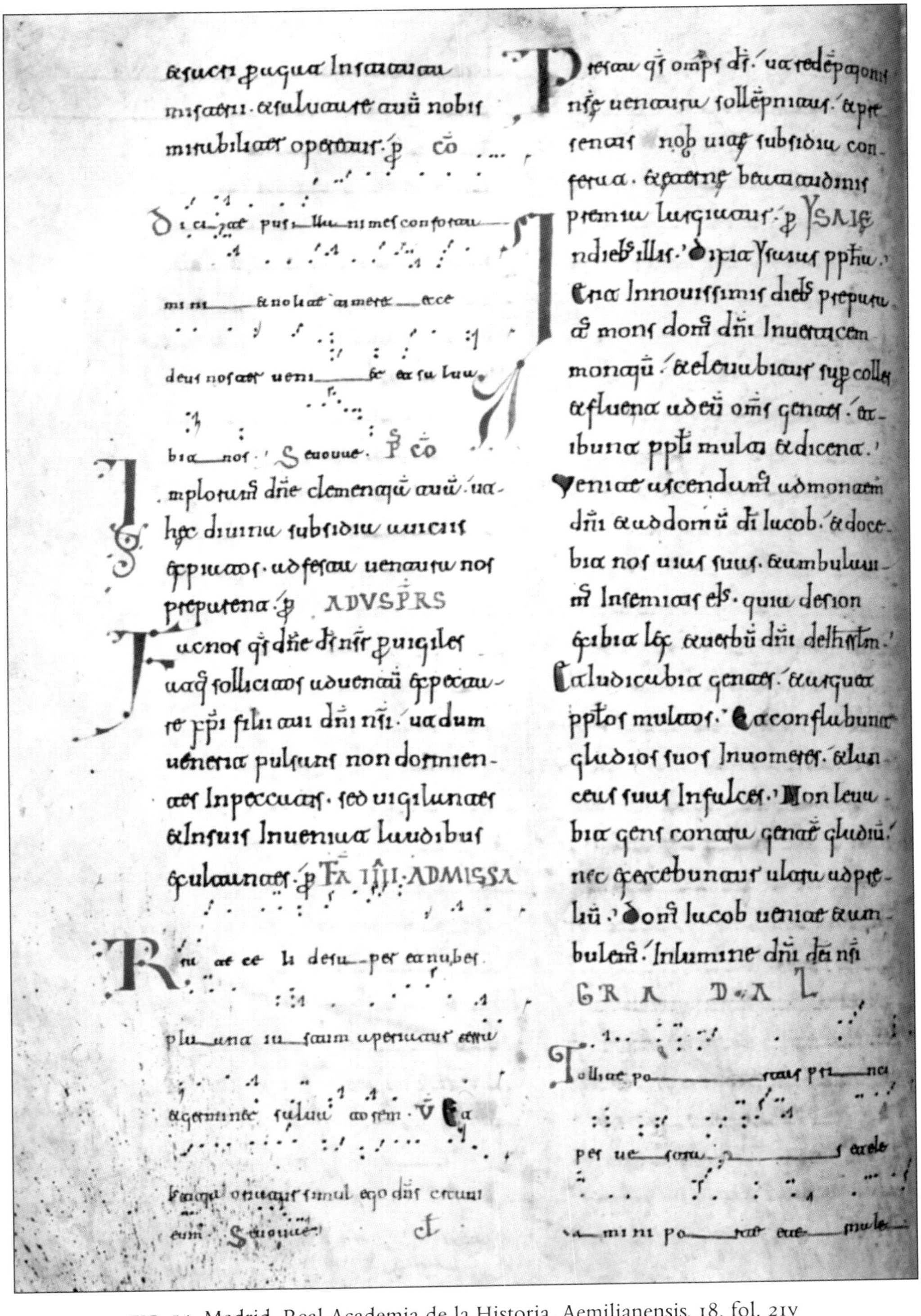

FIG. 54 Madrid, Real Academia de la Historia, Aemilianensis. 18, fol. 21v

more at home, and this initial is executed with more confidence than the figurative initials, which is not surprising because 'Mozarabic' artists were practised in producing interlace monograms, whether *vespertinum* monograms or full-page miniatures as *pages de garde*. Thus this manuscript has all the signs of a 'Romanesque' style executed by a scribe trained in the 'Mozarabic' artistic tradition. The result is routine rather than accomplished, and the lack of decoration has the feel of suppression, which comes out in the few 'Mozarabic' touches and the fantastic flourishes given to some of the letters.

The temporal and sanctoral sections of Vitr. 20–8 are articulated by the regular use of red initials, usually one or two lines high, set in the left-hand margin (e.g. the initial 'd' on fol. 6, FIG. 55). These initials are restrained, mostly geometric in style, with occasional ball decoration, a few crossbars with a strip of exposed vellum left in the centre, and sometimes a rudimentary foliate scroll to form the second stroke of an open letter 'a'. *Vere dignum* monograms also mark the proper prefaces in this manuscript, but here they are formed by two curved bowls with a cross at the join (e.g. fol. 6, FIG. 55).

Unlike the Mozarabic books and Aem.18, not all the feasts in Vitr. 20–8 are treated equally in decorative terms. Particular days are highlighted by the use of an illuminated initial, while others may be given only a rubricated title. The temporal section begins with a fine illuminated initial for the first letter of the first prayer for *Vigilia de Nativitate* (FIG. 55). There is no rubric to mark the day, but another illuminated initial introduces the first prayer for *in die Nativitatis*, also without any rubric (fol. 6v, FIG. 56). Both form the letter 'D' of the word '*Deus*' which is given in its abbreviated form. Both are likely to have been executed by the illuminator of fol. 1 and fol. 2. The first, on fol. 6, is an uncial form of 'D', set in a stepped frame which extends at the top left-hand corner to accommodate the tail of the curved dragon within it. The line of the steps also serves to lead the eye of the reader into the text. The dragon's head, neck and body form the large bowl of the letter. The body coils three times, spaced along its length, and the short wings are folded; the body is decorated with rows of dots and small half ovals, and the eye is delicately drawn, as are the claws on its two front feet, which are held up in heraldic fashion. The bar of the abbreviation is fitted into the first step of the box and the letter 'S', which completes it, is drawn in foliate style with acanthus terminals. The dragons used in several initials in Vitr. 20–8 can be paralleled in various initials of the *Codex Calixtinus*, but that is a much later manuscript dated at the earliest to the 1130s.

The second 'D' is also in a stepped box, although in this case the steps are very irregular and even slope at an angle on the left side. This letter features an acrobat, whose contortions dominate rather than reveal the letter. The figure has its head back, its legs bent at the knees and its feet over its head to form the bowl of the letter, while the arms are stretched forward and hold a foliate spray which spreads to form the tail of the letter. The drapery on the figure is scalloped at the bottom and just breaks across the frame. The use of acrobats in initials may be foreshadowed by the strange figure initials of Add. 30846 and more clearly by the hybrid trapeze artist in the San Millán manuscript,[19] but it is also a popular 'Romanesque' feature. It is likely that the prayer on fol. 8 *Da quaesumus omnipotens deus* was also

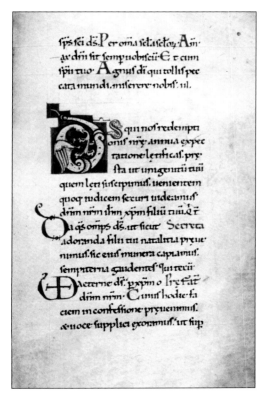

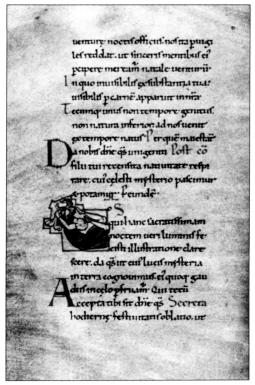

FIG. 55 Madrid, Biblioteca Nacional,
MS Vitr. 20–8, fol. 6

FIG. 56 Madrid, Biblioteca Nacional,
MS Vitr. 20–8, fol. 6v

intended to have an elaborate initial; the space has been left for a letter 'D', but it was never executed. This initial would also have highlighted the feast of the Nativity.

The next illuminated initial does not occur until *in die Ephiphaniae* (fol. 13), again without the rubricated title. Another letter 'D' in a stepped box, it is not figurative, but instead a foliate letter with clasps. Another dragon 'D' (fol. 50v) introduces *Deus qui hanc sacratissimam noctem*. After this there are three more unexecuted initials. One was probably intended to be an elaborate 'E' to judge from the dot and shading decoration given to the rest of the word *'Exultet'* which begins the benediction formula for the Easter candle; this would have drawn attention to the light symbolism of this ceremony (… *laetetur et mater ecclesia tanti luminis adornata*). The next missing initial (fol. 51v) would have been a letter 'D' to highlight the mass for Easter Sunday, and the third would have been a letter 'C' for *Vigilia Ascensionis*. The next illuminated initial in the temporal cycle is the 'D' of *Deus qui corda* on fol. 58v for the feast of Pentecost. This is a plain letter with clasps – one of them filled with interlace – and foliage filling the centre. The plain initials on fol. 64v and 65 are filled with half-shading, and on fol. 71v *Dominica prima Adventus* is given an illuminated letter 'E' with clasps, foliage and infill colour. Fol. 74 leaves space for an initial for *Deus qui salutis*, the fourth Sunday of Advent, but it is again not executed. The last initial in this section is the 'O' of *omnipotens sempiterne Deus* for the feast of *Purificatio Mariae* (fol. 77). The letter is formed by a simple ring which is then entwined with tendrils of foliage including one which pushes through a cut in the ring.

The beginning of the sanctoral is not marked with an illuminated initial and the next one would presumably have been for *Nativitas Iohannis Baptistae* (fol. 89v), as the space is allowed, but again the initial is missing. The feast for *in Natale SS. Petri et Pauli* (fol. 91) is marked with a modest initial 'D' in a square box filled with a simple flower. The next is for *Assumptio Matris Dei* (fol. 99v): *Veneranda* is given an illuminated 'V' of the foliage-and-clasp variety with a filled centre. Thus it is the Marian feasts which receive most decorative attention in this manuscript, while there is acknowledgement of the importance of the patrons of Cluny, Sts Peter and Paul, in the sanctoral.

There are no more illuminated initials until after the end of the sanctoral when the *dedicatio ecclesiae* is given on fol. 117v. The 'D' of *Deus qui nobis* is formed from a four-line square of interlace for the bowl, and a large leaping beast for the shaft (FIG. 57). The beast grips the interlace from the box with its pointed canine teeth. Drawn in outline, with some double lines, the lion-like beast has occasional scalloping and zigzag decoration. This initial has a 'Mozarabic' parallel, not only in the interlace bowl, which can be seen similarly in the Silos Beatus (fol. 8v) and in Add. 30846, but also in the leaping beast. A similar conception is used for an initial in a tenth-century San Millán manuscript (Madrid, RAH, Aem. 8, fol. 15v), *Expositio Psalmorum*, where the tail of the letter is formed by a beast leaping towards the bowl of the letter which is circular, not square, and filled with interlace. In this instance, however, the beast is being killed by a figure with a spear.[20] The idea appears again in another Spanish manuscript, *S. Ephraem sermones*, now in the Bibliothèque nationale in Paris (MS N.a.l. 235). The beast is again depicted in outline and leaps towards a circle of interlace.[21] A third example occurs on the Alpha page of a Beatus Commentary (Burgo de Osma, Cathedral Archive, Cod.1). Here two beasts drawn in outline leap towards each other. From each of their mouths come two strands of interlace which mingle to form a bundle of interlace. Does this indicate a Spanish origin for Vitr. 20–8, which was probably written for a French monk in a Spanish monastery? It certainly demonstrates that an artist who was familiar with 'Mozarabic' techniques worked on the manuscript at some point. There are, however, no other examples of the work of this artist in the manuscript and the beast on fol. 117v has very little in common with the dragons which decorate several of the other initials. The question, therefore, arises as to when the initial on fol. 117v was executed. If most of the manuscript was written and illuminated – leaving several spaces for unexecuted initials – in France, it is possible that one of the spaces was filled by a Spanish scribe during Bernard's time at Sahagún. It is also possible that the manuscript was copied at Sahagún by a French scribe who accompanied Bernard, and decorated by French and/or Spanish artists most of whom were trained in 'Romanesque' techniques. In that situation a locally-trained artist in the same workshop might have been invited to contribute as a gesture of accord.

Vitr. 20–8 has been described as a slavish imitation of its supposed French model.[22] What evidence supports this assertion? The script is indeed a fine example of Protogothic,

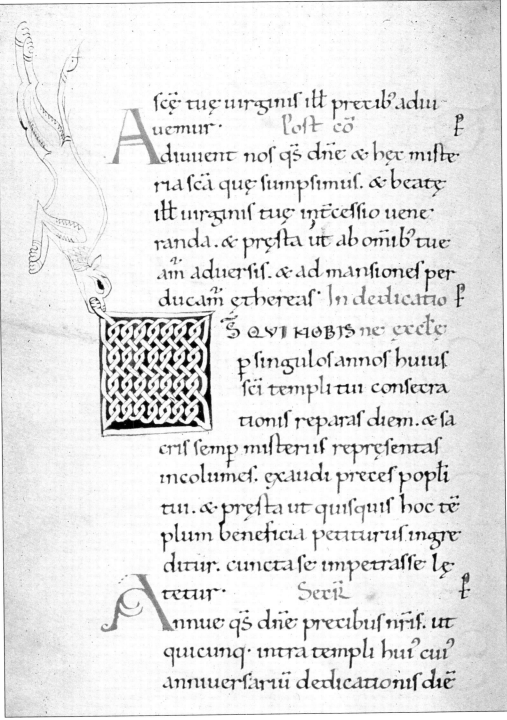

scē tuę uirginis iłł precib̄ adiu-
Auemur· **Poſt cō**   ꝑ
diuuenr nos q̄s dn̄e & hec miſte-
ria ſcā quę ſumpſimuſ. & beatę
iłł uirginis tuę inteceſſio uene-
randa. & preſta ut ab om̄ib̄ tue
am̄ aduerſiſ. & ad manſiones per
ducam̄ ethereaſ· In dedicatio ꝑ
ſ QVI HOBIS ne ercłę
ꝑ ſinguloſ annoſ huiuſ
ſc̄i templi tui conſecra
tioniſ reparaſ diem. & ſa
criſ ſemp miſteriiſ repreſentaſ
incolumeſ. exaudi preceſ popli
tui. & preſta ut quiſquiſ hoc tē
plum beneficia petiturus ingre
ditur. cuncta ſe impetraſſe lę
Atetur·   **Seriī**   ꝑ
nnue q̄s dn̄e precibuſ nr̄iſ. ut
quicunq· intra templi hui cui
anniuerſariū dedicationiſ diē

FIG. 57 Madrid, Biblioteca Nacional, MS Vitr. 20–8, fol. 117v

with no suggestion in its palaeography or orthography that the scribe may once have been familiar with the Visigothic script. The text has been found to be orthodox, and a saint venerated mainly in France and particularly in Dijon, *S. Benignus*, is included in a prominent place in the mass. This is certainly an orthodox manuscript with no sign of any Mozarabic practices. It is, therefore, entirely plausible that a Burgundian manuscript, possibly sent through Cluny, was used as the model for the text.

The French connections proposed for the illumination of this manuscript have included Moissac and Limoges. Schapiro likened the 'P' initial to examples in two Moissac manuscripts,[23] and this link is supported by Moralejo and Williams.[24] Moralejo also offers an Agen-Moissac parallel for the style of the *Te Igitur* initial, but there is little to link the two miniatures: there is some similarity in the drapery but not to a significant degree, and the general aspect is markedly different.[25] I believe that a more striking parallel is offered between the *VD* monogram on fol. IV of Vitr-20–8 and fol. I of another manuscript probably produced near Agen (Paris, BN, MS lat. 2388); the likeness is especially noticeable in the beasts' heads.[26] We should, however, be cautious in our conclusions, as several of these manuscripts have been dated to the twelfth century,[27] that is well after the probable date for the execution of Vitr.20–8. We have good reason to doubt, therefore, that this is a straightforward case of a debt which the Spanish manuscript may owe to Moissac or Moissac-related scriptoria (*see* fig. 58 for another Moissaic manuscript (Paris, BN, MS N.a.l. 1871), which has affinities with Vitr. 20–8).[28] In this context it may be of note that Paris, BN, MS lat. 2388 is a manuscript of Alcuin's *Adversus Elipandum* and Smaragdus's *Diadema Monachorum*, both texts which are linked to Spain by association.

The case is much the same with the Limoges connection, which was suggested by Janini and Serrano.[29] There are parallels in particular with the second Limoges Bible (Paris, BN, MS n.a.l.8, II), dated to the early twelfth century. These can be seen for example in the initial 'A' on fol. 136v, which has close associations with the style of Vitr. 20–8, including the interlace blocks of the 'P' initial and beasts' heads – although these are heads again like those in the *vere dignum* initial, not those in the 'P'.[30] This letter also has men climbing up the letter and vigorously fighting the beasts with spears and knives.

Thus there is little doubt that Vitr. 20–8 was produced in an artistic network which covered the south-west of France. Moreover it is almost certain that the text of Vitr. 20–8 was written by a French scribe, as there are no examples of such an accomplished Caroline script being executed by a Spanish scribe until the twelfth century.[31] Attempts to locate a leading centre within this exchange of ideas have not so far proved convincing. At the risk of entering the endless and generally unhelpful Spain/France debate, we will also consider the possibility that this manuscript could have been illuminated by an artist trained in Spain.

There are precedents in Spain for the methods of decoration used in Vitr. 20–8. Over a generation earlier Fernando I and his wife Sancha had commissioned three manuscripts, which still survive, a copy of Beatus's Commentary on the Apocalypse (Madrid, BN, MS Vitr.14–2), a *Psalterium et Liber Canticorum* (Salamanca, Bibl. Univ., MS 2268), and a Prayer Book (Biblioteca Universitaria de Santiago de Compostela (Rs.I)).[32] These manuscripts have

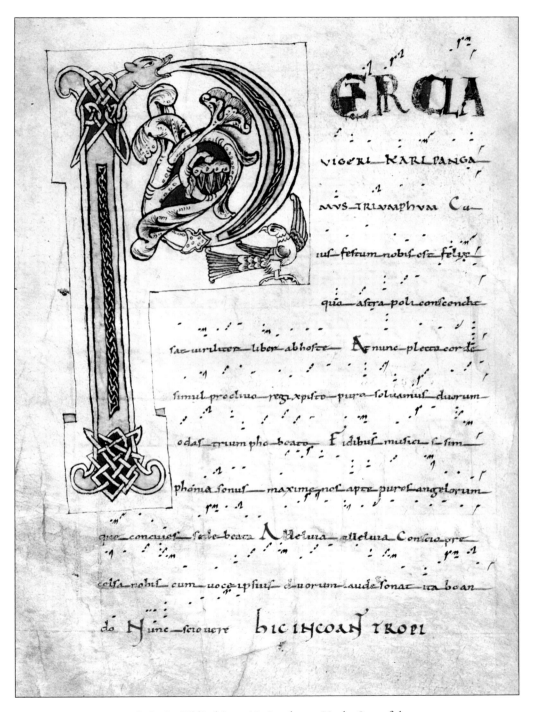

FIG. 58 Paris, Bibliothèque Nationale, MS N.a.l. 18712, fol. 24v

been recognised as introducing Romanesque techniques of illumination into Spain, since they use the artistic vocabulary of the developing 'Romanesque' style alongside text written in Visigothic script. The liturgical texts contained in the Prayer Book – psalms, liturgical canticles and hours – are Mozarabic and the name of the artist is also Spanish (*Fructuosus*), suggesting that some Spanish artists/scribes were capable of using Romanesque techniques by the mid-eleventh century.[33]

It is indeed with this Prayer Book[34] that I believe Vitr. 20–8 may usefully be compared. All the illumination in Vitr. 20–8, however accomplished, is highly calligraphic, and this is especially clear in the construction of the figure of Christ in the Calvary initial. The drapery folds are similar to those on the figure forming the initial on fol. 57v of the Prayer Book and to the curtains on the dedicatory folio. The figures themselves in the Prayer Book are not similar to those in Vitr. 20–8, but some of them stand on mounds decorated with dots and half circles, similar to that at the base of the *Te Igitur* initial.[35]

Recent work has been done on the scriptorium at Sahagún by Barbara Shailor,[36] as a result of which she has attributed the production of the Beatus Commentary now at Burgo de Osma (Burgo de Osma, Cathedral Archive, Cod.1) to the scriptorium at Sahagún. The manuscript is dated by internal evidence to 1086, which is within the 1081–1086 span available for the production of Vitr. 20–8. In many ways the illumination of the manuscript is faithful to the branch of Beatus manuscripts to which it belongs in textual and decorative terms, but there are also several innovatory features including the incorporation of Romanesque elements especially in the treatment of drapery. Williams considers that this manuscript 'reveals the scriptorium of the monastery at Sahagún acting as a foyer for the introduction of the Romanesque style in the painting of the Iberian peninsular'.[37]

We have already seen some similarities between Vitr. 20–8 and the Prayer Book of Fernando and Sancha – placed possibly at Sahagún by Williams, as well as one similarity between Vitr. 20–8 and the Burgo de Osma Beatus Commentary – now placed at Sahagún by Shailor. These similarities, together with the transformed view of the Sahagún scriptorium, could form the basis of an argument for Vitr. 20–8 having been produced under royal patronage with techniques which had developed in Spain since the mid-eleventh century.

As the probable recipient of Vitr. 20–8 was a French monk whose distinguished future lay in leading the Spanish church, it is also possible that this manuscript was a collaborative exercise between a French scribe and a Spanish artist. In any event there is no element of compromise in the production of this manuscript. Its bold illumination thoughtfully applied stands in clear contrast to the uncertain figurative work and undifferentiated initials in Aem. 18. It is an expressive reflection of the crisp structure and positive direction at the centre of the reform movement, while at the fringes the impetus was weak.

Sal. 2637 is clearly the latest of the Roman missals in this study, and, as we have seen, it differs from the others in structure and thus in focus. Lacking a preface and canon section, it spreads its decoration among the texts for the mass throughout the year. It begins with a heading *incipit liber missarum per anni circulum dicendarum*, written in capitals in such a com-

FIG. 59 Salamanca, Biblioteca de la Universidad, MS 2637, fol. 1

plex pattern that it is at first difficult to read: letters are frequently inserted in the bowls of other letters and all the letters of *dicendarum* are placed inside the initial 'D'; the 'A' and 'R' of *missarum* are linked by a common ascender and the first letter 'N' of *anni* is written in reverse, or upside-down (FIG. 59). The letters are decorated with foliate penwork, which protrudes in one or two clumps from the left-hand side of some of the ascenders, and with a shading of fine lines which run parallel with some of the cross-bars. In addition the letter 'S' in both cases is decorated by a dot touching the bowl of the letter, which is then surrounded on the open side by small dots giving the appearance of a half-flower; this

FIG. 60 Silos, Abbey of Santo Domingo, Cloister Capital, Lower North Gallery
(Photo: George Zamecki)

occurs in the top and bottom of the letters. The heading is finished with a vertical line of commas, which could be an echo of the same motif used in the Mozarabic manuscripts. The first sub-heading in the book, which introduces the processional antiphons for Advent, is written in small capitals of a rustic type which are used again, although smaller, in the first line of the first antiphon.

The grandest initial in the manuscript is found on the recto of fol. 2 (PLATE 9). Capitals similar to those used for the sub-heading on fol. 1 state the feast day across the top of the page, *Dominica prima in Adventu Domini officium.* The initial 'A' which fills two-thirds of the page is the first letter of the opening antiphon: *Ad te levavi animam.* It is contained within an irregular frame and is coloured with blocks of blue, red, violet and yellow. The body of the letter is formed of free-form interlace which occasionally sprouts into buds of foliage. The letter is filled with cascading interlace which ends in more extravagant foliate scrolls in various stages of development. At the top the two ascenders meet and cross over one another dissecting a ring, which is itself tied with interlace to a smaller central single ring. The two ascenders continue beyond the ring and become two beasts' heads, from whose mouths pour foliage which scrolls down the sides of the letter. Not content with this effect, the illuminator also places six beasts to inhabit the scrolls. Irregularity rules here, as on the left side the beast at the top reaches back to grip its hindquarters, while the one below raises its front leg and leans its head back to watch; a small third beast emerges from the base of the foliage. On the right side, however, two affronted beasts lean back from one another while a third climbs up the lower foliage to eat a higher leaf. Although likenesses between manuscripts and sculpture are problematic, I wish to propose a sculptural reference for this initial in the cloister at Silos. On the north side of the cloister there is a double capital with a fairly flat carving of lions entwined in foliate interlace, which they reach up to eat, while leaning back from one another as they meet at the volutes (FIG. 60). This may not be a unique subject, but the treatment is sufficiently similar to suggest that the illuminator who decorated Sal. 2637 had seen this capital; the Silos connection for Sal. 2637 is thus strengthened.

The rest of the heading is written in letters similar to those which introduced the manuscript on fol. 1, with the same pen work, patterning and shading in blue and red over a yellow wash. The letter 'A' of *animam* is, like that of *anni*, oddly drawn in that the left ascender bulges at the top as if drawing an 'R' in reverse. A similar letter-form is found on one of the inserted folios in Add. 30849, fol. 294 (FIG. 8), as is the scalloping which occurs on the left of several of the letters in Sal. 2637. A link between these two manuscripts may not localise them to Silos, but together with the other indications it does point in that direction.

Sal. 2637 has numerous other illuminated initials, and several are in a style close to that of the initial on fol. 2. *Dominica III de Adventu* has a 5-line letter 'G' for the introit *Gaudete in domino* (fol. 5). It has a light brown outline, and the centre of the letter is filled with violet, while the body of letter is in red and light brown ink. Its structure is foliate, the letter itself being formed from a long tendril decorated with small circles. The return of the 'G' sprouts rinceaux, some of which curl round the tendril, and three flat hatched leaves; at the top the letter ends in a trumpet-flower.

On fol. 10v *Dominica IIII in Adventu Domini* begins with a 7-line letter 'O' (*O memento nostri domine*), set in an irregular stepped frame, of very dark and very light red ink. It is again mostly foliate with tendrils curling round the body of the letter, but there is also some interlace springing from a wide stem. Occasional bands decorate the stems. The 5-line 'D' of *Dominus dixit ad me*, which opens the *Missa ad galli cantu* on folio 11v, has elements similar to the two previous letters, but a wide foliate band with sections of interlace wraps round the stem and forms the ascender.

Fol. 13 (*Missa ad mane*), has a five-line 'L' for *Lux fulgebit hodie*. Set in an irregular stepped frame filled with pale yellow, it has a short ascender (five-lines) in comparison with the wide horizontal which stretches almost across the column. The body of the letter is drawn in red sections like brickwork, and both terminals are formed from interlace filled with red.

On fol. 14v (FIG. 61), there is a very large initial 'P' (17-lines) to begin the introit for *in die Natale*, *Puer natus est nobis*. The rest of the phrase is also written in capital letters again in a complex pattern. The 'P' is set in a stepped, three-dimensional, light brown frame, which is in its turn filled with violet ink. The letter is mainly of interlace with foliate terminals coming from the two strands of interlace at the top of the ascender and filling the bowl of the letter in red, light and dark blue.

The initial on fol. 20v (FIG. 62) is of a slightly different type. It is an 11-line letter 'I', marking the first Sunday after Epiphany, at the top of which is a mask in yellow wash with red ears, from whose mouth comes a double column decorated with small circles, which ends in interlace knots. Around this column curls a serpent with light brown dots, whose

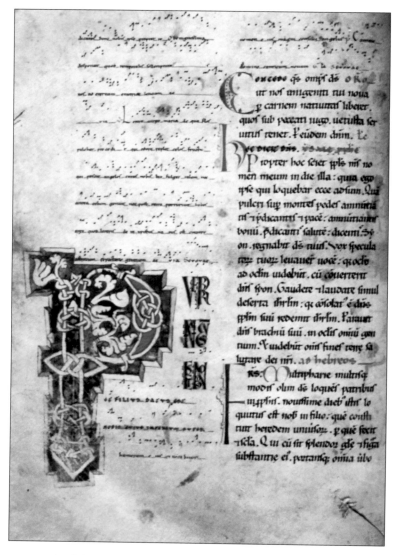

FIG. 61 Salamanca, Biblioteca de la Universidad, MS 2637, fol. 14v

tongue is like a trefoil. The initial on fol. 103, which highlights part of the baptism ceremony, is also somewhat unusual. It has a small font-like basin in the centre from which spring two leafy terminals.

While foliate and interlace initials continue to mark the major feasts, the *lectiones* receive red initials, often of five or six lines, decorated most often with penwork scalloping to the left of the letter, and stripes of exposed vellum showing through the red ink; the letter 'H' sometimes has an arch in the middle of the crossbar. One- or two-line initials are used for responses, verses and other prayers, although the *sacra* receives a three-line initial in one instance. The type of letter used for the readings is also sometimes used for a feast, for

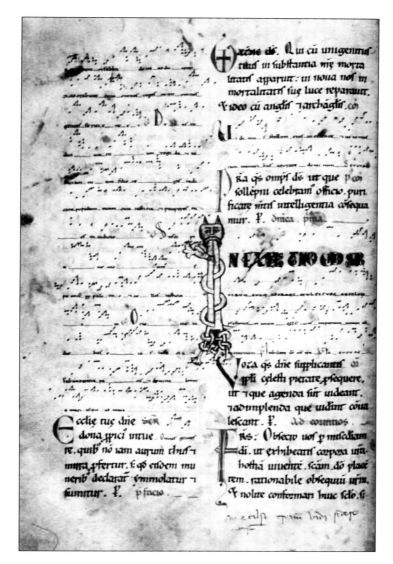

FIG. 62 Salamanca, Biblioteca de la Universidad, MS 2637, fol. 20v

example the 6-line 'P' to begin the first prayer of *dominica ii in Adventu Domini* on fol. 3; this is a geometric letter, with dots, flowers made from dots, and penwork decoration.[38] The rubrics have a yellow wash behind them. The decoration is thus quite even with only occasional highlighted feasts, neither as bland as the decoration in the temporal and sanctoral sections of Aem. 18, nor as partisan in its illumination as those sections in Vitr. 20–8.

Some masses, however, receive particularly fine illumination. The initial 'T' for *Dedicatio ecclesiae* (fol. 168v) has several similarities with the large opening initial 'A' on fol. 2. This eight-line 'T' is set in a light yellow frame surrounded by a stepped box. The bar of the 'T' becomes interlace at each terminal, and the shaft of the letter, decorated with sets of three

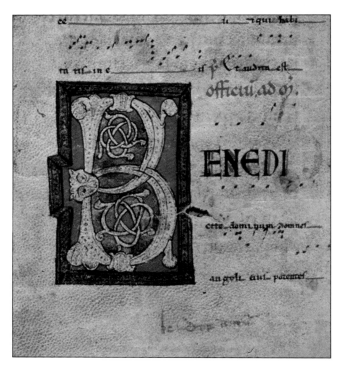

FIG. 63 Salamanca, Biblioteca de la Universidad,
MS 2637, fol. 220v (detail)

dots and bands, is also wrapped in the foliage which comes from a beast's mouth at the base.

In the sanctoral section there is a very large initial 'D' on fol. 194v for the feast of St John the Baptist, with all the familiar foliate interlace, and also a leaf with tight cross-hatching filled with tiny dots. On fol. 220v (FIG. 63) there is another notable initial, a large 'B' (*Benedicite dominum*) introducing the processional anthems for the feast of St Michael. This is decorated with interlace and foliage coming from a mask. The Marian feasts again receive particular attention. A large vegetal 'S' introduces the *Purificatio* (fol. 177v). A fine initial 'G', set in a three-dimensional box, decorates the feast of *Nativitas Mariae* on folio 215v (FIG. 64): the back of the letter 'G' is formed of foliage and interlace, but the return is a beast which leans to the left and lifts its right paw to eat one of the tendrils. The Assumption of the Virgin also receives a fine initial (fol. 210, FIG. 65). So the hierarchy of initials in the sanctoral confirms the manuscript's interest in St Michael and adds St John the Baptist as another possible patron saint. The interest in the Virgin is by this date ubiquitous and not necessarily significant.

The initial which introduces the mass for the Assumption of the Virgin is of interest for another reason. Although only eight lines in height, this letter is executed with meticulous attention. It is set in a frame decorated with small circles through which come foliate tendrils in the same way as they emerge from the frame on fol. IV of Vitr. 20–8. Indeed this large 'A' has other features in common with that *'vere dignum'* initial in Vitr. 20–8. It also has

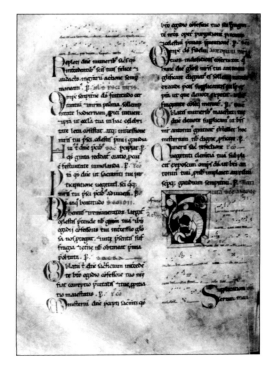

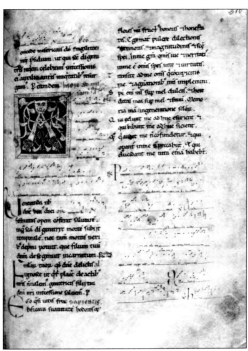

FIG. 64 Salamanca, Biblioteca
de la Universidad, MS 2637, fol. 215v

FIG. 65 Salamanca, Biblioteca
de la Universidad, MS 2637, fol. 210

a beast's head – although in this case only one – which has foliage and interlace coming from its ears as well as from its mouth. The foliage is also similar in profile and the letter itself is formed from foliage and interlace in the same way. The artist of this initial used features which we know from Vitr. 20–8. It is, however, very unlikely that any scribe who worked on Sal. 2637 would have seen Vitr. 20–8, especially if that manuscript was a personal possession of Archbishop Bernard and went to Toledo with him. The appearance of an initial so close to that in Vitr. 20–8 therefore supports the impression gained above, that Vitr. 20–8 might have been a small version of a larger book or books which were circulated as models during the time of the liturgical change.

Apart from this one initial which is so reminiscent of that in Vitr. 20–8, Sal. 2637 is emphatically not a manuscript in the image of the Missal of San Facundo. It is distanced from it not only by over fifty years, but in focus, in structure and in most of its illumination. If Vitr. 20–8 was the model and Aem. 18 is wavering reflection, Sal. 2637 is a new statement, a plenary missal with a strong form of its own, which it expresses clearly through its illumination.

The study of these three missals has established that the association of the new mass text with the new artistic style was very strong. This is reflected very clearly in the way the decoration articulates the text, in two of the manuscripts fixing the reader's attention above all on the preface and canon, which is in marked contrast to the use of illumination in the

Mozarabic books. Moreover in the Roman missals there is no sign of the many 'Mozarabic' motifs which linger in the Roman breviaries; even Aem. 18 has only minimal 'Mozarabic' symptoms in its illumination as in its text. It appears from the illumination, as from the texts, that the liturgical change was uncompromising in the matter of the mass. It demanded a clear declaration of orthodoxy and strict conformity to the new order.

Notes to Chapter Six

1   Gaborit-Chopin, D., *La décoration des manuscrits à Saint-Martial de Limoges et en Limousin du IXe au XIIe siècle*, Geneva, 1969, Pl.70.

2   Guilmain, *as above*, Ch. 3 note 13, Pl.I, Fig. 11 for an elongated Leonese example, and Pl.III, Fig. 3 and 4 for some more developed examples from San Millán.

3   Such beast initials were also in use at San Millán towards the end of the eleventh century, as they can be found in the *Liber Comicus* (MS Aem. 22), e.g. fol. 15v (illustrated in Boylan, *as above* Ch. 1 note 7, p.409, Pl.3).

4   This initial has another parallel, closer than Vitr. 20–8, but probably later than either manuscript, in a codex from Le Mans containing works of St Isidore, Paris, BN, MS lat. 2325 fol. 96v. This is again a letter 'P' where a man forms the shaft of the letter and the dragon the bowl, but in this case the man is killing the dragon with a spear. The details of the initial are not all identical, but the angle of the figure makes this quite a striking likeness. This is illustrated in Stones, A., 'The Decoration and Illumination of the Codex Calixtinus at Santiago de Compostella', p.170, Fig. 10, note 30, in Williams, J. and Stones, A., *as above* Ch. 3 note 43. Stones notes that it is dated by Avril to *c.*1120–30, note 19.

5   I have used Leroquais, *as above* Ch. 5 note 2, Ebner, A., *Quellen und Forschungen zur Geschichte und Kunstgeschichte des Missale Romanum im mittelalter iter italicum*, Freiburg im Breisgau, 1957, and the photograph collection of the Conway Library at the Courtauld Institute of Art to build up a picture of widespread practices of missal illumination in the eleventh and twelfth centuries in Europe. The notable omission in our Spanish manuscripts is the use of the *maiestas domini* iconography to illuminate the preface. It seems a missed opportunity to represent the Roman liturgy as a reflection of the celestial liturgy.

6   Ebner, *as above*, note 5.

7   For example in the Morgan Beatus (New York, Pierpont Morgan Library, MS 644, fol. 87) where the 'angels' are labelled '*cerubim*' and '*serafin*'. Illustrated in Williams, *as above* Ch. 3 note 8, p.73, Pl.17.

8   This date is based on Williams, *as above* Intro. note 51, p.170–84.

9   Williams, J.W., 'Generationes Abrahae: Reconquest Iconography in León', in *Gesta*, 16/2, 1977, p.3–14.

10 Williams, *as above* note 9. Williams takes the interpretation of the tympanum iconography beyond the basic sacrificial level.

11 Madrid, Real Academia de la Historia, MS 33, folio illustrated in Domínguez Bordona, J., *Manuscritos con Pinturas*, vol.I, Madrid, 1933, p.209, Fig. 197.

12 For example in the Silos Beatus, fol. 141v, '*draco princeps diabolus est*', and in Add. 30848, the reading for the Second Sunday after the Octave of Easter: '*draco diabolus simulat se Christum adoraturum per suos ministros in ecclesia ut sicut Herodes intestinus hostis, quem adorare simulabat, occidere quaerebat; ita diabolus natum mulieris ecclesiae per malos Christianos simulando sanctitatem Christum in pectore nostro conatur occidere*'.'

13 Apoc.16:13–6, and in Add. 30848, the reading for the Fourth Sunday after the Octave of Easter: '*draconem iam supra diximus diabolum esse, et bestia, id est, corpus diaboli, quod sunt homines mali et pseudo-prophetae, id est praepositi corporis diaboli, quod sunt sacerdotes et praedictatores mali, unum spiritum habent quasi ranae*'.

14 This is based on the same evidence *as above* in note 5. There is an example from the first half of the twelfth century; *see* Cahn, W., *Romanesque Manuscripts: The Twelfth Century*, Vols 1 & 2, London, 1996, Vol. 1, ill. 10, Vol 2, p.17, Troyes, Bibl. Mun. 894, f.114 (cat. 5).

15 For example the eleventh-century Sacramentary of Figeac (Moissac usage), Paris, BN, MS lat. 2293, fol. 17 has a foliate/interlace 'P' for the Preface with a bird's head at the same point as one of the beast heads in Vitr. 20–8; the eleventh century Sacramentary of St Denis, Paris, BN, MS lat. 9436 fol. 13v, has a foliate/interlace 'P' with a beast's head. Both illustrated in Leroquais, *see above* Ch. 5 note 2, Pl.XXIV and Pl.XXVIII respectively.

16 Chapter 5, p.165.

17 Illustrated in Williams, *as above* Ch. 3 note 8, p.30, Pl.XIV.

18   *See*, for example, Leroquais, V, *as above* Ch. 5, note 2, Pl.XII, the ninth-century Sacramentary of St. Thierry (Bibliothèque Municipale de Reims, MS 213 fol. 13v). Also in the Conway Library of the Courtauld Institute of Art photographs of Vienna, Nationalbibliothek MS 958 and Cologne, Dombibliothek MS 137.

19   Guilmain, *as above* Ch. 3 note 13, Pl.IV, Fig. 6.

20   Guilmain, *as above* Ch. 3 note 13, Plate IV, Fig. 2. Also illustrated in Mentré, *as above* Ch. 3 note 21.

21   Paris, BN, MS N.a.l. 235, fol. 109, illustrated in Avril, F., Aniel, J.-P., Mentré, M., Saulnier, A., Zaluska, Y. (eds), *Manuscrits enluminés de la péninsule ibérique*, Paris (Bibliothèque Nationale), 1982, Pl.V.

22   Domínguez Bordona, J., *Spanish Illumination*, Paris, 1930, vol.I, p.22. Mundó, A., in Janini *as above* Intro. note 116, p.249, also describes the *Vere Dignum* initial as of French inspiration 'con sumisión absoluta al modelo'.

23   Schapiro, M., *as above* note 4, n.161, Paris, BN, MS lat.52, fol. 1 and MS lat.1656A, fol. 16.

24   Moralejo, S., 'The tomb of Alfonso Ansúrez (1093): Its Place and the Role of Sahagún in the Beginnings of Spanish Romanesque Sculpture', in Reilly, B.F., (ed.), *Santiago, Saint-Denis and Saint Peter, The Reception of the Roman Liturgy in León-Castile in 1080*, New York, 1985, p.94, n.74. His comparisons are Paris, BN, MS lat. 2154, fol. 65v, Paris, BN, MS lat. 1797, fol. 2, and Paris, BN, MS lat.1656A, fol. 5. These are illustrated in Dufour, J., *La bibliothèque et le scriptorium de Moissac*, Paris 1972, no. 59 – Pl.LII, no. 47 – Pl.LXI, and no. 41 – Pl.XLIX respectively. John Williams's catalogue entry in *The Art of Medieval Spain*, *as above* Intro. note 14, p.294–5, gives other examples illustrated in Dufour, *as above* note 416, no. 43 – Pl.XLVI for the Te Igitur, and no. 103 – Pl.XXXVIII and no. 59 – Pl.LII for the Preface.

25   Moralejo, *see above* note 24, p.94, n.74, Paris, BN, MS lat. 254, fol. 10. He also compares the miniatures in Vitr. 20–8 to one of the illustrations in a charter of San Salvador de Villacete (Madrid, Archivo Histórico Nacional), but in my opinion the parallels are strained, as the details of the drapery and facial features do not match and the stylistic approach is much cruder in the charter.

26   Dufour, *as above* note 24, no. 67, Pl.LXXIV.

27   Dufour, *as above* note 24. Only Williams's first two examples are dated by Dufour to the eleventh century.

28   It is also interesting to note a close parallel between the letter 'P' on fol. 1 of Add. 30849 and the letter 'P' on fol. 24v of the Moissac manuscript, Paris, BN, MS N.a.l. 1871 (FIG. 58). Although the figurative element is missing, there are marked similarities in the beast's head coming from interlace and the fleshy fruit in the centre of the bowl.

29   Janini and Serrano, *as above* Ch. 4 note 10, pp.248–9. *See also* Yarza Luaces, J., 'La Miniatura Románica en España. Estado de la Cuestión', in *Anuario del Departamento de Historia y Teoría del Arte*, Vol. 2, Universidad Autónoma de Barcelona, 1990, p.21.

30   Gaborit-Chopin, D., *as above* note 1, pp.86–107, Pl.220.

31   *See* Shailor, *as above* Ch. 4 note 16.

32   This manuscript was commissioned by Sancha for Fernando and was completed in 1055. *See* Sicart, A., *Pintura Medieval: La Miniatura*, Santiago de Compostela, 1981; and Janini, *as above* Intro. note 116, no. 290, p.246.

33   Sicart, *as above* note 32, and Janini, *as above* Intro. note 116, no. 290, p.246. The saints included in this book are a typically 'Mozarabic' selection, *Sebastianus, Fructuosus, Babilas, Tirsus, Emeterius et Celedon, Torquatus, Cucufas, Felix, Iustus et Pastoris, Faustus et Ianuarius, Martialis, Servandus et Germanus, Vincentus et Letus, Acisclus, Felix, Emilianus, Prudentius, Isidorus, Victorianus, Eulalia, Leocadia, Baselissa, Nanilo, Elodia, Engratia, Columba, Iusta et Rufina.*

34   Williams, J.W., catalogue entry in *The Art of Medieval Spain, A.D.500–1200*, *as above* Intro. note 14, pp.290–91. Williams proposes Sahagún as one of the possible scriptoria which may have produced the Prayer Book.

35   For example, fol. 29v, illustrated in Sicart, *as above* note 32, p.177, Fig. 1.

36   Shailor, *as above* Ch. 4 note 16, and Shailor, B.A., 'The Beatus of Burgo de Osma: A Paleographical and Codicological Study', in *Apocalipsis Beati Liebanensis. Burgi Oxomensis. Vol.2: El Beato de Osma, Estudios*, Valencia, 1992, pp.29–52.

37   John Williams's, catalogue entry in *The Art of Medieval Spain A.D.500–1200*, *as above* Intro. note 14, pp.159–60.

38 This kind of initial is also found in a manuscript from Moissac, London, British Library, Harley MS 2914, fol. 20 and fol. 181v for example, which shows the continuing connections among methods of illumination in this area of France and northern Spain.

CONCLUSION

──◄○►──

The Reconstruction of Orthodoxy

WE HAVE NOW collected many 'snap-shots' of the liturgical change through comparisons within our group of manuscripts. If we now bring together the evidence from the office texts of part I and the mass texts of part II, what overall impression of the change do we obtain? What exactly happened when the Mozarabic liturgy was replaced by the Roman liturgy? How was the change implemented and how was it received?

All the books in this study are dominated by text, and some of our conclusions are drawn from textual comparison alone, especially those related to the extent and pace of the change in the liturgy. Textual study has revealed that the change was a major upheaval, not merely the alteration of a few phrases or the substitution of this passage for that. Obviously the fundamental beliefs remained the same, the sacraments were in essence unchanged, but the structures used to express them altered enormously. As we traced the change deeper, it became apparent that the differences were no less marked. Whether we consider the structure of an office or of the mass, the terminology used, or the words of the prayers, the changes are considerable. There would have been the occasional familiar antiphon, hymn or even reading, but these were isolated occurrences, and the overwhelming effect for those performing the liturgy must have been one of radical change – of this there can be no doubt.

When we examined the new texts, we found in the centre, at the core of the change, the set piece of the preface and canon of the Roman mass. Here there is remarkable uniformity of text between two Roman missals which contain it: Vitr. 20–8 from the centre of the implementation of the liturgical change at Sahagún, and Aem. 18 from the likely centre of opposition at San Millán de Cogolla. There are variants for some of the mass prayers and embolisms for the preface on important feast days in all three Roman missals, but the often elaborate masses of the Mozarabic liturgy with texts tailored for each temporal feast day and for each saint have been suppressed. Perhaps most tellingly, the many long Mozarabic *inlationes* were replaced totally by the few short Roman prefaces. In comparison with the diversity of the Mozarabic mass texts, where a prayer would not be repeated in identical format until the same day in the following year, the sheer repetition and sameness of the Roman mass – in spite of its initial novelty – must surely have seemed supremely ritualistic (or merely a straitjacket) to those familiar with the Mozarabic masses.

The main features which distinguished the Roman mass on one feast day from that on another were the chants and readings of the foremass. The readings seem to have followed a fairly set pattern over the course of the year with little scope for deviation. We can see this from the almost complete agreement on the *lectiones* within the Roman missals, which present a unified theological vision, quite controlling in its selection of biblical pericopes. In contrast there is very substantial disagreement between the Roman and the Mozarabic choice of readings. Most notably the Mozarabic custom of associating the Apocalypse with Easter week – which was not only Christological but also typological in linking the Easter celebrations with the celestial liturgy – is completely absent from the Roman missals.

The sense of uniformity and tight liturgical structure conveyed by the Roman liturgy is also expressed by the change in the form of the liturgical books themselves. The characteristic Mozarabic book, the 'mixed book' combining office and mass, disappeared entirely. The Mozarabic book had not been conceived as one or two consistent volumes, but rather as a more thematic collection of texts, dividing the liturgical year in accordance with the function of the book in question. In this it reflected the idiosyncratic nature of the Mozarabic liturgy, with its ability to encompass diversity. In contrast to the Mozarabic books the new mass book, whether sacramentary or missal, stands as a symbol of uniformity and solidity, first dividing offices from masses and then encompassing the whole liturgical year in a single volume. In this type of book the rhythms of the year are clearly exposed, as the temporal and sanctoral cycles are given separately. This format seems to have been an immediate requirement for missals. Moreover we found considerable agreement among the missals in the contents of the liturgical year. The strong skeletal structure which this provided for the whole liturgy would have been of great practical use in the organisation of the change-over.

The change seems to have been imposed quite suddenly in the case of the mass. We have no transitional texts, although it is possible that these would not have been allowed to survive. The impression is of a swift and absolute change in the performance of the mass, according to the strict Roman formulae. There are no signs of compromise, not even the inclusion of saints venerated particularly under the Mozarabic liturgy, who could have been included in the lists of saints where additions are explicitly allowed in the Roman mass. There is one Mozarabic prayer included in the missal from San Millán, but this may have been due to a misunderstanding in a missal which otherwise follows the guidance given in the *Micrologus* to a remarkable extent.

Despite the development from sacramentary to plenary missal which is also demonstrated by the Roman manuscripts in this study, there seems to have been firm control throughout. We could attribute this to strict adherence to models which were provided, but the process seems to have been more complex. All the missals are compiled volumes responding to local needs to some extent. Even Vitr. 20–8 has a mass for *SS. Facundus et Primitivus*, which would not have appeared in any French manuscript; the position of the feast for the Purification in this manuscript is also unusual and unlikely to be due to a model. Aem. 18 likewise added masses for its own patron saints and for Santo Domingo of

Silos. Sal. 2637 took the process further by including collects for some traditional 'Mozarabic' saints, not just for Santo Domingo. These features demonstrate that the scribes were not merely reproducing a single exemplar. There is always an element of compilation.

On the evidence supplied by the Roman missals, every aspect of the Mozarabic liturgy seems to have been banished immediately beyond the circle of acceptability and into the category of heresy. In this area adherence to the new regime seems to have been about as absolute as can be imagined.

Between the firm centre provided by the celebration of the mass, and the outer boundaries of liturgical practice beyond which lay 'heresy', there were many grey areas. It was in these areas that we have found the many adjustments and small compromises. We have identified these most clearly in the breviaries.

In striking contrast to the sacramentary/missal, there seems to have been considerable leeway in the structure and consequent image of the breviary in the early stages of the liturgical change. This may have been simply a matter of priorities; if the mass was the essential element, then it was presumably missals which received the most attention at the beginning of the change-over. The less crucial offices may have been allowed to come into line later. Equally the development of the breviary may have been at a less advanced stage than that from sacramentary to missal, and the absence of an accepted model may have left opportunities for compromise. In any event we have been able to follow changes through different stages in the breviaries, which was not the case in the missals.

In the Roman breviaries, which no longer contained any mass texts, two further features of the Mozarabic book were allowed to disappear gradually. One was the mixing of the temporal and sanctoral cycles, which seems to have died out quite slowly as we have two different stages of the separation in Add. 30847 and Add. 30848. This may have been allowed because older Roman missals and breviaries had also mixed the cycles. The other disappearing feature was the habit of splitting the liturgical year into *sui generis* volumes. This seems to have had a briefer respite, as only Add. 30847 serves as an example of a book which does not cover the whole liturgical year, in this case less than half. Quite early in the process, therefore, the breviary was also contained within one volume. These codices thus embodied the new liturgy in two volumes, missal and breviary. Contained and more or less prescriptive, the two books provided a firm basis from which to direct the new liturgical practices.

The changes to the format of the individual offices were not as dramatic as those which affected the mass, except in the case of matins. This night office was augmented significantly in the new liturgy by the introduction of scriptural readings together with their homilies. This new element offered a major opportunity for exposition, which was not present in the Mozarabic liturgy as the manuscripts in this study show it to have been practised. The other offices continued to be dominated by the psalms and their attendant antiphons, verses and responds, some of which were familiar from the Mozarabic liturgy. The inclusion of these familiar elements is probably not evidence of compromise in the introduction of the liturgy, but may merely attest to the distant common roots of the two liturgies in the western tradition. Thus in the office texts there was – as in the mass texts – sudden and – for matins at least – comprehensive change. This makes it likely that precise instructions were issued on the immediate essentials of the liturgical change: that old texts must be put aside, but that the format of the new text was to be flexible within certain boundaries.

We can, for example, see a transition taking place in the choice of readings within the Roman breviaries. This development seems to operate on two fronts. First Add. 30848 incorporated excerpts from Beatus's Commentary on the Apocalypse as the readings for the first and second nocturns from the first until the fourth Sunday after the Easter octave. This choice did not derive from the Mozarabic liturgy, where Beatus does not seem to have been used, but it certainly was not a feature of the Roman liturgy, and there is no trace of this practice in the later breviary, Add. 30849. It may have been a bold interpretation of directions which permitted 'patristic' readings and may exhibit an imaginative attempt to incorporate the familiar in a permissible way. It may even represent the regeneration of Beatus in his original role as champion of orthodoxy against the church of Toledo.

Add. 30848 also included one homily which is also found in the Toledan homilary used in the Mozarabic liturgy. This is not an isolated occurrence, as we know that some Mozarabic homilies were still used in a mainly Roman *homilarium* produced at Silos. Their inclusion may have been thought allowable, as the *ordines* concerning homilies and the directions in the Rule of St Benedict are quite vague, recommending particular authors, but permitting any patristic text.

The change in the choice of homilies, however, involved more than just the gradual elimination of Mozarabic texts. There was also another question: which of the collections of homilies used in the Roman liturgy should be introduced. The homily collection of Paul the Deacon, the 'authentic' text commissioned by Charlemagne, seems to have been adopted eventually, but in the initial phase of the liturgical change the collection of Smaragdus was dominant at least in the area around Silos. It seems to have given way only gradually to a selection from Paul the Deacon. The local nature of this phenomenon implies local direction within the diocese of Burgos rather than instructions from Sahagún. It certainly indicates planning rather than mechanical copying from supplied models. We have seen that Smaragdus was a careful choice, as the text was already familiar in Spain and contained passages which accorded well with the literary symbolism of reform rhetoric. Such a considered decision suggests a figure behind the process, who took the trouble to find a more acceptable text than the first one supplied by Cluny or one of its daughter-houses. The main local candidates for this role are Jimeno, bishop of Burgos, or his successor Gómez.

The breviaries thus give a different picture of the liturgical change from that presented by the missals. Because they appear to operate on the periphery of the process, they reveal more of the transition. The mass texts seem to have been subject to fixed boundaries, but the office texts have shown a less rigid side of the change, where accommodations were made in the early stages before relative uniformity took over.

The texts also provide information on changes in the veneration of saints. We cannot be sure that guidelines were issued on the cults to be abandoned and those to be encouraged, but the evidence from these manuscripts suggests that they may have been. Among the enormous collection of abolished texts were the offices and masses of the 'Mozarabic saints'. A transition took place in the breviaries, as several 'Mozarabic saints' continued to receive offices in the earliest of the breviaries (Add. 30847), although the only text offered is a narrative *passio*. In the later breviaries, the 'Mozarabic saints' were further marginalised to the extent that they appear only in the calendars. Thus the names of the saints were not obliterated absolutely, but, if they were accorded an office or mass under the new regime, it must have been one of the common texts of the Roman liturgy. They were severely marginalised, with no secure anchor in the new liturgy.

The early Roman missals are entirely free from the taint of 'Mozarabic saints' and include texts only for apostles, Roman saints and martyrs and major Gallic saints who also had their place in the early Romano-Gallic sacramentaries. The only exceptions to this are the titular patron saints. Sahagún kept the Spanish martyrs *SS. Facundus* and *Primitivus,* and Cogolla was allowed to keep *'pater noster'*, San Millán, as well as its newer addition San Felices. Silos maintained its allegiance to its first patron St Sebastian, but also keenly developed the new cult of Santo Domingo in parallel, until it eventually displaced the original dedication. Saints and their relics played a key role in attracting pilgrims to visit particular monasteries on their way to Santiago, and thus were a sensitive area closely linked to a house's prosperity. Other saints were introduced, or cults of Roman saints were developed, in an attempt to fill the vacuum left by the marginalization of the Mozarabic saints. Where possible continuity was encouraged. Both the missals and breviaries provide clear evidence of the development of the Marian cult. Already well established in Spain, this cult had been based on the feast of the Virgin, and figured also in the feasts of the Nativity, the Epiphany and the Assumption. In the new liturgy the feast of the Virgin was moved to 27 July, but the cult was expanded to include the Nativity of the Virgin, the Annunciation and the feast of the Purification.

We also see continuity combined with proliferation in feasts for St Peter and St Paul, thereby acknowledging both the papacy and Cluny. Orthodoxy is also apparent in the feasts of the martyr popes made compulsory by Gregory VII, in the missals and in the latest of the breviaries. Likewise the feasts of St Benedict and of St John the Baptist receive increasing attention, as well as those of St James, albeit not to the extent which we might have expected in view of the popularity of the pilgrimage to Santiago.

If we look for new cults, *S. Dionisius,* who is venerated in all three missals and received special attention in the breviary, Add. 30848, is perhaps one of the most significant. There is also St Nicholas, whose rise was presumably due at least in part to the increase in pilgrimages to Santiago. Some of the Gallic saints, for example St Saturninus and St Martin of Tours, were already well established in Spain before the liturgical change and continued to flourish. The other 'new' saints included in the latest missal, Sal. 2637, had their cult centres over quite a wide area of France from Amiens to the Auvergne and from Rouen to Aquitaine, showing the complex network of links which had been built up with many churches and monasteries in France.

These liturgical books are more than just structured text, since they are also illuminated to varying degrees, and the visual presentation and decoration has greatly facilitated analysis and interpretation of the texts. For example the application of decoration to the texts gives a much clearer sense of a hierarchy of feasts than the texts alone. We have seen that the Mozarabic books distinguished very little between the decorative treatment given to major feasts of the Church and the feast days of comparatively minor saints. Just as the (potentially) less important office or mass was given a full text so it also often received elaborate illumination. Some of the Roman books, on the other hand, exhibit a sense of hierarchy, above all the missal Vitr. 20–8 and the breviary Add. 30848. These do not delineate their hierarchies in the same way, the breviary using a combination of headings and small initials, while the missal employs more prominent illuminated initials. Both systems of decoration, nevertheless, promote certain feasts over others and draw the attention of the reader to specific feast days. I would like to take the opportunity of this conclusion to see if the breviary (from part I) and the missal (from part II) present the same map of the liturgical year in their different ways.

Add. 30848 seems to offer more gradations of importance, ranging from two-line headings to full double-page spreads. Vitr. 20–8 on the other hand distinguishes certain feasts by giving them a fine illuminated initial which is often figurative but never historiated. Moreover much of the decorative scheme of Vitr. 20–8 has to be deduced from the blank spaces left for major initials, but for the present purpose such a space will be treated in the same way as an executed initial.

The major Church festivals of Easter and Pentecost receive the most elaborate decoration in Add. 30848 and major initials in Vitr. 20–8. The breviary also gives equal treatment to the first Sunday after Trinity – possibly because such a section had not appeared in Mozarabic breviaries.[1] This structural marker is paralleled in a different way in the missal by the major initial used for *Dominica Prima Adventus*. The missal gives similar treatment to the major festivals of Christmas, *Vigilia de Nativitate, in die Nativitatis* and *die Ephiphaniae*. In contrast the breviary highlights none of these feasts giving them only the one-line headings used for minor feasts.

If we look beyond the major Church festivals, we see that Add. 30848 placed *Officium in Ramis Palmarum* and *Officium in Assumtione Sancte Marie* in the next rank of importance with just as elaborate decoration but only on one folio. Four other feasts receive headings which distinguish them from the others. *Officium de Sancta Trinitate* is the clearest of these with its circle-and-line decoration; the others are the feasts of particular saints: Sts Philip and James, St John the Baptist and St Peter. Vitr. 20–8 concurs with this selection to a significant extent, in that it assigned major initials to the feast of the Assumption of the Virgin, to St John the Baptist and to Sts Peter and Paul. It differs from the breviary, however, in also highlighting *Vigilia Ascensionis, Purificatio Mariae, Dedicatio Ecclesiae* and the fourth Sunday in Advent.

Neither Silos nor Sahagún appear to have held relics of St John or had any other special connection with him, so the emphasis on the feast of St John the Baptist in both these manuscripts presumably had other reasons. It could be due simply to the importance attached to the 'correct' performance of the ritual of baptism. This can be seen in other circumstances of liturgical change such as St Augustine's demands for compliance from the British bishops in the seventh century.[2] It could also be symptomatic of a heightened interest in the idea of redemption. This doctrine of reconciliation between God and man through the atonement of Christ's incarnation and death was expressed for the individual through the act of baptism, a ritual of purification for past sins. And it is in the figure of John that the two concepts of rebirth and redemption were fundamentally combined,[3] as we saw in the passage from Luke's gospel which was highlighted in Add. 30847. Baptism by means of the new liturgy was presumably seen as one of the most significant new rituals. It is very unlikely, however, that members of the Mozarabic Church would have been required to be re-baptised into the Roman Church, as re-baptism was itself considered heretical by Rome.

Alternatively it may be that the ideas of individual rebirth which were associated with baptism were employed in making the liturgical change more acceptable within the overall conceptual framework of reform. Moreover John the Baptist had received considerable veneration in the Mozarabic Church, so there was also an element of continuity in the decision to accentuate the role of this saint.

Continuity may also have figured in the emphasis placed on the feast of Holy Trinity. The Mozarabic Church had been eager to emphasise its orthodoxy in Trinitarian doctrine ever since the Adoptionist controversy, but had not celebrated such a feast. The introduction of a feast of the Trinity in the new liturgy could have been seen on the one hand as the natural culmination of such a claim of orthodoxy, or on the other as a mark of the orthodoxy of the Roman as opposed to the Mozarabic Church. The importance given to the feasts of St Peter and – in the missal the more Cluniac choice – Sts Peter and Paul also seems to be a statement of orthodoxy, giving recognition to the supreme role of the Pope, St Peter's successor.

Both the missal and breviary emphasise devotion to the Virgin and give prominence to the feast of her Assumption, which was also an important feature in the Mozarabic manuscripts (*see* part I). Ideas associated with the Virgin seem to have played an important part in the liturgical change, possibly because they conveniently conflated concepts which had been central to the Mozarabic church with others which formed the core of Gregorian reform.[4] The Virgin could be *Mater Ecclesia* welcoming back her straying children, or *Sedes Sapientiae*, the throne of the wisdom of God. The feast of her Purification, which is carefully placed and illuminated in Vitr. 20–8, was also linked with the light symbolism which was employed by Gregorian reform. This feast with its doctrine of renewal was celebrated with the *benedictio candelae*, a dramatic ritual which heralded the coming of light out of darkness.

The idea of light operated as an image of enlightenment, the 'good', or divinity, in many cultures and for many centuries, but that does not seem to have diminished its usefulness in conveying such concepts positively. We have seen that it was used in the Mozarabic Church, as the word 'LUX' began the Mozarabic antiphoner, and it was incorporated into the inscription on several Cross of Oviedo miniatures. It was also of central importance in the *lucernarium* ceremony of Holy Week. However, the general impression we receive of the use of light in Mozarabic churches is of isolated light in a more pervasive atmosphere of enclosure and darkness, whereas the Roman Church's use of light symbolism seems to have been more celebratory, more open.

In the Roman liturgy we have seen literary references to light in Smaragdus's collection of homilies, and in the ceremonies of the Roman Church, the *benedictio ignis* and the *benedictio cerei*, and above all in the feast of the Purification. We know also that the imagery of light coming into darkness and specifically the phrases from Isaiah were used of the 'mission' in Spain. Hugh of Cluny used them in his letter to Bernard on the latter's appointment as Archbishop of Toledo:

> *per administrationem vestram populus qui in tenebris ambulat lucem magnam visurus sit, et habitantibus in regione umbre mortis lucerne, ipse scilicet Sol iustitie, oriatur eis.*[5]

The use of rubrication in two of the Roman breviaries, moreover, suggests a more theological use of this imagery, based on the metaphysics of light as set out by Pseudo-Dionysius. It seems likely therefore that the liturgical change was represented by a complex matrix of doctrinal concepts. At the core of this was the Divine Light, at once the Word of God and Divine Wisdom as incarnated in Christ. Darkness represented ignorance and error, from which the soul escaped when it received divine illumination from God through the higher levels of the celestial and ecclesiastical hierarchies.

We saw in the Introduction that light symbolism was employed by reformers, as one of the means of making innovation seem natural and acceptable. Other themes related to the creation, to the growth of plants and flowers; others were different versions of light imagery such as fire or the opposition of night and day. It appears, however, that the more metaphysical interpretation of light symbolism was used to present the liturgical change in Spain to those who were to perform the new liturgy. This choice and its intellectual roots in Pseudo-Dionysius suggest that the implementation of the liturgy was planned from Cluny, where such ideas were in fashion, and managed under the close direction of the Cluniac Bernard of Sahagún.

We can perhaps glimpse, however, how impressive such a theologically rigorous campaign might have been, how unacceptable it would have been to wish to remain in darkness, and how well the spiritual ideas of the reform could have matched the intellectual and cultural expansion which Alfonso VI advocated. The effect may perhaps be best captured outside the liturgical manuscripts in one of the central panels of the wall-paintings in the royal pantheon at León: Christ sits in Majesty holding a book, surrounded by the four evangelists in a stance familiar from many other representations, but here the words on the book are '*Ego sum lux mundi*'.

The illumination and presentation of these texts has revealed aspects of the liturgical change not otherwise explicit in the process of mere textual substitution. I will now alter the emphasis slightly and concentrate on the decorated text as image – that is the semiological significance of the overall appearance of the manuscripts.

The script used to write the text does not seem to have had particular 'iconographic' significance, as the Roman liturgy was still written in Visigothic script. The only manuscript, which dates from the early stages of the change, written in 'the French script' is Vitr. 20–8. Although we could argue that this would be expected in a manuscript written for a Frenchman, the fine Protogothic script of this manuscript marks it out as a product with extra-peninsular connections. The implications of this are potentially far-reaching.

The most telling palaeographical evidence, however, may be the apparent confusion in the Roman breviary, Add. 30847, where the scribe changes from one letter-form to another and one spelling to another, sometimes even within one folio. This scribe (or the one he was copying from) could not have been copying from one model, as the manuscript still includes readings for Spanish saints which would not have been found in any Roman book. Perhaps this scribe was himself compiling the volume from different manuscripts, which may account for his lack of consistency. In the act of copying he was apparently translating the Caroline script into Visigothic script and formulating Visigothic abbreviations for the terminology of the Roman liturgy. We cannot helpfully speculate on the mental state of such a scribe, but we can recognise that the consistency seen in the Mozarabic manuscripts has been lost. We may be seeing here a symptom of the cultural adjustment which had to be made when the new liturgy was accepted, and possibly something of the conflicts engendered in those who had to make the adjustment.

The association of the decorative styles – 'Mozarabic' or 'Romanesque' – with the liturgies – Mozarabic or Roman – has also been found to be complex and without predictable semiological significance. The three Mozarabic manuscripts in this study are decorated in styles familiar from other Mozarabic manuscripts whether of tenth- or eleventh-century date. In their illumination they represent a tradition, or more accurately several traditions, since they draw on and recycle different strands of what is recognised as 'Mozarabic' art: a Visigothic foundation, a Franco-Saxon contribution, and the element – which we often perceive as 'fantastic' – developed by the Mozarabs under Moorish rule. The resulting mélange is typical of eleventh-century Mozarabic manuscripts, which rather than closely copying the decoration of earlier codices, as had been the habit in the previous century, often incorporated other 'Mozarabic' motifs. These manuscripts thus conform to one of Schapiro's adjectives: they are 'traditional' in that they represent continuity, although this could be said of any manuscript produced in a developed style and is only meaningful in this context when it is placed alongside what was at that time a new style.

Schapiro also described 'Mozarabic' art as native – that is in opposition to 'international', perhaps in the sense of introverted rather than indigenous, for 'Mozarabic' art was not developed in isolation. It did, however, repeatedly look inwards in its constant copying. The extent to which 'Mozarabic' art was bound up with the identity of the Mozarabic church is, however, a more complex issue. We have seen that the royal Leonese dynasty used works of art to give visual expression to the Neo-Gothic myth in the ninth and tenth centuries, and that the same tactics may have been employed by Fernando I to help to establish his right to rule over León. The cross-fertilisation of royal and ecclesiastical imagery had reflected the close symbiotic nature of the relationship between king and church. Thus if we were to define the identity of 'Mozarabic' art, it would be as 'royal/ecclesiastical' rather than 'national'.[6] This can be seen for example in the figures found in Add. 30845 and Add. 30846 holding staffs of authority, which are also found in manuscripts of councils held by kings and bishops.

If we turn to the Roman manuscripts, we have seen that there was a marked difference between the decoration of the missals and that used in the breviaries. Just as the missals exhibit remarkable textual uniformity, so in broad terms they all receive decoration in an identifiably 'Romanesque' style with almost no 'Mozarabic' elements.

Vitr. 20–8 is the only visual expression we have of the liturgical change which can be securely tied to one of its leading instigators. This manuscript represents the distillation of good practice not only in its text but also in its illumination. Visually it is unequivocal: the style is emphatically 'Romanesque'. This manuscript seems to have textual links with Burgundy, the home of Alfonso VI's second wife, and stylistic links with south-western France (Limoges/Moissac/Agen), the original home of its likely owner. Yet we have seen that it also stands in line with earlier products of Spanish royal patronage and that the illumination could have been executed by a Spanish artist. It is, however, not essential to know the nationality of its executors; it is sufficient that this manuscript was produced in the *milieu* of the new international style introduced to Spain under royal patronage, a style which seems to have exemplified a new self-image for the León/Castile monarchy.

For, although Fernando seems to have built in a traditional style and later dedicated the new palatine church to a quintessentially Spanish saint, St Isidore, he and his Queen, Sancha, also had an interest in the new 'Romanesque' style which was developing in much of Europe during the eleventh century. It was used in the prayer book which Sancha commissioned for Fernando and in the church furniture which they both donated to the new palatine church of San Isidoro at León.[7] These introductions may be linked to the new aspirations of the monarchy, which now placed itself on a level with the German Emperor in its donations to the abbey of Cluny and the intercession received in return. Alfonso VI's ambitions seem to have depended even more on acceptance into the international elite. He married French and Italian wives all connected with lay or ecclesiastical aristocracy; he increased financial support to Cluny, and, of course, by changing the liturgy he brought religious practice in his kingdom into line with that in the rest of western Europe.

The identification of the new style with the new liturgy is, therefore, clear in a manuscript produced for, and probably at, the royal flagship monastery of Sahagún. The identity goes further, moreover, for in spite of the different circumstances of the production of Vitr. 20–8, there are similarities in iconography and style between it and the other missal texts probably dating from the eleventh century, Aem. 18 and folio 1 from Add. 30849. These are centred in the decoration of the preface and canon, as Aem. 18 has only plain geometrical and vegetal initials elsewhere instead of the beasts, figures and foliage found in Vitr. 20–8. In stylistic terms both Aem. 18 and folio 1 from Add. 30849 are explicitly 'Romanesque', but unlike that in Vitr. 20–8 the illumination is tentative, as if copied uncertainly from a model. In Aem. 18 the style is clearly incongruous, fitting ill with the Visigothic script and uneasily in the cramped spaces left for it. This suggests that the new style may have been a requirement when decorating the central text of the new liturgy, rather than an independent decision taken on artistic grounds. The visual impression is of compliance. The scribes translated the text into Visigothic script, but they did not reformulate the decoration in the same way, possibly because they were following instructions which did not allow it. It is difficult to believe that the artists were trained originally to execute 'Romanesque' illumination, considering the awkward execution. Folio 1 of Add. 30849 is similarly uncertain, although here the text is written in Protogothic script.

Only in Sal. 2637 do we find the complete assimilation of the new style. The illumination is richly 'Romanesque', delighting in naturalistic foliate and zoomorphic forms. This manuscript has also abandoned any conformity with a standard model and has its own forthright structure, greatly affected by the large musical content. It seems to have its own identity and form; we have finally reached the end of the period of transition, and the Mozarabic liturgy with its associated decorative repertoire is no longer apparent in the work of the scribes in this manuscript even as something to avoid.

The use of the man-and-dragon iconography – albeit in different guises – in all the missals except Sal. 2637 is striking enough to suggest that they may all have been executed in response to a recommendation. It is as if the use of this iconography were a badge of orthodoxy. As we have not found any examples of its use in this context in surviving French manuscripts, it is difficult to believe that the iconography derives from the copying of independent models. It seems possible, therefore, that manuscripts of a similar character to Vitr. 20–8 may have been circulated during the liturgical change, and that they emanated from Sahagún and may have reached as far as Silos and San Millán. Or at least it is probable that the idea of beginning the missals with a representation of the fight against heresy was disseminated over the same area. If this were so, it would reinforce the idea that the Roman liturgy may have been introduced through a concerted campaign directed by Bernard from Sahagún, employing the new style and iconography to help establish at least the appearance of uniformity in the liturgical change.

The manuscripts have shown, therefore, that where the textual and structural requirements were strongest – in the missals – illumination in the 'Romanesque' style also seems to have been *de rigueur*. The association between the Roman liturgy and what we see with hindsight as 'Romanesque' may therefore have been very close for the members of the Spanish church, outside the royal circle. The royal elite, however as we have noted, had commissioned objects in the 'Romanesque' style many years before the liturgical change, including Mozarabic liturgical manuscripts and other elaborate but small-scale liturgical and cult objects to be used in a Mozarabic liturgical context. For Alfonso VI there was therefore no necessary equivalence between Roman and 'Romanesque'. For him the liturgical change may have been an unexpected and inconvenient repercussion of the other links – political, marital, spiritual as well as artistic – which he and his father had built up with France and other parts of western Europe.

There is no firm evidence, however, that the 'Romanesque' style was employed in Spain in a more public arena before the liturgical change. As Williams has shown, Fernando I built in a traditional style akin to that of the Asturian royal church of San Salvador de Valdediós. The church which Santo Domingo, according to his biographer, restored and rebuilt at Silos was probably also like San Salvador.[8] The chalice of Santo Domingo also lacks the imperial associations of the chalice commissioned by Alfonso VI's sister, Urraca, with its jewels and cameos.[9] Therefore, although the monks and clergy of the Mozarabic church may have heard of the luxurious objects commissioned and donated by the royal family, the 'Romanesque' style does not seem to have impinged on their own ritual or daily lives until the advent of the liturgical change. It is likely, therefore, that the practices of the new liturgy and the new style of illumination may have appeared in the abbeys almost simultaneously and thus have come to signify one another. Whether this was the intention of those who implemented the change, or merely a by-product of the model Roman manuscripts, we cannot be sure.

The view of the liturgical change which we have gained from the missals has been largely that of the instigators rather than of the recipients. The Roman breviaries, on the other hand, give an impression – or rather three different pictures – of the reception of the liturgical change. They exemplify three different responses. Add. 30847 received minimal illumination, and may illustrate the phase of reform which Kitzinger identified, where overt figurative imagery is not found. This bland decorative scheme, with only plain geometric initials which are neither definably 'Mozarabic' nor 'Romanesque', could be the result of earnest attempts to follow a French model, but the inclusion of texts for 'Mozarabic saints' suggests that this may not have been a strong guiding principle. The lack of the 'Mozarabic' figurative and zoomorphic illumination makes an immediate and dramatic impression, nonetheless, if viewed in contrast with the Mozarabic liturgical manuscripts. The rich decorative traditions of the Mozarabic church have been lost. This paucity of decoration, in contrast to the previous elaborate illumination, may be indicative of suppression. We know that the skills had not died out, as they were employed in the Silos Beatus. The scribes may, therefore, have been directed to avoid identifiably 'Mozarabic' decoration and possibly any illumination with specific associations. There is a lack – as well as a loss – of identity in the execution of this manuscript.

Boylan has suggested that Silos was not hostile to the Roman rite because it produced its own liturgical manuscripts in that rite rather than purchasing them from elsewhere. The situation was probably not that simple. It is difficult to envisage where the abbey was going to purchase manuscripts, especially when they would have been in such demand during the liturgical change. It also presupposes that the abbey had the alternative of refusing the new liturgy, which in view of the edict from the Council of Burgos is most unlikely to have been the case. Even if the abbot and other leading figures agreed to implement the change, that does not mean that they or the monks, who were also scribes and artists, were necessarily in favour of it.

The second Roman breviary, Add. 30848, appears to show another adaptation. This manuscript may represent an attempt to accommodate the change by denying it. By producing a Roman codex in a specifically antique 'Mozarabic' style – and even including part of Beatus's long-established text – the scribe of this manuscript seems to construct a past which never was, as if the Roman liturgy had been used in tenth-century Spain. Nevertheless this manuscript also eschews the figurative and zoomorphic aspects of 'Mozarabic' decoration, relying on only the decorative motifs and colour contrasts of the 'Mozarabic' style. There is still no sign of the extravagant decorative style of the Silos Beatus. That Beatus is believed to be a copy of a tenth-century Beatus manuscript, but Add. 30848 is an invention; the design seems to have been very carefully chosen for its traditional nuances and for its purely geometric forms.

In Add. 30849, the third breviary, we saw the last vestiges of 'Mozarabic' decoration in a fundamentally Roman book written in Caroline script. Again the only 'Mozarabic' elements are decorative motifs, which are here restricted to a section of the manuscript. Possibly because the development of the breviary was still in its early stages, we can see in these books something of the various attempts to adjust to the new liturgy within certain constraints. The overall impression is of loss of command, even of identity, which seems to have continued for many years, as none of the examples available to us has confident Romanesque decoration. The process of liturgical change seems to has been carefully directed, but within this there is an apparent sequence of reaction exemplified by the three Roman breviaries, suppression and loss of identity, a re-assertion of tradition so far as it was permitted and the fabrication of a false past, and finally gradual replacement rather than synthesis.

The Roman breviaries have thus given us some insight into the reception of the new liturgy and the processes whereby those who had been members of the Mozarabic church attempted to come to terms with it. In contrast to the positive use of the 'Romanesque' style in the missals, the breviaries demonstrate either a reluctance to employ the new style or a lack of the necessary training. We have not found any examples of 'Mozarabic' style being used as a protest against the new liturgy, as Schapiro suggested was the case with the Silos Beatus. Indeed we have not found any examples in the Roman liturgical manuscripts of the full use of 'Mozarabic' style: dispossession is the dominant theme.

The loss of the traditional visual means of expressing the previously symbiotic identity of king and church, and its replacement by a new style and imagery which operated – albeit with variations – throughout the Roman church, seems to have helped to change the conceptual axis for the members of the Spanish church. The relationship between king and church was no longer necessarily one of mutual benefit, and when the regular income from the Islamic states ceased at the end of Alfonso VI's reign chroniclers did not hesitate to berate Queen Urraca for taking gold and silver from the churches to fund her war with

Aragón.[10] Although the rule of her son, Alfonso VII, was considered to be more successful, the close links which had existed previously between the royal family and the palatine church seem to have been diminished.[11] During the pontificate of Urban II (1088–1099) the Spanish church looked increasingly to the Pope for rewards and defence,[12] and, although Paschal II was a much weaker figure, his successor Pope Calixtus II (1119–1124), uncle to Archbishop Bernard of Toledo, was as much a focus of attention as Urban II.

We have been looking at the processes and the representation of an instance of radical change which took place in the eleventh and twelfth centuries. On a broader level, has it been possible to identify any general characteristics which might indicate a distinctive approach to change during this period? If so, how do these relate to the approaches suggested by the documentary evidence which we considered in the Introduction?

Perhaps we should note first of all that however unacceptable it may have been to acknowledge change, the process itself seems to have been accomplished largely without compromise. We have not found a gradual, almost surreptitious, substitution of old texts with new ones but rather a bold casting away of the past. In this there was no denial of change on the part of those who promoted it. There has been, however, no indication that innovation was celebrated on this occasion. Instead we can see some of the approaches used elsewhere to promote Gregorian Reform: above all reliance on light symbolism and the idea of the Virgin as Mother Church. To the modern reader light symbolism seems a hackneyed choice which gives a very imprecise intellectual framework. It may, however, have been chosen by the reformers for that very reason: if the argument did not sound new, perhaps the object of the argument would also pass as conventional. Although the liturgical change was thorough, the reformers seem to have used continuity wherever possible by developing elements which were shared, thus denying change by expressing it through a series of antitypes. We have not found, however, any evidence of the use of decorative motifs which might be meant to signify the primitive church in Rome, such as Kitzinger found in another reform context. It may be that this was considered an inappropriate approach in Spain where 'the primitive church' was the Visigothic church, which did not employ the same visual vocabulary as the Roman.

Another well-worn concept employed by the reformers was 'heresy'. In some ways this was a bold move, as the same accusation was often used against reformers. The literary evidence is reflected in the missals where we meet recurring use of the man-and-dragon iconography, which might have been intended as a statement for orthodoxy and against heresy, signified by the dragon. At this point the symbolism of the reformers seems to meet and interact with the visual and intellectual vocabulary of the Spanish church. In Beatus's Commentary on the Apocalypse the dragon represented the devil attacking the Church through wicked priests. In choosing this image of heresy, the reformers were again drawing on a long tradition, but it was also a tradition with a central role in one of the most important texts of the Mozarabic Church. The use of Beatus in one of the Roman breviaries may further indicate that concepts familiar from this text were re-interpreted in support of the new liturgy. As Beatus was also known in the Adoptionist controversy as the opponent of Elipandus, the bishop of Toledo who was excommunicated, Beatus himself may have been used for a time – until the conquest of Toledo – as a figure to identify with in opposition to the heresy of the *mos Toletanus*, that is the Mozarabic liturgy. If this is so, it shows that those adjusting to the change also looked for antitypes to make the change seem part of a continuity rather than an innovation, but they looked to the Mozarabic tradition for their re-invention.

How successful were those attempts to adjust to change? In analysing the reaction to the imposition of change, it may be helpful to look at other studies of organisational change which have been undertaken mainly by anthropologists. These have usually, however, investigated the impact of a technologically advanced or 'hot' culture on a traditional or 'cold' culture.[13] Some of the features of acculturation may nevertheless be the same: for example the inconsistent spelling and abbreviating which we found in one of the Roman breviaries could be an example of the dysnomic features usually associated with the conflicts and stresses which arise when one social system displaces another. Anthropological studies have also discovered patterns of organisational change. Firth, for example, has found a sequence of reactions: at first acceptance without modification, then growth of individualism and a split between old and new values, a subsequent hostile reaction and an attempt to revert to traditional practices; finally a synthesis.[14] The circumstances are clearly different in this study of medieval liturgical change, as the difference between the two cultures was much less and both shared a similar heritage to the extent that the Gallican liturgy in use until the time of Charlemagne had much in common with the Mozarabic liturgy. Moreover some of the decorative traditions familiar to 'Mozarabic' art had been adopted from Merovingian manuscripts and only relatively recently displaced by the 'Romanesque' style in France, which was itself still in a developmental phase.

The sequence of reactions to the introduction of the Roman liturgy demonstrated in the manuscripts has little in common with Firth's. We have found an immediate suppression of Mozarabic text and style, and consequently an apparent loss of identity. One tradition is cut off, but there is no immediate embrace of the Romano-Gallic alternative. Our examination of manuscripts from the end of the process has demonstrated that there was no synthesis. A few 'Mozarabic' features might still be found, but they are minor and the overwhelming impression is of total substitution: Roman for Mozarabic and 'Romanesque' for 'Mozarabic'. We have found evidence in the Roman breviaries of a transitional period in certain aspects of the liturgical change. Add. 30848 seems to represent a distinct phase of the change in that visually it appears to be a re-assertion of the 'Mozarabic' tradition although textually it is thoroughly Roman. It is, therefore, not representative of an attempt to revert to past practices but rather of an attempt to give authority to the new liturgy by constructing a false past. It is, therefore, another example of denial of change.

These responses may, perhaps, be expected in a society which had no satisfactory intellectual framework through which to express or accommodate major change. As a whole these manuscripts could be said to have provided a rather despondent picture of the process of change. There is scant evidence for enthusiastic acceptance of the new liturgy among those who produced the new manuscripts for many years after the initial edict. At this level Alfonso's land may have remained *'desolata'* for some time. Thus the symbolism used to promote reform may not have been effective beyond the surface, and the past may not have been satisfactorily re-interpreted or dismissed as misguided or heretical. At this level the promised enlightenment of reform does not seem to have taken hold, and instead there was a prolonged period in which the Spanish Church suffered a loss of identity and only slowly re-constructed a new form of orthodoxy.

Notes to Conclusion

1   I should like to thank Andrea Budgey, of the Pontifical Institute of Medieval Studies, Toronto, for her suggestion that the impressive initial, which begins *Dominica I post Trinitatem*, might be attributed to the copying process, as a summer volume of a two-volume Roman Breviary might well begin with *Dominica I post Trinitatem*.

2   Bede (*Venerabilis Baedae*), *Historiam ecclesiasticam gentis anglorum* (ed. Plummer, C.), Oxford 1896, II2; trans. Sherley-Price, L. and revised Latham, R.E., *A History of the English Church and People*, Harmondsworth, Middx., 1970, p.102, 'to complete the Sacrament of Baptism, by which we are reborn to God, according to the rites of the holy, Roman, and apostolic Church'. The other demands were the timing of Easter and to join in the mission to the English.

3   Wink, W., in Metzger, B.M. and Coogan, M.D. (eds.), *The Oxford Companion to the Bible*, New York and Oxford, 1993, p.372.

4   A sermon on the antiphon *Salve Regina* has been attributed to, among others, Archbishop Bernard of Toledo, *see* Rivera Recio, *as above* Intro. note 103, p.128 and *PL* 184 col. 1059–78. This two-part sermon brings together ideas of error, intercession, and light amid darkness, in its gloss on this antiphon to the Virgin: '... *regina misericordia ... lumen caecorum ... ipsa intercedat pro peccatis nostris*' and '*vanitas erroris est in omnibus quae fidei catholicae et sanae doctrinae contraria sunt ...*'.

5   Férotin, *as above* Ch. 4 note 14. This reference may be to Bernard's work among the *infideles*, rather than the Mozarabic church in Toledo.

6   Linehan, *as above* Intro. note 48, p.174. Linehan makes the 'royal' as opposed to 'national' distinction regarding Isidore's *Historia Gothorum* (i.e. not *Historia Spaniae*). A preference for personal loyalty to a leader rather than national loyalty is also favoured by McCluskey, R., 'Malleable Accounts: Views of the Past in Twelfth-century Iberia', in Magdalino, P. (ed.), *The Perception of the Past in Twelfth-Century Europe*, London and Rio Grande, 1992, p.224.

7   Williams, *see above* Ch. 3 note 3, p.168.

8   Whitehill, *as above* Ch. 3 note 29, p.326.

9   Santo Domingo's chalice is illustrated in Palacios, M, Yarza Luaces, J. and Torres, R., *El Monasterio de Santo Domingo de Silos*, León, 1981, Pl.48. For Queen Urraca's chalice *see* Williams, J.W., catalogue entry in *The Art of Medieval Spain AD 500–1200*, *as above* Intro. note 14, pp.254–5.

10 Falque Rey, E. (ed.), *Historia Compostellana*, Corpus Christianorum, Continuatio Medievalis, vol. k.70, Turnhout, 1988.

11 Williams, *as above* Ch. 3 note 3, p.173.

12 Fletcher, *as above* Intro. note 112, p.184.

13 Beattie, J., *Other Cultures*, London, 1964, p.246–64.

14 Beattie, *as above* note 13, p.249.

APPENDICES

APPENDIX I

A Defence of the Mozarabic Liturgy

The Latin text is written on one of the end folios of a Mozarabic *Liber Comicus* from the abbey of San Millán de la Cogolla, Madrid, Real Academia de la Historia, Aem. 22, fol. 195. *See* part I, p.30. The Latin was transcribed by Pérez de Urbel (as above, Intro. note 83), but the literal translation of the often dubious Latin is mine.

Doctor ayt: audi homo vocem Apostoli dicentem: omnia autem probate, quod bonum est tenete. Non dicet: omnia tenete sed: quod bonum est probate.

The Doctor says: man listen to the voice of the Apostle saying: put all things to the test, cleave to what is good. He will not say: cleave to all things, but test what is good.

Et in dominica oratio, qua Dominus noster discipulos suos orare instituit, dicens: Pater noster qui es in celis. In qua oratione ut patres scribserunt, septem petitiones continentur. Hec sunt itaque septem sacrificii orationes conmendate evangelica epostolicaque doctrina. Cujus numeri ratio instituta videtur vel propter septenariam sancte Ecclesiae universitatem vel propter septiformen gratie spiritum, cujus dono ea que offeruntur sanctificatur.

In the Lord's prayer, by which our Lord taught his disciples to pray, saying: Our Father, who is in heaven. In that prayer, as the fathers have written, are contained seven petitions. These are therefore the seven prayers of sacrifice commanded by the evangelical and apostolical doctrine. The original reason for this number seems to be either because of the seven-fold universal nature of the Holy Church or because of the seven-fold gifts of the Spirit, by whose gift those things which are offered are sanctified.

Dixit canonicus quartus concilium gangrenense. Hos condenamus qui se extollunt adversus scripturas et ecclesiasticos canones et nova introducunt precepta.

The fourth canonical Council of Gangra said: We condemn those who raise themselves up against the scriptures and the church canons and who introduce new precepts.

Item Ormisde Papa ad episcopos Betice: Ut nullus privilegia antiqua convellat, sed in honore suo a patribus decreta servuntur.

Again Pope Hormisdas to the bishops of Baetica: let no one tear up old privileges, but let decrees by the fathers be preserved in their honour.

Tantumque testimonium habentes his quia usi fuerunt libros missales cremare vere apostaticios fuerunt, quia Sancta Trinitate cremaverunt, ut continent missales ab antiquorum patrum laudatos et beatum Petrum. apostolum dicentem. Dignum et justum est nos tibi semper gratias agere, omnipotens Deus noster per Jhesum

And bearing witness to this (?): because they used to burn missal books they were truly apostate, because they burned the Holy Trinity(?), for they contained masses praised by the Fathers of old and the blessed Peter, the apostle saying: it is for us always to give thanks to you, our Almighty

Christum Filium tuum Dominum Nostrum, verum pontificem, et solum sine peccati macula sacerdotem: Et iterum: vere sanctus, vere benedictus Dominus noster Jhesu Christus Filius tuus. Hoc idem procul dubio, que hoc fecerunt arriani fidem in se tenuerunt.

Sed quod? Audi Scripturam dicentem: Confundantur qui me persecuntur. Unde et non canere oportet casum huiusmodo apostaticis, ne similiter plaga feriamur precipiti, et pena puniamur crudeli. Si enim Deus angelis in se peccantibus non pepercit qui per inobedientiam celeste habitaculum perdiderunt, unde per Isaiam dicit: Inebriatus est gladius meus in celo, quanto magis ? nostre salutis interitum timere debemus, ne per apostaticis eodem servientibus Dei gladio pereamus. Quod si divinum iracundiam vitare volumus et veritatem ejus et clementiam provocare cupimus, servemus erga Deum religionis cultum atque timorem, custodiam erga antecenares nostros pollicitatione atque sponsionem. Non sit in nobis, sicut in quibusdam gentis infidelitatis subtilitas impia, non subtio lumenitis (subdola mentis)? perficia, non perjurii nefas nec conjurationum nefanda molimina; nulla re impediante a quolibet nostrum ea que constituta sunt temerari, sed cuncti salubri consilio conservari, quia profectibus eclesie anime conveniunt.

God through Jesus Christ your Son, our Lord, true pontif, and only priest without stain of sin: and again: truly Holy, truly Blessed our Lord Jesus Christ your Son. In this without doubt, the Arians had kept the pledge which they had made.

But what? Listen to the Scripture speaking: Those who persecute me let them be confounded. It does not behove us to sing of the fall of apostatic things in this way, lest we are struck likewise hastily and punished with cruel pain. For if God did not spare the angels sinning against him, who lost their heavenly habitation through disobedience – so he says through Isaiah: [Is 34.5] My sword is bathed in Heaven, – how much more should we fear the destruction of our salvation, lest through serving the same apostatic things we perish by the sword of God. But if we wish to avoid the divine anger and desire to call upon his truth and mercy, let us maintain the cult of worship and fear towards God, guardianship towards our ancestors? by promise and solemn agreement. Let there not be in us, as in some peoples the evil subtlety of infidelity, nor (?) false treachery of the mind, nor the sin of perjury, nor heinous attempts at oaths; the minds of the church agree that without resistance those things of ours which were laid down will be desecrated by progress, but all can be kept safe by firm resolve.

APPENDIX II

A List of Manuscript Contents by Heading

Add. MS 30844

Readings from the *De Virginitate perpetua Sancte Marie* of St Ildephonsus
Magnificamus te domine
Officia et Missa:
Sancte Marie
Sancti Tome (hymn and mass only)
De Nativitate Domini
Sancti Stefani
Sancte Eugenie
Sancti Iacobi (frater Domini),
Sancti Iohannis,
Sancte Columbe
De festo Circumcisionis
Apparitionis
In Catedra Sancti Petri
Ascensionis
De Letanias ante Pentecosten
In sequenti Dominico post Ascensionis
Letanias Canonicas

Add. MS 30845

officia et missa:
Sancti Quirici
Sancti Hieronomi
Sancti Adriani adque Natalie
Sancti Iohannis Babtiste
Sancti Pelagii
Sancti Zoilli
Sanctorum Petri et Pauli
Sancti Cristofori
Sanctarum Iuste et Rufine
Sanctorum Sperati et Marine
De Primitiis
Sancti Cucufati
Sancti Felicis
Sanctorum Iusti et Pastoris
Sancti Mametis
Sancti Laurentii
Sacrationis Sancti Martini
De Asumtio Sancti Marie
Sancti Genesi
Sancti Agustini
Sancti Cipriani
Sancte Eufemie
Decollationis Sancti Iohannis
Sancti Micael Arcangeli
Sanctorum Fausti, Ianuarii et Martialis
Sanctorum Cosme et Damiani
Sanctorum Servandi et Germani
Sanctorum Vincenti, Sabine et Cristete
Sancti Martini
Sancti Milani
Translationis Sancti Saturnini
De Letanias Canonicas
Sancte Cristine
Sancti Bartolomei

Add. MS 30846 [1]

officia et missa
Pasce
Feria II
Feria III
Sancte Engratie
Feria IIII
Feria V
Feria VI
Sabbato
Dominica Octavas Pasce
Feria II
Feria III
Feria IIII
Feria V
Feria VI
Sabbato
canticles and hymns for the period.
Dominica I post octavas pasche
Feria II
Feria III
Sancti Torquati vel socii eius
Dominica II
Sancti Filipi Apostoli
Sancte Crucis
Dominica III
Dominica IV
Ascensionis
Feria VI
Sabbato
Dominica post Ascensionis
Feria II
Letanias Apostolicas
Feria IIII
Feria V
Feria VI
Sabbato ante pentecosten
Pentecosten

1 Texts for *ad vesporum, ad missam* and *ad matutinum* are not given for every feast and there are other irregularities.

Add. MS 30847

officia:
[Dominica II in Adventum]
ebdomada
Sancte Lucie
Dominica III
Dominica IIII de Adventum Domini
In die Sancti Tome
In Vigilia Natalis Domini
In natale Sancti Stefani
in natale Sancti Ihoannis apostoli et
  evangeliste
Adsumtio Sancti Ihoannis apostoli et
  evangeliste
In natale Sanctorum Innocentum
  parvulorum
Dominica infra Natale Domini
Hoctabas natale Domini
in Apparicione Domini [2]

Octabe Ephiphanie Domini
Dominica I post Epiphanie
Dominica II
Dominica III
Dominica IIII

In natale Sancti Sabastiani
Passio Virginum Agnetis et Emerentiane
In natale Sancti Vincenti
In conversione Sancti Pauli
In natale Sancte Agnes
In Purificatione Sancte Marie
Sancte Agate
Passio Sanctorum Fructuosi episcopi,
  Agurii et Eologii
Passio Sanctorum Babile episcopi et
  Trium Puerorum
Passio Sanctorum Tirsi et comitatibus
Passio Sancte Dorote
In natale Sancte Scolastice
Passio Sancte Eolalie
Passio Sancti Pantaleonis et com.
In natale Sancti Valentini
Catedra Sancti Petri
Passio Sanctorum Emeterii et Celedonis
In natale Sancti Benedicti
Dominica in Septuagesima
Dominica in Sexagesima
Dominica in Quinquagesima
Dominica in Quadragesima
Dominia II in Quadragesima
Dominica III in Quadragesima
Dominica IIII in Quadragesima

2 The word apparicio comes from the
   Mozarabic liturgy, where it replaces
   epiphania.

Add. MS 30848 [3]

Calendar
officia:
De Adventu Domini
Dominica II in Adventum
Dominica III in Adventum
Feria IV in Quattuor Tempora
Dominica IV in Adventum
In Sancti Tome
In Vigilia Natalis Domini
Vespera Natalis Domini
In Sancti Stefani
In natale Sancti Iohannis
Sanctorum Innocentum
In Circumcisionis Domini
In Apparitionis Domini

In Sancti Sebastiani
In natale Sancti Agnes
In Dedicationis Ecclesie
In Sancti Vincenti
In Conversione Sancti Pauli
In Purificatio Sancte Marie
In natale Sancte Agate
In kathedra Sancti Petri
In Sancto Benedicto
In Annuntiatio Sancte Marie

Dominica I post Epifanie Domini
Dominica II post Epifania
Dominica III
Dominica IV
Dominica in Septuagesima
Dominica in Sexagesima
Dominica in Quinquagesima
Dominica in Quadragesima
Dominica II
Dominica III
Dominica IV
In Passione Dominica
In Ramis Palmarum
In die festo Pasce
Dominica in Octabis Pasce
Dominica II
Dominica III
Dominica IV
Dominica V
In Evangelistis
In Sanctorum Filippi et Iacobi et de
  aliis
In Sancta Cruce
In Ascensionis Domini
Dominica post Ascensionis Domini
De Sanctam Pentecosten
De Sancta Trinitate

De Sancto Iohanne Babtista
De Sancto Petro
De Vincula Sancti Petri
Inventio Sancti Stefani
In Sancti Laurentii
In Assumtione Sancte Marie
De Sancti Bartolomei
In Decollatio Sancti Iohannis
In Nativitate Sancte Marie
In Exaltacionis Sancte Crucis
In Sancto Mauricio cum soc.
In Sancto Michael Arcangelo
In Sancti Dionisii
In Festivitate Omnium Sanctorum
De Sancto Martino
In die Sancte Cecilie
In die Sancto Clemente
In Sancti Andre
De Sancto Nicholao
De Sancta Lucia

Dominica prima post Sancta Trinitate
Dominica II-XXIV post Sanctam
Trinitatem
In natale Apostolorum
In natale Plurimorum Martirum

3 The Roman manuscripts also give
   regular feriae, IV and VI only or II,
   III, IV, VI and Sabbato for the most
   important weeks.

Add. MS 30849

Calendar
officia:
part of *Dominica I de Adventu Dni*
Dominica II de Adventu Domini
Dominica III de Adventu Domini
Dominica IIII de Adventu Domini
Quattuor Tempora
In Vigilia Nativitatis Domini
In die Sancta Anastasia
In Natale Sancti Stephani
    protomartyr
In Natale Sancti Ihoannis
In Natale SS Innocentorum
Infra Octaba [Domini]
In Vigilia Epiphanie Domni
Octaba Epiphanie
Dominica I post Theophania
Dominica II post Theophania
Dominica in Septuagesima
Dominica in Quinquagesima
Feria iiii In Capite Ieunii
Dominica I in Quadragesima
Dominica II
Dominica III
Dominica IIII
Dominica in Passione Domini
Dominica in Ramis Palmarum
Sabbato in Vigilia Pasche
Dominica I post Octava Pasche
Dominica II post Octava Pasche
Dominica III post Octava Pasche
dominica IIII post Octava Pasche
Dominica V post Octava Pasche
In Vigilia Ascensionis Domni
Dominica I post Ascensionem
In Vigilia Pentecosten
Dominica II post pentecosten

Dominica III-XIX

Sancti Silvestri pappe et confessoris
in Natale Sancti Hilarii episcopi
Sancti Felicis in pincis
Sancti Mauri abbatis
Sancti Marcelli pape
Sancti Prisce virginis
SS Fabiani et Sebastiani
In festivitate Sce Agnetis
In Conversione Sancti Pauli
In Purificatione Sce Marie
In Natale Sce Agate virginis et
    martyris
In Cathedra Sancti Petri
In Natale Sancti Mathie apostoli
In Natale Sancti Benedicti abbatis
In Adnuntiatione Sancte Marie
    virginis
Sancti Georgii martyris
SS Alexandrii, Eventii et Teodoli
In Inventione Sancte Crucis
SS Nerei et Achilei
Sancti Urbani martyris
Sancti Vitalis martyris
SS Philippi et Iacobi
SS Basilidis, Cirini, Naboris et
    Nazarii
SS Gervasi et Protasii
In Vigilia Sancti Iohannis Baptiste
In Natale SS Iohannis et Pauli
In Natale Sancti Petri apostoli
In Natale Sancti Pauli apostoli
In Natale Sancti Martini confessoris
Sancte Marie Magdalene
In Natale Sancti Iacobi apostoli
In Natale Sancti Petri ad Vincula

Sancti Stephani
In Natale Sancti Laurentii
In Adsumptione Sancte Marie
In Natale Sancti Bartolomei
In Decollatione Iohannis Babtiste
In Nativitate Sancte Marie Virginis
Exaltatio Sancte Crucis
SS Cornelii et Cipriani
In Natale Sancti Mathei apostoli et
    evangeliste
SS Mauricii, Exuperii, Canduli
    Victoris
In Festivitate Sancti Michaliel
    archangeli
In Natale SS Simonis et Iude
    apostolorum
In Festivitate Omnium Sanctorum
In Festivitate Sancti Martini episcopi
    et confessoris
De Sancto Briccio
In Festivitate Sancte Cecilie
Sancti Clementis martyris
In Festivitate Sancti Andree apostoli
In Natale Sancte Lucie
Sancti Thome
In Natale Apostolorum
De Plurimorum Apostolorum
In Natale Plurimum Martyrum
In Natale Unius Martyris
In Natale Confessorum
In Natale Virginum
In Dedicatione Templi
Vincenti
In Nativitate Sancte Marie
Evangelistorum
Virginum

A Comparison of the Mozarabic and Roman Liturgical Calendars

DATE	MOZARABIC [1]	ROMAN	ROMAN
	feasts not included in Add. MS 30844, Add. MS 30845 or Add. MS 30846 are bracketed	Add. MS 30848 [2]	Add. 30849

Large sections of the calendars in Add. MS 30848 and Add. MS 30849 are missing or illegible

Date		Mozarabic	Roman (Add. MS 30848)	Roman (Add. 30849)
Jan.	**Ianuarius**			
1	Kal.	circumcisio dni	Circumcisio dni	Circumcisio dni
2	IIII Non.			Oct. sci stephani
3	III Non.		Oct. Sci Iohanni	Oct. sci Iohanni
4	II Non.		Oct. Innocentorum	Oct. innocentorum
5	Non.		Sci Simeonis cf [vigilia]	Vigilia Epiphanie dni Simeonis cf
6	VIII Id.	apparitio dni	Epiphanie Domini	Epiphanie domini
7	VII Id.	(SS Iuliani et Basilisse)	Iuliani et Basilisse et [cinet?] mrm	Iuliani et Basilisse mrm
8	VI Id.	(Allisio Infantum)	epi et ximi mr	
9	V Id.	(SS XLa Martyrum)	quadraginta martyrum	Quadraginta martirum
10	IIII Id.		sci Paulini epi cf	
11	III Id.			Victoriani abbatis
12	II Id.			
13	Idib.			Oct. Epiphanie
14	XVIIII Kal.			Felicis in pincis
15	XVIII Kal.			Mauri abbatis
16	XVII Kal.			Marcelli pp
17	XVI Kal.	(S Antonii)		Antonii monachi
18	XV Kal.			Prisce virginis
19	XIIII Kal.	(S. Sabastiani)		
20	XIII	(S. Agnetis et Emercentiane)		Fabiani et sebastiani mrm
21	XII	(S. Fructuosi epi.)		Agnetis vrg
22	XI	(S. Vincenti)		Vincenci mr
23	X	(S. Ildefonsi epi)	Sci Ildephonsi epi [-?antinis]	Emerenciane vrg
24	VIIII Kal.	(S. Babile epi)	Sci Babilie epi	Babile epi et com eius
25	VIII Kal.		Conversio Sci Pauli	Conversio Sci Pauli
26	VII Kal.		[-?p-] epi mr	
27	VI Kal.		Iohannis os aurei	
28	V Kal.	(S. Tyrsi)	Sci Tirsi	Agnetis scdo Tirsi mr
29	IIII Kal.		Sci [-pot]	
30	III Kal.			
31	II Kal.			

1   This composite Mozarabic list is derived from Vives and Fábrega's revisions of Férotin's composite list; *see* Férotin, as above Intro. note 20, p.XLV–LIII; Vives, J. and Fábrega, A., Calendarios hispánicos anteriores al siglo XII, in *Hispania Sacra*, vol. 2, 1949, pp.119–146, and pp.339–380; and of p.74 the current volume for an elucidation of the selection offered here.

2   In broad schema and in many details the calendar from Add. 30848 is the same as the second calendar in Aem.18, a manuscript from San Millán de la Cogolla dealt with in part II, probably dating from the end of the C11. *See* Janini, J., Dos calendarios emilianenses del siglo XI, in *Hispania Sacra*, No.15, 1962, pp.177–195.

Date		Mozarabic	Roman	Roman
Feb.	Febrarius			
1	Kal.		[column illegible]	Brigide virginis
2	IIII Non.			Papanti domini
3	III Non.			
4	II Non.			
5	Non.	(S. Agate vrg)		Agate
6	VIII Id.			Vedasti et Amandi
7	VII Id.	(S. Dorotee vrg)		Dorotee virginis
8	VI Id.			
9	V Id.			
10	IIII Id.			Scolastice vrg
11	III Id.			
12	II Id.	(S. Eulalie)		Eulalie vrg
13	Idib.			
14	XVI Kal.			Valentini mr
15	XV Kal.			
16	XIV Kal.			
17	XIII Kal.			
18	XII Kal.			
19	XI Kal.	(S. Pantaleonis)		Pantaleonis et com eius
20	X Kal.			
21	VIIII Kal.			
22	VIII Kal.	Kathedra S. Petri	in Catedra Sancti Petri	Kathedra sancti petri
23	VII Kal.			
24	VI Kal.			Matie apli
25	V Kal.			
26	IIII Kal.			
27	III Kal.			
28	II Kal.			
Mar.	Martius			
1	Kal.		Sci Nicepori	Nicefori mr
2	VI Non.			
3	V Non.	(SS. Emeterii et Celidonii)	SS Emeterii et Celedonii mr	Emeterii et Celedonii mrm
4	IIII Non.			
5	III Non.			
6	II Non.		[?Ehita dni] Iuliani epi -	Iuliani epi
7	Non.	(SS. Perpetue et Felicitate)	Perpetue et Felicitate vrg mr	Perpetue et Felicitate vrg
8	VIII Id.			
9	VII Id.			
10	VI Id.			
11	V Id.			
12	IIII Id.		[illegible]	Gregorii epi
13	III Id.		[illegible]	Leandri episcopi
14	II Id.			
15	Idib.			
16	XVII Kal.			
17	XVI Kal.			
18	XV Kal.			
19	XIV Kal.			
20	XIII Kal.			
21	XII Kal.		Benedicti abbatis	
22	XI Kal.			
23	X Kal.			
24	VIIII Kal.			

Date		Mozarabic	Roman	Roman
25	VIII Kal.		[?Annunciatio] Sce Marie vrg	Annunciatio Sce Marie
26	VII Kal.			
27	VI Kal.		S[-?pe] et S[z?]eome mrm	Resurrectio Domini
28	V Kal.			
29	IIII Kal.			
30	III Kal.			
31	II Kal.			
Apr.	Aprilis			
1	Kal.			
2	IIII Non.		Sci Cresegoni et com eius mr	Crisagonii Agappe
3	III Non.	(S. Teodosie)	Sce Teodosie vrg mr	Teodosie vrg
4	II Non.	(S. Isidori epi)	Sci Isidori epi cf	Isidori epi
5	Non.		Sci Ambrosii epi cf	Ambrosii epi
6	VIII Id.			
7	VII Id.			
8	VI Id.			
9	V Id.		Sce Marie egiptie cf	Marie egipcie
10	IIII Id.		Sci Apollonii epi cf	
11	III Id.?			
12	II Id.		Sci Victoris mr -	Victoris mr
13	Idib.			Eufemie vrg
14	XVIII Kal.		Sci Tiburcii et Valeriani	Tiburcii Valeriani et Maximi mr
15	XVII Kal.			
16	XVI Kal.		Sce Engratie milia militum	Engratie et comitum eius
17	XV Kal.			
18	XIIII Kal.		Sci Eleuterii epi cf	Eleutherii epi
19	XIII Kal.			
20	XII Kal.			
21	XI Kal.			
22	X Kal.			
23	VIIII Kal.		Sci Georgii mr felicis et [-?]	Georgii mart
24	VIII Kal.	(S. Georgii)		
25	VII Kal.	(S. Marci evang.)	Sci Marci evangeliste	Marchi evangeliste
26	VI Kal.			
27	V Kal.			
28	IIII Kal.	(S. Prudentii epi)	Sci Prudentii cf et [?-]	Vitalis mr
29	III Kal.			
30	II Kal.			
May	Maius			
1	Kal.		Filippi et Iacobi aplm	Philipi et Iacobi
		SS. Torquati etc.	Torquatus et soc cf	
2	VI Non.	S. Filippi	Sci Atanasii epi cf et Salse vrg mr	Atanasii epi
3	V Non.	Inventio S. Crucis	Inventio Sce Crucis et Teodoli mr	Inventio Sce Crucis
4	IIII Non.		Sci Quiriaci epi	Quiriaci epi
5	III Non.			
6	II Non.			Iohannis apli ante portam latinam
7	Non.			
8	VIII Id.			
9	VII Id.		Gregorii epi ordinatio	Gregorii Nazeni
10	VI Id.			Gordiani et Epimachi
11	V Id.			Maioli abbatis
12	IIII Id.		Sci Pangratis mrt	Nerei et Achilei
13	III Id.			Marie ad matiris

DATE		MOZARABIC	ROMAN	ROMAN
14	II Id.	(S. Isidori)	Sci Victoris et Corone mr et Sci Isidori mr et Pacomii cf	Victoris et Corone
15	Idib.			
16	XVII Kal.			Peregrinis mr
17	XVI Kal.			
18	XV Kal.			
19	XIV Kal.			Potenciane vrg
20	XIII Kal.	(S. Bauduli)	Sci Bauduli mr	Bauduli mr
21	XII Kal.	(S. Manti)	Sci Manji mr	Mancii mrs
22	XI Kal.			
23	X Kal.			
24	VIIII Kal.			Donaciani et ragaciani
25	VIII Kal.			Urbani pape
26	VII Kal.			
27	VI Kal.			
28	V Kal.		Sci Germani epi cf	Germani epi
29	IIII Kal.			
30	III Kal.			
31	II		Petronille vrg	Petronille vrg

June	Iunius			
1	Kal.	(S. Eulogii)	Sci Nicomedis mr	Nichomedis mr
2	IIII Non.		Sci Marcellini et Petri	Marcellini et Petri
3	III Non.			
4	II Non.		Sci Bonifacii epi	Bonifacii epi
5	Non.			
6	VIII Id.			
7	VII Id.			
8	VI Id.			Medardi epi
9	V Id.			Primi et Feliciani
10	IIII Id.			Barnabe apli
11	III Id.			Basilidis [?cirini] mrm
12	II Id.			
13	Idib.	S. Quirici (et Iulite)		Sci Quirici sci [?] viglia
14	XVIII Kal.			Viti et Modesti
15	XVII Kal.			Cirici et Iulite
16	XVI Kal.	S. Adriani et Natalie		
17	XV Kal.		?Quirici et Iulite	Marci et Marcelliani mrm
18	XIIII Kal.	(S. Ciriaci)	[?Theod]uli mr	
19	XIII Kal.	(S. Gervasi)	SS Gervasi et Protasi mrm	Gervasi et Protasii
20	XII Kal.			
21	XI Kal.			Vigilia Sci Iohannis
22	X Kal.			Nativitas eiusdem
23	VIIII Kal.		Vigilia	
24	VIII Kal.	Nativitas S. Iohannis	Nativitas Sci Iohanni Babt.	Iohannis et Pauli
25	VII Kal.			Ireni cum sociis
26	VI Kal.	S. Pelagii	Sci Iohannis et Pauli mr [?] mr	Vigilia aplm Petri et Pauli
27	V Kal.	S. Zoili	Sci Zoilli SS Germanorum	Sci Zoili mr et Natale eorundem
28	IIII Kal.	(S. Iuliane)	Sce Iuliane vrg [?] vigilia	
29	III Kal.	SS. Petri et Pauli	SS Petri et Pauli	SS apls Petri et Pauli
30	II Kal.	(S. Lucidie)	Sci Marcialis epi [?] Lucide vrg	

DATE		MOZARABIC	ROMAN	ROMAN
July	Iulius			
1	Kal.	(SS. Simonis et Iude)		Oct Sci Iohannis bte
2	VI Non.			Procesti et Marciniani
3	V Non.			
4	IIII Non.	(Translatio S. Martini)	Translatio Sci Martini epi et ordinatio	Translatio Sci Martini
5	III Non.			
6	II Non.			Oct aplm Petri et Pauli
			Sci Apollonis [?]arionis et [?]	
7	Non.			
8	VIII Id.			
9	VII Id.			
10	VI Id.	S. Christofori	Septem fratrum filii mrm	Septem fratrum filii
11	V Id.		Translatio Sci Benedicti Sce Marciane vrg mr	Translacio Sci Benedicti
12	IIII Id.			
13	III Id.			
14	II Id.			
15	Idib.			
16	XVII Kal.			Narionis
17	XVI Kal.	SS. Iuste et Rufine	SS Iuste et Rufine vrg mr	Iuste et Rufine mr
18	XV Kal.	SS. Sperati et Marine		Oct Sci Benedicti
19	XIIII Kal.		SS Sperati mr et [marine] vrg mr	Sperati et marine
20	XIII Kal.			Margarite vrg
21	XII Kal.			Praxedis vrg
22	XI Kal.		Victoris mr cf Marie Maidalena	Marie Maidalene
23	X Kal.			Apollinaris epi
24	VIIII	S. Bartolomei	Sci [iacobi] vigilia	Vigilia Iacobi apli
25	VIII	S. Cucufatis	Sci Iacobi apostoli et Sci Christofori et [?cin] mr et Cucufatis mr	Iacobi apli
26	VII	S. Christine	Sce Christine vrg	Christine vrg
27	VI	S. Felicis nolensis	Sci Felicis epi nolensis mr Sce Marie vrg ma[?]	felicitate epi
28	V Kal.			Maire vrg
29	IIII Kal.			Felicis in pincis
30	III Kal.		SS Abdon et Senesi mrm	Abdon et Sennesi mr
31	II Kal.	(S. Fabi)	SS Favi et Germani episcopi	Germani episcopi
Aug	**Augustus**			
1	Kal.		Viincula Sci Petri et	Vincula Petri
		(S. Felicis ierunda)	Sci Felicis epi mr et maccabeorum mrm	
2	IIII Non.		Stephani pape	Stephani ppe mr
3	III Non.		Inventio Sci Stefani et soc eius	Invencio Sci Stephani
4	II Non.			
5	Non.			
6	VIII Id.	SS. Iusti et Pastoris	SS iusti et Pastoris mr et Sci Sixti epi mr	Iusti et Pastoris mrm
7	VII Id.	S. Mametis	Sci Mametis mr et Donati epi cf	Mametis mr
8	VI Id.			Ciriaci Largi
9	V Id.		Vigilia	Laurenci [?sptem]

DATE		MOZARABIC	ROMAN	ROMAN
10	IIII Id.	(SS Sixti et) Laurentii	Sci Laurenti mr	Natalis eiusdem
11	III Id.	S. Martini sacratio	Tiburcii mr	Tiburcii mr
12	II Id.			
13	Idib.		Sci Crisanti et Darie mr et	
			Ippoliti d[ucis roma]	Ipoliti mr
14	XVIIII Kal.		Sci Eusebii epi	
15	XVIII Kal.	Adsumtio S. Marie V.	Assumtio Sce Marie vrg	Assuncio Sce Marie
16	XVII Kal.			
17	XVI Kal.		Oct Laurenti	Oct Laurenci
18	XV Kal.			Acapite mr
19	XIII Kal.			Magni mr
20	XIII Kal.			Phioti abbatis
21	XII Kal.		Sci Privati mr	
22	XI Kal.		Oct Marie	Oct Marie
23	X Kal.		SS Claudii Asterineonis domini?	Sci Claudii cum sociis
24	VIIII Kal.		Sci Bartolemei apl mr	Bartolomei apl
25	VIII Kal.	S. Genesi	Sci Genesi mr	Genesi mr
26	VII Kal.	(S. Geronti)	Sci Victoris mr	Sci Victoris
27	VI Kal.	(S. Victoris)	Cesarii mr	
28	V Kal.	S. Augustini	Sci Agustini epi cf	Agustini epi
29	IIII Kal.		Decollatio Sci Iohannis et	Decollatio Sci Iohannis
			Sc[?spei et] fida[?]	
30	III Kal.	(S. Felicis)	Sci Felicis epi mr	Felicis et Audacti
				Paulini epi
31	II Kal.		Octabe	
Sept	**September**			
1	Kal.	(S. Vincenti et Leti)		Gorgoni et Dorotei mr
2	IIII Non.			
3	III Non.			
4	II Non.			
5	Non.			
6	VIII Id.			
7	VII Id.			
8	VI Id.			
9	V Id.			
10	IIII Id.			
11	III Id.			Proti et Iacinti
12	II Id.			
13	Idib.			
14	XVIII Kal.	S. Ciprani		Exaltacio Sce Crucis
15	XVII Kal.			Nicomedis et Valeriani
16	XVI Kal.	S. Eufemie	Sce Eufemie	Eufemie
17	XV Kal.			
18	XIIII Kal.			Iustine
19	XIII Kal.			
20	XII Kal.			Vigilia mathei apli
21	XI Kal.	(S. Mathie)		Mathei apli et evangeliste
22	X Kal.			Mauricii et sociorum
23	VIIII Kal.			[An]doch[ii] [Thy]rsi fel[icis]
24	VIII Kal.	Decollatio S. Iohannis		[?]
25	VII Kal.			Cosme et Damiani
26	VI Kal.			
27	V Kal.			
28	IIII Kal			
29	III Kal.	Dedicatio S. Micaelis		C[?-] Vigilia Sci Micheli archangeli

DATE		MOZARABIC	ROMAN	ROMAN
30	II Kal.	(S. Iheronimi)		
Oct.	**October**			
1	Kal.	(S. Luce evang.)		[column severely damaged]
2	VI Non.			
3	V Non.			
4	IIII Non.			
5	III Non.			
6	II Non.			
7	Non.			
8	VIII Id.			
9	VII Id.			
10	VI Id.			
11	V Id.			
12	IIII Id.			
13	III Id.	SS. Fausti, Ianuarii et Martialis		
14	II Id.			
15	Idib.			Calixti ppe
16	XVII Kal.			
17	XVI Kal.			
18	XV Kal.	(S. Luce evang.)		Luche evangeliste
19	XIIII Kal.			
20	XIII Kal.	(S. Caprasi)		
21	XII Kal.	(SS. Nunilonis et Elodie)		
22	XI Kal.	SS. Cosme et Damiani		
23	X Kal.	SS. Servandi et Germani		[?] Gera et [?] mr
24	VIIII Kal.			
25	VIII Kal.			Crispini et eius
26	VII Kal.			
27	VI Kal.			Vigilia [Vincenti]
28	V Kal.	SS. Vincenti, Sabine et Cristete		Natalis eiusdem
29	IIII Kal.	(S. Marcelli)		[Marc]elli mr
30	III Kal.	(SS Claudi et Luperci)		[Lu]perci et Victoris
31	II Kal.			[Saturn]ini mr
Nov	**November**			
1	Kal.	S. Saturnini		Festivitas Omnium Sanctorum
2	IIII Non.			Lauteni abbatis
3	III Non.			Valentini et Ilarii mrm
4	II Non.			
5	Non.			
6	VIII Id.			
7	VII Id.			
8	VI Id.			Quatuor coronatorum
9	V Id.			Teodori
10	IIII Id.			Martini [vigilia]
11	III Id.	Obitum S. Martini		Martini [?]
12	II Id.	Obitum S. Emiliani		Emiliani
13	Idib.			Briccii
14	XVIII Kal.			
15	XVII Kal.			
16	XVI Kal.			Eucherii epi
17	XV Kal.	(S. Aciscli)		Aciscli et Victorie mr
18	XIIII Kal.	(S. Romani)		Romani et com eius
19	XIII Kal.			Odoni abbatis
20	XII Kal.	(S. Crispini)		

DATE		MOZARABIC	ROMAN	ROMAN
21	XI Kal.			Longini
22	X Kal.	(S. Cecilie)		Cecilie vrg
23	VIIII Kal.	(S. Clementis)		Clementis epi
24	VIII Kal.			Crisogoni martyris
25	VII Kal.			Petri epi et mr
26	VI Kal.			
27	V Kal.	(SS. Facundi et Primitivi)		
28	IIII Kal.			
29	III Kal.	(S. Saturnini)		Saturnini mr
30	II Kal.	(S. Andree)		Andree apli
Dec	December			
1	Kal.	(S. Longini)		Crisanti et Darie
2	IIII Non.			
3	III Non.			
4	II Non.			
5	Non.			
6	VIII Id.	(S. Nicholai)		Nicholae epi
7	VII Id.			Oct Sci Andree
8	VI Id.			
9	V Id.	(S. Leocadie)		Leocadi vrg
10	IIII Id.	(S. Eulalie)		[Eulalie] vrg
11	III Id.			[Dam]-asi epi
12	II Id.			
13	Idib.			Lucie
14	XVIIII Kal.			Iusti et Habundi
15	XVIII Kal.			
16	XVII Kal.			
17	XVI Kal.			[La]zarii epi
18	XV Kal.	S. Marie	Sce Marie	Expectacio Sce Marie
19	XIIII Kal.			
20	XIII Kal.			Dominici abbatis
21	XII Kal.	S. Tome apost	Sci Tome	Tome apli
22	XI Kal.	(Translacio S. Isidori)		Translacio S. Isidori
23	X Kal.			
24	VIIII Kal.	(S. Gregorii)		Vigilia Natalis Domini
25	VIII	Nativitas dni	de Nativitate	Nativitas Domini
26	VII Kal.	S. Stefani	Sci Stefani	Stephani protomartir
27	VI Kal.	S. Eugenie	Sci Iohannis	Iohannis apl et evang
28	V Kal.	S. Iacobi	SS Innocentorum	
29	IIII Kal.	S. Iohannis		Translacio Sci Iacobi
30	III Kal.	(S. Iacobi Maioris)		
31	II	S. Columbe	Sce Columbe	Sci Silvestre ppe Columbe vrg

APPENDIX IV

A Comparison of Selected Readings and Homilies from the Roman Breviaries, London, British Library

Add. MS 30847, Add. MS 30848 and Add. MS 30849

Key to Abbreviations for the Collections of Homilies:

PD = Paul the Deacon, S = Smaragdus, F = Alan of Farfa, T = Toledo, B = Beatus of Liébana's Commentary on the Apocalypse, U = Not yet identified

FEAST	LECTIO (incipit)	BIBLICAL REF. OF INCIPIT	HOMILY	COLLECTION	MS
Dominica I de Adventu Domini					
noc.I	Visio esaie filii amos quam vidit super Iudam	Is.1:1			48
noc.II	Verbum domini quod vidit esaias filius amos	Is.2:1	Bethphage autem domus buccae	S	48
noc.III	quum adproprinquasset ihesus Iherosolimis	Mt 21:1	Ico VIII: Quasi Iherosolimam venturus salvator	U	49
Dominica II de Adventu Domini					
noc.I	In die illa erit germen domini	Is:4:2			48
	Et creavit dominus	Is.4:5			48
	Nunc ergo havitator Iherusalem	Is.5:3			48
	Verbum misit in Iacob	Is.9:8			48
noc.II	Ve qui consurgitis mane	Is.5:8			48
	Et pascentur agni iuxta	Is.5:17			48
	Propter hoc sicut devorat	Is.5:24			48
	Et levabit signum	Is. 5:26			48
noc.I	In die illa proiciet homo idola	Is.2:20			49
	Et dabo pueros principes eorum	Is:3:4			49
	Popule meus qui beatum te	Is.3:12			49
noc.II	Et erit omnis qui relictus	Is.4:3			49
	Cantabo dilecto meo canticum	Is.5:1			49
	Ve qui coniungitis domum	Is.5:8			49
noc.III	Erunt signa in sole	Lc 21:25	Quod vero dicit: erunt signa	S	48
			Dominus ac redemptor noster	PD	49

FEAST	LECTIO (incipit)	BIBLICAL REF. OF INCIPIT	HOMILY	COLLECTION	MS
Dominica III de Adventu Domini					
noc.I	Quomodo cecidisti de caelo lucifer	Is.14:12			47 48 49
	In anno quo mortuus est rex ozias	Is.6:1			49
noc.II	cont.				47 48
noc.III	Quum audisset Ihoannes in vinculis	Mt.11:2	Legimus sanctum Moisen populo Dei	PD	49
			Qui venturus es(t) id est	S	47 48
			Querendum nobis fratres kmi Iohannes	PD	49
Dominica IIII de Adventu Domini					
noc.I	Et erit in die illa adtenuabitur gloria Iacob	Is.17:4			47 48
					49
noc.II			Vos inquam convenio o Iudei	PD	47 48
					49
noc.III	Miserunt Iudei ab Ierosolimis.	Jo.1:19	Ex huius nobis lectionis verbis frs. kmi. Iohannes humilitas	PD	47 48 49
Feria ii			Et amico veri sponsi	U	49
Feria iii			Igitur quoniam post tempus	PD	49
Feria iiii	Missus est angelus gabriel	Lc.1:26	Exordium nostre redemptionis f.k. hodierna	PD	47 49
Feria v			Notandum est	U	49
Feria vi	Exurgens maria abiit in montana	Lc.1:39	Lectio quam audivimus sancti evangelii	PD	47 48* 49
Sabbato	Anno quinto decimo imperii tiberii cesaris	Lc.3:1	Redemptoris (nostri) precursor quo tempore	PD	47 48* 49
in die sancti Tome apostoli (no proper readings given in 49)					
	Quum sanctus apostolus tomas qui et didimus esset apud cesaream				47 48 [1]
	Vidit Iohannes ihesum venientem ad se	Jo.1:29	Iohannes babtista et precursor domini	PD	48

vigilia natalis / nativitatis domini

	Incipit	Reference		Source	
noc.I	Cum esset desponsata mater ihesu Maria	Mt.1:18-	Quum esset desponsata mater	PD	49
	Propter sion non tacebo	Is.62:1	Hic prophete introducitur persona dicentis	S	47 48
	Paulus servus Ihesu Christi vocatus	Rom.1:1-3			48
	Primo tempore adleviatur est	Is.9:1		PD	49
	Consolamini, consolamini	Is.40:1		PD	49
	Consurge, consurge	Is.52:1-		PD	49
	Populus gentium qui ambulabat in tenebris	Is.9:2	Hic locus ita explanatur adveniente	S	47 48
noc.II	Multipharie et multis modis deus..	Heb.1:1-	Dicendo enim multifarie et multis modis	S	47 48
			Natalis dies domini eadem causa a patribus	PD	49
noc.III	(order varies between 48 and 49) In principio erat verbum	Jo.1:1	Assidue enim dicenda nomina verborum	S	47
			Quia temporalem mediatoris dei et hominum	PD	48 49
	Exiit edictum a cesare	Lc.2:1	Quia largiente domino missarum	PD	48 49
	Pastores loquebantur	Lc.2:15	Nato in bethle(e)m domino salvatore	PD	48 49
	Liber generationis	Mt.1:1	In exordio satis ostendit generationem	RM[2]	48

In natale sci stefani

	Incipit	Reference		Source	
noc.I	Heri celebravimus temporalem sempiterni		Heri celebravimus temporalem sempiterni	PD	49
noc.II	cont.		cont.		49
noc.I	Ad aquas stabilitanas episcopo adferente prolecto			PD[3]	47 48
noc.II	cont.		Et sapientes et scribas...	S	47
noc.III	Ecce mitto ad vos prophetas	Mt.23;34	Hoc (autem) quod ante(a) dixeramus	PD	48 49

In natale sci Ihoannis apostoli et evangeliste

	Incipit	Reference		Source	
noc.I	Melito servus Christi episcopus Laudocie[4]				47 48
noc.II	Sicut enim qui non manducat aut non bibit		cont.		48
noc.I	Secundam post Neronem persequacionem		cont.		49
noc.II	Unde accidit ut quid in eum vinere		cont.		49
noc.III	Dixit Iesus Petro sequere me	Jo.1:43	Sequere me ac si aperte dicat	S	47
			Lectio sci evangelii que nobis modo lecta	PD	48 49

In natale sanctorum innocentium / parvorum

	Incipit	Reference		Source	
noc.I	Vidi supra montem agnum stantem	Apc.14:1	Hodie fratres kmi natale illorum infantum	F & T	48
			Agnus Christus de quo Iohannes ait	S	47
			Zelus quo tendat quo siliat livor	PD	49

FEAST	LECTIO (incipit) of INCIPIT	BIBLICAL REF.	HOMILY	COLLECTION	MS
noc.II	cont.				
noc.III	Angelus domini apparuit in somnis Ioseph	Mt.2:13	Non dicit tuum puerum neque mulieris	S	47
			De morte pretiosa martyrum christi	PD	48 49
In circumcisionis domini/infra octaba					
-			Cupientes aliquid de huius diei sollempnitate	PD	49
noc.I			Unus igitur dies eternitatis	U	49
noc.II			cont.		49
noc.III	Postquam/(Cum) consummati sunt dies octo	Lc.2:21	Sanctam venerandam que presentis	PD	48 49
Vigilia epiphanie					
noc.I	Surge in luminare iherusalem	Is.60:1	Ecclesiae dicitur que primum de Iudaico	S	47 48
			Celebrato quo proximo diequo intemerata	PD	49
noc.II		cont.			47 48 49
noc.III	Quum natus esset Ihesus in bethlem Iudee	Mt.2:1	Pulchre autem dicitur Bethlem Iudae	S	47
			Sicut in lectione evangelica fratres	PD	48 49
De die sancto pasche					
	Maria macdalene et maria Iacobi et salome	Mc.16:1	Multis vobis lectionibus fratres kmi predicatum	PD	48 49
Feria ii					
	Exeuntes duo ex discipulis	Lc.24:13	Stadium quod greci auctore ut dicunt ercule	S	48
			In cotidiana vobis sollempnitate	PD	49
Feria iii					
	Stetit Ihesus in medio discipulorum	Lc.24:36	Hanc hostendionem domini post resurrectionem	S	48 49
Feria iiii					
	Manifestavit se iterum dominus ihesus	Io.21:1	Lectio sci evangelii que modo	PD	48 49
Feria v					
	Maria stabat ad monumentum	Jo.20:11	Pensandum est huius mulieris mentem	S	48
			Maria Magtlalene que fuerat in civitate peccatrix	PD	49
Feria vi					
	undecim discipuli habierunt	Mt.28:16	Evangelica lectio fratres kmi quam modo	PD	48 49

Reading	Reference	Incipit	Source	MS
Sabbato post pascha				
Una sabbati maria magdalene venit	Jo.20:1	[Sicut] in principio mulier auctor culpe	S	48
		Lectio sci evangelii quam modo frs audistis		49
Dominica octava pasche (for 49 see Dom. I post pasche below)				
Omne quod natum vincit mundum	1Jo.5:4	Illa fides quia eius humiliter auxilium	S	48
Quum sero esset die illo una sabbatorum	Jo.20:19	Quid mirum si clausis ianuis	S	48
Dominica I post octava pasche				
noc.I Primum quidem sermonem	Act.1:1	Iohannes quod dum vaticanio ex merito	B	48
	48 49			49
noc.II cont.		Quum [sic] dominus boni pastoris opus ostendere	S	48
Ego sum pastor bonus	Jo.10:11			
noc.III Cum esset sero die illo una sabbatorum	Jo.20:19	Prima leccionis huius evangelice questio	PD	49
Dominica II post octaba pasche				
noc.I Apocalypsis ihesu christi quam dedit illis	Apc 1:1	De ore eorum exiit ignis et fumis et sulfur	B	49
noc.II cont.				48
noc.III Ego sum pastor bonus	Jo.10:11	Audistis frs. kmi. ex leccione evangelice	PD	49
Modicum et iam non videbitis me	Jo.16:16-22	Ad illos specialiter hecque dicta sunt	S	48
Dominica III				
noc.I		Et septimus angelus tuba cecinit	B	48
noc.II cont.		Duobus modis intelligi potes	S	48
amen amen dico vobis si quid petieritis	Jo.16:23	Leta domini et salvatoris nostri fratres kmi	PD	49
noc.III Modicum et iam non videbitis me	Jo.16:16			
Dominica IIII				
noc.I Iacobus Dei et domini nostri ihesu Christi	Iac.1:1-	Et primus angelus effudit	B	48
				49
noc.II Et vidi celum apertum ecce equus			B	48
cont.				49
noc.III Vado ad eum qui misit me	Jo.16:5	Significat sic se iturum ad eum	S	48
Hec loqutus sum vobis tristicia implevit cor	Jo.16:6	Sicut ex leccione evangelica fr. kmi.	PD	49

Feast	Lectio (incipit)	Biblical Ref. of Incipit	Homily	Collection	MS
Dominica V					
noc.I	Petrus apostolus Ihesu christi electis advenis	I Pt.1:1			
noc. II	cont.				49
noc. III	Amen dico vobis Si quid peteritis	Jo.16:23	Potest movere infirmos auditores	PD	49
In Vigilia ascensa domini					
noc.I	Primum quidem sermonem	Act.1:1			48
	Qui crediderit et babtizatus fuerit	Mc.16:16			49
noc.II	Neque enim misterium babtizandi cont.??				48
noc.III	Recumbentibus undecim discipulis apparuit	Mc.16:14	Quod post resurrectionem dominicam discipuli	PD	48 49
	(49 Euntes in mundum huniversum predicate)	Mc.16:15			
Dominica post ascensionem					
noc.I	Estote prudentes et vigilate	I Pt.4:7	Et dominus in evangelium nos incerti finis institui	48	
noc.II			Post beatam et gloriosam resurrectionem	PD	49
			Sed hoc specialiter de karitate dicitur cont.		48
noc.III	Quum venerit paraclitus	Jo.15:26	Ex multis sancti evangelii locis invenimus	PD	49 / 48 49
vigila pentecosten					
	Si quis diligit me sermonem	Io.14:23	Audistis fratres kmi quia spiritus sanctus discipulos	U	49
			Libet fratres kmi evangelice verba lectionis	PD	48 49

1 Readings from a *passio* of St. Thomas, *see Bibliotheca Hagiographica Latina*, I–Z, Brussels, 1900–1901, p.1179.

2 Rabanus Maurus, In Matt. *PL* 107,col.731–732.

3 Readings from St. Augustine's *De Civitate Dei*, XXII c. viii, also used in the Mozarabic liturgy; see appendix VI. The rubric which introduces these readings in Add.30847 is: *lectio ecclesiastica de mirabilibus sancti stefani martiris ... cbristi ex libris de civitate beati agustini episcopi*

4 Readings from an apocryphal life of St. John, Vita Auct. Pseudo-Mellito, *see Bibliotheca Hagiographica Latina*, A–I, Brussels, 1898–1899, p.639

APPENDIX V

A Comparison of the Sanctoral Cycles in the Roman Missals

Vitr. 20–8	Aem. 18	Sal. 2637
Sanctoral	*Sanctoral*	*Sanctoral*
silvestri pape	natale sci silvestre pape	sci silvestri
		sce columbe
	genevefe virginis	sce genovefe
		ss Iuliani et basilisse
felicis confessoris	sci felicis confessoris	sci felicis confessoris
marcelli	natale sci marcelli	sci marcelli pape et martyris
		sulpicii confessoris
prisce martyris	natale sce prisce virginis	sce prisce virginis
	ss marii et marthe	ss marii et marthe
	eodem die sci lavnomari	
fabiani martyris	ss fabiani et sebastiani	ss fabiani et sebastiani
eodem die sebastiani		
agnetis martyris	sce agnetis martyris	natalis agnetis virginis
vincentii martyris	natale sci vincenti martyris	natale sci vincenti
		ss emerentiane et macharii martyrum
conversio sci pauli	conversio sci pauli	conversio sci pauli
	eodem die sci proiecti	eodem die sci proiecti martyris
		sci iuliani confessoris
(oct.) agnetis virginis	octavas sce agnetis	(oct) sce agnetis martyris
		sce brigide virginis
purificatio sce marie	purificatio sce marie	in purificatione sce marie
placed between the temporal and sanctoral cycles	benedictio ignis	
	eodem die ad missam	
agathe virginis	natale agate virginis	natale sce agathe
		sci vedasti
	scolastice virginis	sce scolastice
	eodem die sce sotheris	sotheri martyris
	eodem die dorothee virginis	
valentini martyris	natale sci valentini martyris	sci valentini martyris
	sci vitalis felicule et zenonis	ss vitalis, felicule et zenon martyrum
	natale sce iuliane virginis	sce iuliane martyris
cathedra sci petri	cathedra sci petri	cathedra sci petri
mathiae apostoli	natale sci mathie apostoli	natale sci mathie apostoli
	sci albini	natale sci albini confessoris
	natale sce perpetue et felicitatis	ss perpetuae et felicitatis
gregorii papae	depositio sci gregorii pape	sci gregori confessoris
beati benedicti abbatis	natale sci benedicti abbatis	benedicti abbatis
Annuntiatio sancte mariae	annuntiatio sce mariae	annunciatio sce mariae
	natale sci leonis	sci leonis pape
	natale sce eufemie	eufemie virginis
valeriani, maximi	natale tiburcii valeriani et maximi	tyburcii et valeriani
georgii, fortunati, felicis, achillei	natale sci georgii	sci georgii martyris
		sydrach, misac et abdenago
marci evangeliste	natale sci marci	sci marchi evangeliste
		sci richarii confessoris

Vitr. 20–8 *Sanctoral*	Aem. 18 *Sanctoral*	Sal. 2637 *Sanctoral*
vitalis martyris	sci vitalis	sci vitalis martyris
		sci germani
phillippi et iacobi	natale apostolorum philippi et iacobi	natale apostolorum philippi et iacobi
sancti alexandri, eventii et theodoli	natale ss alexandri eventi et theodoli	siccharii martyris ss alexandri, eventi et theodoli
inventio sanctae crucis	eodem die inventio sce crucis	eodem die inventio sce crucis
iohannis apostoli	Iohannis apostoli	Iohannis ante portam latinam
gordiani epimachi	gordiani et epimachi	ss gordiani atque epimachi
nerei et achillei, pancratii	nerei achillei et panchratii	ss nerei et achillei atque pancracii
	potentiane virginis	potentiane virginis
urbani martyris	urbani episcopi	urbani pape et martyris
		eodem die caprasii confessoris
	sci germani episcopi	
	natale sce petronille martyris	petronille virginis
	dedicatio sci nichomedis martyris	nichomedis martyris
marcellini et petri	sci marcellini et petri	ss marcellini et petri
primi et feliciani	natale ss primi et feliciani	ss primi et feliciani
		in die barnabe apostoli
basilidis, cyrini, naboris, nazarii	natale sci basilidis cirini naboris et nazarii	ss basilidis +n+cirini et nazarii martyrum
	natale sci viti et modesti et crescentie	ss viti et modesti
	natale sci cirici et iulite	cyrici et iulite
marci et marcelliani	natale sci marci et marcelliani	ss marci et marcelliani
gervasii et protasii	natale gervasii et protasi	ss gervasi et protasi
vigilia nativitatis precursoris domini	vigilia sci iohannis babtiste	in vigilia sci iohannis baptiste
missa in mane	in prima missa de nocte	in die missa matutinalis
nativitas sancti iohannis baptiste	natale sci iohannis babtiste	in die ad missam
s iohannis et pauli	natale iohannis et pauli	natale ss iohannis et pauli
	natale sci leonis pape	sci leonis pape
vigilia apostolorum petri et pauli	vigilia apostolorum petri et pauli	vigilia apostolorum petri et pauli
natale apostolorum petri et pauli	natale apostolorum petri et pauli	in die ad missam
commemoratio sancti pauli apostoli	commemoratio sci pauli apostoli	in commemoratione sci pauli
processi et martiniani	natale sci processi et martiniani	processi et martinani
translatio sancti martini	translatio et ordinatio sci martini	in die translationis sci martini
octave apostolorum	octavas apostolorum petri et pauli	octabe apostolorum Petri et Pauli
septem fratrum	ss septem fratrum	ss felicis sociorumque eius
translatio sancti benedicti	translatione sci benedicti	translatio sci benedicti
		ss iuste et rufine
		sce margaritae martyris
		sci arnulfi confessoris
	natale sci praxedis	praxedis virginis
marie magdalenae	natale sce marie magdalene	sce marie magdalene
		ss nichasii et eutropii
apollinaris martyris	natale sci apollinaris episcopi	sci apollinaris
iacobi apostoli	natale sci iacobi apostoli	natale iacobi apostoli
	eodem die ss cristofori et cucufatis	eodem die christofori et cucufati sociorumque eorum
		sci samsonis episcopi
		ss nazarii et celsi
simplicii felicis faustini et beatricis	natale sci felicis	ss felicis, simplicii, faustini et beatricis
	ss simplicii faustini et beatricis martyrum	
abdon et sennem	natale ss abdon et sennen	ss martyrum abdon et sennen
	natale sci germani episcopi	germani confessoris
ad sanctum petrum ad vincula	sci petri apostoli ad vincula	vincula sci petri

246

Vitr. 20–8	Aem. 18	Sal. 2637
Sanctoral	*Sanctoral*	*Sanctoral*
		in natale plurimorum martyrum
stephani pape et martyris	natale sci stephani episcopi	sci stephani pape martyris
	inventio corpris sci stephani martyris	inventio sci stephani
		nichodemi gamal atque abibon
		in transfiguratione domini
	natale sci sixti episcopi	sci syxti episcopi
christi felicissimi agapiti	eodem die ss felicissimi et agapiti	eodem die felicissimi et agapitis
iusti et pastoris		
	natale sci donati episcopi	
cyriaci largi et smaragdi	natale sci chiriaci martyris	in natale cyriaci largi et smaragdi
vigilia beati laurentii martyris	vigilia sci laurentii	in vigilia sci laurentii
in die	natale sci laurentii	in die
natalis sancti tyburtii	natale sci tiburcii	natale sci tiburcii
sancti yppoliti	natale sci ipoliti	sci ypoliti martyris
eusebii confessoris	sci eusebii confessoris	eusebii confessoris
vigilia sanctae mariae	eodem die vigilia sce marie	in vigilia assumptionis sce marie
missa		
assumptio matris dei	in assumptione sce marie	in die ad missam
octave s laurentii	octavas sci laurentii	oct sci laurentii
agapiti martyris	natale sci agapiti martyris	natale sci agapiti martyris
	sci magni martyris	natale sci magni martyris
	timothei et simphoriani martyrum	timothei et sinphoriani
	sci timothei martyris	timothei et apollinaris
bartholomei apostoli	natale sci bartolomei apostoli	sci bartholomei apostoli
		sci audoeni confessoris
	natale sci rufi martyris	in natale ruphi martyris
iuliani et hermetis	natale sci hermetis atque iuliani	in natale hermetis martyris
		iuliani martyris
augustini confessoris	eodem die natale sci agustini episcopi	augustini confessoris
sabinae virginis	natale sci sabine martyris	natale sce savinae virginis
decollatio precursoris domini	eodem die decollatio sci iohannis babtiste	decollatio sci iohannis
	sci felicis et audacti martyrum	felicis et audacti
	sci prisci martyris	natale sci prisci martyris
		sci egidii
		sci antonini martyris
nativitas matris dei	vigilia sce marie virginis	nativitas sce mariae
	nativitas sce marie	
		sci adriani martyris
		sci gorgonii martyris
gorgonii martyris proti et iacinti	s proti et iacincti martyrum	ss prothi et iacinti
exaltatio sancte crucis	exaltatio sce crucis	in exaltatione sce crucis
cornelii et cyriani	ipso die ss cornelii et cipriani	ss cornelii et cipriani
luci et geminiani		natale sci nichomedis martyris
eufemiae martyris	eufemie virginis	euphemie virginis
vigilia mathie apostoli	vigilia sci mathie apostoli	vigilia sci mathie apostoli
in die	in die festo	in die ad missam
mauritii cum sociis suis	sci mauricii cum sociis	ss mauricii sociorumque eius
		tecle virginis
		paterni confessoris
sanctorum cosme et damiani	sci cosme et damiani	ss cosme et damiani
	vigilia sci michaelis	in die sci micheli processiones
michaelis archangeli	in die festo	ad missam

Vitr. 20–8	Aem. 18	Sal. 2637
Sanctoral	*Sanctoral*	*Sanctoral*
iheronimi	sci iheronomi confessoris	sci iheronimi confessoris
	sci remigii et sociorum eius	ss remigii, germani vel sociorumque
eorum		
		natale sci leodegarii
		sce fidis virginis
marci pape	sci marci pape	sci marchi confessoris
		sci giraldi confessoris
		ss marci et apulei
dyonisii rustici eleutherii	sci dionisii martyris	dionisii cum sociis suis
calixti pape		sci calixti pape et martyris
lucae evangeliste	sce luce evangeliste	sci luche evangeliste
vigilia simonis et iude	vigilia ss apostolorum simonis et iude	vigilia apostolorum symonis et iude
in die	in die festo	in die ad missam
		crispini et crispiniani
		sci quintini martyris
vigilia omnium sanctorum	vigilia omnium sanctorum	vigilia omnium sanctorum
in die	in die festo	in die ad missam
		sci cesarii martyris
		sci austremonii
	translatio corporis sci Felicis presbyteri confessoris	
	quatuor coronatorum	ss quatuor coronatorum
theodori martyris		sci theodori martyris
mennae martyris		menne martyris
martini episcopi	vigilia sci martini	in vigilia sci martini episcopi
	eodem die octabas omnium sanctorum	
		in die ad missam
	natale sci emiliani presbytri	
	sci briccii confessoris	sci bricii confessoris
		sci macuti confessoris
		ss augustini et felicitatis
	octavas sci martini	
	oct sci emiliani	
cecilie virginis	sce ceciliae	sce cecilie virginis
clementis	sci clementis	sci clementis martyris
felicitatis martyris		sci felicitatis martyris
crisogoni martyris		natale sci grisogonii martyris
	sci chrisanti et darie	crisanti martyris (the order varies from Vitr. 20-8 & Aem. 18 after this point)
saturnini martyris	sci saturnini martyris	sci saturnini martyris
in vigilia sancti andree apostoli	vigilia sci andree apostoli	in vigilia sci andree
in die	in die festo	in die ad missam
sanctorum facundi et primitivi		
nicholai confessoris	sci nicholai episcopi	in die sci nicholay
oct sancti andree	octavas sci andree apostoli	oct sci andree
		Damasi confessoris
luciae virginis	sce lucie virginis	sce lucie virginis
	missa in veneratione beati Dominici confessoris	sci dominici confessoris
	in die festo	
thome apostoli	sci thome apostoli	sci thome apostoli

A Comparison of Selected Readings used in Masses of the Mozarabic and Roman Liturgies

The Roman Liturgy (Sal. 2637 [A], where Aem. 18 agrees [B])			The Mozarabic Liturgy (based mainly on Morin: Liber Comicus/Add. MS 30844 agrees), [C] = Add. MS 30846 disagrees	
Dominica prima in adventu domini				
Scientes quia hora est	Rm.13:11–14	A	Verbum quod vidit Isaias	Is.2:1–5, 4:2–3
Cum appropinquasset ihesus iherolimis	Mt.21:1–9	A B	Nolo enim vos ignorare fratres	Rm.11:25–31
			In diebus autem illis venit Iohannes	Mt.3:1–11
Feria iiii				
Erit radix Iesse	Is.11:10–13	A		
Cum videritis circumdari iherusalem (wrongly labelled in Sal.2637 as John)	Lc.21:20–24	A		
Feria vi				
Gratias agere debemus deo (wrongly labelled in Sal.2637 as Romans)	IITh.1:3–10	A		
Vigilate et orate	Mc.13:33–37	A		
Dominica II				
Quecumque scripta sunt ad nostram doctrinam	Rm.15:4–13	A B	Idcirco haec dicit Dominus Deus	Is.28:16–17, 29:17–24
Erunt signa in sole et luna	Lc.21:25–33	A B	Sic nos existimet homo	ICor.4:1–5
			Iohannes autem cum audisset in vinculis	Mt.11:2–15
Feria iiii				
Pacientes estote	Iac.5:7–10	A		
Venit iohannis baptista predicans	Mt.3:1–4	A		
Feria vi				
Redemptor vir .... Primus ad Sion (wrongly labelled in Sal.2637 as Malachie)	Is.41:27, 42:1–9, 13	A		
De die autem illa nemo scit (wrongly labelled in Sal.2637 as John)	Mt.24:36–40	A		

Dominica III

Sic nos existimet homo	ICor.4:1-5	A B	Idcirco vaticinare super humum Israhel	Ez.36:6-11
Cum audisset iohannis	Mt.11:2-10	A B	Cum Christus apparuerit vita vestra	Col.3:4-11
			Et cum adpropinquassent Hierosolymis	Mt.21:1-9

Feria iiii

Ecce ego mitto angelum meum	Mal.3:1-4	A		
Amen dico vobis: nonsurrexit inter natos	Mt.11:11-15	A		

Feria iiii in quattuor temporum

Erit in novissimis	Is.2:15	A B
Locutus est dominus	Is.7:10-15	A B
Missus est angelus	Lc.1:26-38	A B

Feria vi

Egreditur virga de radice	Is.11:1-5	A B
Exurgens maria	Lc.1:39-47	A B

Sabbato in xii

Clamabunt ad dominum	Is.19:20-22	A B
Letabitur deserta et invia	Is.35:1-17	A B
Super montem excelsum	Is.40:9-11	A B
Christo meo cyro	Is.45:1-8	A B
Angelus domini descendit	Dn.3:49-55	A
Rogamus vos per adventum	IITh.2:1-8	A
Anno quinto decimo	Lc.3:1-6	A B

Dominica IIII

Gaudete in domino	Phil.4:4-7	A B	Ecce ego mittam angelum meum	Mal.3:1-4
(wrongly labelled in 2637 as ad corinth)			Rogamus autem vos fratres	ITh.5:14-23
Miserunt iudei ab iherosolimis	Io.9:19-28	A B	Initium evangelii Iesu Christi Filii Dei	Mk.1:1-8

Dominica V

			Laetabitur deserta et invia	Is: 35:1-2
			Gaudete in Domino semper	Phil.4:4-7
			Anno autem quintodecimo imperii	Lc.3:1-8

Incipit		Reference	Incipit		Reference
in Vigilia Natalis Domini					
Propter Sion non tacebo	A B	Is.62:1–4			
Paulus servus Christi vocatus apostolus	A B	Rm.1:1–6			
Cum esset desponsata mater	A	Mt.1:18–21			
ad galli cantu					
Populus gentium qui ambulabat in tenebris	A B	Is.9:2,6,7			
Apparuit gratia dei salutaris	A B	Tit.2:11–15			
Exiit edictum a cesare augusto	A B	Lc.2:1–14			
(wrongly labelled in 2637 as Marchum)					
(de nocte)Missa ad mane					
Spiritus domini super me	A B	Is.61:1–3 & 62.11,12	Adiecit Dominus loqui ad Ahaz	A B	Is.7:10–16, 9:1–7
Cum autem benignitas et humanitas apparuit	A B	Tit.3:4–7	Multifariam et multis modis	A B	Hb.1:1–12
Pastores loquebantur	A B	Lc.2:15–20	Factum est autem in diebus illis exiit edictum	A B	Lc.2:1–20
Propter hoc sciet populus meus	A B	Is.52:6–10			
Multipharie multique	A B	Hbr.1:1–12			
In principio erat verbum	A B	Io.1:1–14			
Sancti Stephani					
			Lectio eclesiastica de miraculibus sancti stephani martyris		Aug. XXII,viii 10–22
Stephanus autem plenus gratia	A B	Act.6:8–10, 7,54–60	In diebus illis autem illis crescente numero	A B	Act.6:1–7, 7:51, 8:4
Dicebat dominus ihesus turbis iudeorum	A B	Mt.23:24–39	Ideo ecce ego mitto ad vos prophetas	A B	Mt.23:34–39
in die pasche					
			Apocalypsis Iesu Christi quam dedit		Apc.1, 1–18
Expurgate vetus sermentum	A B	1Cor.5:7,8	Notum autem vobis facio fratres	A B	1Cor.15:1–11
Maria Magdalene et Marie Iacobi	A B	Mc.16:1–7	Et exierunt cito de monumento	A B	Mt.28:8–20
feria ii					
			Angelo Ephesi ecclesiae scribe		Apc.2:1–7 [C]
Stans petrus in medio plebis	A B	Act.10:37–43	Exsurgens Petrus in medio fratrum	A B	Acts1:15–26
Exeuntes duo ex discipulis ihesus	A B	Lc.24:13–35	Maria Magdalene et Maria Iacobi	A B	Mc.16:1–7 [C]
feria iii					
			Et angelo Zmyrnae ecclesiae scribe		Apc.2:8–11 [C]

Surgens paulus et manu silentium indicens	Act.13:16, 26–33	A B	Viri israhelitae audite verba haec	Acts2:22–41 [C]
Stetit ihesus in medio discipulis	Lc.24:36–47	A B	Duo ex illis ibant ipsa die in castellum	Lc.24:13–35 [C]
feria iiii			Et angelo Philadelphiae ecclesiae scribe	Apc.3;7–13
Aperiens petrus os suum deleantur	Act.10:34, 3:12–19	A B	Erant autem perservantes in doctrina	Act.2:42–47
Manifestavit se dominus ihesus ad mare	Io.21:1–14	A B	Una autem sabbati valde diluculo	Lc.24:1–12
feria v			Et angelo Pergami ecclesiae scribe	Apc.2:12–17
Angelus domini loqutus est ad phyllippum	Act.8:26–40	A B	Et factum est cum introisset Petrus	Act.10:25–43
Maria stabat ad monumentum	Io.20:11–18	A B	Una autem sabbati Maria Magdalene	Jo.20:1–9
feria vi			Et angelo Thyatirae ecclesiae scribe	Apc.2:18–29
Christus semel pro peccatis nostris	IPt.3:18–22	A B	Per manus autem apostolorum fiebant	Act.5;12–16
Undecim discipuli abierant in galileam .	Mt.28:16–20	A B	Maria autem stabat ad monumentum	Jo.20:11–18
sabbato			Et angelo ecclesiae Sardis scribe	Apc.3:1–16
Deponentes omnem malitiam	IPt.2:1–10	A B	Viri fratres filii generis Abraham	Act.13:26–39 [C]
Una sabbati maria magdalene venit mane	Io.20:1–10	A B	Postea manifestavit se iterum	Jo.21:1–14
Dominica Octava Pasche			Et vidi quattuor angelos stantes	Apc.7:2–12
Omne quod natum est ex Deo	IIo.5:4–10	A B	Angelus autem Domini locutus est ad Philippum	Act.8:26–40
Cum esset sero die illa sabbatos	Io.20:19–23	A B	Cum esset ergo sero die illo	Jo.20:19–31
Pascha annotina:				
Non cesso gratias agens pro vobis	Rm.	B		
Erat homo ex phariseis nichodemis	Io.3:1–15	B		
Obedite prepositis	Hbr.13:17–21	B		
Exierunt mulieres	Mt.28:8–15	B		
Dominica 1 Post Pascham			Et venit unus de septem angelis	Apc.21:9–23
Christus passus est pro nobis	IPt.2,:21–25	A	Saulus autem adhuc inspirans minarum	Act.9:1–22
Ego sum pastor bonus	Io.10:11–16	A	Post haec erat dies festus ludeorum	Jo.5:1–18

BIBLIOGRAPHY OF WORKS CITED

MANUSCRIPT SOURCES

London, British Library, Add. MS 11695
London, British Library, Add. MS 30844
London, British Library, Add. MS 30845
London, British Library, Add. MS 30846
London, British Library, Add. MS 30847
London, British Library, Add. MS 30848
London, British Library, Add. MS 30849
Salamanca, Biblioteca de la Universidad, MS 2637
Madrid, Biblioteca Nacional, MS Vitr. 20–8
Madrid, Real Academia de la Historia, Aemilianensis 18

PRINTED PRIMARY SOURCES

ANDRIEU, M., *Les Ordines Romani du haut moyen âge*, vol.2, Louvain, 1931–61

BEDE, (*Venerabilis Baedae*) *Historiam ecclesiasticam gentis anglorum* (Plummer, C. ed) vol.1, Oxford, 1896.

Bibliotheca Hagiographica Latina, A–I, Brussels, 1898–1899

Bibliotheca Hagiographica Latina, I–Z, Brussels, 1900–1901

Chronica de Nájera, 10, Cirot, J. (ed.), *Bulletin hispanique*, 11, 1909

ESCALONA, R., *Historia del Real Monasterio de Sahagún*, (facsimile edition), León, 1982

EUSEBIUS OF CAESAREA, *The Ecclesiastical History*, (Lake, K., trans.), London and New York, 1926

FÉROTIN, M., *Recueil des chartes de l'abbaye de Silos*, Paris, 1896

    Le liber mozarabicus sacramentorum et les manuscrits mozarabes, Paris, 1912, vol. 6 of Monumenta Ecclesiae Liturgica, Cabrol, Leclercq and Férotin (eds.)

    Le Liber ordinum en usage dans l'église wisigothique et mozarabe d'Espagne du cinquième au onzième siècle, Paris, 1904

    'Une lettre inédite de saint Hugues, abbé de Cluny, à Bernard d'Agen, archevêque de Tolède (1087)', in *Bibliothèque de l'école des chartes*, 61, 1900, pp.339–45

    'Complément de la lettre de saint Hugues, abbé de Cluny, à Bernard d'Agen, archevêque de Tolède, in *Bibliothèque de l'école des chartes*, 63, 1902, pp.682–6.

FLÓREZ, H. (ed.) *España Sagrada*, Madrid, 1749–1879, t.23

FRANCE, J. (ed.), *Radulfi Glabri, Historiarum Libri Quinque, Ralph Glaber, Historiarum*, Oxford, 1989

GARCÍA LARRAGUETA, S., *Colección de documentos de la catedral de Oviedo*, Oviedo, 1962

GIL FERNÁNDEZ, J., MORALEJO, J. L., and RUIZ DE LA PEÑA, J. L., *Crónicas asturianas: Crónica Albeldense*, Universidad de Oviedo, Publicaciones del Departamento de Historia Medieval, 2, Oviedo, 1985

JAFFÉ, P., '*Monachus Sangallensis de Carolo Magno*,' in *Bibliotheca Rerum Germanicarum*, vol. 4, *Monumenta Carolina*, Berlin, 1867, pp.628–700.

LÖFSTEDT, B. (ed.), *Beatus Liebanensis et Eterii Oxomensis, Adversus Elipandum libri duo*, Turnholt, 1984

MANSI, J.D., *Sacrorum Conciliorum Nova et Amplissima Collectio*, vol.10, Graz, 1960 (reprint)

MIGNE, J.P., *Patrologia Latina*, Paris, 1844– 64

MIGUEL, C., *Fuentes Medievales Castellano-leonesas 50*, Burgos, 1988

MORIN, G., *Liber Comicus* (Anecdota Maredsolana vol.1), Maredsous, 1893

MUÑOZ Y ROMERO, T., *Colección de fueros municipales y cartas pueblas* 1, Madrid, 1847

PÉREZ DE URBEL, J.and RUIZ-ZORRILLA, A. G. (eds.), *Historia Silense*, Madrid, 1959

PSEUDO-DIONYSIUS, *The Complete Works,* Luibheid, C. (trans.), London, 1987

VALCÁRCEL, V., *La 'Vita Dominici Siliensis' de Grimaldo*, Logroño, 1982

VIVANCOS GÓMEZ, M.C., *Documentación del Monasterio de Santo Domingo de Silos (954–1254)*, Burgos, 1988

BIBLIOGRAPHY OF OTHER WORKS CITED

ARBEITER, A., and NOACK-HALEY, S., 'The Kingdom of Asturias', in *The Art of Medieval Spain A.D. 500–1200*, New York, 1993, pp.113–119

The Art of Medieval Spain A.D.500–1200, The Metropolitan Museum of Art, New York, 1993

AVRIL, F., ANIEL, J.-P., MENTRÉ, M., SAULNIER, A., ZALUSKA, Y. (eds.), *Manuscrits enluminés de la péninsule ibérique*, Paris (Bibliothèque Nationale), 1982

BARRÉ, H., *Les homéliaires carolingiens de l'école d'Auxerre*, Vatican, 1962

BEATTIE, J., *Other Cultures*, London, 1964

BENSON, R.L. and CONSTABLE, G.(eds), *Renaissance and Renewal in the Twelfth Century*, Oxford, 1982

BESSE, J-M, 'Histoire d'un dépôt littéraire, l'abbaye de Silos', *Revue Bénédictine*, 14, Abbaye de Maredsous, 1897, pp.210–225 and pp.241–252.

BISCHOFF, B., *Latin Palaeography: Antiquity and the Middle Ages*, Cambridge, 1990

BISHKO, C.J., 'Salvus of Albelda and Frontier Monasticism in Tenth-century Navarre', in *Speculum*, no.23, 1948, pp.559–590 (repr. *Studies in Medieval Spanish Frontier History*)

'Fernando I y los origenes de la alianza castellano-leonesa con Cluny', C.H.E., XLVII–VIII, 1968, pp. 31–135; reprinted as 'Fernando I and the Origins of the Leonese-Castilian Alliance with Cluny', in Bishko, C.J., *Studies in Medieval Spanish Frontier History*, London, 1980, II: pp.1–136

'Liturgical Intercession at Cluny for the King-Emperors of León' in *Studia Monastica* 3 1961, pp.53–81[A]

BOYLAN, A., *Manuscript Illumination at Santo Domingo de Silos (Xth to XIIth Centuries)*, Ph.D. diss., University of Pittsburgh, 1990 (Ann Arbor, 1992)

BRAEGELMANN, A., *The Life and Writings of Saint Ildefonsus of Toledo*, Washington, 1942

BRIEGER, P.H., 'Bible Illustration and Gregorian Reform', in Cuming, G.J. (ed.), *Studies in Church History*, vol. 2, Oxford, 1963, pp.154–164

BROU, L., 'Les plus anciennes prières liturgiques adressées a la Vierge en occident', in *Hispania Sacra*, 3, 1950, pp.371–381

'Un nouvel homiliaire en écriture wisigothique – Le codex Sheffield 'Ruskin Museum' 7', in *Hispania Sacra*, 2, 1949, p.147–191

'Un antiphonaire mozarabe de Silos d'après les fragments du British Museum', in *Hispania Sacra*, vol. 5, 1952, pp.341–366

BROWN, M.P., *A Guide to Western Historical Scripts from Antiquity to 1600*, London, 1990

BULLOUGH, D.A., 'Roman Books and Carolingian *Renovatio*', in Baker, D. (ed.), *Renaissance and Renewal in Christian History*, Studies in Church History, vol. 14, Oxford, 1977, pp.23–50

CAHN, W., Romanesque Manuscripts: The Twelfth Century, vol. 1, 2, London, 1996.

COWDREY, H.E.J., *The Cluniacs and the Gregorian Reform*, Oxford, 1970 'Unions and Confraternity with Cluny', *Journal of Ecclesiastical History*, 16, 1965, pp.152–62

DAVID, P., *Études historiques sur la Galice et le Portugal du VIe au XIIe siècle*, Lisbon-Paris, 1947

DAVIES, J.G. (ed.), *New Dictionary of Liturgy and Worship*, London, 1986

DELISLE, L., 'Manuscrits de l'abbaye de Silos acquis par la Bibliothèque Nationale', in *Mélanges de Paléographie et de Bibliographie*, Paris, 1880, pp.53–116

Inventaire des Manuscrits de la Bibliothèque Nationale – Fonds de Cluni, Paris, 1884

DÍAZ Y DÍAZ, M. C., 'Literary Aspects of the Visigothic Liturgy', in James, E. (ed.), *Visigothic Spain: New Approaches*, Oxford, 1980

Códices Visigóticos en la Monarquía Leonesa, León, 1983

El Codice Calixtino de la Catedral de Santiago, Santiago de Compostela, 1988

Diccionario de Historia Eclesiastica, Aldea Vaquero, Q., Marín Martínez, T. and Vives Gatell, J. (ed.), vol. 2, Madrid, 1970

DODDS, J.D., 'Islam, Christianity, and the problem of religious art', in *The Art of Medieval Spain A.D.500–1200*, New York, 1993, pp.27–37

DOMÍNGUEZ BORDONA, J., *Spanish Illumination*, vol. I, Florence and Paris, 1930

Manuscritos con pinturas, Vol. 1 & 2, Madrid, 1933

DUFOUR, J. *La bibliothèque et le scriptorium de Moissac*, Paris, 1972

DUFFY, E., *The Stripping of the Altars*, New Haven CT and London, 1992

EBNER, A., *Quellen und Forschungen zur Geschichte und Kunstgeschichte des Missale Romanum im mittelalter iter italicum*, Freiburg im Breisgau, 1957

El románico en Silos: IX centenario de la consagración de la iglesia y claustro, 1088–1988 (Studia Silensia, Series Maior, 1) Burgos: Abadía de Silos, 1990

EMMERSON, R.K. and McGINN, B. (eds.), *The Apocalypse in the Middle Ages*, Ithaca and London, 1992

ÉTAIX, R., 'Le lectionnaire de l'office à Cluny', in *Recherches Augustiniennes*, vol. 11, Paris, 1976, p.91–159

    'Homiliaires wisigothiques provenant de Silos à la Bibliothèque Nationale de Paris', in *Hispania Sacra*, 12, 1959, p.213–220

    'L'homéliaire composé par Raban Maur pour l'empereur Lothaire', in *Recherches Augustiniennes*, vol. 19, Paris, 1984, p.211–240

FALQUE REY, F. (ed.), *Historia Compostellana*, Corpus Christianorum, Continuatio Medievalis, vol. 70, Turnhout, 1988

Fälschungen im Mittelalter, teil 1 and 2, Hannover, 1988

FERNÁNDEZ DE LA CUESTA, I, 'Notas paleográficas al Antiphonario Silense', in *Homenaje Fr. J. Pérez de Urbel*, Studia Silense 3, vol. 1, pp.233–256

FÉROTIN, M., *Histoire de l'abbaye de Silos*, Paris 1897

FISHER, J.D.C., *Christian Initiation: Baptism in the Medieval West*, ACC 47, London, 1965

FITA, F., 'El concilio nacional de Burgos en 1080', in *Boletín de la real academia de la historia*, 49, 1906, pp.337–84.

FLETCHER, R., *The Episcopate in the Kingdom of León in the Twelfth Century*, Oxford, 1978

FORSYTH, I.F., *The Throne of Wisdom: Wood Sculptures of the Madonna in Romanesque France*, Princeton, 1972

GABORIT-CHOPIN, D., *La décoration des manuscrits à Saint-Martial de Limoges et en Limousin du IXe au XIIe siècle*, Geneva, 1969

GARAND, M., 'Le Scriptorium de Cluny, carrefour d'influences au 11e siècle: Le manuscrit Paris, BN, nouv. acq. lat. 1548', in *Journal des Savants*, 1977, pp.257–283

GARCÍA RODRÍGUEZ, C., *El culto de los santos en la España Romana y Visigoda*, Madrid, 1966

GEARY, P.J., *Living with the Dead in the Middle Ages*, Ithaca and London, 1994

GIBERT TARRUELL, J., 'El sistema de lecturas de la cincuenta pascual de la liturgia hispánica, según la tradición B', in *Liturgia y Música Mozárabes*, Instituto de Estudios Visigótico–Mozárabes de San Eugenio – Toledo, Serie D, Núm. 1, (Ponencias y Comunicaciónes presentadas al I Congreso Internacional de Estudios Mozárabes), Toledo, 1975, pp.111–124

GRÉGOIRE, R., *Les homéliares carolingiens de l'école d'Auxerre*, Vatican, 1962

    Les homéliares du moyen âge, Rome, 1966,

GUILMAIN, J., 'On the chronological development and classification of decorated initials in Latin manuscripts of tenth-century Spain', in *Bulletin of the John Rylands University Library of Manchester*, vol. 63, Spring 1981, pp.369–401

GY, P.-M., 'La mise en page du bréviaire', in Martin, H.-J., and Vezin, J. (eds), *Mise en page et mise en texte du livre manuscrit*, Paris, 1990, pp.117–120

    'La mise en page du Canon de la messe', as above, pp.113–116.

HEARN, M.F., *Romanesque Sculpture*, Oxford, 1981

HEFELE, C.J., *Histoire des Conciles*, t.1, partie.2, Paris, 1907

HERNÁNDEZ, F.J., 'La cathédrale, instrument d'assimilation', in Cardaillac, L. (ed.), *Tolède, XIIe–XIIIe: Musulmans, chrétiens et juifs: Le Savoir et la Tolérance*, Paris, 1991, pp.75–91

HERRGOTT, M., (ed.), *Vetus disciplina monastica*, Paris, 1726

HUGHES, A., *Medieval Manuscripts for Mass and Office, A Guide to their Organization and Terminology*, Toronto, 1982

HUNT, N., *Cluny under Saint Hugh 1049–1109*, London, 1967

JAMES, E. (ed.), *Visigothic Spain: New Approaches*, Oxford, 1980

JANINI, J. 'Dos calendarios emilianenses del siglo XI', in *Hispania Sacra*, no.15, 1962, pp.177–95

    and Serrano, J., *Manuscritos litúrgicos de la Biblioteca Nacional*, Madrid, 1969

(ed.), *Manuscritos Litúrgicos de las Bibliotecas de España, T.1, Castilla y Navarra*, Burgos, 1977

and González, R., *Catálogo de los manuscritos litúrgicos de la Catedral de Toledo*, Toledo, 1977

'Officia silensia, Liber Misticus III', in *Hispania Sacra*, 31, 1978–79, p.357–483

JONES, L.W., 'Pricking Manuscripts: the Instruments and their Significance', in *Speculum*, 21, 1946, pp.389–403

JUNGMANN, J.A., *The Mass of the Roman Rite: its Origin and Development* (vol. I & II), New York, 1955

KATZENELLENBOGEN, A., *The Sculptural Programs of Chartres Cathedral*, Baltimore, 1959

KEMP, A., *The Estrangement of the Past: a Study in the Origins of Modern Historical Consciousness*, Oxford, 1991

KING, A. A., *Liturgies of the Primatial Sees*, London, 1957

KITZINGER, E., 'The Gregorian Reform and the Visual Arts: a Problem of Method', in *Transactions of the Royal Historical Society*, 5th series, vol. 22, 1972 pp.87–102

KNOWLES, D., *The Evolution of Medieval Thought*, London, 1962

LAWRENCE, C.H., *Medieval Monasticism*, London and New York, (2nd edition), 1989

LECLERCQ, J., 'Les Manuscripts des bibliothèques d'Espagne, Notes de Voyages', in *Scriptorium*, 3, 1949, pp.140–144

LEMAIRIÉ, J., *Le bréviaire de Ripoll*, Abadía de Montserrat, 1965

LEROQUAIS, V., *Les sacramentaires et les missels manuscrits des bibliothèques publiques de France*, Paris, 1924

Les bréviaires des bibliothèques françaises, Paris, 1934

LINAGE CONDE, A., *Los origenes del monacato benedictino en la península ibérica*, León, 1973, 3 vols.

LINEHAN, P.A., 'Religion, Nationalism and National Identity in Medieval Spain and Portugal', in Mews, S. (ed.), *Religion and National Identity*, Studies in Church History, vol. 18, Oxford, 1982, pp.161–199

History and the Historians of Medieval Spain, Oxford, 1993

LOUTH, A., *Denys the Areopagite*, Wilton CT, 1989

McCLUSKEY, R., 'Malleable Accounts: Views of the Past in Twelfth-century Iberia', in Magdalino, P. (ed.), *The Perception of the Past in Twelfth-Century Europe*, London and Rio Grande, 1992, pp.211–225.

MacGREGOR, A.J., *Fire and Light in the Western Triduum, Their use at Tenebrae and at the Paschal Vigil*, Alcuin Club Collection 71, Minnesota, 1992

McKITTERICK, R., *The Frankish Church and the Carolingian Reforms, 789–895*, London, 1977

(ed.) *Carolingian Culture: emulation and innovation*, Cambridge, 1994

'Unity and Diversity in the Carolingian Church', in Swanson, R.N. (ed.), *Unity and Diversity in the Church*, Studies in Church History, vol. 32, Oxford, 1996, pp.59–82.

MANSILLA, D., *La Curia romana y el reino de Castilla en un momento decisivo de su historia, 1065–1085*, Burgos, 1944

'Dos Códices visigóticos de la catedral de Burgos', in *Hispania Sacra*, 2, 1949, p.381–418

MENÉNDEZ PIDAL, R., 'El Lábaro Primitivo de la Reconquista – Cruces Asturianas y Cruces Visigodos', in *Boletín de la Real Academia de la Historia*, t. 136, pp.275–296

MENTRÉ, M., *La Miniatura en Leon y Castilla en la alta media*, León, 1976

La Peinture Mozarabe, Paris, 1984

El Estilo Mozarabe, La pintura cristiana hispánica en torno al año 1000, Madrid, 1994

METROPOLITAN MUSEUM OF ART, *The Art of Medieval Spain A.D.500–1200*, New York, 1993

METZGER, B.M. and COOGAN, M.D. (eds.), *The Oxford Companion to the Bible*, New York and Oxford, 1993

MILLARES CARLO, A., *Tratado de Paleografía Española*, vol. 1–3 Madrid, 1983

MOORE, R.I., *The Formation of a Persecuting Society: Power and Deviance in Western Europe, 950–1250*, Oxford, 1987

MORALEJO, S., 'The tomb of Alfonso Ansúrez (1093): Its Place and the Role of Sahagún in the Beginnings of Spanish Romanesque Sculpture', in Reilly B.F. (ed.), *Santiago, Saint-Denis and Saint Peter, The Reception of the Roman Liturgy in León-Castile in 1080*, New York, 1985, pp.63–100

'On the Road, the Camino de Santiago', in *The Art of Medieval Spain A.D.500–1200*, The Metropolitan Museum of Art, New York, 1993, pp.175–183

O'MEARA, J.J., *Eriugena*, Oxford, 1988

PALACIOS, M, YARZA LUACES, J. and TORRES, R., *El Monasterio de Santo Domingo de Silos*, León, 1981

PALAZZO, E., 'L'iconographie des fresques de Berzé-la-Ville dans le contexte de la Reforme Grégorienne et de la liturgie Clunisienne', in *Les Cahiers de Saint-Michel de Cuxa*, no.19, 1988, pp.169–186

PARKES, M.B., *Pause and Effect. An Introduction to the History of Punctuation in the West*, Scolar Press (Aldershot), 1992

PÉREZ DE URBEL, J., 'El último defensor de la liturgia mozárabe', in *Miscellanea Liturgica in honorem L. Cuniberti Mohlberg*, vol. 2, Rome, 1949, pp.189–197

PINELL, J.M., 'Liturgia Hispanica', in *Diccionario de Historia Eclesiástica*, Aldea Vaquero, Q., Marin Martinez, T. and Vives Gatell, J. (ed.), vol. 2, Madrid, 1970

    Boletín de Liturgia Hispano-Visigótica (1949–1956) in *Hispania Sacra*, 9, 1956, pp.405–428

RÄDLE, F., *Studien zu Smaragd von Saint-Mihiel*, Munich, 1974

RANKIN, S., 'Carolingian Music', in McKitterick, R. (ed.), *Carolingian Culture: emulation and innovation*, Cambridge, 1994, pp.274–316

REILLY, B. F., *The Kingdom of León-Castilla under Queen Urraca, 1109–1126*, Princeton, 1982

    (ed.), *Santiago, Saint-Denis and Saint Peter, The Reception of the Roman Liturgy in León-Castile in 1080*, New York, 1985

    The Kingdom of León-Castilla under King Alfonso VI 1065–1109, Princeton, 1988

REYNOLDS, R. E., 'The Ordination Rite in Medieval Spain:Hispanic, Roman, and Hybrid', in Reilly, B.F. (ed.), *Santiago, Saint-Denis and Saint Peter, The Reception of the Roman Liturgy in León-Castile in 1080*, New York, 1985, pp.131–155

    'Rites and Signs of Conciliar Decisions in the Early Middle Ages', in *Settimane di Studio del Centro Italiano di Studi sull'alto medioevo* (*Segni e Riti Nella Chiesa Altomedievale Occidentale – 1985*), Spoleto, 1987, pp.207–244

    'Pseudonymous liturgica in early medieval canon law collections', in *Fälschungen im Mittelalter*, teil 2 (Gefälschte Rechtstexte der bestrafte Fälscher), Hannover, 1988, pp.67–77

RIVERA RECIO, J.F., *La Iglesia de Toledo en el siglo XII (1086–1208)*, vol. 1, Roma, 1966

ROBIN, M., *Bernard de La Sauvetat, abbé de Sahagún, archevêque de Tolède (v.1040–1124) et la réforme clunisienne en Espagne au XIe et XIIe siècle*, École nationale des chartes, Positions des thèses de 1907 (unpublished thesis)

RODRÍGUEZ, A., and LOJENDIO, L. M. de, *Castille romane*, La Pierre-qui-Vire, 1966

El Romanico en Silos, IX Centenario de la consagracion de la iglesia y claustro, 1088–1988, (Studia Silensia, Series Maior 1), Silos, 1990

ROREM, P., *Pseudo-Dionysius – A Commentary on the Texts and an Introduction to Their Influence*, New York and Oxford, 1993

RUIZ, T.F., 'Burgos and the Council of 1080', in Reilly, B.F. (ed.), *Santiago, Saint-Denis, Saint Peter, The Reception of the Roman liturgy in León-Castile in 1080*, New York, 1985, pp.121–130

SALMON, P., *L'office divin au moyen âge: Histoire de la formation du bréviaire du IXe au XVIe siècle*, Paris, 1967

SÁNCHEZ ALBORNOZ, C., *Los Estampos de la vida en León durante el siglo X*, Madrid, 1926

SCHAPIRO, M., *The Parma Ildefonsus, A Romanesque Illuminated Manuscript from Cluny and Related Works*, New York, 1964

    'From Mozarabic to Romanesque in Silos', in *Romanesque Art*, reprinted in Schapiro, M., *Romanesque Art. Selected Papers*, pp.28–101, London, 1977

SCHILLER, G., *The Iconography of Christian Art*, vol. 1, London, 1971

SCHLUNCK, H., 'La Iglesia de San Julián de los Prados (Oviedo) y la arquitectura de Alfonso el Casto', in *Estudios sobre la monarquia asturiana. Colección de trabajos realizada con motivo del XI centenario de Alfonso II el Casto, celebrado en 1942*, (2 ed. Oviedo 1971) pp.405–465

Shailor, B.A., 'The Scriptorium of San Sahagún: A Period of Transition', in Reilly, B.F. (ed.), *Santiago, Saint-Denis, Saint Peter, The Reception of the Roman liturgy in León-Castile in 1080*, New York, 1985, pp.41–61

    'The Beatus of Burgo de Osma: A Paleographical and Codicological Study', in *Apocalipsis Beati Liebanensis. Burgi Oxomensis. Vol. 2: El Beato de Osma, Estudios*, Valencia, 1992, pp.29–52

SICART, A., *Pintura Medieval: La Miniatura*, Santiago de Compostela, 1981

SMALLEY, B., 'Ecclesiastical Attitudes to Novelty c.1100–c.1250', in *Church, Society and Politics,* Studies in Church History, vol. 12: , Oxford, 1975, pp.113–131

SUÑOL, G., *Introduction a la paléographie Grégorienne*, Tournai, 1935

THOMPSON, E.M., *Catalogue of the Additions to the British Museum in the Years MDCCCLXXVI–MDCCCLXXXI,* vol. 13, London, 1882 (reprinted 1968)

THOMPSON, J, W., *The Medieval Library,* repnt. New York and London, 1965

TOUBERT, H., *Un Art Dirigé,* Paris, 1990

TYRER, J.W., *Historical Survey of Holy Week its services and ceremonial,* ACC 29, London, 1932

VIVES, J. and FÁBREGA, A., 'Calendarios hispánicos anteriores al siglo XII', in *Hispania Sacra,* vol. 2, 1949, pp.119–146, and pp.339–380

VOGEL, C. *Medieval Liturgy: An Introduction to the Sources,* Washington, 1986 (revised version by Storey, W.G. and Rasmussen, N.K.)

WERCKMEISTER, O., review of Schapiro, M., Romanesque Art, in *Art Quarterly,* n.s.2, 2, 1979

'The First Romanesque Beatus Manuscripts and the Liturgy of Death', in *Actas del simposio para el estudio de los códices del 'Comentario al Apocalypsis' de Beato de Liébana,* vol. 2, Madrid, 1980, pp.167–200

'Art of the Frontier: Mozarabic Monasticism', in *The Art of Medieval Spain A.D.500–1200,* The Metropolitan Museum of Art, New York, 1993, pp.121–132

WHITEHILL, W. M., 'A Mozarabic Psalter from Santo Domingo de Silos', in *Speculum,* 4, 1929, pp.461–468

and Pérez de Urbel, 'Los manuscritos del Real Monasterio de Santo Domingo de Silos', in *Boletín de la Real Academia de la Historia,* t.95, Madrid, 1929

'The Manuscripts of Santo Domingo de Silos (à la recherche du temps perdu)', in *Homenaje a Fray Justo Pérez de Urbel,* Studia Silense 3, vol. 1, Silos, 1976, pp.271–303

'The Destroyed Church of Santo Domingo de Silos', in *Art Bulletin,* XIV, 1932, pp.316–343

WILLIAMS, J.W., 'A Contribution to the History of the Castilian Monastery of Valeránica and the Scribe Florentius', in *Madrider Mitteilungen,* 2, 1970, pp.231–248

'San Isidoro in León: Evidence for a New History', in *Art Bulletin,* vol. 55, no.2 1973, pp.170–184

Early Spanish Manuscript Illumination, New York and London, 1977

'Generationes Abrahae: Reconquest Iconography in León', in *Gesta,* 16/2, 1977, p.3–14

'Tours and Early Medieval Art', in *Florilegium in Honorem Carl Nordenfalk Octogenarium Contextum,* Stockholm, 1987, pp.197–208

'Cluny and Spain', *Gesta,* vol. 27, 1988, pp.93–101

and Stones, A., *The Codex Calixtinus and the Shrine of St James,* Tübingen, 1992

review of 'El románico en Silos: IX centenario de la consagración de la iglesia y claustro, 1088–1988' (Studia Silensia, Series Maior, 1) Burgos: Abadía de Silos, 1990, in *Speculum,* vol. 68 (2), 1993, pp.873–877

'Orientations: Christian Spain and the art of its neighbours',in *The Art of Medieval Spain,* in *The Art of Medieval Spain A.D.500–1200,* The Metropolitan Museum of Art, New York, 1993, pp.13–25

'León and the Beginnings of the Spanish Romanesque', in *The Art of Medieval Spain A.D.500–1200,* New York, 1993, pp.167–173

The Illustrated Beatus: A Corpus of the Illustrations of the Commentary on the Apocalypse, 5 vol. , London, 1994–

WRIGHT, R., *Late Latin and Early Romance in Spain and Carolingian France,* Liverpool, 1982

YARZA LUACES, J., 'La Miniatura Románica en España. Estado de la Cuestión', in *Anuario del Departamento de Historia y Teoría del Arte,* Vol. II, Universidad Autónoma de Barcelona, 1990, pp.9–25

'Nuevos Hallazgos Románicos en el Monasterio de Silos', in *Goya,* no.46, Madrid, 1970, pp.342–345.

INDEX
OF MANUSCRIPTS CITED

259

INDEX